MW01228069

MEMOIRS OF
MYTHS
AND
TRUTHS

MEMOIRS OF
MYTHS
AND
TRUTHS

*In an
Ordinary Pebble's
Extraordinary Life*

CARL B. ALLEN

Library of Congress Control Number: 2008901810
ISBN: Hardcover   978-1-4363-2555-4
                   Softcover   978-1-4363-2554-7

To order additional copies of this book, contact:
Xlibris Corporation
1-888-795-4274
www.Xlibris.com
Orders@Xlibris.com
45049

DEDICATION

This wonderment part of my life's stream came from my clan, my kin, family and friends, but most of all from my parents, wife's, and children, of whom gave me courage and believe there is no mountain too high or valley to low for pebbles to find their voice. Thank you, especially to Kathy for all the lost hours, days, and years not shared with her because I was on that damn computer.

To Carmyn,
Who has shared the joy
and pain of being apart
of this family tree. You
have enriched this journey and
memories of myths & dreams.
There has been gold shared in
our streams with each new day
unforseen in each bend and
turn of our extraordinary life.
always love
Carl

PROLOGUE

Without a great writing ability, but with the help of a few photos added, I hope to bring you into my memories and times with some "Myths" emerged from stories being retold countless times, then became truths after the memories got cloudy. I now find myself being in the fall of my years, having a sense of belonging, a sense of family, and the closeness of friends, which has brought me to this place of wonderment that continued from those wonderful past years of youth. They have brought me to these joyous thoughts as I wrote these memoirs, and into thinking about my "extraordinary life." First for myself, for all my kin or others within my stream, but I'm also hoping other pebbles of my time can recall and reflect on these times with a little smile but some sadness. I may have wandered through my youthful years winding through life's paths and finding I was running on empty or full or too fast or too slow at the time. Being nurtured as a child was not always satisfying, but it did start, however, when I built many protective walls around myself. Yet like James Dean in *East of Eden, or Rebel Without a Cause, or Giant,* there was this desperate search for love and approval, which was not always available for many reasons. Seeking my own needs just as an ordinary pebble has resulted in finding an extraordinary life. I'll continue expressing any visions of what my heart and mind may be trying to embrace although so much of me is hidden deeper within myself. But I'm always trying to hold and consider that these parts of life, like beauty and sadness, may be viewed as an expression of my soul some day. I've been trying to use my painting, and now the written word, in expressing some of my myths, whether truths may be spoken or memories can be trusted. They carry simple but complex myths in the life of an ordinary pebble's life, always amazed by the course of streams found.

These memoirs are a reflection of my times, history, love of the automobile, encounters with lovers in those places I've traveled. It's also about people encountered in my stream, which may have reflected just a little light about whom I am as I went through my journeys, gathering memories, myths or truths, that sustained my notions of an ordinary pebble's extraordinary life. Within some happiness there is sadness, whether it comes with sex or fights, in dangerous or peaceful places. It gets me to reflect on my morals issues or things that may have been questionable by my judgment. I hope, however, that you enjoy this time traveling in my stream. Pebbles or not, we are the most important part in the stream surrounding us, and everyone else's lives continue similarly within the same small stream, or another that's larger. We all do have more impact on ourselves then others, but while sharing our life's stream with others, they matter more then we think possible. I feel we all must continue on learning about what love is, and maybe we should be fighting our way up streams like the salmon, because we all will die, or cross onto the other side. We must all keep our soul's eye on the scales of how our lives are measured, be it daily or at the end. We must all find our own forms of gold by sharing with others as much as we can with those we love, because those who love us are the greatest part of any interaction, our myths, our songs. Sharing of ourselves is the mark that continues to be recalled in time, as music notes of an extraordinary song.

Finding myself, reacting to having happiness and sadness at the same time while the gathering those expressions or emotions, I'm traveling in these memories once again with a different view. Yet altogether they have become sometimes a great source of much-growing energy, opening many of my past emotions. Reliving those moments has caused reflection on the past, some myths and some truths, with so much more pleasure, then I would have known or found before. While knowing the ending story is coming nearer in my life, I continue finding that life still has that new meaning within old paths, new days and new streams to travel. The past can become baggage, or it can be a greater gift, the most important thing, whether within our past or present, while our dealing with life continues. We have a short time here to learn the many lessons on relationships, how we should feel, how we handle adversity, and how to treat those others surrounding us, no matter where we are or who they are or whoever we are, and then finding there is greater joy in the end because that right thing can give us rewards and can be done over again. September 11 should've taught us something about living every day: we never know what will happen in the next moment. So with an almost daily quotation, I read written on my morning coffee cup,

"Dream as if you'll live forever. Live as if you'll die today."
—James Dean

PEBBLES

Let me make my case for using ordinary pebbles. Pebbles are larger than sand and smaller than rocks, easily moved by wind or streams, and they are like ordinary people meandering through life. There are billions covering the earth, and yet most of us don't pay much attention to them. Though traveling through many different times, pebbles and we may have been a part of a comet, joined together. If only the whole story could be told. While we are prospecting for gold in pebbles, this can be like looking for good people. Sometimes you can find a nugget, but first you've got to shift through allot of sand and rocks, and through many rivers as well, with mostly a lot of good luck or fate, it's been said. Therefore, I may carry on a little to long with these next thoughts and words in these next few pages, while hoping you don't get lost, while this gives you something to ponder on regarding our being mere pebbles or person of interest or not. So, not to bore you, you can just skip this part and go on to "My Story," part 1, if you like, but not without reminding yourself to come back and read the rest of my thoughts here regarding ordinary pebbles.

You ask, how do ordinary people like small pebbles running in streams, become extraordinary too? Most of us are only within a few steps or streams from what we consider bigger, grander, or extraordinary. However, our surrounding within any gathering of events can bring and make extraordinary pebbles or people, without them even knowing it at that time, or maybe move them through it into a new light just by finding those extraordinary actions in others, or their own, within that simple mix of the surrounding stream of life. We can make some extraordinary things happen as humans. We all are surrounded by extraordinary times, extraordinary people, and these daily events bring forth something in those ordinary people or pebbles, into becoming and finding they are now standing in the forefront that forms extraordinary pebbles. For some reason, those taking one extra, or more, step can change those around them or themselves forever with just one action through those so-called ordinary people.

Let's just look within others, and ourselves and maybe we could begin to understand and see just how anyone of us could be or have been part of something, or someone's life, that has made a great impact on others' or our own paths, leading us to some form of reflecting to hold on to. Writing of our life's memoirs, by looking back, may open yours and others' eyes or minds to see an unordinary life's story. That's because by just being there at that moment in time and adding just a little more weight in the world's turning, or just being a companion for a moment or just pushing them on, or ourselves, we can help others along those many streams and courses into finding and making those changes around us all. Making those things that may have never been does make a difference for so many because like in the movie It's a Wonderful Life, any ordinary pebble's life did make a difference in my life and others'. By simply engaging others in some form of interaction, we can find means to liven up and that makes new traveling, changing paths within others, and our streams measurement to be a greater in heights. By going it alone though, we miss so many opportunities in finding those golden nuggets of life in our streams, and no stories can be told without a listener. This is what makes life a little richer for us all. We all are extraordinary pebbles.

What are truths, what are dreams, what are myths, while all of them are getting mixed up in our stories or minds like our thoughts do, in a way that makes them myths or truths? While believing they are being told in the best means or interest to bring together their own forms of truths. There's poetry, tragedy, and joy inside each and every one of us, making complex or simple stores grow somehow into our lives and our own worlds, just like we read from William Shakespeare's or other playwrights' plays. We all are within our own plays, but with far more acts and within a much longer story, with different times, stops, and it goes on like the pebble in its stream.

Some can become tragedy, romance, or comedy, but most people, like pebbles, are hidden in the flowing stream being layered leading to much larger rivers further away, never closely seen by anyone or told of, except when taken closer to the surface like our pebble being explained and told to others to pass on their stories for some reason.

Small pebbles or ordinary people can become myths, bigger and larger because their stories are told through many centuries, through use in great writings and by story tellers, like the Greeks stories or maybe scriptures writings passed on. We become something within these faiths by rising or falling like our own gods or god, with our own designs, to our own destiny's that may hold us too. Then only to find these paths chosen are always our own destined truths, hopes, and myths within the gods or god stories, but without our own control. It may have been by some miracle or luck or gods or god shown or given to us that most believe in the saying "The Gods may have been looking down on us," like it's was told in earlier dreams of man, or seen in a vision, or read by our fellow men. However, we fumble around in our earthly forms, or in our pebbles forms, deeply being moved by everything surrounding us, by unknown forces surrounding us, or not, and doing our uncontrolled travels in our streams. The gods or god watching from their viewing points as only the gods can do, during each of our own turning events and points, may bring these events with some connection to us. We ask what can be next, what meaning it has, or what moving force is now forming us into what we are becoming or causing occurring events to happen as we try to reason with life. Yet we may be knowing and viewing things happening to others or ourselves, or maybe believing in some form of prediction on our streams' action, but never knowing for sure why or how. We all want or expect someone to be in control, while streams fade somewhere, and at sometime find their way into dry sand or earth while disappearing into time at the end. Yet I've believed in guardian angels being there for me all along, it maybe unrealistic, or hoping without merit.

Yet as people we mostly compare ourselves with other pebbles, without looking deeper within our own surroundings, other than that where we stand. We would find stories with myths, and truths of gold surround most of us, if we looked deep and listen to others, finding maybe something apart from ourselves. Sometimes there's something within ours and any ordinary pebble's life's stories, which can turn out to be extraordinary, and becomes just as important in viewing or told, becoming our own myths or stories to others close to us. If we try, and by knowing those stories, it can make some pebbles stand much taller and in a larger mountain's perspective, rising among or above or along those other pebbles seen in their surrounding greatness of highs, becoming extraordinary, and within their own surrounding. Those within those "famous fifteen minutes of fame" who are moving pebbles into those great mountains or streams are for just that moment becoming extraordinary in many views, at levels much higher than us in stories or myths and truths. But it doesn't always have that shine that lasts in those views or heights. Then if we do examine closely those surrounding us like we do with the pebbles found in streams, along the way we'll find something beyond ordinary in most of us. Pebbles are like ordinary people, which can have so much more than what's found on the surface in life's streams. There are those seen in the fifteen minutes of fame, but our inner worth must last much longer. So there are those found not always easily visible by just looking at the outer shell, but they can surface with the right events and timing, when the conditions are perfect to become extraordinary

Life can run up hills, but like the streams it always runs downhill to the very end, where it ends and mixes with the earth's or stars' energy again. As found, not all the same pebbles are always in the same surrounding rocks, streams, or neighboring streams, but we all can relate to good stories within the connection of all mankind, allowing us to be there.

Many are found far from their beginnings, and yet still can be traced back to that same beginning and in similar parts of that one history. An extraordinary pebble may have come to be through many different means and through many different times. If only it could be told, then most small stories can be very surprising. Seemingly, we have been apart of something much greater than ourselves, but it's very important to claim ours too, adding our own wealth to the stream.

After most of our deaths, we are missed by others, and maybe only then can our stories come to light, but till then we can still lose any chance of hearing the whole story as it was felt or told by the person affected by the events in the story and those living it. Others' and our stories are lost in the sands of time and streams of life for the most part. Most of us in this world are ordinary people leading ordinary lives, surrounded by even more similarly ordinary people traveling in our currents and streams, but because we are here, our life's still can be extraordinary to many.

However, because those close to us do become even more important, they are part of us, and for whatever reasons they have had their effect on us, in some big or small ways, bringing us to their mix of energy. So let us do that examination of what can be known, told, and revealed for our minds or eyes, the truths connecting us all. Like the stars, we hold each other's energy together, making starlight grow in us all.

Now looking beyond pebbles, let's examine my thoughts regarding these two words, "extra" and "ordinary," and their difference in meaning when brought together to form a single word—"a greater ordinary." By using them together as one word, you'll now find them forming another word with meaning and direction. In many ways, becoming now sometimes, that has caused a new view of information in its usage. These two words together give our pebble a new form, making it extraordinary. Its new meaning is something liking in reflection, and growing into "not following the usual; going far beyond the ordinary; very unusual, exceptional and remarkable." Now it is beyond being "ordinary." Bringing them together gives them a new appearance and a great meaning, finding it in some kind of new level of expansion and much higher than ordinary. Also, with even further examination, you'll find that many of us are always moving into different levels, and that does appear to be beyond our control because of our surrounding is filled with so many other streams that we move into those streams in the ever-changing moments of life, even those of us who stand alone. So you never know when or how you can be exceptionable or when it occurs.

So let's go see if maybe we can understand what I've tried to say through all these prior thoughts, and shift through my life's streams with all those other pebbles' stories and memories, making a very extraordinary pebble's life story either myth or truth. You'll find no heroes, just my presence in being part of so many streams, of others surrounding me. Let's begin with my history and an examination of my family elements, mostly seen within my own human eyes from the very start of my story, and then telling of the times I moved along in my streams with the growth of my soul. But let me first say this story looks back from my now older age, and from my present thoughts, and whether it's made up of myths or truths, it doesn't really make me feel extraordinary, or does it? Whether the life I've experienced is extraordinary or not only rests on your own judgment. Knowing the glowing energy within people and that amazing energy of love in this world we're in, ordinary or not, being in this journey has given me an extraordinary life.

ONE

My Beginning Streams
My Story

This story starts before my birth. Like all pebbles, we are small pieces of energy coming from other energies in a much larger and older source in the universe, mostly made up of water and then more elements, such as minerals. All things are made up of energy in someway or another. Pebbles are related to the formation of our world, our geography, and our people through genesis. They are part of events reaching thousands of years. Our family trees come from seeds growing through time, as the pebbles are chips from larger energy-filled stones mixed into that magic formula. Man started covering the earth with his family going back through time. We have traveled so many different streams before we became what we are now.

Like all, we have changed from mixtures of many elements, like pebbles. These various elements of my life began slowly, carrying me into my own stream where my life started to take shape. We are cut loose as a new pebble from our mother into a measured starting point, with a given date, and mine was June 25, in 1939, within that part of history. I found the genesis of my life's stream there.

Once we are in that stream, we keep moving, continuing at our own pace, and even after our deaths our sprits are still imparted in a continuing stream of energy through time, unseen by many. The time we find our stream is the beginning of an extraordinary pebble's life story.

In 1939, the first year of my existence, the Great Depression came to its hopeful ending, but with many other signs of a sparkling energy of a greater hell for mankind. The continuation of the Great War was seen on the horizon. This year was the real start of World War II for the world, and historically it was really only a continuation of World War I. Times were hard but there were also signs of a much better for the world, at least for the first part. This was the year for all "small people" with the release of the movie *The Wizard of Oz*, about Dorothy following the yellow brick road to Emerald City. With it the world believed we could fly "Over the Rainbow" to find ourselves, and that we were better off with love and family at home.

Irish

The Great Irish Famine started around 1850 and through 1875, killing many thousands in Ireland and the many other thousands traveling here from the British Isles. Again it was the America Dream that made these people become part of this great land. These pebbles traveled on the ocean, as grain of sand travels with the winds, to find their streams of life. Of course, it takes very strong winds and waves to move these many pebbles. Those waves took her children here during the eighteen-century.

My Irish descendants came to America's streams because of the Great Irish Famine in their land. Seeing death, starvation, they left everything they had behind them. Upon their arrival, the Irish were used as the lowest form of labor, and they were increasingly found working for railroads during the drive from the East to West. They where used in most other lower tasks in greater numbers before this as well, because of their availability in larger numbers. Most of us didn't know, but they were used as substitutes for blacks for cleaning sewers in New Orleans because the blacks were worth more than the Irish. This applied truly in other parts of nation as well. There were larger numbers than most think, who came through the South, and not just Boston or New York as most would think.

They came anyway, with more dying in much larger numbers at sea or even more after arrival because of starvation and diseases, but never without looking for that rainbow. This was the time for the greatest movement toward the West from the eastern cities. It normally took six months or longer to cross this country before the connection between the railroads, but after its completion only six days. The Irish and other working people came because there was a prospect of food, making a living, the hope of bettering themselves, and above all becoming freemen from the English rule. Others, like the Chinese, wanted to return home rich with gold. However, for the Irish, they became known as drinkers, fighters, outcast, and did find their place in the American Dream. From these people came farmers, ranchers, outlaws, storytellers, playwrights, dreamers, and one would become president of the United States.

Black Irish

Grandfather Allen was known to be black Irish, and there are many stories as to why there is black Irish. Some say they are the result of the Spanish armada battleships being destroyed off the cost of Northern Ireland in 1588, but the Irish say they killed all they found, and this still leaves many questions. However, the Irish and Spanish, being Catholics, had more in common than the Irish had with the English. Further, for some reason the black Irish are found only in the northern part of Ireland, which is nearest to were the battle was fought. Most of Northern Ireland, because of British control, is Orangeman Protestant, continuing the war until today between both religions.

Others just say they've been here since the Romans. We, black Irish, have dark hair, dark skin, blue eyes, which is not the way one would think of the normal appearance of an Irishman. You figure it out, because most just don't know where we came from. My grandfather, dad, and I still bear these genetic in our appearance. Oh for sure, we all three have that gift of a tall tale too. Which is Irish? Any of these colors can be Black, Orange, or green? I intend on doing some further research into my family tree one of these days; there are some untold stories here.

The Irish Family Process

One other thing, talking of my dad's family history, as each son would think he's became of age speaking up or having their own opinion was seen as "talking back" or disrespect to my grandfather. Therefore, they would have to go outside and fight him for that right to be heard or have a say about family matters. One would know this beforehand before saying anything. This was part of the process since the beginning of man, but now times are a-changing. This clan was made up of four girls, one dying very young at the age of two, and seven boys who were all older then my dad, who was the baby boy. They all shared with him their experiences and many examples of why he shouldn't take that step of challenging my grandfather's authority. The girls learned to stay quite until they got married and had their own families. Plus, it happened my grandfather was in his fifties when my dad reached his teen years. My dad's day of "up and comings," as his family would say, was skipped. Luckily, this was never apart of his process or my process, but much later it did play out again, except in a different way. There was a reflection of a dad brighter enlighenment and in each following generation as each moved on. My grandfather occasionally found it necessary to use his razor strap on my father's backside, and my father used this same penalty instrument a few times on me, but maybe not as many times with that same instrument as he had received. However, in the passing of time, my grandfather and everyone else seen usage of this instrument had brought varying views on its past usage, value or history of usage. My mother, grandmother, and grandfather had reversed their view during my growing-up period and as their truths faded. Even now, my father doesn't recall the number of times it was used on him or me, but does recall its effectiveness to change views. At times though, my mother would use a newly picked small swift switch for enforcement of her rules too. I do suppose it hurts them somewhere more than us victim, as we are repeatedly told at the time it's being applied to our backside. This custom was not passed on by me to my children; however, my wife and I did use an open hand across the "rear running gear" during their early years before their capacity to reason beyond their actions, somewhere around ages two through five, but once I did lose my temper with our oldest daughter during her teen years by slaping her face for disrespecting her parents. I found that Middle-Age Irish weapons had no benefits in this age, and other means could be skillfully used to reinforcing lessons and control. The usage of love is stronger and with adding clear strong boundary adds greater bonding, while giving the feeling of protection, and finding real communication is the answer in molding and instilling the wanted values in our children's morals and respect. A repeated example from our own action does a better job influential effect and greater rewarding. This is something we all have to learn and pass on to our pebbles.

My Father

My father was twenty when I was born. He was the youngest of a family of eleven children, mostly English-Irish, and yet not knowing the past. He was born in 1920 in Grayrocks, Wyoming. His families known roots started in Kansas, and I found out there is a county that still bears our family's name in a section of this state. Allen County was a part of the roots of my granddad's clan, who were known as mostly descendants of Irish railroad workers, cattlemen, and farmers starting there.

Allen Family Beginnings

Ida holding Henry "Lee" and Isaac "Burt" holding Grace

Kansas

My grandparents were married in Kansas. Grandfather would tell me stories about the outlaw Jesse James with his gang coming to his farm when he was a small boy. They would have dinner, leave a dollar under their plates, and be gone in the morning before the family would rise to farm. After some time and much later in my life, I found out the James family had been apart of my family through bloodlines. His grandmother was a James family member. My dad's brother was also named Jessie to honor the outlaw. The legendary Jesse started out fighting the railroads after fighting the Union and became an outlaw because of his problems with the railroad over the family's land. It was not because he wanted to steal, rob, and kill. Was it because of the war? This was a result of big business taking people's land for the good of the nation and their own profits seen throughout the southern states. The farmland, the war, and survival is what made this man what he became. He tried to put it behind him, but one of his own shot him in the back. So my grandfather had been a part of Kansas and Missouri history. He now shared and started his own mixed of eliminates with his bride.

Dad's Mother

Dad's mother, Ada Angelina Whitaker, was born in Morris, Kansas, on 1876 to William W. Whitaker, who was born in London, England, 1842 and died November 20, 1934. Her mother was, Elizabeth Jane Whitaker, born 1844 in Dublin, Ireland, and had a total of nine children. I don't know why they went or how they got to America, but someday I'd like to do some research into that as well. Also, William McKinley was known to be a relative to her family. I do know she reflected a warm light with her Irish smile burning into my heart.

Dad's Dad

Dad's dad was a cowboy and worked for the railroads, which was why the family came to Cheyenne. These were the short methodical ending days of the cowboy and the West. He with his family had started in Kansas, then Nebraska, and then Wyoming. In those days, Cheyenne was where the railroads met as the hub to serve the northwestern, southwestern, and eastern connections. Also, in these beginning of the late eighteen hundreds, there was plenty of cattle work with the railroads, and ranches meeting here to feed America. He was also a carpenter by trade; he invented a procedure for making the floors and putting them together in the boxcars for the railroad the fastest manners yet seen. He won many races supervising the assembly of boxcars for the railroad. Also, he did other things like singing, calling square dances, and sometimes a little farming. He made a lot of mistakes, losing much of his money on deals in land, drinking, gambling, womanizing, and doing business he knew nothing about. Many Irish had made bad bets during their lives, and this cost their families much pain too.

He had owned land in Wyoming where oil was found later, only after it had been sold for taxes. He lost his strong light and became a flickering energy at the end.

Uncle William "Bid"(Named after my Grandmother's father)
& Tom (who was standing on right in previous photo)

Wyoming

Wyoming loses its people to wind, cold and no more than a low to average income for most. Its harsh environment is too hash for most dreams or pebbles. Most can't accept more than what is called a simple living for the most part. However, there is some coming to this land making wealth in many forms, but not all are in monetary form. That's a part of the nature of the land and this state. It largest and oldest income comes from oil and cattle ranching, but now with an ever-increasing amount of dependence on tourism. It brings most people here because of its large open lands reflecting that great diversity of natural beauty. Its existing abundance of great natural wonders have brought and forged men like Teddy Roosevelt, Buffalo Bill Cody, and many others through this beauty found in the wide open wilderness that exhibits the need for survival for all living things within it. Its many parks reflect this, like in Yellowstone National Park, the Great Teton National Park, Jackson Hole, and Medicine Bowl National Forest. Here is where the Great Plains open to badlands and then the Continental Divide, a place you must travel through to get across this country; therefore not many wanted to stay for the most part. Starting from historical Fort Laramie, where the settlers were protected from the plains' Indian tribes after leaving Pine Bluffs, Nebraska, when their great wagon schooners began traveling through this dangerous land, here is where the great trails of ruts from the wagon wheels can still be seen traveling west into the waves of grass inviting travelers before revealing their great tasks ahead. I too love its beauty, but we all must move on. This is also the first state to give women the right to vote.

Cheyenne

Wyoming lost most families following the lost of the railroad, which moved it's hub to Salt Lake City, Utah, during the late sixties, and I learned both of my grandfathers had worked for the railroads in Cheyenne until my dad's father moved on. However, my mother's father died working his last days around the railroad, and my mother's brother Paul worked for the railroad like his dad, but did move from Cheyenne to Salt Lake City. He paid the same price as his parents, with a stroke after retiring. Cheyenne has its strokes as well, but oil and coal helped bring it back to life. Cheyenne now has the retired Big Bertha; the largest steam engine in the world, reminding us of it's past glory when it dragged cargos for the railroad up that great gateway through the Rocky Mountains. It's mostly famous for its Frontier Days Rodeo, that's "the Daddy of 'Em All," with cowboys as reminders of its cattle town days, and with native Indians reminding us of days before the cattle days. It's a very small city, yet it's the capital of the state, and there aren't too many towns in Wyo. This is for my parents, the beginning of their life together, bringing me, and then my younger sister into the world with their energy.

My Parents Starting Together

Earlier in his presidency, President Franklin Delano Roosevelt said in his inaugural address, "The only thing we have to fear is fear itself," but our nation would now have to endure much greater trials and tribulations within itself and the surrounding world than ever before in its history. It rose to become the most powerful nation in the world.

My parents had no fear like most of the country, and they believed Mr. Roosevelt. Things get better when you're young, and there is nothing you can't do or overcome. It has been said "children are the promise of the future," and children believe everything is possible. They are the future as we are the present, and while all are moving together, that promise fades into the past. Understanding the times during the thirties, my parents believed in working and helping with the feeding of their own large family. Life could've been much easier just feeding themselves as a married couple. Hard times brought families to a point where shrinking the numbers to feed was the only way to address these troubled times.

My dad's education never went past the seventh grade, and my mother would get her high school diploma a year before my graduation from high school in 1957. Dad learned many trades during his lifetime and was always able to find work to support his family, like his father and the rest of his family, because that's what you did—that's what had to be done in order to eat, provide for yourself and family.

Mom's Family

Mother was the oldest of seven children, with the youngest only twenty months older than me. Her parents were English-Dutch-German, the rest I'm not really sure of. This family came traveling with all their worldly goods toward the advertised "Golden Cost of Milk and Honey," seen to be in the state of Washington during those late nineteen thirties days, not yet recovered from the Great Depression as it was seen in newspapers and reported on radios. My grandfather maybe have been a dreamer, but he lost his footing in Illinois before seeing they could have a better life out west. Moving from the small town of Lewistown in Illinois, where Mom was born, they where on their way like many Americans from the Midwest, in their car and a homemade trailer on a car frame, with wooden boards and canvas sides, carrying all they could. Packed with furniture and small spaces to rest, the trailer had live rabbits in small wire cages along the undersides for the family's food. They had to survive the heat and six children in an old two-door Dodge pulling it all. It was like ridding a great beast of burden up a great hill. It stopped in Cheyenne, Wyoming, and couldn't and wouldn't go any further. My mom had a strong hidden light in her soul, which gave her strength, keeping everything going straight within her while everything around was spinning out of control in that event of her life in her stream. I think she received this from both of her parents' energy, and that's what it took to survive those hard times for all in this country.

Mom's dad found work as painter and wallpaperier after a long waiting list to becoming a member of the union and then leader of it, while attempting some small farming to feed his family on their newfound land, working and living in this make shift house trailer until able to build a house. He always believed there was a better life in Walla Walla picking apples when they left Illinois, but never did travel much beyond here. No more mountains to climb.

Cheyenne, Wyoming, was his last place fighting the winds. It did get better, but he just never was able to reach his dreams. He found his stream of life carried him here, leaving him in this dry, cold, and windy spot of earth to his final journey, which came after many turns, hard work, and raising his children. All of his children, except for my mother and her younger sister, would stay and live in Wyoming or its nearby states for the rest of their lives. The family found their spots for a long stop and let their life's streams move them into new but slow-moving small streams near this place. Her youngest brother still lives in Cheyenne and another now in northern Wyoming. My grandparents were survivors of the times and land, dying here, but many years apart, from the same cause—stroke—but not before adding one more son much later to pay this same piper.

Dating and Mom's Animals

My dad tells, when he first dated my mother, he drove the family convertible to my mother's house in efforts to impress her, but most cars were soft tops during the early nineteen twenties anyway. Her parents lived on the outskirts of Cheyenne, shared with many small farm animals roaming around in the yard, while some were kept behind fences because this was open land outside of town. Kids and animals found interest in my dad upon his visit, before going into house for a time, and when he came back out, three goat kids were on top of his car, trying to eat the car's top. He was so mad. He almost didn't come back. Plus, while Mom wasn't looking, her littlest brother at the time would step on his toes. Oh the pain of love.

Dad & me & Mom

TWO

My Mother

My mother and I began our journey when she was only sixteen, just a kid herself. She had told my dad while they were dating that she was sixteen. That must have been something for her family to deal with, and therefore, she must have really wanted to get married because it would take something very important for my mother to bend the truth like that.

She believed in love, and made a very strong argument for all to reason with, about beginning together and starting her new life full of stories of truths and myths. Like it has been said, "The bubbling brook would lose its song if you removed the rocks." There were not many times that I could tell you when she would do this or couldn't tell the truth. I've always had very good scenery for untruths, but when it comes from your mother, your eyes are very unclear and blinded; you never see untruths coming from and told by your mother. What maybe in her view of truths may have been very necessary at the time? It never had any bearing on my parents love for each other, which continuing for forty-two years. They loved each other, and that's all that mattered.

My Beginning

We all start as small parts of a cell, known now as DNA, which combines for our magical beginning. It then develops into a group of cells the size of a fine grain of sand, and then takes form, resembling a human being during a period of nine months more or less. We form into a new baby, becoming "a chip off our family lines." Our birthday is the day we become breathing individuals with less dependence on our mother against the world and now on the road of learning how to become human.

Now pushed into the world by my mother's body on that date, through her pain, joys, and absence of fear yet unknown on our part. I'm sure for my part; this world was a feeling of being much colder, a feeling of that great push into something of the unknown, a sense of fear from disconnection. My perfect world was gone.

We all must go through this at birth in a physical and psychodynamic manner. I'm sure this is true for all babies coming into this world. It's shocking to us all, coming from a warm environment with total protection and all our needs on natural auto apparatus gone. For our mothers, who are a waiting this periodic to end, after that moment, their memories of pain fade after seeing the results. This important event in their lives and ours is what raises us above all the pain, and this is all that matters. However, for us we don't recall the event at all.

It's funny, we're never told about the weather or kind of day it was on June 25, 1939. We all celebrate this day as ours from that moment on, but more important, we become apart of a family with links to the past and future. Most of all, for our parents, we are their child, a piece of their life from that day on. This is what is known as part of the miracle of life. However, the question remains still over the centuries: when is the human soul born? We grow from this small human fertilized egg to cells, with all the genetics in place, then into thinking adult. We're molded from complete innocence to a being with the ability to choose in our own stream of life as a growing soul in a process. This process is important to who we are, where we are going, and what we are becoming. Our soul! God is apart of that growing and testing the soul. The sprit is that energy that becomes a soul in a never-ending process of learning.

Given Family Names

Mom's family does a lot of book reading. A mother would read books, and then afterward use a name for her next child after somebody in the book, and this was how my mother got the name of Cleo from Shakespeare's Anthony and Cleopatra. Funny how sometimes stories fit within life's real stories. I see my mom and dad somewhat in the frame of that story, looking at their characters now. My mom was strong but weak like Cleopatra. My dad let his ego always get the best of him, like Mark Anthony.

Dad was named Orval, and I'm sure that was because his was the time of the famous flying brothers. But as you can see, it wasn't spelled the same way as the famous Wright brother. This shows a trait of the family and their educational level too. Also, his middle name is Floyd, which is believed to come from my dad's older sister's husband. But no one in the family trusted him, so it's hard to believe, but possible. My grandfather didn't like him either and always said, "He's a horse thief." Dad likes to tell a story of walking on a street as a kid in Lincoln, Nebraska when Pretty Boy Floyd was driving and shooting at the Police after a bank robbery, and ducking bullets flying over his head. He didn't know from which side the bullets came from since there where many coming from both sides. Some other kids did get injured during these battles as he recalled. But what an irony that would have been if he were killed or shot by someone with the same name as the outlaw of his time. However, he didn't think his name came from that outlaw, but I could be wrong. Knowing my grandfathers flair for outlaws and the times, maybe Floyd, his new son-in-law, was a horse thief or wasn't a horse thief yet.

Mother's dad was Carl B. Mitchell, and being his first grandchild, combined with the fact that my dad's closest friend was named Carl too, of course it followed that I'd be named Carl, but my grandfather's middle name was Bruce, and mine became Benjamin after my dad's favored brother whom had died young. So it was Carl B for us both.

Benjamin

Dad's favorite brother was named Benjamin, known as Bennie by all who knew him, who had been shot and killed while in his twenties, in Cheyenne by an unknown killer, before I was born. He was shot in the back from a hotel window, or some said, driving a truck or while getting on a train across from the train station. He may have been another Jesse James. As the song went, "Who was the little coward that shot Mr. Howard [a.k.a Jessie James] in the back?" As that song continues, it was the Ford brothers, who got a pardon after being friends and "outlaws with Jesse." By chance, was Bennie another outlaw who was shot by another outlaw?

Last Photo of "Burt & I before his death

Many years before my uncle's triggered tragedy, he had move out of my granddad's household, maybe married, but would bring food or money in, helping out his the family. My dad got his candy or something extra, being the youngest, from his older brother, and that's why, I believe, he was my father's favorite brother. Although he may have been another Jesse James in this family, he may not have been a train robber shot in the back. He was known for wearing nice clothes and having money during a very hard time for most others of this area and era. Beside these facts, my dad tells stories of him and his brothers driving to small towns delivering homemade bootleg booze under the guise of a book salesmen and being chased by the local lawmen in their car.

So, Carl Benjamin Allen is my given name, but the Allen part is still a mystery for the most part, regarding my grandfather's family, but it was known to have those connections to the James family and Kansas. While you get to know me in my early twenties and see my life's integrated faults, this bring to mind more reasons for reflecting on these inherited initials of C. B. A. from my clan, a long inherited questionable judgment and seeing other reasons why they being ABC backwards, are a symbolic undercurrent which strongly effects this extraordinary life.

Grandfather Isaac

Recalling my grandfather from my very youngest of age, he was tall, very thin like an old white birch tree, mixed with long legs and arms like a king crab. His shallow face was topped by gray hair with tracks of dark blue-black lines running straight over his head and around his large ears. The hair would curve down round his light blue eyes at times, which were set above his very high cheekbones. His bushy eyebrows surrounded those sunken eyes that had seen the world change with the rise of this nation. His voice was low, and he was very quite. When I looked up at him, he would only smile a little from the side of his mouth. After going to school and seeing pictures of Abraham Lincoln, I could see my granddad had a similar physique as Abe. Lincoln, who was killed seven years before my grandfather was born, but Kansas and Missouri were the first mixer in states fighting slavery because of them being on the Mason-Dixon Line of this area, dividing North and South.

Bert

He was known as Bert, but the whole name was Isaac Albert Allen born 1872, in Lost Springs, Kansas. It's very funny also because my dad's best friend in life was named Albert too.

His mother was born in Missouri, and his grandmother was known to be apart of the James family. His mother was Elizabeth Mary (Allen) Keck, who died February 23, 1928, at eighty-three years old, in Cheyenne, Wyoming. She was born in Dever, Missouri, but not much is known of either side of his family. His father is believed maybe to been named William, who had died while he was young. His mother remarried another man, Mr. Keck, who had two daughters from previous marriage. His two or one brother was fathered during the first marriage with his father, and one brother was believed to have died, with one of the stepsisters having a hand in it. He didn't talk much about his family, or his youth, to his own family, so much is unknown. All as hard working, hard drinking, smoking, and living a "very hard, hard, hard life" best describes Isaac "Bert" Allen and Clan. It ended with him paying a very hard price at the end. He would die small in size, sad, poor and without much respect from his family, after eighty-three years, because of heart and many cancer problems. He could dance a jig at seventy-three, drink, cry, and sing at the wakes of his children, along with his wife passing on after forty years of togetherness. He lived longer than all his sons expect for my father, and he believed himself a ladies' man until he died. However, he let a younger woman make a fool of him by taking his money until the family stepped in. This was his last embrace of embarrassment. He had done this while as a younger man as well. My dad too also carries that same belief of being a ladies' man, and each birthday—he is now in his eighties—he tells me he wants to die by the hand of a jealous husband. He only wishes he could still get it up for that kind of occasion. Yes, that black Irish mind-set—mostly Irish or maybe Spanish.

Grandmother Ada

My grandmother Ada Allen died in 1952. I have a memory of her as a very small woman with a hunchback from her osteoporosis. Her back may have been bent and deformed then, but her heart and soul were straighter than anyone else in my dad's family, always warm and never complaining about what life gave her. There was always love in her eyes and warmth in her smile, but she showed the hard face of time in all the wrinkles in her face. She was always a glass of milk with honey toast and some apple butter for me.

Grandmother's Passing

My dad's mother, Adie, passed away in California. She was the beginning of this clan, and this was seen also as the Allen family's shift into a new script and stream. With her passing, I found myself missing her love at age twelve, and it brought deep sorrow, deeper than any other passing in my clan, or that of my grandfather. He would pass on much later in life. But before he did, his two eldest sons had died in Wyoming, and then two other sons living in California in their midlives before him. My dad was the only son left, with his sisters' still living into there eighties. An unknown assassin shot one son, Benjamin, in his early twenties, and a daughter just over one year had died, before their streams had widened.

Hazel and Carl Mitchell

THREE

My other grandmother, Hazel Mitchell, born April of 1900, passed away on October of 1960, and my grandfather Carl, born November of 1896, had died in August of 1970 while his two sons, Paul and Frank, were still living at home in Cheyenne.

All of their other children were married and had moved out, but they had came home to live with him after being in the military and seeing the world because this still was home. But they both moved on after my grandparent's deaths. My mother being the oldest was placed in charge of my grandfather's affairs and debts after his death. With my grandparents' deaths, my parents and I made our trip to Wyoming along with other family members, but I have little memory of that time except that I did so with great respect.

The Tree in the Rock

On one occasion, during on one of our trips while I was still very young, we where traveling by car and stopped, I believe somewhere in Wyoming, where there was this large bolder with a small tree growing out of its large crack in the middle. My dad lifted me up on it then took a photo of my mom and I. When I look at that photo now, I see that like that tree we both started life in a small crack, and that surrounding rock split, allowing for the beginning of a seed. It provided it with its needs, holding water and food and giving a holding place needed for that seed's growth into a young tree. Like my pebble or seed, we both had that strong stone foundation supporting us in our growth against the wind, snow, and rain, until came those days when we could stand larger than our own foundations. That's what your family can do for you too.

It's funny many years later, we drove there again, and there it was now surround by a fence and had parking spaces. We took another photo of it. The tree was presumed protected from us humans, and now that rock couldn't no longer perform its duty. The tree had now outgrown it, and that's why it now needs a fence for protection from others elements, like humans and not mother earth. We all also are growing beyond our boulders or families or fences, as we become adults moving into our streams. Many are lost and forgotten without any roots to hold them. We need photos to remind us where we came from, to give us something to keep us moving downstream.

Mitichell Family House

Remembering My Mom's Parents' House

As a young boy, I recall our visits to Mom's parents' house and my grandmother hatching chicks with a light bulb hanging above a large wooden box for warmth, with a screen over the box. It lies on the floor inside the house during the winter, keeping them safe. But when it was spring, they would become spring chicken. That's where that saying comes from. In spring is when they were put outside in a fenced yard and house, awaiting their fate. And when we would come to visit, when we open our house doors, every now and then adult chickens would escape running or flying into the house. This made us very watchful when going in or out, but still many times the old rooster got past us. My parents would yell, "Don't let the chickens in the house!" Most of the time it happened because we wren not mindful of them, but sometimes it was just fun when it happened. For a city kid it was great fun trying to get him back out again, with feathers flying everywhere. On the farm I was almost always with my uncle Frank, who was closest to my age. Things got boring for a city kid after a few days of interest, and as it turned out there is more work than fun. However, there's a lot of stories that I now recall about their house, with it's many farm animals for a city kid, during these few visits I had, but most of them recall were fun. I recall feeling terrified when a large mama pig and her piglets knocked down an enclosure fences and chased me into the house. Another when the geese acting in the form of watchdogs chased me around the yard with wings flying almost the height of my shoulders and pecking at my butt. I don't recall any dogs, but perhaps they didn't need any because of the geese. Then of course there was the stupid turkey, and everyone knows the stories, if they looked up with their mouths open during a rain, they could drown, but who knows if that's myth or truths. Picking fresh foods, like raw rhubarb and eating a few with salt before going into the house, but the most fun was finding eggs hidden in the chicken coup brings me back to my childhood vestibule memories, good and bad. One bad memory was that the house had no bathrooms inside, and its inside walls were never finished. There was only a one- or two-seater outhouse with a Sears Catalog for toilet paper.

So when you got out of bed in the morning and desperately needed to get to that small smelly, cold house, you never want to sit on that cold and damp wood, therefore placing your hands between you and the seat to save some warmth.

That's the way it was, and after living in California with all those modern bathrooms, you felt like you've moved back into the dark ages. After that, we didn't make many trips to my grandparents except for those sad times to follow, but it will always be apart of me, and I look at it differently now.

The Mitchell Family

My uncle Frank was the closest to me in so many ways and still is. He lived with his dad until the latter's passing many years after my grandmother's passing. Frank got married for a very short time, during the nineteen seventies, and never thought about trying it again. On the other hand, my mom's youngest sister Iris, born in February of 1935, has been married over forty years now too, having a son and daughter after moving to California in the late fifties like we did earlier during the forties. We saw her and her family more often than the rest because the other members of mom's family had children who continued their lives around parts of Wyoming or Colorado. However, sorry to say, they had very little contact or closeness with my parents during most of the years of my growing up because of the distance holding them apart, which was in contrast to the Allen clan. It was mostly because of the distance, but they where more independent with their own family lives as well.

The Mitchells all had their own lives without much closeness to each other's streams. Their streams separated them until only death could bring them together. Now only the three youngest members are alive, and that has now brought the two last brothers together throughout the years because of their missing dates with death.

One of Mom's other sisters, Charlotte, born March of 1925, became a teacher and married a fellow teacher, who later became a school superintendent in their small town. They stayed around the state and had a daughter, who also continued to collage and now has her own family too. Later came two more children, who grew into their own worlds too. Mom's sister has now passed on from Alzheimer's, failing to recognize my mother's face or name just before her death after the disease completely took over her mind and body at the end. Her husband and son later moved to Southern California many years later, and the husband has now passed on too. It's funny, I just recently got to read her diary when she was sixteen, getting an insight into how hard she worked in keeping house for the richer families and helping her family pool with every penny from work after my mother's marriage and we had moved away. She found her husband after working for his family during this time.

Uncle Paul

Paul was born on May of 1926 and got married late in life after being in the navy at the end of World War II, then living at home before finding his partner for life, then moving in with his wife, who had a son by her previous marriage. They did the best they could raising him, but drugs claimed the boy's life at an early age, but not before marrying and leaving his young wife to his family, which couldn't handle life's challenges either. Unlike that rock with a small tree along the road, Paul and his wife couldn't protect their children from his surroundings and what it brought. It destroyed his life. Later the wife couldn't handle the death of Paul either and was lost without her rock. Paul was the closest to my mom's age and my family and always came to visit us even after getting married. He would watch my children at their school or during games and visited with my mom throughout the years. For most of his life he worked for the railroad, but those years working for the railroad took its toll on his health. Before he could retire, death came robbing him of happiness not many years afterward.

Her other sister, Eloise, born November of 1923, passed on from heart problems like my mother, but she did after my mother. She had children too, but like Paul she couldn't protect them from the surrounding bad human habits and drugs.

Uncle Myron

The other middle brother, Myron, born on September of 1928, became one of the youngest linemen at sixteen and later trained other young men while in the US Army Communication Corps. He got married a few days before going to work for Uncle Sam's army during the Korean War. He returned to be with the love of his life and worked for a telephone company within the western states until his retirement after a heart attack. After becoming one of the higher-ranked men in management, the stress took its toll on him too. In most of his earlier years, he lived with his family in the wild, a part of or nearby Yellowstone Park, repairing downed lines. He now lives in Powell, Wyoming, near Montana and Bighorn Canyon National Park. After retiring, he and his wife completed many years of traveling in a fifth-wheel trailer from Alaska, north to the south through the Copper Canyon in Mexico during these pass years. Myron has two daughters and a son, who now have their own children now too. One of his granddaughters would come up to his house to ride Grandfather's horses, and she became his sunshine. The son lives in Arizona with his family and has his own horses and a lot of sunshine, but is still very close to all of the family. Talking about of his son, Frank brought him to California for a visit, and country met city. The son learned his lessons and has traveled throughout the world now.

Country Meets City

During the nineteen seventies Frank came out to California and brought Myron's son Kenny, who was just twenty years old and wanted to go experience the wild life of Southern California's topless bars at the time. He had been a country boy for most of his life.

During this time, I was married and had two children and worked as an insurance investigator in the local San Gabriel area. Naturally, knowing many great topless club locations was just as part of the job. I fixed him up with a passable ID with a draft card, and we took my car because it was raining, and my wife said, "OK, it's the boy's night." Plus she wasn't feeling well. We started in Pasadena in a place where coworkers and I had been before and it had very interesting lunches. It was called Genino's, a respectful Italian restaurant on North Lake and one of the first topless places around to have something to eat while girls performed with some class for the businessmen. We all believed the shady owners had some mob connection. The mob took control of its interest by providing dancers. I knew this after interviewing many girls in my investigations.

Kenny's ID worked out fine, so we continued our quest. We visited three or four more on our way back to Monrovia, where my wife and I were living. Mom was still living on Alta Street. Our last stop was only a block away from Mom's house, where the boy's were staying. It was called the Gilled Cage, a small bar with a good local standing, without the bad element. You could bring your wife or girlfriend here, plus I heard they had some nice, good-looking younger girls with some class. It was late, and this was going to become our last stop.

We entered after the doorman showed a flashlight in our faces at the entrance. It was dark with red interior lighting and took a while for our eyes to get used to seeing further in with a few faces of people only few feet ahead. We made our way closer to the small stage where one girl was performing. Three stools at the stage edge were empty, only a foot away from the dancing girl.

The waitress came over taking our order, and while giving our order I noticed two guys sitting at a table a few feet behind us farther back in the darkness. One of them was looking straight at me and motioning for me to come over closer. Being in Monrovia, knowing a lot of people here for years, I didn't give it a thought. So I walked over to him while the music played loudly and faced him with only few feet between us. This one guy was saying something, looking very intense. Not hearing him very clearly, I bent over closer, trying to hear what he was saying. He repeated, "Your eyes are looking through me." This is what I heard, and as he repeated it, he hit me in the middle of my chest, around the breastbone. My reaction was to return that with my own left hand to his forehead, following with my right to the other side of his head, but while I pulled my left hand after delivering its blow, there was pain. It started stinging at the edge of my palm, but without stopping, I continuing to strike him again anyway as he was falling back in his chair to the floor. The next blow was a right foot to his chest while he hit the floor. The other guy was surprised now, and he was trying to move out of his chair while falling backwards too and trying to find his feet. That's when I saw where and why my left hand was stinging. He had cut it open with a very sharp short knife. So backing away now while he was attempting to get to his feet, I began yelling, "He got a knife!" to Frank and Kenny, who where now coming toward my direction. They, with everyone else surrounding me, got out of the way. I was now jumping up on one of stool next to the stage, then on up with the dancing girl under her spotlight. Ready with my feet, for any further attempt by him to cut me, I saw the blood running down my shirt in a strong flow of red where I believed he first just had hit me. But now I knew he had actually stabbed me in the chest. The dancer screamed scrambling off the stage. If he hadn't hit a rib, there's no doubt I would have been dead from his blow. It was only a small turn of my body from hitting my heart; the doctor had told me while treating me. With the girl screaming and my blood turning my shirt red, these two guys were now making a dash towards the door with the bartender and bouncer running out after them. Frank grabbed Kenny because of his age and got him outside and told him how to walk home to Mom's from there. By that time, they had me lying down on a bench seat next to the stage with bar towels full of ice were placed on my chest and hand. The ambulance came and took me to the Arcadia Methodist Hospital ER, which I visiting many years earlier during my teens. They told Frank where they were taking me, and he drove to my Mom's in my car, got her, and then came to the hospital, where the doctors stitched me back together. They told me I was very lucky, and there's only a small scar now.

The Monrovia police came over to the ER taking the information and they had gotten the call from the bartender and because with his fast action, clear reaction, while it was going down, they, the police were able find these two guys racing down Huntington Drive in an old Mustang. The bouncer watched and had gotten the license number while they raced away. The police stopped them in Monrovia Park, around six or seven miles away from the bar. One was running through the park and the other stupid one who stabbed me was trying to hide under the dash. They both were high on drugs and worked at a car wash on the boarder of Monrovia and Arcadia. After finding out about this later, I went to court, and the judge order them to pay my medical bills, but they ran out of town before any payment or their jail term was served. Frank drove me home in my car, and my mother followed him.

It was around three and still raining when they dropped me off. I went in the house with my wife still asleep in the bedroom. She awoke when I turned on the bedroom light, and seeing my blood and bandages asked, "Did you wreck my car?" I replied, "No, I was stabbed in a Bar!" She was wide-awake now as I asked, "Help me out of my clothes and into bed, please." I took a few days off work after that. It made the local newspapers, and Kenny will never forget the wild time in California, nor will his dad. Myron was mad at Frank and me for getting his son from the country into this big city crime scene. Many years later at my thirty-fifth class reunion, the first thing my present wife asked me—after being told about this (and other things of my past) by our high school friend Jim Rood, who had read about this in the newspaper—was "You don't do those things anymore, do you?" Kenny, Frank, and I don't do those things anymore.

Suspects questioned in stabbing

MONROVIA — Police are questioning two suspects here in a stabbing at the Gilded Cage, 531 W. Huntington Drive.

Russell Edward Harrison, 26 of 423 W. Colorado Blvd. and Michael Eshanissey Anderson, 27, of the same address were arrested early Thursday, minutes after the alleged stabbing and have been charged with suspicion of assault with the intent to commit murder.

Witnesses said Carl B. Allen, 33, of 2468 Evergreen Ave., Monrovia, became involved in a fight with Harrison. Allen is said to have jumped up on the dancing bar, yelling, "He's got a knife!"

Harrison and Anderson allegedly fled from the bar but a witness reported the license number of the car in which they drove away. Allen was taken to Arcadia Methodist Hospital, where it was determined he had been stabbed in the upper right chest and left hand. The chest wound, according to police reports, did not penetrate the rib cage. His hand required eight stitches. He was released after treatment.

Police officers spotted the suspects' car from the description given and signaled the driver to stop. When the car stopped in the West 400 block of Olive Avenue, Anderson fled from the car but was apprehended behind a nearby house, police said.

Both suspects, police said, are in custody. Police added that Harrison is on parole from an earlier offense.

City Meets Country

During the nineteen eighties, after Myron came to California for a visit with my mother and my family, he showed interest in visiting with the boys during one of our Boy Scout meetings, where I was acting as my son's Boy Scout leader. He told the boys all about Wyoming, and he held their interest because Myron must be a little Irish too, and those boys saw Wyoming through his eyes, as he knows and loves it. Therefore, it was decided that night, during the next coming summer, our next trip would be to his Yellowstone Park, and a visit with him at his home in Powell, just north of Cody, Wyoming. They already completed trips to the high country of California's Kings Canyon National Park for a fifty-mile hike loop, climbing above ten thousand feet. They where ready for another national park peak. We made this trip with six boys and two adults in my crew cab truck with a large overhead camper that slept six, but had room for eight adding the two seats in the four-door truck. But it was summer time, and everybody slept outside under the stars most of the time. Our first stop was Las Vegas at Circus Circus trailer park. The boys stayed up seeing the circus until midnight, then slept on the warm pavement next to the truck on a tarp in the parking lot space for RV's. It was around eighty degrees at night under those thousands of manmade lights. So thinking of this heat, with no air-conditioning for those who were riding in the camper, we left before the sun came up again. The boys slept, as teens do, while we traveled along to our next resting stop in Zion National Park for a much cooler night. We visited the river and saw the beginning of the natural grandeur of this trip before moving on to our next stop, which was Paul's house in Salt Lake City, Utah, with his talking parrot. The boys loved his performance. We spent some more time cooling and relaxing before heading north to the Great Salt Lake Desert and mountain area. This also was the last time I saw him and his wife together, seeing that small smile of his and his bright blue eyes. Our next stop was Idaho because Yellowstone is closer to it in the northwest corner of Wyoming. We stayed overnight along a river, where the boys had tubed all day and slept under the stars on a tarp, watching the greatest meteor showers that come this time of the year. That was the biggest shower that we saw, and the falling-star show continued all night to our surprise as, and we made lots of wishes. This may have been the way early man saw this part of our world, with fire coming across the sky, and this is what John Denver had written and sang about in his songs. It was what he loved so much about this area. We also stopped in another town that had hot springs for a quick swim. Then the truck climbed the mountains into Yellowstone Park, where we stopped to watch moose and elk grazing along a river, before we went on to the Old Faithful geyser and the rest of the sights of this park, with it's bubbling heat, muddy spots, bright colors, smells, and waters. Just like the earth were forming millions of years before man. There was a big wildfire in this area the year before, and it left the forest blackened forest scars. This was a new world to most of these city kids.

Before going to Myron's, we stopped in Cody, Wyoming, and went through the Wild Bill Cody Guns and Art Museum. There was a staged gunfight in the street with cowboys falling and sheriffs bringing peace to the town. Now the boys were ready for the West, and Myron was trying to get us set up with a horseback camping trip into the wilds, but couldn't get enough horses. However, he made up for it later with something just as good in the eyes of the boys, after only having two horses, the camping trip didn't work out, but even better, he had his own shooting range in his backyard. I brought my guns, and Myron took out his whole range of guns because he also does his own gunsmithing. To the delight of all, he had his own quick-draw machine in his own backyard, consisting of a large pipe standing upright with two large metal paddles on each side. We draw the line on the ground, placing two boys facing it, side by side. After allowing a few shots with each type of gun first, they were ready now, standing still, awaiting the order "draw." The first to hit the paddle was the winner. My son learned my semiautomatic .32 was not strong enough to move his paddle after hitting it first. But with more shots it would have been deadlier. While Myron's .357 or .38 Special had a harder hit with the first bullet. I also brought along my old western Winchester.30-.30 rifle, and with this the boys learned more about the Old West. Against Myron's single shot rifles, it would have been like having wild Indians or buffalo's charging you. That's why the repeating weapons won the West and the American Civil War.

The boys slept on the top floor of his barn for a few nights, and then we went back to Yellowstone for a two-day hiking trip in the backcountry with some fishing before returning home. We stopped in Jackson Hole next to the Bridger-Teton National Forest shaping the Snake River. They had crossed many streams on this trip, climbing many heights and returning home with a better understanding of these great states of the west. Myron's energy was opened to them and me, exposing us to new roads that have been traveled in myths and truths and bringing us all to a new way home. We thanked him.

Uncle Frank

My uncle Frank, who is only twenty months older then I, was born in September 1937, being the youngest in his family next to my aunt Iris. My first memories of my grandparents' house were formed with him, and aunt Iris, who was away at collage, being the only children living at home during those early years. My sleeping upstairs in his bed, but at his feet, while my parents slept downstairs. This brought on the beginning of a never-ending tournament, which resulted in an instinctive infighting, him being the youngest and me being the only child. We fought for control of the turf, but I recall fondly one occasion, when we forgot about our self-centeredness. We enjoyed an overnight snowstorm and awoke with snow piled almost over the front door. We both thought about and wanted to use the upstairs window to exit, but a combination of parents with the sun halted our skew, but we did some hard work shoveling aside my dad before playing after clearing it away. It brought us together in action without us thinking only of ourselves. We did have fun jumping and throwing snowballs at each other, and this was also a release for both of us without lost of our monarch state. We learned we can't always be in the winner's light, and that winning was not the most important of things. We grew up together in sharing so many similar interest and ways.

Again much later, while both of us were teenagers, on another of my trips, Frank was working at a gas station with a junkyard next door, not far from his house. We would walk through the junkyard, dreaming what we could do with these old cars or parts, which we still do, but there was a girl who lived close by, and I guess, but I did not know it at the time, she took a liking to me. Anyway, to this day, Frank says, "You took away my girl." I guess it was mostly because of me being from California, a stranger in town, which caused her to shift her interest to me. In the mixing streams, pebbles from other places sometimes begin looking for other interests. During that time, he also had an old Jeep truck with a small 265 CI Chevy V8. He had fitted it with motorcycle exhaust pipes coming out under the sides. It was very loud, but anyway, one night we went for a ride in it to the lower parts of some nearby hills. After doing a lot of four wheeling around until dark, he said, "Hold on!" He turned off the headlights and we went up this very steep hill, trying to be stealthy with this thing the best we could. We went flying in the air, and at the crest he turned on his headlights and stopped just for a few seconds. We were now facing about two or three cars facing the town lights where we had just came from seconds ago, and there were couples jumping around coving their faces and other parts seen through those bright lights from the truck as we surprised everybody. We were laughing for the rest of the night, but everybody knew it was us. Afterward in town, as it was told around for a few days, we heard some people had some not-so-friendly feelings for what we did, but some laughed even more than we did as the story was told. We've always been closer because of our interests and age than any other members of Mom's family or the Allen family.

He got married during the nineteen seventies and came to California for a visit with his new wife. Everywhere we went, Universal Studios and others places, people would ask if we were twins or at lease brothers. "Nope, he's my uncle Frank!" We would laugh at the expression of bewilderment. His marriage didn't last long, but now he has girlfriends. Just like with my present wife I, they also connected after one of their class reunions. We are still connected because I've brought both of my wives to Cheyenne to visit with him, but my first marriage lasted much longer than his. Both of us are extraordinary pebbles, and in our cases it can be very difficult to be around us at times, but now it's time to look closer at "that Allen clan."

FOUR

The Allen Clan

The Allen clan stayed closer because of most of them moved to California, but my dad's two older brothers, Henry, known as Lee, the first child, born 1894, and Benjamin, known as Bennie, the fifth child, born 1903, had died in 1930 in Wyoming before the Allen clan moved west to California. Most found they're way west.

Henry's son Harry, who grew up with my dad (they were closer than Frank and I), was the first to move to California, and finding a job started it all. He got married and stayed in the San Francisco area, had two daughters much younger than I. He died in the late nineteen fifties of a heart attack too, and then his wife and girls moved to Southern California in the newly developed desert city of Apple Valley, until she remarried moving back north. So, I never knew this part of the family much.

The last son living in Wyoming was William, known as Bid, born in 1898, married his wife Fanny in 1918, and they died many years later after Jessie's and Harold's heart attacks in the nineteen seventies. Their only son known as Buddy died a drunk after serving in the army during World War II, and had children, but not much is known about them. When I was a teenager my parents visited with Bid and Fanny for a few days on their small cattle ranch, where I learned to ride and work fences. They came to California a few times, visiting my parents before their deaths. I had my last visit with them in Wyoming after getting out of the service in 1965 on my way home.

Grace

My aunt Grace was the second child, born in 1896, the first girl for my grandparents. She married Floyd, who had a wooden leg by the time I knew him. My grandfather told me, "Floyd's a horse thief, and should've been hung!" He reminded me more of the pirate Long John Silver. He had a limp and would talk from the side of his mouth with one eye squinted just for fun with us kids. My dad said he wasn't worth the powder to blow him up. I never saw him as a young man and only saw him for short periods and did not know him for what he really was, but I knew you couldn't trust him. My aunt Grace had three daughters, all marrying young. They had kids, and during Christmas

40

we all got together for family gatherings. Grace lived well into her eighties and died during the nineteen seventies too. My dad and mother never trusted anyone from that side of the family in telling the real truth, but thinking about my dad's middle name being Floyd too, maybe it's because of some favorable things her parents saw in Aunt Grace.

Aunt Lemoine's Family

My aunt Lamoine was the fourth child, born 1900, and had three daughters and one son, Eddie, named after his father, Eddie Sr., who was a prize fighter, which is like being a movie star now, when they first got married. He was not very big, but had the biggest heart and always had a smile for anyone. Lamoine was a big woman and ruled her family. Sometimes she was too interfering with all those surrounding her, and more so with her daughter's lives.

These families started out renting water trucks while the rest of my dad's brothers were in California with construction jobs that always had them running. Ed Sr. had also started his own masonry business and brought in his son, Eddie. It became Losinski and Son's, and they were close in every way. Ed Sr. died in the nineteen seventies as a result of an auto accident when my aunt lost control driving home from Arizona. She lived well into her eighties. Their only son, Eddie, was the second oldest of their children.

Eddie

Eddie got married very young, but the marriage ended in an early divorce after two kids, twin sons. He took custody of one of them, naming him Edward too. He became know as Little Ed throughout the family because there was now three Ed's. Eddie later remarried with Pat, and they remained married until the nineties. She had a daughter from a previous marriage. When they got together, the kids were raised as brother and sister, closer than blood. Eddie was closer to my dad's age and got in the navy at the very end of World War II at age eighteen, but never went overseas. He was like my dad, with an overwhelming love for speed and cars, which consumed him and his son too.

During Ed's early twenties, my dad drove a 1939 Ford coupe, which was fast, and my dad still thinks that's what started Eddie's hunt for something to beat him with, but knowing Eddie, it's just part of us. He loved and felt the danger of speed, like the rest of us as teenagers, and after the war he had fast cars and was everywhere with friends. It's still lives within him.

Well, Eddie found a 1929 Ford roadster on 1932 rails with a Flathead engine. He would take it out on their dead-end street when we came over and then show off how fast it would go for my dad and I. Seeing it whizzing past in a loud roar would get us all charged up. He began setting records with it at the new drag strips, with more now appearing throughout the area and the country. He was featured in Hot Rod magazine for many achievements. One was for reaching 132 mph in a quarter mile in 1953, and then later driving another car over 200 mph. I've a photo of me sitting in this car at the local Pomona Dragstrip with him and my dad, who had his leg in a cast from a motorcycle accident. Not too much later, my dad started racing his cars on circle tracks too. While Eddie later also built a dragster that was one of the first to reach 150 mph in the quarter mile, and I got to set behind the wheel of it as a teenager too. Eddie's son, Little Eddie, also got the speed bug early, racing around age five or earlier. In the nineteen fifties, cars and hot rods were making waves across the country. What a golden age for teenagers who loved cars and the highway.

Frances

Aunt Lemoyne's oldest child and daughter, Frances, or Frannie as she was known, was a larger and louder than her mother. Her presence was always known, and she was a little on the crazy side, but she had a big heart too. She had a son, David, who was one year younger than I, and I didn't know who his father was. David was my aunt Lamoines's first grandchild and was always getting her attention. Frances and David lived on and off with my aunt and uncle for different reasons, but during the nineteen fifties she remarried a sailor, Carl, and they had twin daughters and a son, Carl Jr. They were around six to seven years younger than David and I. I became known, because of the other Carls, as Carl Benny.

David was a teenager during the nineteen fifties, and his idol was Elvis. He died his hair black, had long sideburns and a big "waterfall" do. He was tall like his mom and wore thin clothes, the likes of Elvis's in those early years. Then in the nineteen sixties, he got married and began his own family working for both Ed's and with their same rental trucks, helping him make a good living too. He moved to a small horse ranch north of Newhall with his wife and daughters. However, cancer took his life at a very early age. He was in his early thirties, leaving a young widow and two children. Frannie's husband would also die of cancer much later. He was a quiet man who let his wife rule their world around family, like her mother did, but he was in charge the rest of the time. Their son, Carl Jr., went into the navy too and made it a career. One of their twins would die young too, while the other would stay on caring for her mother until her death this year.

Juanita

Aunt Lamoine's next daughter was Juanita, known as Pee Wee because she was less than five feet tall. She was very cute, with dark hair, and always reminded me of Shirley Temple. Sometimes she would be my babysitter, and that became the first time I found puppy love. I was in my preteen years. However, she married a fast talker from Oklahoma by the name of George, who sang country and western in bars and shows or anything for fast bucks. He was always a high roller without the money to back it up, and joined in on the family trucking rental business too. They started out young too and had a son, Billy Ray, and a daughter, Candy. Both were younger then I. Billy Ray soon became the godfather of my middle daughter and died of cancer at an early age, in his middle thirties as well. He had been close and best friends with his cousin, Little Ed, who had died before him in a racing accident.

Now they lay side by side in the graveyard with their grandparents and their great-grandparents. Candy is living, but is divorced, with two children near my children's ages, now owning the water truck business. However, Pee Wee decreed her life was not worth continuing after years of fighting with life, George, and divorce around fifteen years ago, and had ended her own life by overdosing on pills and alcohol.

Velma

The last daughter was Velma. She was more of a tomboy type, with a face like Buckwheat in the movie Our Gang, with a freckled face and sometimes his voice. She married young also during the same time as her sister. Then she had two boys nearing the age of Billy Ray, Candy, and Little Ed. She divorced her husband after many years of abuse and problems as well. The husband died of cancer at an early age too after they parted. One son has had problems with drugs; the other is a truck driver and is doing business with his cousin Candy. Velma remarried and just lost her husband of many years this year.

The whole Aunt Lamione family, plus Mom, Dad & Me
I'm 2nd left in 2nd lower row

Christmas Days

Mom, Dad, and I would go to my aunt Lamione's on Christmas Day for dinners. My mother would bring cooked turkey, pie, and her famous Jell-O fruit salad with walnuts and mixed canned fruits. My aunt Lamione would always have new furniture, and every other year a new car. Depending on the weather and how many people were expected, there was always room for more at the long table. There was a small one for the younger family members and there were always leftovers to take home, along with new toys and clothes everywhere. Kids were running, laughing, playing with all these new things in and out the house. You could smell the food cooking, and women were caring for their children while listening to the latest stories about the family's businesses, each one trying to outshine the other.

When dinner was served, the men would find a seat next to their favorite dish so they could get it first and then barter with the others for what they wanted next. This became another enterprise and the biggest game every year, with all the women getting mad at them waiting for theirs and the children's share. But it was always done in fun, and the children had fun watching the men play this game. After dinner the men would have a poker game, playing for pennies most of the time, but sometimes for much more. When I became a teenager, with my own money I would join the men's game. It was done for fun, but at times later in years, during the nineteen seventies after my aunt and uncle passed on, there were motor homes ownership pink slips on the table to cover the bet. That wasn't funny any longer. The family became smaller each year.

Also at the beginning, Jessie with his family, then Harold with his family, plus my grandfather would show up after dinner, and then aunt Grace with all of her family would drop by for some pumpkin pie. There was always a disagreement between the four families, and as the years passed with deaths, our number dwindled along with the disagreements. There was less and less of these get-togethers until there was no clan left. However, Aunt Lamoine and Eddie continued this dinner until after I was married and had my own family. After my parents were divorce, my mom still brought that Jell-O fruit salad for Christmas dinner until her death.

Family Business

There are two of my dad's brothers and their families, and two of his sisters and their families now living here in Southern California. The two brothers went into business together at times and my dad would work for them when he had no work to do. They drove, rented out, or sold used trucks during the years of home-building boom, which was gaining in the area during the nineteen fifties. Jessie had two daughters, who were teenagers older than I. Harold had two boys, one older by a year and one younger than I. Also there was Grace's family, with three daughters who were in their midthirties then, and they had husbands working with water trucks as well, but Lomoine's family did this the best. However, dad's two brothers became very successful too, but both died in their midfifties from heart attacks. Their families never did recover; there was money, but they had many problems: drinking, drugs, and broken marriages.

Jessie, the Seventh Son

Dad's brother Jessie was the seventh child and fourth son, born in 1910. He was a quiet man with a bigger-than-life smile, but worried too much about his brothers and their families. He was thin in build and looked a lot like his dad. He loved his horses and worked hard at the trucking business with Harold. Jessie had two daughters, and they would baby-sit me at times too. The oldest was Betty. She married a guy named Snooky, a name that fit him well. He wasn't much, not worth much either, and a waste of a human being, like the other guy named George who married Juanita. They later would divorce, and she'd become a drunk. The other daughter, Pat, married and took care of her mother as well after my uncle died in his early fifties with a heart attack.

The Unknown Laura Marie Allen

She was the eighth child and born between Jessie and Harold. She died at a very young age in Wyoming, with not much ever said about how, why, or when. I found out about her death in the family bible announcement with her picture and date of death, March 15, 1915, at age two years, one month, and ten days. This was much like my sister's death too.

Uncle Harold

Harold was the ninth child, born in 1915, the fifth son, built like a tank, stocky, and was always a fighter. When he was a teenager, he and his brothers were hunting with Floyd, and as he sat down on a rock over a cliff, rolling a cigarette, his .22-caliber rifle slipped off his lap and went off when it hit the ground below. The bullet stopped an inch or less from his heart and was never removed. He was wounded with alcoholism for the rest of his life too. He would go on drinking binges for days and completely disappear. He was the most successful businessman of all the Allen's but just couldn't keep himself under control. He also died in his midfifties from a heart attack too. His son Delmar, one a year older than I, had a sleeping problem, just falling asleep anywhere. That happened while he was behind the wheel at night on two occasions. Later he had a heroin habit and died in his early thirties. The other son, Donny, was one year younger than I and also had some drug problems for a while when he was young. After their father died, their mother remarried their business's bookkeeper and moved to Las Vegas with Donny. The last I heard, Donny was a cross-country truck driver. We are the only sons able to carry the Allen clan's name into the next generation as far as I know. After all those pebbles of ten children from my grandfather, only two can carried the name into the stream of life.

Aunt Nellie's Family

Aunt Nellie, the sixth child, born in 1905, brought up my father like a mother, he would say. She came out with her husband, Julie, to California for my grandmother's funeral. He was big bear of a man with hair covering most of his back while she was a very pretty woman like her mother. They stayed with us, and he would lie down on our rug and have me scratched his back over and over again, begging for more. I would give up with much disinterest after completing this task. They had an adopted son, Jimmy, but no other children back in Cheyenne. About a year later, Jimmy lived with us for a time and worked in my dad's delivery business while in his early twenties. Dad owned a three-wheel Harley Davidson, and Jimmy used it in the business. I recall Jimmy and I would go flying down the street, with me in the back hanging on to the bike's two rear bars while sitting on the metal compartment over the back wheels just for fun. He did something very wrong because Dad fired him for some reason without me knowing what it was or why. Then he moved back to Wyoming, doing many different jobs before losing both my aunt and uncle. He now his own family and has not kept in touch with mine.

Earlier, when at around ages ten or eleven, while visiting my aunt at their house in Cheyenne, Julie took me hunting for deer. At about age twelve, my dad did buy me a Red Rider BB gun for Christmas, but before that, I went hunting with Julie carring a 22 rifle in my hunting trip with Julie. During that hunt, after coming around a mound of rocks, I saw this big buck standing on the side of a small hill eating only twenty or less feet away. He looked up, and I looked into his eyes, but after seeing the movie Bambi, I couldn't pull the trigger, and I'd had been told not to shoot anything right from the start by my uncle. He heard my uncle coming and flew over the hill. However, my uncle had already shot another one on the other side of the hill anyway, and had already cut its neck upon calling me. We dragged the poor thing on a canvas to his truck.

Later at night my aunt froze it after my uncle stripped it down. My aunt had years of experience cooking wild game, and we had a piece of another kill the year before for our dinner that night. It was very good. However, after remembering those eyes looking deep into mine and dragging the other dead deer home, I didn't have much desire for killing animals from then on. I've never told this to anyone, but maybe my dad bought me that BB gun because he sensed that maybe my hunting experience would bring out something different in me. After that trip, perhaps my uncle told him I could be trusted.

My First Fishing Stories

Julie also took me fishing as a very young boy. While he would distract me for some reason, like sending me to retrieve something from the truck, he would put a fish that he had caught on my line without me knowing. Then I would come back and feel it on my line, fighting for the second time for its life until to my delight it would be netted again. He'd told me, "You'll have to spit on the hook with tobacco juice, that's what gets the fish attracted to the hook." I would get so excited it was hard to do two things at once. He showed me how to pull in the thin line without breaking it and not let the fish get away. However, I never tried that tobacco juice bait. I always knew there was love in that man with his respect for the outdoors.

I learned on my own respect for Mother Nature through his world, but not too many years later he died of a heart attack, and my aunt Nellie lost her will to live without him. She turned to drinking, which filled her wasted days. She was a lost, sad person without her sunshine and great bear.

The Bear

Much later in life, some friends went hunting and killed a bear in northern California. They followed its tracks back and found out it was following them. After the skinning, I tried picking up the box with the skin and head in it, but found way too heavy for one person to lift. As I looked back at its hanging body, it almost appeared to me as a skinned human being hanging on that tree. It gave me chills as they finished cutting it apart. We all tried a piece of the bear meat after getting it home, and it tasted OK but very chewy. Now after having this new insight into killing our fellow animals, I'm starting to see the way the American Indian's looked upon him as their brother, and I'm starting to see that we are a part of the bear clan. The streams of nature surrounding us are apart of us all, as we are moving together in its energies.

Grandparents and their Cheyenne House
Garandparent Allen's House

Moving Back in Time

Today the clan has diminished in number and is far from those days when we were a large family. However, now I'll giving you a little of what role my clan played in my foundation, my rocks surrounding me and giving off energy in so many ways as apart of my life. They were very important as I started from this small pebble in those early days described in these memoirs of myths and truths began.

Starting with Cheyenne, this was the place of my childhood where I heard the often-repeated stories of my family. This landscape is where my steam of life starts. As very little children, we naturally trust in our parents, and our adventures with them make our growing-up years filled with love, and without fear.

My parents brought me home from the hospital to our old bus on blocks, sitting on the back part of my dad's father's land at the top of a hill, next to the railroad tracks not far from town. My dad's parents lived in an old house in the front lower part of their property. My dad and grandfather had converted the bus into two small rooms, a bedroom, a kitchen, and it's a place to sit. An old potbelly wood-burning stove placed in the middle kept it warm and was used for some cooking. My bed was an old dresser drawer pulled out halfway, while my parents had their own bed in the back of the bus. See, we lived on the wrong side of the track and in the back of the bus too. Poor white Irish had a lot in common with blacks or poor whites during those times. We would have a good laugh about this later in the nineteen sixties. We didn't worry much about the bathroom, but it was outside, the outhouse. It didn't matter much to me since Mom took caring of me. Then my sister would come a year later, and I'd move into a small bed made by my grandfather. My mother worked cleaning houses, and my dad drove trucks, taxis, and did other odd jobs he could find. While my grandmother would baby-set or one of dad's older sisters, took care of me during the times Mom worked.

I was a handful, and I always remember that one day I was climbing a chair. I stood up, but then I fell onto the red-hot potbelly stove, burning my right hand. I was screaming in pain afterward, and that event would affect me the rest of my life. I learned to eat left-handed, but I still wrote with my right hand in school, so I would cry, "It hurts, I can't do it." Now left-handed, I'm not sure that was the only reason.

I do many things with both hands and also do things with both feet, like kicking. But I throw right-handed only and kick mostly with my left foot. Hitting a baseball from either side is sometimes very helpful. However, I see things in a more abstract form than others, outside the box as they say. I see them from the right side of my brain, which indicates being really left-handed. Looking at drawings and pictures more than reading words, I found out much later in life, is the cause of my trouble with words. I also found out later my sister had six fingers on her left hand at birth.

FIVE

This is the very beginning of an extraordinary pebble. This also brings a deeper infusion with elements and all the other energies in my early life's stream.

Dad loves telling the story when I began walking. There came a time when walking under the table in the middle of our bus became a problem. It just happened I could no longer clear the tabletop when I tried walking under it, and I bumped my head and fell to the floor in a fit of anger. I got up and continued doing the same thing again, again and again. Then my dad grabbed me, gave me a swat across the butt, telling me to knock it off while I cried. He told me sternly, "It's time to bend down or go around," showing me how to bended down, but oh no, that would be too easy. It took a long time for me to learn that bending down or going around would be easier.

Much later in my growing-up years, I learned, thankfully. But I tell this story to people who have had similar experience with me. I tell them, "This is what you'll be dealing with, and I'm hardheaded at times." It came naturally, seeing this in my father, grandfathers on both sides of my family, and in most of the other family members on both sides. Our Irish, English, and German family lines, as it's called, instilled this bullheadedness, I guess, and I've repeatedly been told so. This has to be the only reason for our "head-on" way of thinking. Of course I write this with a little laughter.

Believe me now, learning after many years of dealing with this problem, there still are those occasional running head on with my headstrong thinking that must be under control. There are fewer little tables now, but I still need to go around, under, or if needed, climb over. Trying to learn this is naturally harder on those of us of older age, but it's seen in my children as well just as another "big way." We must carry that genotype in growing up, but for some of us that quality is stronger in our life's streams.

I'm hoping we learn with age, as did our fathers or mothers, in keeping that damage to a minimal lost. We need to control fear and anger in our lives from the top to bottom of the tables.

My Moving World

Changing streams is not easy on pebbles or any of us, as said before. Most people do leave Wyoming, sooner or later. My father was like my mother's dad. He had big dreams and heard about a lot more work in California, in "the Land of Golden Dreams." He left my mother with me around January of 1942. Later my baby sister, Elizabeth Jane Allen, named after Dad's Grandmother and was born on September 1941 in Cheyenne. This was just after hell's fire had come to America, with even deeper and larger effect for the rest of the world. America was now at war, moving its people to mobilize all its recourses, and very soon afterward it would prove its place in world power. The stream of life had made a drastic turn for everyone on December 7, 1941.

Leaving Cheyenne

I think it was because of the war mostly that his cousin Harry, who was now working in California, gave Dad a job opportunity. They had worked together in a government CC camp, while both were single and younger, before my mother had come along. They were very close during their youth because of their age, like Frank and I. I also believe he was the best man at my parents wedding. Harry had written my dad telling him about the many jobs.

Once my dad was in California, he found work right away with a pipe company and later with the shipyards in Oakland. His new employer was Mr. Kaiser, who was building ships before the attack on Pearl Harbor.

Mr. Kaiser had made a promise to Mr. Roosevelt, which he was making good on, the turning out of one ship every two weeks for the war effort to help supply England with equipment to fight Germany. It later became a twenty-four-hour operation, with more and more people working seven days a week. Mr. Kaiser would become very wealthy from this, but would lose some of his money after the war through his involvement with other ventures, one being Kaiser Motors, which became apart of the Hudson and Nash Automobile failure after the war. But he did make it back in the steel business and hospital foundations.

Buddy, his Mom and "Bid"

War Loss

Dad's job was very important to the war effort, and since he also had family, this made him exempted from the draft. So were his older brothers because of their age and family. However, his older brother William, known as Bid, had a son, Buddy, who went into the army and became another victim of the war. He survived the Battle of the Bulge in Belgium, but he returned with deformed hands and feet from the extreme cold, other than the war scars he hid within. He died much later from his involvement in one of the war's major battles that became the enemy's breaking point. Many like Buddy, Mr. Kaiser, and my dad would pay their debts later, for what they thought was a great opportunity. Dad had become a welder, without knowing at the time the gases from the types of steels used was destroying his health. The job would affect him, my mother, and me with many drastic turns. He saved all the money he could in three short months and sent for his family, with the help of his cousin Harry, who had also set in motion his own drastic changes. He was twenty-one and would be another year older on March 13. He was struggling but learning in his new job, and he had found a place to live with his new family. He was standing on his own two feet now, and it brought much hope. He was now making more money then anyone else in his family, and proud of the work he was doing for the country. He was a shinning pebble now.

Three Leave, One Left Behind

The three of us—Mom, my sister, and I—had left Cheyenne on a train for Oakland, California, in a bitter winter, with snow on the ground on March 10, which was not unusual. My mother was looking forward to moving to the Golden State. The tickets were for the cheapest of seats, where you sleep, eat and tried keeping warm for three or four days on a drafty train car, and also trying to handle one small child and a baby would be enough for anyone. I was now two years and nine months old was in an age of no defiance, as everyone who has or had children know. My sister was five months old and needed much care, and to top this all, we both had bad colds that day we left Cheyenne. Somewhere, somehow, we both even became much sicker, and my mother got off the train in Salt Lake City, Utah, finding her way and taking us straight to the hospital from the train. She didn't know anyone here, no family, but she knew it was what was needed. The two of us had pneumonia, but only after a few days, only one would leave with Mom to California, the other staying in a small plot of earth.

There was no cure for pneumonia then, and so my sister died on March 12, 1942, one day before my father's birthday, she being only less than six months old. My mother was nineteen and now had to deal with the death of her youngest child alone, with me still sick but getting better. There was no one around her to hold on to for any support, no one to give her a warm hug or cry with her while traveling this turn in her stream. My mother must have been a very strong person to keep herself in control throughout all this, but I do believe this made her a very much colder human, taking some of her energy away with this death. A mother's pain in the loss of a child can never be measured. We lost a third of my mother too that day. Dad did leave his job for a few days, but didn't have any money left or anywhere to get the money now. There were no credit cards then. He was only able to get there for my mother three days later, but they had no money for the doctors and hospital debts. So they had to borrow it from anyone they could get it from. My mother's mother and dad's parents came to Salt Lake to help too, bringing some money from both families for the debts. They had to turn to church charity to bury my sister in an unmarked grave for children. It would be well into the nineteen seventies before they would buy a grave marker for my sister.

I got better after weeks, and we boarded an Oakland-bound train again. Now there were three again, but there was a difference kind of chill in the air. It must have been a emotional time for us all leaving Elizabeth Jane behind, like my grandparent's had done with their Laura Marie Allen, who was nearing the same in age too. However, they had more children, but my mother never wanted to have another child again. There is no greater loss than the death of a child, but my parents being young, that must have been of some help in moving on in their stream. The world was losing babies, mothers, and young men in the war during 1942, but again Mr. Roosevelt was telling the world to overcome and stand up with a sword because there were battles to be won, and the fight had just begun. The world believed they could, would, and history proved him right again.

Oakland, California

Dad had found an apartment not too far from work. It was upstairs on the side of a hill and within walking distance from the Oakland Bridge or some other bridge, I'm not sure which, but this is how I remember those days. I had been playing downstairs, putting on my dad's Hard-hat before I started walking to the street with his lunch box in my hands. After going down the bridge, this policeman stopped me, asking "Where are you going, big boy?" I replied, "I'm going to work with my dad, at the shit yard." He then picked me up, and off we went to the police station, and I became the center of the show watched by an attentive audience in blue. After waking my dad, who was supposed to be watching me, my mother discovered during midway through her doing laundry, I was missing. They had gone from top to bottom of the building before calling the station. She found me with a policeman's hat on eating ice cream and sitting on the top of the sergeant's desk in the middle of the biggest gathering known to this prince or newspaper coverage. There was so much laughter, and I thanked the crowd with a smile of dipping sweetness. Dad's hat had his name on it, and I knew my first name, so the police identified me and told Mom about my adventure when she called in her panicky state.

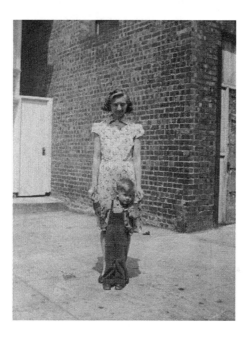

Mother had tears at first, but by the time we got home, my ears were red inside and out from her pinching them while shouting at my dad and me. I was helpless again without my eager audience of protectors, and my dad warned me very loudly about never leaving without them for anywhere, or I would be answerable to his belt. My dad was working the night shift, and my mother thought I was upstairs asleep with him while she was doing our laundry downstairs. Laundry became a problem in our lives many times. We didn't forget this adventure where we learned policemen are equipped for anything that can happen—with ice cream, hats, and a good audience. I have dim memories of happy days playing in the sand on the beaches within the Bay Area, and I have few photos to remind me of those times. My parents liked being with their friends, being young, and having fun during this time in their lives while the world was going mad. I recall my dad trying to play a banjo and his coworkers coming over to drink his homemade wines, dancing, and laughing for hours. We always had our own car with gas stamps, which limited our travels because of the war, for those trips to the beach or anywhere else on his days off. There are many things that were rare because of the cutbacks for the war. You got stamps for gas, food, and other item like clothes too or tires for the car. There were two things about that war that I remember that was the most important to me as a child: there were no metal toys and eating horsemeat.

San Rafael

We moved to the very beautiful city of close to San Rafael in Larkspur, across Richmond, with trees making the surroundings much better, as my mother would say. It was still like the rest of the surrounding bay cities, up-and-down streets on hills, but not as many apartments or people. There were a lot more open spaces. It was smaller and felt more like a small town too.

One day my dad washed our car on his day off, getting the car out of the garage to the alley behind the house, where there were wild berries growing on one side. My mother and I would pick as much berries as we could reach for our sweet treats. She would make so many great things like jelly, jam, pies, or just put them over ice cream or sometimes just plain milk. My dad would make wine from them and other fruits he could find, but his black cherry wine was his best.

Going to the Store

Back to the car washing, Mother asked Dad to go to the store for something, and he asked me to ride along. I took with me a wooden toy gun with a bayonet Dad made me just a few weeks earlier. For those who don't know what a bayonet is, it's a knife attached to the end of a gun used for charging the enemy. Our car was a coupe, a two-door. It wouldn't start because the wires were wet; lacking rubber protection lay most cars during those years. Also, the cars in those days had only six-volt batteries and starters, which is half of today's standard systems. He tried to start the motor over and over, and it was getting slower each time until the battery was dead. He figured it out and got out and started wiping out the cap and wires with a dry rag. He was sure it would start now, but the battery was still dead. Now angry, he got out and pushed then jumping back in. We started moving down the alleyway, and he turned the key, put it in gear, and popped the clutch. He didn't know why, but it still wasn't starting, and now the still-wet tires were sliding on the dirt. Then we began swerving off the road and into the air, ending sideways in the wild berry bushes just like Br'er Rabbit in *The Song of the South*. I recall flying and then landing sideways on my dad's side, the car surrounded by berries. There were no seatbelts invented yet those days, and when it was over I was crying louder than a puppy that got its paw stuck. My dad asked, "Are you alright?" I stopped crying for that one short breath and started hitting him. "You broke my gun!"

Dad struggle up through the door window and lifted me outside. My dad carried me back up the hill, and with each step came a harsh set of words that I was never to repeat. I don't recall much else, but you bet my mother was not happy with this event, nor was my dad. When the car was pulled out, it only had some scratches on the paintjob and started right up after the battery was charged at a gas station. We crashed while traveling around 10-15 mph or less, and cars those days were made of heavy steel metal fenders. It would have taken more to wreck it. In the end we had more scratches than the car after climbing out through those berries. You can tell there was no forgiveness for Dad, and there were many other accidents to come.

Ending the War

America and the world had done its job, but in this process they both had changed. The world had learned what real evil was. Now came the lessons on rebuilding and healing. By 1944 the war was ending, and my dad's health had become a major issue. The doctor's told him we had to get out of this wet, foggy, and cold weather. It was mostly caused by his job, welding. His lungs were filling with fluid, and he was losing weight and coughing up blood and had many other problems. My mother told him maybe Southern California would be better. Our lives' streams got bigger and made another wide turn for us all.

SIX

Southern California Stream

Los Angeles

We moved south to sunshine, to a much warmer climate for Dad's health, where my parents both found work. Within months my dad's health started improving. We found a house on a street going up a hill. Most of the country thinks of LA as flat when they look at it from the Pacific Ocean to the west and with mountains on the backside east. It's not as hilly as San Francisco, but if looking from the older El Pueblo de Los Angeles, there are still hills surrounding all of downtown in all directions. There is Angel Flight, China Town, Dodger Stadium, East LA, Westlake, Silver Lake, Lincoln Heights, and Mt. Washington without traveling into the Hollywood Hills. However, we soon found it was not the City of Angeles.

Bonnie Bra Street

We lived not far from downtown on a hill close to Echo Park, which has a small lake with ducks and old men in small rented paddle boats fishing along its banks. Now turning five years old, I went to my first school only a few blocks from home and just past the park. I remember one day walking home after school with a friend, a neighbor, and his mother, and seeing a man beheaded probably by the blast of a shotgun. We couldn't get close for a better look but could hear people who had gathered around talking about it. This stuck in my young mind, and when my mother heard about it from the neighbors, I could hear her yelling at my dad that night when he came home. A child's mind doesn't know death, but I did know my sister was no longer with us. "She's in heaven," my mother would tell me when I'd ask where she was, until I let it go. However, that person in the park was now in two parts, and I did understand someone had done that to him. There was fear, and we all felt it.

Trapdoor Spiders

From this house, on another hill behind you could see a hospital along with other clustered houses on all sides. After living here a few days, I found trapdoor spiders in the grass in the front and back yards. They dig a burrow and cover the entrance with a hinged lid, like a trapdoor, and wait for their victim to come by. We had fun by getting a stick, putting a bug at the tip, dangling it in front of the small trapdoor, and waiting for the spider to come get its prize.

My Trapdoor

At that time I didn't think we could all become baits to things lying behind traps, things bigger than any spider. My parents never knew of this, and I've never told anyone what had happen to me until only a few years ago. If my dad had known, someone would have been dead; and if my mother knew, there's no knowing what she would have done. This stayed deeply hidden in my mind, affecting the rest of my travels within my stream of life until I faced it, which is only now. I was totally innocent before this place and this trapdoor, but in the darkest part of my young mind it affected me and changed my views of the world forever.

Dad had become a millwright setting up machinery for large companies, and my mother went to work for the President Ship lines. My parents were at work, and a neighbor with three children was watching me. I slipped off into the rear of our house like I usually did. Since it sat on the side of a hill, there was a small space under it on one side. Normally, I was able to walk under it almost standing up, but any adult would have had to bend over to get in, and it got smaller the closer you got to the front of the house. Wooden slats with a small door enclosed this lower section. It was a cage of white slats with dark holes like a hidden trapdoor.

This was a hot day, and I usually go there to play because it was cooler in the summer. I was busy playing with my toy trucks and did not hear him come in. The spider was now in the hole. He grabbed me from behind by my neck and turned me around. He had it in his other hand already and put my nose against it and told me to lick it.

He was bent over, and since it was very dark I could only see his thing in his hand. I could smell it when he told me to lick it in his very low voice. He was a huge man. I opened my mouth to start yelling, but at that same moment he forced it into my mouth. It was salty, sticky, gagging me. He told me to hold still and keep my mouth open, or he would hurt me.

In a few minutes it was over, and he threw me down into the dirt and told me that if I ever told anybody, "You'll end up dead, like that man found in the park with no head!" He turned; walked bent over through the door lit by sunshine, and disappeared, leaving me crying with my face covered with him and dirt. Any child who has been abused this way by an adult is forever damaged; he no longer trusts the world.

I don't remember anything about his face because I never saw it. I just remember that voice and what he said. I didn't get out of there for a long time, just sat there afraid of what could still be out there, hidden from sight. Then I slowly came out looking at every direction at first, shaking all over. When I was sure no one was there, I found a water hose on the side of house and washed my mouth and face because I couldn't stand the taste. Even so, after washing I still felt dirty. Luckily no one was home yet. I never played under the house again and never told anyone what happened that day, but I had many bad dreams and refused to go by the park on the way to school. This haunting abuse was buried, hidden away in my mind forever. My mother had to walk me, or I wouldn't go to school or the park. We moved by the time I was in the next grade. I was just five years old.

The Suburban Valley Living

Duarte, California

This is a city next to the San Gabriel Mountains on the outer eastern part of LA in the San Gabriel Valley. US Route 66 travels through the center of town with motels, bars, restaurants, groves of oranges and avocado trees. There was also a mix of palms and pine trees scattered along the way up to the base of the mountains. But it had more rocks than trees, and more trees than houses when we moved there. There was a large sandy and rocky area where the San Gabriel River runs along the city of Azusa. This is the place where rocks become pebbles, and then sand after thousands of year. It's been there before any man was there. This river in the winter has water making its way all the way to the Pacific Ocean.

When we moved there, the Red Car traveled on tracks to downtown LA and on to Long Beach. This should have never been disassembled; it was the best form of transportation this area ever had. A freeway off-ramp is now in place where we moved to then. I never knew why we moved here or whether it had anything to do with my dad's work, but we were not on any hills any longer. This town is at the base of some very high mountains ranges and was still almost desert wilderness at that time, with its dry riverbed only a small distance away from our trailer.

Now being almost six, I sensed a much larger world around me seeing these wide-open spaces surrounding us. It was like being a part of the Western movement, with this pebble now moving in a wider stream, but rolling in a very slow way to a bigger part of my life.

Red Car

One day on the weekend, my mother and I rode the Red Car, the electric train, from Royal Oaks Avenue in Duarte to downtown LA. It was the week before Christmas, and with no school, we left in the morning, traveling a little over an hour even with all the stops. I'd never seen so many people, lights, music, and stores widows filled with moving dolls, clowns, trains, and toys. It was like being in a dream, yet it was really happening. We walked the streets and stopped at the May Company, plus many others that I don't recall. We stopped and stood in line for a long time so I can sit on Santa Claus's lap and tell him what I wanted for Christmas. But I could tell he wasn't listening to me because there were so many children and so much noise. I told him first I wanted a Red Rider BB gun, but it didn't appear under our tree on Christmas Day. So then I knew he didn't hear me, probably because I didn't speak up loud enough, but I was hopeful the next year he could hear me.

Clifton's Cafeteria

However, best of all, we went to Clifton's Cafeteria afterward for lunch. Wow, you could pick out so many different things, but I just couldn't make up my mind. It was unbelievable having so many kinds of food at once in such a big restaurant, and you could go back for more too.

Mom reminded me to use my manners I learned from my grandparents. "Don't wasted the food," my mother had told me in her lowest and stern voice. As we finished, Mom got a big smile on her face, and away we went finding a special place on the side of a hill. We boarded the small train car Angels Fight on the side of a hill towards the top of Bunker Hill. The cars would cross each other, with one going up and the other going down. Another wow. It was fun watching, and riding them was even neater. She bought a couple more packages at other stores as we made on our way, and at last back on the Red Car for home as the lights came on in the streets, stores, and autos. It made the appearance of a make-believe place in my small mind. It got cold as we got on the train, and I snuggled up to my mother.

I got deeper into my make-believe world when our train gave off a big rain of sparks, with sounds of popping coming from the top as we started whipping along toward home. Now I was off into my dreamland with a short sleep, and I awoke to my mother shaking me before we got off. My dad was waiting for us with a big smile as we to stepped off at the platform. He was there, waiting to drive us home. Seeing him, I became wide-awake again and tried to tell him everything at once. It was a wonderful time and place for a child of six. It even got better later on in that summer when we went on another trip to the beach in Long Beach on the same train, only 25 cents one way to the beach and fun zone with a big roller coaster.

The Trailer Park

We lived in a very small trailer, maybe ten to twelve feet long, which my dad had traded for our rental house in LA somehow. He had it fixed before we moved, and I believe he was now closer to his work with us now in this old trailer park on the south side of US

Route 66. Our trailer was in the front part of the park and not far from the bathrooms with showers. I don't recall exactly when, but my grandparents on my father's side moved into a small old house down aways on a dirt road at the end of the trailer park. It was a long walk and took a good while to get there for a six-year-old.

The Hunter

What a place it was for a six-year-old boy with all the wild things around. I discovered a newfound friend in an old man who had an old dog and lived across the way in the park. The three of us would walk into the surrounding rocks and desert sands whenever we felt like it. He must have been retired or something, but full of wisdom. Sometimes we would go out with his .410 shotguns early or late in the day, shooting rabbits, rattlesnakes, and quail for his dinner. He would skin them and hanging them up to dry all around his trailer. I ate my first rattlesnake, and as they say, it tasted like chicken. This was after that day we came upon a rattlesnake trying to get away from his dog. It was longer than I, and the old man blew its head off. Later, he made a slingshot for me from an old bicycle tube, forked wood, and some leather from the tongue of an old shoe. From then on I would practice shooting old cans and bottles on sticks to make sure no predator could bring me fear. There were plenty of pebbles, but this one was now ready for any snake or wild things that got in his sights, big or small. Checking further in our park, I found some other kids too, and we would find many adventures hunting lizards, horny toads, snakes, and spiders without fear because of my skill with my weapon.

The Desert Ship

There were three or four other kids with me on one of our adventures when we came across a giant desert tortoise, and when we got near him, he stopped and hid in his shell, knowing there was danger. Then two brothers ran back to their trailer and got a big old washtub that you would wash clothes in, and while we surrounded this creature of hundreds of years, we placed the washtub over him. He filled almost 70 percent of the space inside that tub, and one kid sat down on top of it. We were surprised to see the washtub move a few times with the kid on top. The rest of us rolled big rocks into a big circle to surround him and keep him from leaving without our approval. We then took off the washtub and waited for movement. While we waited, one of us kids went for some lettuce and attached some of it to a stick with a string. When it smelled the lettuce, its head came out very slowly for a bite. He liked it and wanted more as it gave it a taste. While eating, one of the smaller of us kids got slowly up on his back—honest, that tortoise was that large—and some other kid put some more lettuce on a stick inches away from its mouth. It started moving toward it, and sometimes we would let it have a few bites to keep it going. We all tried riding him around the circle, but it was very slow, and with most of us too heavy, it would just stop. However, being smaller and thinner than most, I got my short ride on this great desert ship. The next day he was gone, just like a slow-moving ghost of the desert. He had found the weakest link in our stone fence during the night and got away with some lettuce for his troublesome visit with us kids.

Wash Day

Mother had an old wringer washing machine outside the trailer, and that machine got me by the hand one day while I was trying to help. My hand got too close just as I was putting in some clothes; the wringer caught me with a big bang! It got my fingers, hand, then started for my arm, but my mother's quick action, she being only a few steps away, got my hand out with only a few smashed fingers. I was very lucky, but it wasn't done yet. I did have a fear for this machine with its grinding and whirring.

To get hot water into it, my mother would heat a large pan on the stove inside the trailer. The washer was sitting on some small wooden boards next to the steps. One day she filled it almost to the top with clothes, soap, and lastly, boiling water. But on her way out with the last pan of hot water, she slipped on the wet steps, hitting the pan against the washer and spilling boiling water over her upper body. She landed on the boards supporting the washing machine, causing the machine to fall on her. She was now pinned by the machine, screaming. A neighbor and friend of my parents came out running and pulled the machine off her and picked her up from the wreck. But when he pulled the wet soapy clothes from her body, she screamed even louder because her burnt skin had stuck with fabric, and it was now being ripped off her. He took the clothes, including the ones she wore, because their weight alone caused her pain. It ripped off more skin, which came off in rolls when he touched every burned part of her body. He took her into his car, rushed her to the hospital still screaming, and her screams were muffled by the screeching tires and my screams.

One of the neighbors took me to my grandparents down the road to wait for my dad, but he went straight to the hospital from work. He didn't get to my grandparents until after the hospital visiting hours were over. My father and mother had agreed it would be better for me to stay with my grandparents. She was in the hospital for a very long time, and I got to visit her only once, but behind a glass window in a door. I saw only a bandaged woman sleeping until, after a long wait, seeing her awaken up. I threw her a kiss, and she tried moving one arm, but the pain stopped her movement. I guess I still had memories of my sister in the back of my head that time, and combining it with the memory of my mother screaming the last time made me cry myself to sleep almost every night for weeks.

Dad brought her home, but I was still to stay with my grandparents for over three or four months while she was recovering. I did not get to see her until after about one month at our trailer, and she was still covered with bandages from the chin down, so

64

again I was unable to touch her or give or get any hugs. We would just stand there crying as I looked through her loving eyes while my grandmother held me back. I found out later in life that my mother had filed for divorce prior to her accident, and this was another reason they let me live with my grandparents. She believed my dad was having an affair with another woman after work. True or not, it will never be known.

Grand father Isaac & Ida Allen

My Allen Grandparents' House

My grandparents had moved west too after we moved to Duarte. They lived in a small two-bedroom house at the end of a dirt road near our trailer park. My grandfather was at age sixty-seven when I was born, and he was now seventy-two and my grandmother sixty-eight. They had raised their ten children, and now their youngling grandson had come to live with them. My grandmother would get me ready for school and make sure, I was clean behind the ears. I loved her apple butter sandwiches, which she maded for school with some fruit in a brown bag. You could feel love from my grandmother, but with my grandfather you weren't sure. He would kill and clean a chicken or rabbit or shoot a dog without any expression of emotion that could be seen in his face or eyes. He did laugh and sing my songs, and that's when his eyes sparkled, but he was a man of few words. He once told me, "You're the old man, and your parents are still the kids."

Maybe my seriousness at a young age and my parents' unstable emotions made him think this way. My dad was loud, always the center of attention, and that came from being the youngest in his family, I guess. My mom was the oldest of her family, always the one who had to pay bills and worry about the money throughout her life. My grandfather also said, "Your mother has to raise two kids, your dad and you."

They had a few small chickens and rabbits raised by my grandfather for food along with some garden-grown stuff. My job was feeding, watering, helping with weeding and picking. There were no fast food or supermarkets, and you ate what was put on the table or you didn't eat at all. Plus, you had to wait for grace before beginning, and you're not excused until everyone was done.

"Burt with his grandsons, Delmar, Donny and me

We had a radio and loads of stories from my grandfathers long life. He would also teach me how to play checkers and think ahead of your opponent. He would sing me his songs, "The Streets of Laredo," "Big Rock Candy Mountain," and "You Are My

Sunshine." I became very proud when I could sing "You Are My Sunshine" too for my mom and dad. This being my first song, it was special for my mom and me. After my mother was healed of her burns for the most part, and my dad was pardoned for his possible affair, I was able to return home to our trailer. It was something special for all. She was covered with bandages from her chin down to her arms, and I still was not able to touch her other than her face. Not being able to hug caused us tears. Things had changed for all, but my grandparents still treated me better than any of the grandkids. They were my role models, and receiving their love, protection, and education instilled in me values and morals for the short period we were together. I still feel their presence around me today.

My Beginnings at School

I first went to school in LA for only a year of kindergarten, where you're prepared for primary school by learning to go to the bathroom by yourself along with some social behavior through games, exercises, music, and handicrafts. But now I was in first grade, learning the first steps in a very large old two-story building surrounded by a large surrounding schoolyard. The school is still there, off the 210 freeway, but now it's the Spaghetti Factory restaurant with a big parking lot. We would hear the large bell in the tower ring, announcing for all to line up and standing in front of the building for our classes.

The day started with all the classes saying the Pledge of Allegiance before the Red, White, and Blue as it rose high on the flagpole in the front of school. Then we would begin filing into our classrooms, awaiting the teacher to say, and "be seated." This wouldn't happen until everyone was standing by his or her desk and quiet. The row would be called, and then you could open your desk, get your paper and pencil ready, and put your lunch in it. Again we must be totally quiet before the teacher would start class, and if you didn't follow instructions, the amount of time you wasted became the amount of time taken away from your playtime. You or the whole class stayed in the room while the rest got to go out and play at recess time. You went to the bathroom and learn what being part of a group is all about. At the end of the day came the ride home on the bus to your waiting parents. I always showed my mother the handful of papers I wrote on for a day's learning.

My writing became the biggest problem for the teacher and me because I refused to use my right hand. I would reason, "It hurts!" Then when it came to reading, I felt I was a little different from the rest of the kids since those new jeans were too hot. You couldn't move, you couldn't play, you couldn't talk, you couldn't draw, and you couldn't hear your mother's voice or find her when you fell down. You could stand in a corner or go to the vice-principal's office, but pebbles don't cry. You had to be a big man and learn to be a rock. You had to get up early, get dressed, eat, and run for the school bus stop. What was there to like? I didn't like this new stream. It would rain, but you still had to go to school anyway. But after school you could run in the puddles, splashing around, free at last. I missed the surrounding desert where I chased birds, wild animals, and shot cans with pebbles with my old friend and his dog. Books didn't work unless you could read them or someone had time to listen. Who cared about Dick and Jane and Spot? But my mother told me books are the key to a bigger world, and it would open many worlds, but I couldn't find any keys. She kept trying telling me this was a stream where you must become a part of—sink or swim—and you must keeping trying in order to travel within it for the rest of your life. Mother would read books of adventures, like that of Tom Sawyer and Huck Finn to me, but by the end of the school year I still found school as a mixed place with mixed people and mixed pleasures.

SEVEN

Finding Our Home

Monrovia

Monrovia is the next town west of Duarte, and this is a small city at the base of the same mountains as Duarte, with some small canyons running up and down, and one large canyon known as Monrovia Canyon to many. There were many older houses in and below some more hills, with a much older downtown than its neighboring towns, except for Pasadena, which is older and has bigger, older homes. There are old hotels, a main street with small stores, and a city park with a library. It had its own Santa Fe Railroad station and the Red Car on different tracks coming in and out of town. So traveling here was done in many ways, like cars, trains, and even a small airport for small airplanes. There were more schools, parks, and land for growing things on in Monrovia than Duarte with all its rocks. This would become my real home, my path of life, for over twenty years, and later for my own children too. This is the place that I would grow up in, become a part of, and would mold me. It affected most my youth, which brought the greatest changes for me. This small pebble was being washed around in steams. It would pull me back into its pools of memories, as it did many.

548 Alta Street

My parents found a piece of land which had been a part of a farm with walnuts and other fruit trees, one block down from Route 66, named by the cities as Huntington Drive running from Los Angeles until changing into Foothill Boulevard in Azusa. There was a small old barn to the rear of our property, which had smaller lot that became a playground and junkyard for cars over the years. On the west side of the existing barn was a small wash, about twenty feet wide and ten feet deep. It had rocks in cement for its walls and sand with weeds growing on its bottom. Only when it rained did it get water, but when the water would come, it would fill it almost to the top. One day I caught a small cottontail rabbit in it after it tried to escape from our dogs. It had small cuts inflicted by the dogs, so I gave it to my grandfather so he could take care of it. He raised it in his cage, but I learned later that, like all his rabbits, he had eaten that one too. Now I was very upset with him and never trusted him again, not understanding him.

The barn became the main part of our house, only a few feet from the edge of the wash. This was where my many childhood adventures happened. Also surrounding our lot were some old and new homes. My dad moved our trailer from Duarte to the property and added four closed walls and a roof. My grandfather, uncles, family friends, and my dad started the work by taking off one end of the barn, the remaining section becoming our two bedrooms. They built a bathroom, next a kitchen and dinning room, and a larger living room toward the front of the house facing the street. This larger room was not finished into a living room until I was almost through high school. Then much later, a garage was added to the rear corner and a patio added on the front of the house. But there was always a large section of grass in front of the house reaching all the way to the street with a long gravel driveway in the middle, dividing the grass and the extra lot on our eastside that would always stay just dirt until the house was sold twenty or more years later. There was a big old pepper tree at one time, always weeping sap, and small red berries until the patio was built in its place at the front of the house. A very large eucalyptus tree stood near the front-street curb of our lot, and was over seventy to eighty feet tall, always dropping leaves and bark, with an occasional large branch, which made a loud cracking sound before hitting the ground, except during heavy storms.

More than this, this was our house, a house with two hanging plates which were hand-painted and placed over the kitchen wall saying, "Cleo Put On Kettle" and the other "Put On Another Pot Of Coffee" because there was always a pot on, welcoming all who came through the door. There were always friends coming over, and we had welcome matt that seemed to greet with open arms all who made their way into our kitchen to share food, coffee, and laughter. It was the richest place in everybody's stream as it welcomed and knew friendship.

Mom's House

Mother painted, wallpapered, and helped build this old barn into a home while working for the Monrovia Blue Seal Laundry as a steam iron operator in order to help pay the bills. So the laundering, in some way, repaid my mom for that earlier pain it caused in the trailer. She worked very hard to get this house and maintain it for many years after I grew into manhood and had my own family and home. She was the last person to live there before it was sold for redevelopment, and later a shopping center was built there. It was always "her" house even after she moved to her last house in West Covina, which she bought with the money given to her by the city for the house's sale. There is only a small oak tree now in that shopping center parking lot to mark where the house once had its place, across from the wash that is also gone forever. The only thing remaining is that small tree standing with other trees in that parking lot's islands. Along the way I had helped it in its lonely stand against the sands of times. The tree is surrounded with asphalt now, where I'm sure a bird left its seed for me beneath the earth. I began helping it grow among those surrounding weeds as a boy, and now it shades parked cars from the sun. So it reminds me of what was there, still standing there among progress, as a headstone marking my passage, yet still living part of me that will continue beyond my streams. That young oak tree is a silent marker of my past. Maybe someday I may secretly request to have my ashes placed around its roots, and like that tree fenced in Wyoming, I'll help it stand against the winds of time and let it continue living for hundreds of years with a my added energy.

548 Alta Street

My Dad's House

Dad worked very hard with his dad in building that house, but it just didn't have the same meaning as it had with my mom. There was always a problem with him, so he started things without finishing them. I too walk into these same shoes throughout my life's streams. He just didn't take the same pride in the house like my mother did, but I guess most women have that in their genes more then men do. My dad brought his motorcycles, cars, tools, junk, or any other projects, including his mix of male buddies home with him without any thoughts of how it may have appeared to anyone else. It reminds me of an old junkyard; he'll let you look around some, but don't try to take anything or say anything to cheapen his world when you leave it. It was his home, and he was always very protective of it and his junk, and it stayed that way until his death. My job was always helping my mother paint, clean the yard, cut the grass, and picking up dog shit. However, later I also became more like my dad, gathering cars and junk and staying in one place, but I tried like my mother to keep the house clean, hiding my junk most of the time. But perhaps it wasn't enough. It's very hard for some to move on to a new land, new life, and new streams in our travels without leaving or taking some of those pebbles or things we've gathered. He always said, "Broken things can still have some use or be fixed," but he did not understanding that they lost their value every day, and they just didn't fit the present world.

My House

It seams the bigger and older you become, things become much smaller, but it became my house and home with long-lasting memories holding its place in my heart. The house, like memories of changing times, is a part of my being. It was our house, and it started, as I recall, with me helping my grandfather cut broads and hammer nails (with his bad eyesight both of our aims were way off most of the time), and my dad redoing most things we had done, doubling his work without a complaint.

My grandfather, now around Seventy-four or older, had many problems with his health, staying with us, and one problems he played up was having poor eye sight, but when he would asked me to buy something for him at the corner little market, I found out he could still tell the difference between a $1 and $10 bill in his wallet when giving me some money. Women was always his biggest weakness, not his health until much later, and after grandmother's passing, he would hock up with younger women getting into his wallet and never have his own house to stay in, or die in.

Then much later in my teenager years, I laid a cement slap area by myself for our washing machine with some pride. We remember that encounter with that menace. Then came another menace for my mother outside the house. She was hanging clothes on clothesline outside since there were no clothes dryers in the houses during those days, and I found her bent over. She had pulled those wet, heavy clothes out of her basket, and suddenly she was unable to move. She was crying in pain; her back had given out.

I hurried into the house and dialed up the doctor, who came as fast as he could. He gave her a shot to relax her, and then straightened her out on the floor in the house. She would stay in bed for a few days afterward, not able to work or do anything. I believe it was caused by her years of steam ironing, doing the same motion day after day.

But that wasn't the only thing that made her freeze in fear. She also had fear of heights, and when she found herself close to the edge of anything high, she would get a bad case of vertigo just thinking of falling over. Therefore, I became the house painter.

One summer I helped around the house, again during my teenager years, and by now we had a patio at the front of the house. Mother requested I paint the outside of our house, but I didn't like heights either. I started by painting the pediment in front of the house, which peaks at about twelve to fourteen feet high, and went down until my feet were on the patio again, giving me the greatest relief. It was now time to move the ladder, but my mind was on the newly painted surface. Then I climbed up the ladder with a newly opened full gallon of paint, and just as I got back to the top, it slipped under my feet. Now I suddenly was standing on the patio again, feeling shorter by a few inches and half of the paint covering the sliding glass door and the cement patio. Luckily, my mother had just gone into the house, or we may have had a grumpy little spitfire with burning blue eyes, which my dad and I had learned to fear. She was very unhappy in the loss of a half-gallon of paint, but she was glad I wasn't hurt. Since the paint was oil-based, it took some time and a lot of paint thinner and rags to get it all cleaned up before dad got home. I learned about painting houses, ladders, and how she controlled her temper with both dad and me most of the time.

Before this, I was always trying to please my mother by helping cook our dinners so that once she was home, she could get off her feet for a while. Therefore, many times before she got home, I'd peel potatoes or carrots, readying them for cooking because they took a long time. There were no microwaves or quick-fix frozen foods then. We had an electric stove, refrigerator, and running hot water with a sink, but no dishwasher. We didn't have a refrigerator until after the war. I recall the iceman's deliveries and Mom draining the icebox every few days. The milkman also brought milk in bottles daily to our front door, but it wasn't like today's water bottles.

Trash Days

It was my job taking out the trash and burning it in an incendiary box in our side yard. No bottles or cans, but sometimes you could get it hot enough to melt the cans if you just happen to put one in by mistake. The milk cartons would burn, changing colors from blue to green and then red to black as they turned to ash because of the wax coating burning. Egg cartons would get the fire going real good too. Newspaper, especially the funnies on Sunday, would change colors too. But during the fifties, this was stopped because of the smog laws. Kids loved watching things burn before there were too many pebbles or cars gathering in the valley.

Bed Wetting

Moving into our house and having my own room, I had a new problem at seven years old. I've been told it took a while for me to be potty trained, and I hear that's not uncommon for boys. However, there was an even bigger problem for me hidden deeper in my little boy mind or dreams that my parents didn't know about, which may have been responsible for wetting my bed. My now knowing through my past memory about that Trapdoor Spider. My mom and dad did everything that they could think of in order to make me stop. My dad tried spanking me, and my mom would get me up and take me to the bathroom before she would go to bed, but nothing was working. Was I lazy? Finally, one day my dad made me stand out in the front yard holding the wet sheets on the clothesline until they were dry, before washing them. This smelled, and my eyes watered with embarrassment as the sheets whipped around me in the wind for the neighborhood to see. My dad's reasoning was this is what stopped it. He may have been right, but that way of thinking thankfully has changed, and the actions of present-day parents have changed with books that keep them informed on the problems in the field of child development. Now there are other manners of helping with the greater availability of information on raising children.

There was a deeper underlying reason for me, causing this type reaction and behavior problems. That my parents didn't know of the Spider in LA, and in my dreams my mind unconsciously released what I had been hiding deeply. Dr. Sigmund Freud and other psychologist have revealed in their books and studies the causes of this problems.

Many years later, many things hidden in my mind as a child affected me, and I needed help to make changes in my stream of thinking. These things became a large bag of rocks that I had carried around with me until there was a way of ridding myself of this burden. Until they surface, we can't face them, and when they do come up, it's the only way we can begin ridding ourselves of those baggage. Life is a matter of testing our mind, the building of our sprit.

Building Neighborhoods

This was a colorful new beginning with many old houses, tree groves with walnuts, citrus and other fruits for picking in nearby yards. Then there were more new houses, new businesses, and new friends taking root. A new school brought me better awareness of my ever-growing stream in this neighborhood. There were new kids only a block or two away by 1947 when the world believed in peace and the middle class was becoming richer throughout America and making many changes in the country. My mother was now working at the laundry in town while my dad was working off and on, like so many parents did then. My grandfather was leaving for varying period's length of times after the loss of my grandmother. I felt safe around these faces that knew me. It was becoming a new neighborhood for all pebbles. Our house was always a work in progress as my parents built it piece-by-piece, dollar-by-dollar for over twenty years with their own hands, minds, and souls. Like this house, my soul was being built in the process piece-by-piece, day-by-day, and year-by-year. The surrounding neighborhood was being built much faster than our house, but as this was going on the neighbors was still very close during the fifties. It didn't reflect any Rockwell painting for it was too new, but it was a mix of the fifties TV families. It could be seen as more of a Mayberry R. F. D. town without the country part. It was real and not a wishful dream for most. Every day in this small town, kids would play, eat, and learn with each other. Our parents were working to make a better life for us. During the war they worked together to overcome evil, and now they won the right for a new life, with a promise of a better things in the future.

Building Imagination

Imagination is that little spark that starts mental growth, making extra thoughts, bringing many extraordinary things to begin developing into much larger things. That's what makes the difference between most pebbles. You see new questions, wanting to investigate, wanting more new answers, and opening thoughts to anything possible. If you can just find that big new dream, you can envision newer, wider worlds that start you on that larger, more fulfilling trip. We all are the same yet different, and our streams reshape pebbles. Sometimes I'm the leader, sometimes second in the pecking order, but never at the bottom being walked on. This had always fit me. As we integrate our dreams with imagination, it will bring these small sparks to start our mental growth, and extraordinary things to begin to develop. The differences between others and ourselves started showing during those years, we must begin to either conform or start becoming a leader or an outsider of any group. For me, it was always one step outside and one step in for most of my life, just trying to find myself was the hill to climb. I guess this fits most of us pebbles.

When we go to school or find friends, it's like small drops of oil on water; we float on top and gather in small rainbow groups, and then something larger than all of us comes along. But we never really mix with the water because we are kids. But as we get older, we become more watered down, less concentrated than that small drop of oil as we were in the beginning.

We would leave home in the morning and play all day, and we were home when the streetlight came on. It was worry free for our parents. Then we'd have our dinner and get back out during the summer months. During those days, we played kick the can, hide-and-seek, jump rope, and rode bikes until bedtime. Most important of all, we traveled into space and other realms with our imagination in our childhood plays.

We had friends, we went outside, and found them in our neighborhood, real or not. We interacted, without TV sets yet, only those Saturday movies and radio shows for images, role models, and heroes.

We would go to the Saturday matinee, costing 10¢-25¢, and returned as pirates, cowboys, Tarzan, or Flash Gordon, doing our battle with evil for good. We collected pop bottles in our wagons for spending money. Like Our Gang in the movies, outside of my house there were sewer pipes, all sizes of woodpiles, all sizes wooden boxes, cement blocks, and an ever-growing amount of old wheels to help our imagination grow on that large lot next to the house. No one in the neighborhood had these things to build forts, planes, ships, rocket ships, or racecars. We dug holes, and rode bicycles, tricycles over the many mounds that appeared at different times in my yard. We made bows and arrows from sticks or guns from pieces of available wood or a fort.

We took the sewer pipes, put them with stacks of wood and wooden boxes, and we had a pirate ship with canyons. Then we slid cans in one end of the pipes, and a broomstick or any stick in the other end, and with a big push upon the order "fire!" the can came flying at the Spanish galleon. Now it was time to swing over on ropes hanging from a big Chinese maple tree above us. With masks and wooden swords, we yelled as we charged bravely to capture the enemy crew and booty from the box ship alongside ours. The next week we would play *Tarzan or Jungle Jim or Red Ryder*. All kids did these things, wishing to be like *Spanky and Our Gang.*

Another part of my life was two big lovable boxer dogs. One moved on and never returned, but Duke, with a white marking around his eye, loved playing football with us boys. Upon getting our ball he would start running and running with everybody chasing him until two or three of we tackled him. Whether you had the ball or not, he also loved tackling you with his front paws. For everyone it was a problem. Even if you were just running around in the yard, you'd get tackled when you least expected it. I would get up yelling with anger as he ran away. I'd look for rocks, which had my dad laughing. Then he would warn me, "You, and not him, made this game." You see, he waited all day for me to come within reach because he was often chained to a car axle driven into the ground because there were no fences, and his job was to protect the yard from real intruders.

City of Arcadia

What a lucky surrounding we had as well, having another town on the border of Monrovia, which was Arcadia, California, because just between both these cities, on Huntington Drive or Route 66, was a collection of old railroad cars next to what would become the Northwood's Restaurant's location. They moved it to the city of Rosemead. But before that, we could play train robbers like Jesse James or engineers or whatever before the restaurant was built. They moved the trains farther down Huntington Drive across from the Santa Anita Park for a few years before moving them again to what is known as the Gene Autry Museum, just north of Los Angeles, and called something like Trains Town now, where you have to pay to play on them.

Traveling farther into the hidden places of Arcadia on our bikes, on Colorado Boulevard a few miles from Pasadena, before any freeways was even thought of or planed, we found Tarzan and Jungle Jim's hidden home. It was really there, just like in the movies. We rode our bikes to a large fenced area with large bushes hiding a wonderland, just a short distance from the Santa Anita racetrack. We would hear the screams all a round us as we found a hole leading to the deepest jungles of Africa. There was a large, deep dark lagoon with large trees and bushes around it that made it hard to find your way through, until you found bushes shaped like tunnels that took you through a maze. And then came a big old house sitting by the water. On the other side were large trees, and there it was, the big tree house. We all knew who lived there. This was where they filmed Tarzan and Jungle Jim movies, but there was no muscular body swimming or swinging or loud chimpanzees, just birds, ducks, and fish. We found our way up the tree house and became real explorers. Next we found an old log cabin across from the old mansion beside the lagoon. There were wild birds, with squawking peacocks that would scare you to death at those most unexpected moments, and they surrounded the lagoon. We could've gotten in trouble if found, but we were only seen once, and we disappeared like natives into the bush, finding our quick exits. Now it's owned and ran by the County of Los Angeles, for the public usage, known as the Arcadia Arboretum. Most of us know now it was also used in the filming of *Fantasy Island*, as shown in the show, but it was better known as the estate of Mr. Lucky Baldwin, who built it and owned the surrounding cities. Wow, we lived our fantasies there. As for Tarzan and Jungle Jim, they are now only dim memories on films.

My first attempt to fly came when I got a metal pedal car-airplane one Christmas. I was around six or seven. With the help of three other kids we got it atop my house with some ropes. Just as I was sitting in the cockpit, ready for takeoff, my father came home, saw us and stopped my first flight, but that never stopped us or me from trying other ways of flying. Later, we used big bed sheets tied together and used a capes as we jumped into that empty wash from ten to eight feet into its sandy bottom. We were light enough then and had enough sheet to brake our falls. Boys always want to fly like Superman or Flash Gordon, with rocket packs or capes on our backs, with visions of saving the world. They did it in the movies, didn't they?

The Piano Man

You can fly with music too, and we discovered this when Dad made friends with a neighbor who had a piano in his garage. He would sing and play it without sheet music. He just had to hear a song and could just play it. He was always fun, flying with his music, and he made us enjoy it. He also had piles and piles of horse racing forms and studied them hour after hour. He was always playing the ponies and had his big dreams too. He was home a lot, a house painter I'm guessing. He was trying to find his rainbow among the paper and ponies. There were three girls and one boy, Ronnie, in the Van Gundy's, so the girls always outnumbered the boys. Mom ruled the roost, and I guessing because the father was a dreamer. It was like a three-ring circus every day at their house with other kids from the neighborhood in and out.

The son, Ronnie, was one year older then I. There was a spark of self-confidence in him and had something extra. He always attempted to stand taller than most of kids in the neighborhood. He and his sisters were into 4-H and raising things like rabbits. He killed and a skinned rabbits like my grandfather, and it was no big thing to him either.

One day, I was around when Ronnie hit the victim behind the back of the head with a small pipe. He thought it had gone on to rabbit heaven. He started the process of skinning it, with its paws nailed to a board and its insides hanging, but then it started making noises and moving all around. It had only been knocked out, and it was now waking up in pain. Ronnie finished the job as quick as possible with his knife, but I'd never forget that sound. It was hard thinking of becoming a farmer or eating rabbit. It was just as hard trusting him again; he wasn't like my grandfather either. Of course, seeing chickens running headless with blood flying everywhere was even worse for me. There was a lot of eating of rabbits during those days.

Ronnie would die later in his life when he crashed his motorcycle in the desert sands. Knowing his family's closeness, they must miss him. His mother and sisters are still alive and in contact with others in the neighborhood.

Beside this family there were other families with a number of sons and daughters known as the baby boomers. We also learned a lot about doctors and nurses through some girls in those eager ages of childhood incidents. We completed many physicals exanimations of looking at, but not touching, each other's private parts. These were our discoveries by eleven or twelve. There was no real sex, or anything harmful other then seeing what was hidden in those places. "That's why you have to sit down to pee?" we asked even after we were told, "You will be sent to hell," if anyone knew we'd seen what was there. There was no one to talk about birds or bees, but we knew there was a big word called "sex" even then. What was the big deal? There wasn't anything there, why the secrets? Our minds and bodies were making many changes, though, without us knowing it.

Hot Wheels

One day I took my tricycle apart, removed the front handle bar and fork, then turned the bike over and put the fork back through. Before the word was even made, it was our "hot wheels." Some other kids did the same with theirs too, not knowing who did it first. It was so low, fast, and sometimes with a holed drilled for the seat (without it we'd just sit on the rear part of the frame). It was the first hot wheels in the early fifties. These things didn't become popular until the seventies, when it came out in stores. Believe it or not, I rode this thing to school three or four miles occasionally, with the front wheel just getting bigger and bigger until I got my bike later on.

My First Bike

Later came my first bike, a J. C. Higgins from Sears, Roebuck, and Co. It was way too cool with its bell and had a headlight on the front fender, a tank with a horn in the middle bars, chrome wheels and fenders, and a rack on the back with twin taillights. It was red and black with white wall balloon tires. Later within a year or two of getting it, I saw this movie about J. C. Higgins. It told of him as the first person to build a glider in the U.S. before the Wright brothers' powered flights. So now I was flying down the streets and picturing myself lifting off into the clouds, but I also knew he died at the end of the movie, like most dreams.

However, growing older, I began stripping my bike to its bare bones. My dad later told me, "I'll never buy you another bike again" after seeing what my bike had become and after making all those monthly payments just to get it for me. Afterward I got my first paper route, and I was working on buying my own three-speed racing bike, which everybody wanted in those days. I found out it wasn't made to carry big bags of newspapers with those thin tires, and it was a lesson about life. I learned this lesson about things: some just do not fit in with your dreams for a reason. You don't use a racehorse to pull a wagon. The thing you are wishing for may not be what you thought it would be or worth what you thought it was. You learn the value of many things when you work for it.

EIGHT

Santa Fe School

After coming into our neighborhood and starting school anew, many new doors for learning opened for me, and this had always been my mother's hope. At first my mom drove me in our old 1930 Model-A cabriolet while on her way to work at the Blue Seal laundry in downtown Monrovia. Then later she trusted me enough to let me walk, knowing I wouldn't get lost. Even though there were no buses during those years, there were lots of kids in the neighborhood walking together or riding with neighbors. The school's name was Santa Fe because of its location just across the way from the Santa Fe Railroad tracks and the Santa Fe Railroad Station for Monrovia. Halfway there, you would cross the railroad tracks on your way to school, and if you walked along those rails, you could cut the distance down into half. There where cows and other things to see along this way, and I felt like Huckleberry Fin traveling along the river. It would slow me down. You could see just off those tracks many hobo camps too, with spots under bushes or under bridges. The boys kept a watchful eye for those wonders. It drew our interest to investigate even though we were scared. These left behind open cans and fire-blackened ground and rocks, easy signs of them being there, but what we didn't know was where they went. Was it the Big Rock Candy Mountain in the song? And where did they come from? We had lots of questions as we looked sharply from the safe distance of those tracks, letting our mind travel on those long tracks into the distance. What kind of men where they? Could they be something like the trapdoor spiders too hidden deep in my mind?

Most kids didn't walk there, just us few brave souls did in spite of our mothers pointing a finger and warning us of "bad men" hiding in bushes.

The richer kids where becoming greater in numbers, living below the tracks in newly built housing tracks in what was known then as Mayflower Village or other similar so-called villages raised from tree groves. We hadn't encountered those people living above Foothill Boulevard as yet, not until we gathered for junior high in what is now called middle school. They were from well-established, wealthy, and prosperous older families for the most part. People were moving into that area, as they were to the rest of Southern California, in waves, setting records after the war and buying these new homes during the baby boom years to start their families as America grew.

First Grade

My first class had twenty-four boys and eleven girls. Some of them I would know throughout high school and longer. We learned quickly that our teacher favored the girls after sizing her up. She was middle aged, short, wearing glasses, and didn't like my shirt hanging out. The girls followed her every command while the boys only wanted more playtime, which didn't please her at all. Very early I found out my right hand still hurt when I wrote. But she insisted and tried to help me. "But you must learn to make letters," she said. So with that I started learning to write using my left hand, which didn't look normal. She and others told me it was "the devil's hand."

My left-handedness was always in the way of how I saw things, and without much help and the teacher not knowing its deep reasons, which became clearer to me later in life, it became even harder for me to write. The desks weren't made for left-handers, and my papers and books would fall to the floor when I wrote. And after I wrote a line, it would be difficult to add letters since I couldn't see what I wrote because it was covered by my twisted left hand.

My education was on a slow track, and I got into bigger trouble throughout my school years. "It was not caused by that mishap," my parents believed.

In my classes from 1946 to '50, from ages seven to twelve, the kids grew faster than we thought we would, both mentally and physically. Radical changes came through experiments, experience, and education surrounding us like the winds, and we did not notice it until it almost knocked us down. We grew in time, and we all went along at our own pace, moving into our own streams. I found out I can't just stay with one type of group or wear just one social coat, which most kids did. Then I put on of my own rebel coat and moved a little further to the edge, but there was stillroom for growth in many areas.

I found others like me. One classmate who loved drawing too had a mind-set in like mine in many ways, but he was also much different for many reasons. I also got into sports, and this would also help me find friends too. Another area I found interesting was math and science, pushing the mind to ask questions and grow. However, reading and writing was still a great wall standing in my way, in the way of progress. So drawing became the easiest stream of escape and my best subject for the soul.

My dad was doing pencil drawings of cartoons from the Sunday funnies and comic books during my early years too. I began penciling with my left hand even before school to avoid the pain in my other hand. By the fifth and sixth grades, I found David Renaker, and as I said before, he was always drawing too. He and I would combine our skills into drawing a complex and a complete drawing of the Battle of Troy, with the Trojan horse within the walls and the warriors in the pitch of battle. It was done on a large sheet of butcher paper, three or four feet linear in a panorama view. We both were in the same class, got A's for history and our artwork, but we got mixed reviews from our fellow students. However, drawing was distracting both of us in our other subjects often. Later on it even became my diversion from other subjects. David's family owned a pottery business, making art very important to him. When it became his birthday for example, the family would give out small pottery figurines as gifts to all the kids at the parties. Now if only I had just had one of them now, I believe it would be worth a lot. Art too continued to take its hold on my mind and life, but it also brought a curious curse to both.

When it came to football and track, it had been established in repeated racing events that I was the second fastest fifty-yard dash runner in the whole school until my seventh grade when I got into a larger school, where I competed with more seventh and eighth graders at Clifton Junior High. I found other friends too who had been moved much farther down the standings. However, the guys were still looking to me for speed, plus I did bring some sprit and was a good team player. I had some moves, was still pretty quick, and had no fear. I was never the first pick in those small drafts, but was never the last either, neither all the way in or all the way out, as my buddies said.

Buddies

When I was around eleven or twelve, at someone's birthday party I was drinking a Coke from a bottle, and someone thought it would be funny to hit the bottom of my bottle. It broke one of my front teeth right in the middle, and this wasn't fixed until I reached my high school years. From then on I mostly covered my smile. I learned to hold back my smiles for pictures in school photos. This just added more to my feeling of being different, a rebel for some.

Kids can hurt each other without knowing how long the hurt may remain, or what effect a stupid action will have on the image of others. However, some kids remain outstanding in your memory for many reasons, and others for a short amount of time. Others, for their friendlessness, last well into your life, and others end up in your memoirs for their unthinking actions, even nameless ones.

Some of my offbeat buddies were two guys with their own worlds, with their own centers of thinking—David R. and another kid named Johnny Patton. Both were more interested in science, star travel, and history, flying around the world, and finding high adventures as explorers. For example, Johnny had his pet turtle in his back yard named G.I. Joe. I was never sure why he named it so, but maybe he had thoughts of himself becoming General Patton, with the turtle being his tank and going to war. We had fun searching for him in the backyard when he disappeared for the winter, and we wondered how Joe slept for months. Maybe he found something he could use for his star travels.

Roger Albo & me fifth Grade

Gary's Specialty House

There were two other guys who many were drawn to because of their self-confidence; they were extraordinary pebbles then too. Roger Albo and Gary White would go on to become yell leaders in high school and were my friends before they became popular. Roger and I stayed overnight at Gary's house way before we all moved on into junior high and high school. Gary's parents owned a large steakhouse called the Plantation, next to the Monrovia Airport, just off Route 66. Their small house sat behind the restaurant. This became a very successful business, with his family moving to a much larger home on the side of the hills in the much wealthier upper part of the city. Confidence makes pebbles sparkle, and the more it shines, the more it becomes worthy and popular.

Gary went on to own his own restaurant in northern California, along a river in the mountain country of California. Much later in life I would bring my son's Boy Scout troop there when we had a chance to stop for a short visit with him before going up the mountain for our fifty-mile summer hike into Kings Canyon National Park. Gary only had a short moment with us, but he still sparkled.

Roger, being Italian, always sparkled too, and inside his house smelled of great food. He still loves the very best of foods and drinks, even adding his personal touch to them over the years, which has brought its rewards for him too. He became a very successful salesman dealing machinery tools and equipment. Roger and I are still in touch, remaining buddies from that railroad track at Santa Fe.

Flying Dreams

Back to those early days, we visited Gary's house and the restaurant; we would be treated to the best smells and, some great tasting food, which we didn't really care about at that time. But we were happiest with having that great amount of freedom given us while the rest of his family and surrounding people were very busy. We loved the freedoms to have so many of choices of food available from their menu for that day too. The people in the surrounding towns also loved their food. This place was listed among highest in approval rating with our parents and would also refer to it as—one of the best in the area. My parents would go to Gary's family restaurant only on those big special occasions and when they had found some extra money.

My mom was not the best of cooks and didn't have much time being homemaker and working all week in a sweatshop. Early came my learning at age six or seven, what it was about and what steps it took to prepare for dinner—by stagiest pealing of potatoes and other ingredients for any meal. As they trusted me more as I grown older, I would cook many complete meals for us all. However, our large and special family meals was always cooked by my mother and we ate together always with set-down meals on Sundays and relaxing together as a family—until my dad started racing on Sundays.

Back to those sleepovers at Gary's house, it became like going to a special place for me with my two close friends, not just because of the restaurant, but more so, because the Monrovia Airport was operating just outside next to his house. When night came within those moments of quietness between buddies before sleep fell, my mind would lose their presents or any other distractions, and my mind would drift to the sounds of engines raving up for take off or far away returning to earth. Seeing lights mixing with shadows and listen to the sounds of the various sizes of planes landing or taking off soon brought clear pictures in my mind of myself flying with them. The sounds were always changing as the airplanes engines speed was rising, disappearing, and landing, and they would be the last I hear before sleep overcame my youthful imagination. This was the best of times for a young dreamer. I had a greater interest in airplanes than most my age, and never question whether I would becoming a pilot, all the way into my teen years. It was always present with my drawing airplane and flying machines through those early years. In many daydreams, this combined speed and adventure taking my spirit to the heavens. Most other pebbles, like Gary and Roger, stayed traveling on their own beginning paths, having their own energies and streams that brought them to were they find their self now.

As a teenager, one of my dad's closest friends, a brother biker buddies, who did the tile work in our house, who also played Badminton and did many other things too, but the best for me was him also being a pilot and loved to fly. On top of all that, he was one of the best giving humans souls with a smile for life among all my dad's friends. He would pick me up on the weekends, with me now age fifteen, and he would rent an airplane in El Monte Airport for a few hours or all day. Then once we're in the air, he would turn the controls over to me while giving me instructions. He always did the landing while I'd loosely feel the controls. We loved the freedom but while flying over mountains, where it got getting bumpy, hitting big downdraft with free fall a few hundred feet in seconds and then rise like a silver bird again in an updraft he would take the controls. We did rolls and loopy loops through the clouds free of Mother Earth's hold. One weekend we flew to Santa Catalina Island for a day, which even deepened my love of flying, seeing the coastline and ocean change colors below. The landing and take off from the island gave the scent jumping on and off a cliff. Money became more of a growing problem following this dream. My dad didn't have the money to pay for this, and without the money, you stand on earth with only your dreams. However after asking around at the airport, I found a job for one summer after turning sixteen. The job was gassing up and tying down planes, which allowing me to talk with pilots, and from whom I got firsthand accounts, giving me greater dreams of really flying off into that wild big blue yonder on my own someday. Even pebbles want to rise up above the earth searching for thier dreams.

I began reading books about the World War I and II aces like "On a wing and prayer," and few others, which brought me even closer to dreams with my drawings of all those famous planes during my high school classes and kept my dreams flying. Later on, I joined the Civil Air Patrol, thinking it would take me closer to being apart of that dream, but instead I found it a lot of marching and "Yes Sir's" without any real flying at all. We did some searching for missing planes but only on the ground. So that didn't last long. I was not into the "Yes Sir's" thing. Then later during my junior year in high school, I discovered something, which changed my dreams and course by a simple school eye exanimation, and finding that my eyes were not 20/20, and that flamed out my dreams of becoming a jet pilot. It was another change in direction and falling. Without my dreams of flying left my sprit falling because I'd gotten too close to the sun and couldn't see any new horizons or direction from this cavern.

NINE

Me driving dad's home made Model-A Tracker

Driving

At age eight, my dad let me drive Mom's old Ford Model A around our front yard. He put big wooden blocks on the two main pedals, but its control for the gas was by use of a handle on the steering column and on the other side was a spark retard or advance for starting. Therefore, there wasn't much need for any pedals while driving around in first gear most of the time except for starting or stopping. To stop it, you had to stand as hard as you could on the brake pedal, pulling on the steering wheel with all the means my body could make. You see it had mechanical brakes—without help from any hydraulic brakes—until Ford put them in their cars in 1939. But circle after circle, as if racing on my own small track and winning that big race started my dreams and the need of speed. This was my first feeling of power through a machine, and having total control. Like all youth, I was driving on my own for the first time and the feeling of real speed, mostly because it was an open car, and it gave the feeling of the wind flying into your face that gives even more a feeling of speed, even thought it maybe at only five miles per hour or more. And that's all that was possible in first gear.

Horse Power

Another school friend from my earliest grade school days also had a jackass horse, which we rode after school throughout his walnut groves within the Mayflower Village housing area. Then one summer at age fifteen, my family went back to Wyoming on vacation, where one of my dad's brother Uncle Bid, also had a real ranch, giving me another occasion to ride his old paint, a good cowpony. One who knew more about what needed to be done than its rider, but still following my lead. He knew those cows and their moves while my job was just to stay with him as he was working. Our job was to check on my uncle's ranch fences for a week with his other grandkids. I learned from that horse how to take care of his needs and how to bind animals with humans as a working team. I also learned that each horse is different, like humans, and expect their respect with the need of your control. Horses can't see very far off in distances; they usually use their senses of smelling and hearing with added guidance from you. It is the bonding and gaining of trust in you that is a must and more important for both of you.

Still speaking of that summer, a good example was while we worked on those broken fences on this very hot July 4 day, we came upon a large open water tank, which looked cool. We stopped for a drink and some cooling off, and next came our jumping from the horses' backs into that cool water with just our jean pants on for a few moment then getting out. Just as the winds started to blow very hard with the horse telling us something was coming our way. Now with those water-soaked jeans weighting very heavy, within just a few mounts, it became colder quickly with increasing dark clouds rolling in like a herd of stamping cattle with even heavier blowing movement coming in our direction. We got back on the horses and headed back to the barn and the house with increasing speed as it brought small flying cold white flakes to our faces. The faster we rode for some reason that brought out laughter all the way there; but by the time we got there, it was now snowing harder, and those cold, wet jeans were holding court regarding our foolish judgment. So running into the house as fast we could to get out of those jeans was all that was on our minds. My uncle made us get back out there and take care for those horses once we had gotten out of those jeans first that refused into coming off. We learned Wyoming weather can change, and without the horses, we would have been in big trouble. We made sure they were cared for and did take our responsibility seriously.

Again my dad's other brother Jesse, now living in California too, also owned a prize winning Palomino horse, which he rode in parades and later rented to Roy Rogers to be used as a double for Trigger in some movies and on his TV shows later. They had met after a horse show and became friends because of their love of palomino horses, and that had brought them together. This again came with only one opportunity for me to ride this beautiful animal in its corral because of his worth being much more than mine. This came around before my riding and connection in Wyoming. Of course my uncle kept a rope on him to lead, and the horse wasn't sure if he wanted some kid on him being smarter than its rider and able to do tricks like Trigger following any of my uncle's commands while I was on his back just holding the saddle. Now I know why Roy liked playing cowboy or any human would.

Following this at eighteen, during another summer, the stream continued with me working with horses as an "exercise boy and walker" for a horse trainer at Santa Anita and Del Mar race tracks but more about that later. My dad's parents and family all had horse in Wyoming before my birth, and now I have photos with my grandmother standing on a hill with my uncle Benny on another hill while both were on horseback looking at the open west around them. What a gift horses are to man's history, they combine man's dreams, travels and experiences through the ages, until machines replaced them.

Wild Mustang

Now for another type of horse, on my twelfth birthday, my dad bought me a real motorcycle; it was smaller but very powerful—a real mustang by name like the horse and way before the car with the same name. My dad, with his best friend Albert, who was the best motorcycle rider I'd ever known, and with me of course drove over to pick up my new bike. We went in dad's car traveling only a few miles where he gave the seller the rest of his money, and with that, my dad started it up. He had already gone over before this, looking at it and hearing it run before deciding it was to become my birthday gift. My heart was racing, just waiting to get it home. Dad started moving like a wild horse with a new rider when the front wheel came in the air, and it almost dumped him on his backside. But now, he's holding on with everything he had with his feet hitting from side to side. And after he made it to his feet for just a second while letting off the gas in a running manner, still he does not have total control of this wild little horse. Now again on the gas still bouncing side to side with his feet out, with some swooping and holding on with his full determination, he was now heading his weary way toward home and getting control, but his trouble now was that his big feet and legs were hanging in space. Albert was laughing so hard he couldn't move while I was standing wide-eyed and mouth opened wider until I joined in with my own nervous laughter after the shock had passed.

Finally, we got in the car and headed home. My dad was waiting there. As we drove up and got out of the car, we all started laughing then, and I was still so nervous I didn't know what to do next. Then my dad said, "OK, now I want you to run down this street as fast as you can and throw yourself down on it." I looked at him and thought, He must have lost his mind and what was he thinking? Then he said, "If you don't, no motorcycle!" Knowing he meant it, so this was what's going through my mind with a lot of, what the hell? I did it then got up and walked back rubbing my knees. He then said, "OK, now you know what it feels like eating the asphalt. The faster you run, the harder that asphalt will be; and the faster you ride that mustang and fall, the more it's going to hurt." I got his point, and after that, he made me wear an old World War II helmet shell liner, which he had painted black with yellow and red flames to wear while riding that "little wild mustang."

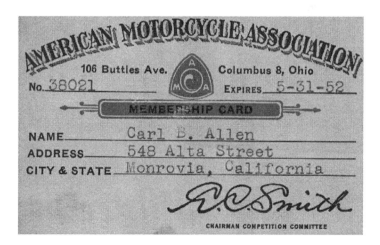

Our Club

My dad belonged to a motorcycle club called Santa Anita MC with a group of guys and girls mostly all riding Hogs known also as Harleys with some mixing in of Indians and other heavy bikers of the times. This was during the late nineteen forties or during the making of *The Wild One* movie. These guys called Mr. Marlon Brando a big sissy after seeing the movie. Just for example, in order to become a member of his club, you would have to go out with the club on a night's run throughout the city of Pasadena. And when finding a cop, who would usually start following "the pack," they would ride faster and faster until it was time for them all to bust away in all directions, leaving you to deal with the cop on your own—now having to ditch him in some way on your own. In those days, there weren't a lot of motorcycle cops or having good radio communication to pinpoint or get help in chasing someone who is running away. However, my becoming a mascot was much easier with my "wild mustang" into this club because my dad and all of these guys hang out at our house and was taking in by me too. Besides, I could challenge anyone of them in a hill-climbing event and could ride across any trails in the dirt better and faster than most of them with their heavy bikes. Except on one of those days, the mustang threw me off into a patch of cactus with Dad enjoying getting a pair of pliers and pulling out all the needles in my butt while my riding for the rest of the day was by standing up. The rest of the club enjoyed my learned position more than I do. Riding mostly in the dirt until around fifteen, then I began riding bigger and more powerful bikes for my size. By seventeen, there was a few times of riding my dad's BSA 150cc, which he later turned into a racing-only bike. It wasn't until much later into the nineteen sixties did I ride a bike again with friends. But in those years in between, I had lost interest in riding on the streets after my dad's accident that almost killed him under a garbage truck after it had made a left turn in front of him in Monrovia's midday heavy traffic.

He was rushing home to take his other motorcycle, the BSA, to a race for circle dirt track racing with Albert, his bike's rider. This type of flat-track racing happen mostly at night with their metal shoes shooting sparks from the bottom of their boots and spraying rocks from the friction between the rocks. And the leaning riders does, making always an exciting experience with these men riding wild machines, but it was not for me to try. There were no brakes used, only your hand on the gas, skill, and how long you could chance going into the turns before letting only a small amount of a second off then back into full throttle going through the corners taking more nerves than I had.

Dad & Albert

At that time, Albert was my dad's rider on the quarter mile or longer flat dirt tracks around Southern California. My dad had a broken compound fracture of one leg and had steel bolts in his shoulder—all because of one leg with his head hitting on the truck's bottom without a helmet while sliding under that truck and coming out on the other side lucky to be alive with its bent steel parts and his body. He couldn't walk or work for six months afterward, but he still rode on the streets and in the dirt for many years afterward until he started racing cars in 1955. My dad smoked a carton of Lucky Strike every week, and every other word spoken was a curse word without any meaning. He drank plenty too, and it was always a part of him then. These were the real "wild ones." He is still alive but stopped smoking during the nineteen sixties and doesn't drink much now. After this accident, we'd gotten on each other's nerves more because of my being a teenager and being a little shit with him most of the time. We became closer during his car-racing days.

My dad's motorcycle club entered a race competition once a year on Santa Catalina Island. We took the Great White Steamer with our motorcycles to race during the summer with some other thousands of bikers on this small island racing around the whole island all day then partying at night. It became one mass of partygoers' fun-filled crowd in the center of town after the sun went down, and this was a small town. One of my dad's closest friends had broke his leg that day, and all of the club members would put him on the back of their motorcycles at different times, letting him ride into a bar for a few drinks and then moving on to the next until he couldn't stay on the back of the bike any longer.

They did this for my dad at another race a few years later after a race on Red Mountain. He broke his foot, hit a turtle in the desert, and flipped on his bike. The club was a fellowship of pebbles within surrounding "sharks" that appear to be very friendly and fun, but we all know, sharks will eat anything. And too many drunks become sharks when there's blood in the water, and fights will start effortlessly among friends. There were so many drunks during these events that when a few had gotten out of hand, the sheriffs would grab them up and take them to the other side of the island in their jeeps, let them walk, and find their way back. Later they would check on them at each time dropping a new load and doing each run almost hourly. This would last for the whole weekend with bikers seen sleeping in bars, motels, with many others in or outside of houses, or within sleeping bags in tents while the jail was filling up with the more problematic ones. Nowadays, none of this could or would happen.

One of my dad's other close friends Manner had more guts than anyone I'd ever seen or known. There was a large pool in the middle of town with live ocean fish swimming around, and among these fish were a few small baby sharks. So one night, he reached down into the pool while his buddies held him at the waist while he pulled out one small shark by holding it by the top fin and putting his arm around its head very careful where those teeth where while placing it under his leather jacket. They proceeded into the bars for a few bottles of beers until a sheriff heard about it and made him put it back into the pool without either ones carelessly getting bitten. We believed that shark may have even liked the small amount of beer received in its traveling because it never bite the hand that fed him beer or the one who freed him from that pool's circling crowd.

Many years later, Dad saved Manner's life while they were riding in the San Gabriel riverbeds. Manner had hit a rock and had fallen, broke a rib while not knowing it yet and was bleeding internally. He got up but couldn't breathe. So my dad, with some others' help, put him in front of my dad's bike, and they rode as fast as hell would take them to the nearest hospital. My dad got him to the hospital just in time, and they had to remove his spleen.

These were the wild times, and yet they were like brothers being part of those men riding these undependable machines and became legendary. Funny years before my dad had known him, Manner had gotten into a fight with his own brother while working on their parents' house; and in the heat of the fight, Manner knocked him off the roof, resulting to his brother's death. Most of the time, he was always just joking around, but that time, he wasn't joking around. There were many practical jokes between him and my dad, but there was always a drinking everyday for him.

One day, while my dad was working on his motorcycle in our uncompleted living room, Manner, seeing an open can of paint my dad was using, took the wet brush full of paint to some of the tools my dad was using while my dad wasn't looking. My dad picked up the tool, not knowing or looking until he felt and saw what Manner had just done; but by now, he had it on everything he picks up. Albert was there, and they both began laughing as my dad now reached for some rags and used his favorite sailor's words for both of them while cleaning his hands, tools, and motorcycle parts covered in paint.

However a little later, both had left to get some other parts for my dad, and it was now raining. Upon their return, Albert, being the first to reach for the doorknob, noticed some small blue sparks jumping at his ring before his hand even gabbed it; good thing he was wearing rubber boots because of the rain or he would have gotten hit much harder too. Now turning away from the door, he let Manner open it, knowing something was up. They learned much later that my dad had hooked up an Old Model T magneto wires to the door and connected it with a small electric motor running it. Manner couldn't let go and was crying for Dad's release and forgiveness while fire was flying from his heels on the wet puddle steps. Manner hated fire more than anything else in the world, and now Albert was laughing with Dad. Albert was the type of person who uses words or stories for laughter, but never exposes himself to be caught in the fire. There was always someone around who could come up with the next joke and try to top the others. Questioning that's why, while a teenager with my friends, we tried some crazy things too.

Manner and my dad were very close friends as was Albert, but Dad then had also worked at different time off and on with Manner and his family during those many different times and throughout the years when there was no work for my dad as a millwright. Manner's family owned a cesspool business, and this was one of the worst and lowest of all jobs for any human being to do; but the Irish before my dad made it though with Manner beside him. They would drink a few beers after being in those smelliest of working conditions, and this had always became part of their day's ending. The beer won the battle with Manner; he died at an early age, not learning how to cope with a man's shit or your brother's death while trying to wash your hands. I guess that was too heavy a load.

My Sharks

On one of those occasions when we came to the Santa Catalina races and I was around fourteen, I brought along my swim fins, a mask with snorkel, a truck inner tube, a small fisherman's catching net, a potato sack, and my long five-foot spear made with some surgery rubber bands hooked on one end and three fishing fork head on the other. This was the first type of spear guns in a simple manner while putting your wrist through the rubber tubes having a strong, heavy fishing line attached into the spear's end, then pulling it back with your hand and moving forward up on the spear shaft as far as you could grab it. Then holding it while swimming until it gets close to a victim and then releasing your hand pointing at the fish with the spear jumping forward with a great amount of force. Then hoping you could have a fish attached on the other end, trying to pull you with the spear line attached on your wrist, awaiting a prize while pulling it up to the surface.

My parents were at the race while I was preparing all my equipment to explore the clear deep water for my prey. The water around Catalina Island is cold and very clear, and you can see clearly down forty to sixty feet like looking in a swimming pool full of sea animals. So walking down some steps on the pier while wrapping the potato bag over the inner tube and placing the net in its center, I began swimming out fifty or more yards from the pier across from the Great White Steamer dock. Looking down through the mask, I was seeing all kinds of fish; while snorkeling, my heart began quaking upon seeing a large halibut on the bottom trying to hide its self in that bottom. This fish has both eyes on one side of its head. As I was leaving the tube with a deep breath and kicking with all my force and pulling back my spear inch by inch ready for its release at the same time I had my eyes fixed on my target getting as closer as possible and dreaded that it sees me before I caught it. Now being within three or four feet, I released my rod hitting the bottom but completely missed my spot while I ran out of breath too. So turning to the surface and looking back at where I thought it still was and seeing some sand moving from my hit, my knee hit a pile of something on the bottom—rocks or something with barnacles living on it. Now feeling a sharp, cold pain from that encounter while fighting my way back to the surface, I then saw this new trail of red following me. I had cut a large vein on the side of my knee with blood flowing very rapidly, now starting to show its signs surrounding the cut, by the time I had gotten air and to the tube. Then just as I had gotten on top of the tube with my stomach and with my knee still hanging in the water, I could now see the cut with the blood just flowing everywhere. Now because the water was so clear, I also then saw two large dark shadows coming in my direction from much-deeper water. It was two sharks picking up and following my trail as it washed away from me toward them under the waves. Now I pulled myself farther up the tube with my shoulders now in the water because of the tube's size. And I pulled up with both my arms as hard as possible while trying to keep my knees out of the water without any kicking and without leaving a red trail with my spear on its line still following toward the closest point to get out of the water on to the pier. By the time I gotten to the pier, the sharks were only a few yards right behind me with their fins pointed on the surface for me. Pulling myself out with all the strength I had, seeing the blood pumping in small squirts, I pulled back my spear gun ready for defense while they just kept going under me around the pillars.

Finding the steps while fighting my way up, out, and off the tube, I found my towel left on the pier deck where I left it before going into the water, and I now wrapped it around my bleeding knee. Seeing where the blood was flowing from, with it turning from light blue to red with each wipe and looking again closer, there was a small white vein sticking out within the cut, and the blood was pumping in short squirts.

Now, just leaving my equipment there on the pier, I started walking to a drugstore seen only a short distance away form the pier. Walking in the store, I found some peroxide, medical tape, and big Band-Aids, then paid the clerk who was now looking at the trail of blood on her floor as I walked outside with a limp and with almost completely red towel. Upon getting outside and sitting down, I began pouring the peroxide over the cut, watching the forming bubbles in the center while using my knife in cutting the tape into small butterflies to close the open cut. This stopped most of the bleeding—closing the opening while I put pressure on it with the towel. Then I finished it with a larger Band-Aid over my patch job as the chilling and shaking started throughout my body. I didn't care about the bloody towel wrapped around me as I walked over to some grass in the sun to warm up. My parents had given me five dollars for lunch, but I wasn't hungry now. Waiting awhile, feeling a little lightheaded, I then followed my bloody trail on the walkway to my equipment, thanking and thinking, my guardian angel must now have been with me on this day again, but quickly putting that youthful center strength in charge. I've used up my share of them throughout my life. Pebbles and I do believe they are out there when you need them. But I've must have used mine plus some others as well. My parents found me on board the ship asleep and safe without knowing anything about the sharks. My first aid had worked, but the medical aide on board the ship looked at it while adding some new dressing and said, "You may need a few stitches upon getting back to Long Beach." Then after my mother and my dad had gotten on board, I neglected to tell them about the possibility of my becoming the prey after missing mine and only having a brush with the rocks. Never again I did swim in those cold Catalina waters until much later in my life with my son and his Boy Scouts camping trips.

TEN

Dining Table Injuries

One night, months after my dad's accident on his motorcycle, we had been sitting at the dining table, waiting for my mom to bring the food to the table for dinner. I can't recall what was said between us, but he was sitting across from me with my back to the wall in our small dining room, which was maybe eight by eight feet. Then before knowing what happened or any warning, Dad threw a fork at me with it stuck in the wall, only inches from my head in the heat of our moment. My mom put down the serving dishes and got a broom from behind the door, yelling while coming at us, and started with hitting him behind his head, neck, and shoulders. Then she came with a wild swing at me and hit my head a few times and her yelling become louder with each swing then again returned to my dad, now being a less movable target. It was easy chasing both of us around that small table, and we were trying to hide our heads looking for our escape. Yelling, she said, "I never wanted to be present or see or hear this type of behavior again" and then she started to cry as she just stopped. You see, my dad's leg was still in a long cast, and he couldn't get his hands on me or get away from mom or her broom, and he knew how wrong this was. There were others like Manner and others of dad's friends, who met that broom on some occasions as well. She being only five foot four but had a temper that was released in a fire of energy. We never eat our dinner that night. She went out the kitchen door crying, and I exited out the front door going for a hamburger at Burger Lane in Arcadia and returned at bedtime later.

Dad's Irish Temper

Later on, Dad's Irish temper became a much larger problem for us all with his increased drinking; he became abusive and always angry. For some reason, while drinking, that temper would go wild for no apparent reason, and I could only guess where it was coming from. Many times, during his racing days, he would jump out of his car, race over, jump on some other driver, and they would do battle even not drunk. He wasn't the only one during those days or now that are still seen in today's racing. He had many demons for his drinking too. However, later in life, his drinking came to a stop. It was after receiving his three drunk driving arrest, a divorce, and moving out of state because he may lose his driver's license again, and then did he finally quit drinking.

The Wrong Turn

On one of his drinking occasions, with me now being around seventeen, he came home drunk around two in the morning, and I was awaken to his loud yelling at my mom. He was becoming more abusive, and I gotten up because it was time to see what was going on. They were in the kitchen and I was coming down the hall when I saw him hit mom and pushed her away while yelling down at her. My first reaction was I stepped between them, put my hands up, and yelled at him to "knock it off." He then said, "You want some too?" And with that, there was a wild swing with his right fist at me, but with my just stepping back, his body continued around following his fist and completely missing me with him losing his balance and then falling like a broken tree with legs crossing at the ankles and his face finding every handle on the series of drawers on the left side of our kitchen. He was out cold on the floor because of the drinking or the impact of the fall. Who knows? Then I asked my mother if she was all right. She responded, looking down at him. "Yes, I'm OK." We slowly picked him up and carried him with him mumbling something on the way of taking him into their bedroom and placed him on their bed. She took care of him from that point on and I returned to bed.

The next day, he started to work earlier than my getting up, so we didn't see each other until I'd got home from school. And by the time I had gotten home, he wasn't home yet either. Then when he came home around six, I saw his face with cuts over one eye, a big black eye, his nose much larger in size, and another cut on his cheek that wasn't normal in size either. Not one word was said between us that night, and neither of us said a word about that night ever. As a result, he never came at me again as long as I was living with him in our house. Drinking or otherwise, thinking back on it, he wasn't sure and just didn't remember what happened or wasn't sure if I'd done all that damage to him. It worked for me; and I guess that in this way, he did get the Irish family's father's up-and-coming lessons in life from his father or son—only from his drinking.

One time, I being around twenty-nine years old, married, and have a house party in my own house. He came by himself after his being drunk. I asked him to leave, took him outside and again told him, "Leave, you're not welcome."

Again he tried a swing at me and again he fell, but this time he fell into a hedge of bushes next to our front walkway. Without my responding other than just looking at him in the eye while he got up on his own just turning and leaving. With me not saying anything, he knew my response was, "Walk away" or I will respond, "And don't try that again" just by looking at my face. My wife at the time and many friends lost total respect for him for being a "dirty old drunk man" saying things to my friends' wives and being mean drunk.

ELEVEN

Changing Times, 1949-1952

FDR had died on April 12, 1945, and Harry S. Truman was vice president, and it became his responsibility to end the war. Truman ended World War II with the use of the first atomic bomb, but another newer evil had already started sweeping wider into the world. Winston Churchill tried to warn the world after World War II about the communism principles and the spread of its doctrines. The USSR and China were now moving over major parts of their surrounding countries and pushing their power into those other more weakened parts of both sides of the world, left with no understructures governments. The Korean People's Democratic Republic (North Korea) had shortly afterward attacked the Republic of Korea (South Korea) on June 25, 1950, on my eleventh birthday. Truman had to respond and now brought most of the world through the UN to help fight this war or police action, as it was called, and this war didn't end until 1953. Until under a new president known as IKE, the general of World War II who saved Europe from Hitler and now through a cease-fire had to reaffirm the division of Korea. Communism was now becoming the biggest threat to freedom. This was the beginning of the cold war years and with the iron curtain descending throughout the world. We were now into the Atomic Age but still some believe this is our happiest age with a greater amount of fear deeper in our minds. The world saw the results of the war on Japan, with it being the first to pay the price and hoping it would never ever be used again. Now in the present years of 2000, we now have North Korea with its atomic bomb threatening upon us again, but China is now in the middle. China will become the newest growing greater power in the world with its biggest contribution of bringing in greater number of humans with guns into the battle to keep the North Korea government standing. Maybe General MacArthur was right with his dealing with them both and suggesting we use the bomb on them too.

There was now television coming into our homes in 1947-1949, and my dad's brother Harold had purchased one of the very first ones other than the ones seen in stores.

So we would drive over to his house on the weekends just to watch it and have a visit with my two cousins, one older and one younger than me. These were the only two other boys left with the last name of Allen besides myself in continuing our clan's name that I knew of then. They lived in Downey, California, with my other cousins, aunts, and uncles within those surrounding towns of that greater building area, which was growing with new housings, cities, and jobs every day. Only dad's two oldest brothers and one sister as family members of the Allen clan were still living in Wyoming. Therefore, we in California were becoming part of a new age of a faster movement—more information, entertainment, and enterprise. Only a few were out of touch, but like the TVs having only first three channels on the air in the LA area then, we had increased with four Allen families now living within five or ten-mile radius away from each other. My parents, living twenty or more miles away from the rest of the clan, kept us away from the "families in fighting" that was increasing because of wealth. However, we got our TV a year later than Harold, an easy vision Hawthorne with its green screen. Gone were the times with my mom making chocolate fudge and listening to the radio on the weekends. No one knew what this thing could do to the family units and could bring so many changes to our streams and the world to come. We started watching Milton "Uncle Miltie" Berle, Pinky Lee, and my favorites Space Patrol and Beanie and Cecil in the afternoons. Then there came four major stations, then five, and then more stations as the years moved on to now in the hundreds and thousands over the world. My mother's brother Paul got out of the military service and then went back to live in Cheyenne but built his own first TV with Heath kits through the mail. So he drove all the way to our house in California for a visit and to see if it would work and it did! There was no local station around him yet in Cheyenne.

The times where changing in some other ways in our smaller world too. One early morning in 1952, just before the sun came up, I been awakened with my bed shaking and moving across the floor. At first, with my partial-awaked mind, I was thinking my dad was fooling around with my bed, but then I realized there was no one there, and I saw that my bed is still moving across the floor. It was an earthquake, and by the time it had stopped, my parents were up with everybody else in Southern California. The radio stations told of buildings falling, and we learned that Bakersfield was the center of the quake. Thinking it would never stop at the time, but this became something you live with from that time on.

Before TV, you could build a crystal set, which was a crudely simple, primitive radio receiver with a crystal detector instead of electron tubes. One of my friends in another neighborhood but close by, living about a mile from my house, was interested in radios too. So we put together a crystal set radio of our own at around age ten. It could only pick up a few stations, but we did it too. It's funny now; his family had a color wheel in front of their TV trying but not making it into color yet. However, you got the feeling of color. It was like the colored glasses of the first 3-D movies and hard on the eyes, but at least they did work. They also lived in a big four- or five-bedroom, two-story house with only two children and two large Great Dane dogs and have many new toys of the times. But the best of all, his step dad had two new Jaguars XK120, which were the first two-seated sports cars from England, and he raced them as well. He worked for a foreign car dealership in Pasadena, and we would go for test rides. It was so much fun; the two Great Dane dogs got their rides too in the passenger seat with their heads above the windshields as we go down the street. When it was our turn, one could ride on a small rear bench seat sideways, the passenger seat moved up with the top down, and with the wind flying your hair and with blurry watery eyes. It sure would be great to have one of those cars now too.

They had lots of money, or we believed they did anyway. What was funny, I found out later that my friend was related to Albert and some way with the Van Gundy family as well. Also funny was the fact that Albert was worth more money than them all during and after this time because his dad was a family doctor, who was given land all over Southern California in payment for treatment during those Depression years. Albert, my dad's best friend for life and also my older brother throughout these many years died of a heart attack while dancing with his ex-wife on New Year's Eve just a few years ago. He loved life and dancing from the day we first met.

Those Happy Days

Junior high in 1952-1953 at Clifton Junior High was the beginning of those happy days seen so much later on TV depicting those fifties. We rode our bikes, played with yo-yos, and this was how our emotions ran too-fast, slow, high, and low. However, one other thing changed my stableness now—from staying in one classroom the whole day during those years through six grades to a new system of many classrooms changing all day. Being in charge of your self brought on its own easiness in becoming a loner. You no longer stay with one teacher's class for the whole day, and therefore the classmates changed too. We also learned to drop, hide, and cover from girls, teachers, and parents while practicing to "drop, get down under your desk, protect your neck, and cover your ass" with or without those "the bomb" drills. It was now the Atomic Age.

My sports activity of running track like the fifty-yard dash, broad jump, and high jump gave me some standing and placement within the social standings with other boys. My simple standing was being judged as a member of the third-place relay team; but my winning later in the intramural football, basketball, and being a member of the track champion team gave me a greater standing among my peers. With all that said, I was still not much more than a small pebble in a bigger stream here, who was crossing back and forth over the social tracks in town with puppy love for two girls.

Learning Social Change

There were social changes too, which at puberty brings on that finding of a new and strange wanting to find out "What are Girls" and the watching of girls in a new kind of viewing and thinking what it would be like to kissing a girl or just maybe hold hands. I was also learning their powers when they became women too because I noticed the greater amount of controls placed over our social approvals. We all did anything just for that approval whether it was a teacher or anyone else surrounding you whenever you could find it and look for someone to notice.

Eight Grade Cool

We like almost all of the guys or gals our age started worrying about our appearance more each day. The hair had to be just right; the shoes had to be cool with the pants and shirts. Socks had to be matched, and jackets had to fit in within your crowd's social fashions too. Also came the crew cuts, flattops, ducktails, waterfalls, and Princeton cuts. However, no long hair was seen yet and was still not cool. It started there, and by high school, it was your mainstream of thinking and actions. Most were growing into their fixed suits or clicks whether it is short or long relationships by the eight grades. I was still smaller than most of the other boys; but for some reason, those girls had become taller, smarter, and much prettier for the most part. However, us boys were still "The Kings" over the seventh graders under us; most of them were still much shorter than us, and we now held our one short year advantage like they learned in sixth grade over others below them. Pebbles are being pushed, washed, and moved into many streams coming their ways at this age. Some guys were faster than others without seeing the long-term effects, and many never recovered from junior high or judgment decreed there upon them. Your circles of friends either became members of those small groups of so called in crowd or maybe just not caring but found yourself in the mainstreams of those mostly just looking in and much more standing outside of everyone else's small social class.

Some of the guys you had become friends with during these middle junior high school years wouldn't spend much time with you later in high school because of the allegiance made during these earlier formations, or just form their own groups. Changing, channeling their characters into different social levels was started here for the most part. There were three guys that came to mind: Don Everett, Tom Grondzik, and Gary White with some others for me. And for whatever reasons, they believed they should be looked upon at high social levels and in gatherings in high school, disregarding their friends from the past. I guess that's what's called climbing those social steps to success. I was again just an ordinary pebble in the middle of any social success.

In these younger days, we went to the smaller and cheaper movies at the Monrovia Theater on our Saturday afternoons by riding our bikes, but our parents would take us to the Lyric Theater farther uptown on the weekends mostly at night. It had its much larger plusher seats with its much-higher ticket price and its newer or bigger released movies. You were demanded to be on your best behavior at that theater or with your parents. This became also the same behavior with your relations with girls; by twelve, you would want to be cool with your buddies, but watching your favorite girls from a distance at the Monrovian or the Lyric theaters was completely two different worlds. When face-to-face with a girl you liked either you would be on your best behavior or make a complete ass of yourself. For some reason it was never in between the two, and the same for the girl's reactions too. Knowing how to dance later and knowing that some of the girls from that social dance thing that my mother made me join later was a plus. Also knowing some of the older guys from within my neighborhood with their sisters gave me a little knowledge in this area, my just knowing something of what most girls were and like but not much more.

Our parents, teachers, and older surrounding kids showed us how to act, but sometimes that didn't stick. But as we grew older, we started having more interaction and started finding our roles within both sexes easier and how to define that behavior. Sex, well you always knew about it through the outside world, but not through your family's little talks and always before their sit-down discussions while thinking it was now time to talk to you about "the birds and bees." So right or wrong, you had some ideas of what was going on. Your parents didn't talk about it either, and that wasn't talked with them until the Kinsey Report was talked about among themselves and sometimes never thought about telling us either. My mother was worried about my social skills and me by this time, especially now being in the seventh grade; you see, she was married at fifteen. So she signed me up for a society dance club and class for Jr. High Kids called the Teenage Trotters Dance Club that met once a week after school for its club activities. Here you learned to dance, meet girls, drink punch, and find your two left feet; but being left-handed, it did help in overcoming that foot part but still not handling those other un-dancing parts yet. The meeting of girls did become easier later on in life as you'll find out. The funny thing about all this, this was where my social life started, and this was where I celebrated my first day of marriage much later in life.

This society function setting was used for my wedding reception was held at the same Monrovia Women's Club above Foothill Boulevard and not too far from Clifton Junior High because my mother much later became its president after my high school days. This was why we used it for my wedding party and in learning another type of social dance with the beginning of another type of social beginning. This building was a beautiful large old white southern style mansion with its well-kept gardens and large old oak trees in the surroundings. Its large ballroom in the middle center area had stairways winding up like in *Gone with the Wind* and saw many large parties and balls, but it's all gone now too with its social presents.

Clarence "Pee Wee" Kirchefer

New Kids on the Block

There came a new kid on the block with his family moving into the neighborhood, the Kirchefers, while I was around age ten. His first name was Clarence, but everybody called him Pee Wee because he was small like me but one year older, and we became buddies for five or six years. He always had self-confidence; all the guys wanted to be his buddy for many other reasons too. Also, there was another guy Ronnie Van Gundy, who had been here at first on the same street only a few houses separating them at first. So during that time, it always became a struggle over who would hold on to the greater numbers in his court and the largest control over our small groups of guys surrounding them and the neighborhood. After a few years though, Ronnie's family moved a few blocks away into a new house and neighborhood but still holding on to many of us from the old one. My bet and standing was always with Pee Wee. But not like Ronnie's family, there was an older brother, sister, and mother, but no dad around. For whatever reason, this wasn't discussed, but his mother was always the best and very cool mom. She now is still living across the street from him. I spent a lot of time watching both families closely and being there during their interactions with their different streams. I found both are trying out their independence, and both families have a piano.

While Ronnie's dad played in his garage, Pee Wee's piano was played in the living room with us all singing songs together like from the movie the *Song of the South* and other pop songs of the day before TVs were in our homes. My mother also had received her piano in her living room from that garage; it was for many years too, but not before it became a furnished social room much later during the nineteen sixties after I was gone. Both our moms liked country music best too, but also loving all kinds of pop music was very important as it was with Ronnie's dad with his ragtime.

Pee Wee was also very good in sports and a few steps faster than me. While he was standing up to anybody, who thought about pushing either of us around, plus having his older brother with his friends, including (Reggie Jack) Bob Turner at the time, who was very close also with Ronnie's family as well, there wasn't much need to worry about help in or out of the neighborhood. However, that didn't keep us out of fight though because you see, we didn't need much backup.

Also, there came my going to church with them too and playing sports with him in his church's group leagues, which gave me something without knowing it. And seeing their holding-on togetherness as family with a very hardworking mother and their fun-loving surroundings made a lasting impression on me too. His family was into bowling, and now that he is retired, he works part-time with his brother-in-law running a bowling alley.

We both where on the championship C football team of 1954 in high school; he was co captain, playing the left running back while I was second string right running back behind Ray Reyes during my first, second, and third years. We won the CIF championship with us both running with Ray Reyes plus having Keith Lincoln, our quarterback. Pee Wee moved up into the B team in the next year of 1955, but he didn't play in his senior year. For Lincoln, he moved on up to varsity the next year and became a standout in CIF. And from high school, he went on to Washington State playing in the Rose Bowl and then continued playing pro-ball in the NFL. However, before all that, Keith and I too had lots of fun with girls, learning about French kissing during our first few years of junior high at Clifton and earlier times during our freshmen years at the old' Monrovian Theater. However, during our first year of football, he had knocked me out during one of our practice while I was trying to make a tackle on him. He was a freight train coming at you even then, and I had walked home, not knowing or recalling taking a shower. He moved up while I stayed thin, small, and played three years on the C team, but still we stayed undefeated again in the next year again without him or Pee Wee. In that first championship, no one scored any points on us until the last game of that year, but we still won thirteen to six without it becoming close.

However, before my senior year, during my summer vacation with my parents at Bass Lake in Northern California, I fell breaking my ankle while fishing with my dad. No more football for me; being out before the season even started, I kept my old football shoes, hanging them up in my old dreams, and that also was my last fishing trip with my dad. He had never taken any time off work or interest in watching me play football either, but I made sure later in my life to see my kids try anytime in their sports.

Divers

Pee Wee got his driver's license a year before mine while driving his mom's '47 Chevy two-door Fleetliner most of the time when he could get it. It was a stick shifter on the column, which was always getting stuck at the wrong time with us stopping and fixing it right where we got stuck. We drove it on the back streets and roads within some still-dirt roads and mostly tree groves than throughout La Puente growth area. We

Richard "Dick" Dane

listened to country and rock and roll music on the radio while we're on our way in picking up his mother from work. Then later on, when I got my first car at fifteen, he drove another kid to school in my car Dick Dane, who didn't have a driver's license either. Dick was a little older than both of us but in the same grade with Pee Wee, who also had a lot of self-confidence and with us meeting him only during the high school years. He also had a brother older than Pee Wee's brother by the name of Skip, and Skip was working for the LA Times, owned a car, and had married early.

Dick was the only one among us with a job, working at the Budget Town market where his mother also worked. So he helped with the gas, which was at fifteen to twenty cents a gallon then. We went to school for a whole week on one dollar worth of gas. However, there were times that we did some pushing and walking for gas. We would also go to the drive-in theaters watching movies like The Big Sky and others while hiding guys or girls in the trunk of those big cars of those days parking in the rear parking areas of the lot. After getting into the theater, watching and waiting until it was dark enough and clear, we all would cream into the cars' doors with a finger on the door light's button and breathe better.

The trickiest part was always going around and opening the trunk while the kids now slip into the rear seat without being seen or caught. You don't do this on dates of course, and we always had to play the radio loud when paying at the booth for the tickets to cover any sounds coming from within the trunk.

Pee Wee's Girls

Pee Wee bought his new 1957 Chevy two-door black hardtop after his high school days. It was fast and beautiful, but before owning this car, we only had my car or his mom's or possibly his brother's. So we all drove around together until I got my own driver's license at sixteen with Dick still riding with me, but Pee Wee started dating now. Pee Wee, Dick, and I had became the Three Musketeers up until then, hanging out together for about a year. Most girls thought he was cute, cool, and as they said, "Well put together," which had also got the attention of one girl in my class, Donna Gill. She lived above Foothill Boulevard with a much-younger brother. She also had it with that same "well put together" looks that most other boys had openly thought about when looking or thinking about her.

So after school, we (Pee Wee and I) would drop by her house, which just happened to be close to another guy's house on our football team by the name of Lonny DeBoisblanc, who was in my class too and who just lived down around on the next street through an alley on the next street from her house. We would occasionally drive him home after our football practice or just drop by her house. I believe Lonny liked her too but was always saying she was "only like a sister," which became much truer as the years went on, and he also had twin younger brothers Bobby and Billy, who also played later on the same C and B football teams. They on their own became very famous in their own right, "Yo-yo men," and still involved.

Now with all of us at Donna's house, Donna's mother had a lot to watch over. She furnished food and kept a close watch on us buddies with her one girl, who loved getting all that attention. Donna's young brother would bug us all most of the times too like all little brothers do; plus with Lonny's two younger brothers there too, there was always something going on. Pee Wee and Donna still were able to get together for dates until he moved on, or she did without him. Afterward, Donna became very popular in our senior year; she become a song leader and ended up dating our former buddy Gary White, now the head yell leader. Along with my other old friend Roger from our Santa Fe Grade School days, who also became a yell leader and then Lonny the other friend became the third yell leader. My other close friend Jim Rood wanted to become a yell leader like his older brother before him in the class before ours but didn't make it. Also, his younger brother had been a mascot yell leader before going into high school with their older brother in that year.

Jim had also become very close friends with Lonny and myself during these years. Jim Rood would also become my dentist for many years and a very good friend afterward while seeing me through both my marriages after his return to Monrovia from dental college. Then he moved into a house close to his parents' house just below the Big M, which just happened to be rising on the hill behind his house. He with his teacher wife Lynn became a part of that town's sprit and was involved longer with living there in the city of Monrovia more than Gary, Roger, Lonny, his brothers, or myself.

For Donna, much later after high school, she went on to marry a Monrovia policeman, who went into business for himself and became very successful after his injury on the job. She also became a stepsister to another friend of mine, Lloyd Eggstaff from high school. Because her mother married his dad after he became a widower and lived down the street from Jim Rood. Her mother had worked with me after my high school days in the West Arcadia Shopping Center in the Green Stamp redemption store. For Pee Wee, after high school, he found the love of his life in Linda while both were working for Avon in Pasadena and became married partners for thirty-five years before she passed away from cancer. Dick Vaile, another friend named Dick, stayed on to become his closest friend throughout the years after high school and after their beginning meeting in their car club. Now we all are resting pebbles in life's streams.

See Dick Can Drive

Our first buddy Dick from the original the Three Musketeers didn't have a car, but his brother had a 1939 Ford two-door sedan. And sometimes with his brother, we (Dick and I or the four of us with Pee Wee) would drive around looking for chicks around downtown, at the high school, at the public pool during the summer—where we spent most of our summer—and parks, or drive-in food spots. This was cursing the mating social trend during these times, which was only in America because of the automobile. There were no shopping malls then to hang out in. Funny during that time, Dick's brother Skip was working for the Los Angeles Times in the printing section and was working with Mickey Thompson, who was working there at that time too. Later on, Mickey Thompson became a big car racer in drags against my cousin, plus off-road racing with land speed records and brought so much more into the whole wide world of racing. We would meet much later, but sadly, he and his wife were killed by two guys on bicycles many years later in 1988 with an unsolved hit contract in the small city next to Monrovia called the Bradbury Estates. During Dick's senior year, he found love without yet owning a driver's license or car. So I became his driver and escort on dates, and on one of these occasions, we had borrowed his brother's car for a double date, which was set up by his girlfriend and one of her friends for me. We had done something, a movie or something, and ended up on the mountains in Arcadia known as Chantry Flats or Lovers' Flats. He and Lynn were in the backseat while I was in the front seat with Lynn's girlfriend, who was older than me. The girlfriend moved over closer to me in the middle of the seat with my arm placed around her. And then turning to her, we kissed with her saying, "Oh, Carl." Grabbing me around the waist, pulling me over her, and hitting the floor shifter of the car that was still left in third gear. I hadn't put on the brake lever, and the car popped out of gear at the same time, and she continued pulling me down on her with me hearing that big pop and knowing it came from the transmission. I've got to break free and stop the car because we were now moving forward with my trying everything to get lose from her grip.

Now finding both feet on that foot brake, I kept pushing, pulling, trying to stop the car only a few feet short before it could run off the edge of this cliff, where we had been sitting only few seconds before. Luckily, we went only a few feet before stopping, but with all of our hearts racing for many reasons during that short moment. However the next day, everybody was coming up to me at school saying, "Oh, Carl! You really rock my world!" then laughed their heads off. There weren't any more double dates with Dick and Lynn. They both graduated that year from high school, and then Lynn with her parents moved to a small beach town. It was still my duty to continue my driving for Dick on the weekends to her new house, but now in his own two-door 1951 Ford that he bought. We spend many early mornings seeing the dark changing into morning on the weekends, driving along Beach Boulevard through those hills before any freeways. Dick finely passed his test and got both license, married Lynn, and moved to Cost Mesa too. I don't know were they are now, but Dick got a great job, maybe moved to Texas and was a great friend for years afterward. We all moved on in our streams.

My First Car

My first car was a 1941 Ford Business Coupe customized with frenched headlights my dad and I did with 1953 ford headlight rims. Both the two-side grills were already removed; and we filled, noised, and decked it with razing up in the rear putting it on rack, and therefore the gas gauge was way off. However, before getting my car, Dad again played teacher telling me, "See that car over there? (A 1934 Ford Coupe.) Before you can have your own car, you'll have to take that one apart, check its running gear parts like trans, engine, etc., etc. Then put it back together, and it must run!" So I started on it at fourteen, and by fifteen, it was running. And within weeks, he let me pick out my own car on the used-car lot that I've seen on the way home from school. He paid twenty-five dollars for it, and to me, it was a black beauty but with some cracked paint with blinded young eyes. But later within one month, the engine broke down, and we found out why. The used-car dealer had used tin cans to shim up the engine rod bearings. Plus, it was an early twenty-one stud engine, not the twenty-four that should have came in that year from the factory with many more miles than the car had. But the funny thing was that the engine my dad had me took apart in that learning-lesson car was the same twenty-one stud too. We pulled them out, now using the engine in the learning-lesson car to replace my car's engine. But later we got a hot twenty-four stud, '49 Merc 59AB block used by my cousin Eddy in his racecar.

My First Ticket

Now sixteen, having my driver's license for only five or six months and just replacing the engine from that '34 Ford. Now, unable to recall who was with me, but we went to Carpenter's on a Saturday night to hang out. We picked up two girls and asked them if they wanted to go for a ride. So while we're driving down Route 66 into the city of Duarte going east toward Azusa, some Spanish guys came up beside us in a low rider. Not recalling why or how other than being teenage boys words were said with these five or six mucho guys in their car. It was we, my buddy and I with the two girls being cool. We speeded up with them following us now and giving us the finger. During the time of changing the engine, I made changes to my suspension like lowering it all around, changed it's shocks to tubs, a new heavy sway bar on the front and rear. This thing would really go around corners now. We raced through Azusa's side streets and back on to the main part of Route 66. I'd lost them, but within a few miles they were back only a few feet and was behind us again.

We were now in Glendora, and they were right back on my tail again. Next, we came under an overhead railroad crossing bridge area with a dropping down of the roadway and now throwing my car into a full big U-turn under the bridge, not seeing or thinking this was a double white-line area or a headlight coming from the other direction. Well, the other car didn't make that turn and kept going. It couldn't turn like my car. And I was thinking we've lost them now, but just within a moment later, out of nowhere came some red lights behind me. Now pulling over, I saw there was an officer in a motorcycle coming up and stopping behind me. He asked for my driver's license and registration. While getting the requested things, he asked where we were going. So now very nervous, I was trying to tell him about the car full of guys chasing us. He didn't believe us and gave me a ticket for the U-turn over the double line and added reckless driving. Being only sixteen, it was required that you had to bring your parents to court in front of a juvenile court judge. On my court date, my buddy came along as a witness, and we told our story, but the judge told us, "Next time that happens, drive into a police station and ask for help." If that will happen again, let me think where the nearest policeman or station is while six crazy guys are looking to beat the "crap out of you." I got my license put on probation for three months. One of those ironies of this story was that many, many years later, during my years living in Glendora with my own teenage kids we lived only a few miles away from that bridge in Glendora, and my kids drove under this same bridge going to lunch during their high school years. Plus, my son got his first ticket for showing off by going around a corner too fast, close to our house, on Old Foothill Boulevard by one of Glendora's finest motorcycle cops following him into his high school parking lot a mile or so away. My son said it was the water on the street, and the cop wanted to make a point to him in front of all the others.

My New Engine

In my junior year of high school, I got that new flathead engine from my cousin Eddie, a three by eight by one-half '49AB Merc with a broken crankshaft, three-fourth race cam with three 97 crabs intake, Edelbrock heads, a Lincoln distributor with dual coils. And my dad placed Lincoln gears in a '39 transmission on the floor, which came from Eddie's drag roadster after breaking its crank in racing, so we put in a new one from a '49 Merc that was made into to a three-eight inch stroker at Hal's Auto Parts on Shamrock in Monrovia. So now it was three-eight by three-eight. "Ahh, that speed! That feeling and that sound!" Needless to say, the car would never run a week on "one dollar" of gas again. However, it would beat any new '55 or '56 Hot Chevy V-8 cars around. The front wheels came off the ground the first time; we started that new engine up by accident while being pulled behind my dad's truck. When this engine started, my dad was pulling me around the block with no front fenders. And in order to pump up the oil pressure at first, I'd turned on the switch to look at the oil gauge, and it fired up with the front wheels coming up, flying in the air toward the back of my dad's 1956 Ford pickup while on a long log chain hooked to the truck's bumper. Like a mad chained dog rushing after a bone and now being awakened from a nap, it was out of control. I'd gotten the switch shut off just as I was about to land the front wheels in the rear bed of his truck but landing only inches from his bumper and next time pushing in the clutched pedal and keeping it running for a few minutes now. The car only had a six-volts type starter like all cars of those early years, and when the engine got hot, it didn't want to start without some help and also because of its high compression. So still many days afterward, I would have to park on small hills and use the starter as well while popping it in first gear at the same time to start it. But after it gotten more broken in, it was a little better, faster, and more engine than I ever needed, always being near the edge of how fast you can go; that's what it's all about without coming apart in those days.

Old Killer

One day, while stopping at a four-way stop sign and then starting forward, another car was slowing and should have came to a stop at the sign while on my left, but he didn't stop. He running from the stop sign, speeding up even more, hitting me in the left front fenders, pushing my engine back into the driver's compartment, then bouncing off me, crossing the street and crashing into a church's door. It was an old man; he wasn't hurt, but said he had hit the gas instead of the brake pedal after my flying over to confront him. He had only bent his front fender and bumper on his old Dodge, but my car was a total lost and was being towed home for its last trip. The police tried placing the blame on me. "A teenager with a hot rod." But my dad got a statement from the old man, which he signed for the police and the insurance company over who was at fault. It took three to four months to get my money and another car. My Ford Hot Rod was dead, and Dad took out my engine, put it in one of his racecars as the rest were junked out. The engine did well for him, but in the meantime, I had found an old' stock 1929 Ford Roadster Pickup for twenty-five dollars until I received

50' OLDS with wrecked 41' on left rear

my money from the insurance company. After a fight with the insurance company, I found a beautiful 1950 two-door black Olds and drove it until I went to the army at the end of 1961 and, of course unable to leave it stock! In time, it got a newer CJ engine with three crabs and put a shift kit in the four-speed automatic trans after I replaced it two times because of my racing it.

My Girlfriends

Now I fell in love at lease three to four times a year during these early teen years, but without most of these girls knowing about my passions for them. However, the few who knew, had little interest in me. There were a few in our eight-grade years who where willing to play the old "spin the bottle" kissing game and didn't care to whom it was pointing at. We all had given that game a spin. On my freshman year, I found Helen. She and her sisters lived in Duarte, which was a great distance for two lovers. Ronnie and I rode our bikes for about six or seven miles to see these two sisters. He was dating Helen's older sister. Mostly we met in school, at the movies, or in the football games, and mostly on Friday nights.

The Monrovian Theater at that time had all of those first original-made "old horror" films from the thirties playing on Friday nights. That worked great for us, getting our arms around our girl in the balcony and getting a first "French kissing." During other times, we would just be out front in their yard under a big tree, kissing, and hidden under the shadows. Helen was worth many long rides into the dark.

Then there was Sherry, sweet as cherries and hot as chili. She lived down the street, about a block away from my house. When Jerry Lee Lewis's hit songs "Whole Lotta Shaking Going On" and later "Great Balls of Fire" came out, she loved him; and I loved her. She was two years younger than I, but she was wilder. We became the rising "fireworks" on July and during those very hot summer month's nights inside a wrapped-up blanket, lying on that cooling grass. We spent our time finding things that had gotten us both "very hot," but trying to cool down was a much bigger problem for me, trying to walk home without any sexual relieve, effecting problems for your whole body or sleep.

Across the street lived another girl, Judy, with her younger brother and parents. There were times I felt some attraction for THAT girl next door and she for me, but we became more like a brother and sister in our relationship while time went on. She liked having all the boys around, and she sometimes came around my house to watch those across the street. She was pretty much a "rebel" too. Her father and mother became like family to me over the years too. Later, her brother followed me around with one of his friends, and they became big help to my dad with his racecars, while I was in my military years. This was after his getting out of high school too. Judy got married, but wasn't very happy, getting a divorce after a few years. After seeing them at a Monrovia High School reunion a few years ago, I found they, sister and brother are now living together.

Trouble with Halloween

Her father was a sergeant on the Monrovia Police Force. Being a stupid kid at twelve with two other neighborhood guys, we stole some of his pumpkins from his garden just before Halloween. The next day, we were found out in some way. He got to the other two boys first and had them confessed, telling on me too. He picked me up in his police car, taking us to the police station for questioning. Not knowing at the time that he'd talked with my dad before we went to the station. Upon arranging our arrival and after questioning, the "three little pigs" were placed in a cell next to two drunks, who had gotten sick sometime before this, filling the area with a smell. After we were left, with prospects of our fate running through our minds, the drunks were then again moved into another cell. We were in theirs and were handed mops to clean up their cell floor. We were gagging and turning green, trying not to have their sickness as well. I held myself together, but the other two got sick. My dad then came and got me out, but upon getting me home, I was treated to his belt and was grounded for a week, learning well the lesson about stealing and never getting caught by the law again, or getting in with drunks.

"Just a Lonely Boy"

My dogs were my closest friends ever. By the time I turned seventeen, I hadn't found any girl for me, or one who could be really interested in me whom I knew of. Most of the younger girls weren't it for me, and not one of the girls in my class appeared to think much of me either. During my high school freshman year, there was Helen, but it was more of a young guy learning about kissing and holding hands and sexual attraction. Being very thin in build, like Frank Sinatra during his early 1940s, didn't help. However, I'd gone out occasionally with a few girls who were one or two years older than me during high school—that was because of my older friends and their girlfriends who would make me double date. But we saw that it didn't work, it was simply pointless.

The Older Women

Then at seventeen, there was a horse trainer who was a former jockey living next door with his family. He was a New Yorker and Italian. He would go for long periods of time, working the horse racetracks across the nation. I played with their two younger kids at times while I was working around in our yard. They didn't have any kids their ages close around. We played ball in the street; or I would just chase them around in their yard at different times, and sometimes, I would baby-sit them too. They had lived here for a few years and during one summer day, the wife being a young woman in her mid-twenties then, tall with dark eyes and long dark hair hanging down, which was up off her neck most of the time, motioned me over after seeing me walk down our street toward home. We talked and I felt something was wrong, she wouldn't look in the eye while we talked. She asked if I'd keep her company while her two kids were down for the afternoon nap. We went inside and she had been drinking red wine while crying and playing records. We talked for a while; then she put on Sinatra and wanted to dance. At first, I found it uneasy; then feeling her put her head on my shoulder, we danced closer. And then she said, "Have some wine too." We stopped while she poured me a glass. It went to my head very quickly because it was warm that day and I wasn't used to drinking wine. We then continued to dance very closely, with her crying, her tears running down her checks. But she wouldn't tell me why she was crying, only hiding behind the words of the songs. We ended our dancing into her bedroom, with the door not all the way closed. This was my first "taste of honey with a good Italian wine." It lingers on for the rest of my life, never to be found again or forgotten. It was never to happen again, with both of us taking time before looking each other in the eyes. But much later, I learned her reason for crying. It was because she learned that her husband's been cheating on her.

The funny thing about this was within that next year, her husband got me a job as an exercise boy and walker in his stable at Santa Anita. I also worked at the Del Mar track with him that summer. With that came my going to the jockey's ball, and there I met HIM! Frank Sinatra with Kim Novak, Bing Crosby, and other stars! It became another completely different dream world of mine, or of any Homemaker's world with two children. Now and then, just thinking about both Kim Novak and Sinatra—because he had it all and I was in love with her after seeing her in Picnic with that dancing scene being so "hot" and in Bell, Book and Candle—was WOW! Of course! Mr. Sinatra was the coolest of all the cool things, with his "I Did It My Way." But anyways, back to the husband. Because everybody at the ball was having fun and drinking, and so was he that night with another women, while his wife was miles away and not in his mind. So after seeing that, it was easier to never feel bad about my, or her, actions. GOOD AND EVIL, maybe it's gray like Frank's life. Pebbles and rivers move on down into new territories without looking ahead much farther than the next bend, or seeing clearly in the rear mirror, or around us sometimes until it's too late.

TWELVE

GOOD OR EVIL

Looking back, seeing the task of learning what's "good and evil" was in play, more so, during my years of pupilage and purity. The choice of right and wrong was being formed and tested, as we get older. This is part of finding our soul. That knowing in our soul what is right and wrong with the presentation of many choices can bend our directions. It is hoped—you know from the age of twelve—by our learning from everything surrounding us and teaching from others. You begin and start narrowing down and nearing the right paths to follow. Teenagers are not interested in being saved, or thinking about death. As teenagers, we are left with many doors of choices—many closed, many partly open, many open wide—just waiting for us to enter. Some of us know what's awaiting us, but most of us don't. That's why we are in need of guidance, and most need to be guarded during these hard choices. Which paths will you choose, and which guards will be in place? I did a painting of a "mixed-up" teenager during my junior year in high school, with paths running away in all directions from his hill—depicted as "good and bad." My dad always liked that painting, keeping it for many years before giving it back to me. It was the thoughts, not the work, that he liked and maybe he saw himself too. I think, he related to it in his own way. We all can—at times, throughout our lives or streams—look for the right paths.

"The Devil Made Me Do It"

On one occasion in my senior year during spring break week, five of us couldn't find a place to stay, other than with a few girls we knew too well. They had rented houses at the beach with two mother hens watching over them, and our parents thought we would be staying down there with them. One guy suggested, "Let's go to TJ's." Away we went, and after walking over the border, and starting at the nearest strip bar then to another because there was no age limits then, the fun began.

It was my first time there as well as most of the others. There were a lot of sailors and Marines everywhere, and I bet it was the same for some of them, too, to be in this city of sin. What some of these guys were doing to the dancers, "holy big bull" or "crazy dog things," I'd never seen before or afterward except in hidden XXX films. It was something we had never seen anywhere before. "It" was the devil's playground—beginning with "sex, bad girls, beer, and bad boys"—everywhere inside these clubs brought temptation. We could have only dreamt of seeing or joining in the eating at the Blue Fox club or seeing the lady with her donkey doing unbelievable acts. You could, also get rubbers and bennies at any drug store. So now, we were ready for "Sin City." However by 1:00 am, there wasn't any action, and after taking some bennies to stay awake, we were now wired up for anything. The taxicab drivers were on every corner, telling us about young women just awaiting for us young studs, saying, "Come on, guys, just take a ride and look them over, you won't be disappointed," and continuing, "These stupid sailors are wasting their time and money on these bar girls." We had enough of this watching and drinking and just couldn't turn down the devil's words. We all jumped in his cab, and away we went down a dirt road into the dark. There were no lights in that direction we were traveling, and about ten minutes later, the cab's lights showed us a two-story building with nothing surrounding it, but who cared? The taxi stopped. We got out and could see the city lights over the bear hills. The large red door downstairs opened, and three or four young women came out, dressed only in bras and panties. The devil hit us with the news; it would now cost ten dollars each for the ride there and back, plus ten dollars a girl. So now, we were in deep, and maybe we had ten dollars each, if that much together, period. We started looking in our wallets, while knowing, we all were way short that amount.

So now again, the devil with his big smile and mustache said, "Boys, don't waste my time" while pulling his large switchblade out of his back pocket. Now why did he do that? I was thinking there were five young guys wanting girls, sex, wired on bennies, with the three guys being very large football linemen; and I saw the talking was over. The devil was very small, as small as me, maybe weighing one hundred pounds, but all of us at the same time took a step forward without thinking or saying anything. The devil started thinking to and backed off some with a surprise look. One of the women screamed as he flashed the blade, but he made a big mistake in reaction by turning to look at her, while one guy grabbed him from one side and the others grabbed his arms from behind him. By then, everyone had grabbed his arms, waist, and knife. The knife fell to the ground. We just took him to the red door, with the girls now laughing at him, and smiling at the bigger guys. One of our guys spoke some Spanish and the devil told him in Spanish, "And you'll all be in Tijuana Jail soon." Then, we all started laughing after it was explained, and for that moment, we forgot where we were. One of the guys reached over, taking a robe belt off one of the girls and tied the devil's hands behind him and then his feet. While another girl said, "Put him in that closet over there," while laughing. And we locked him inside with a chair while hearing the increasing loudest Spanish words I'd ever known and all bad words. He could only now muster up in anger, and kicking at the door, but soon stopped. Now, we were left with the beer, six girls, five young studs: and what should we do? We all took what you would expect, but first, we checked for any telephones lines first. There was only one telephone and we pull that and any line, wanting no messages, we were save for a while. We found those bennies and rubbers served us well. Within a few hours, now exhausted and thinking about our other problems as it was starting to get light outside, we told the girls, "Don't let him out until we are gone." We left all the cash, except for one dollar each, in a Mexican hat on the table to be shared by all. We made it back to toward TJ, but couldn't find the keys and wasn't going to open that door again. So with my mechanical skills, I hot-wired the taxicab, which we parked only a few blocks from the crossing bridge. As the sun was coming up now, we sang our songs of pleasure, joined arms with two drunken sailors crossing the bridge, while walking home free and having new meaning to songs like "Tequila Sunrise." We knew we got lucky in more than one way and done something very stupid as well. All started breathing easier with each step, but knowing we had to tell every guy we knew about it. After all, us being around seventeen-to-eighteen-year-old males, it's a must to brag—but only with other guys of course and not ever, ever with any parents or girls.

One of the guys kept the switchblade, but our guardian angels had kept us from falling too far into hell. The next spring break, all of us returned only to Thousand Steps in Laguna Beach or Huntington Beach for surfing and girls or to college. But in much later years, I returned there only for some betting on horse race, jai alai games, and bullfights—the only danger or devil's temptations to remind me of my lessons learned. But years later, on one of our honeymoon trips with my first wife on a dark street in TJ, I fell into a hole while we were walking after just telling her, "I'll protect you."

Bad Boys Myths

While working on cars or just hanging out, we would meet a mix of "wild" guys, but most not. However, it only took one of these guys to come up with an idea for something to do because teenagers have a lot of time on their hands. "Boring time! The devil's time!" While one guy brought an idea out loud or spoken of it, someone else would add or try to top his original idea, or another guy would think of something even better. We would laugh just thinking of ways of doing it, real or not; but by then, someone had now started putting it together. Those hot rods and B movies didn't know really how or what made us work or think, or maybe we were just stupid, but not that stupid. These movie writers were trying to make money and stupider than us, and it wasn't until James Dean's Rebel without a Cause did someone get it close. Almost always, the next thing you knew, we were in the process of doing it. The most important thing was it was just fun; and most of the time, we never destroyed or hurt anyone, like they did in those movies. We just brought havoc in our wake, and that's what bad boys do. These were our showoff life-stream stories, but fun. Teenagers just want attention and something different than their boring parents or their boring-viewed lives.

Good Guys Myths

Some teenagers bring their or other's pain upon their own as it happened one night while I was running with the "in" crowd, or good guys, who were made up of sports lettermen and "the social group" who were the occupants sitting on "the wall" at school. With their mixture of guys and girls from this crowd, we drove three or four cars to the end of Lake Boulevard above Pasadena and parked where there was a known real "haunted house," which was the remains of an old mansion up and off a path that had been built during the 1930s. It burned down, and there had been a large hotel with a cable car that ran all the way to the top of Mount Wilson, a famous area for the rich, coming to Pasadena's during it's hay days. There was nearly a full moon and wild animals sounds in the distance. It was and is part of the national forestry up there still. We broke up into smaller groups to go exploring you could easily hear things. Your imagination or someone messing in your head may only have invented those. Then came the sound of a girl's scream as some joker threw something in the bushes next to her. This caused everybody else to jump. From then on, the girls would either get closer to a guy they liked, trying to get him alone or into their own small chicken-holding groups, hanging together in three or four. Most of us would laugh and chase each other around while making low sounds. It was like the mansion in Rebel without a Cause in some ways, with an empty pond or pool and other emptiness of ruins, but there was no James Dean to protect the weak.

However, these weren't the real "good guys" in my thinking, but they where the "bad guys" like you would think of in the movies in a different way. But they believed themselves to be good guys. They did many other things that may have been worse in my eyes or others. But I wasn't around or taking part of their fun. I dismissed their kind of fun, being seen by most as just "fooling around." But it was more than that; it was their demeanor of who could take advantage of whom. It was using their social powers to gain a greater advance into the next higher social levels over the pebbles, and it wasn't my kind of fun. It was a game they learned early, and most carried it over into their present lives. It's still very much present at our class reunions with peacocks and chickens.

"Rebels and James Dean"

Before this, some also found me quite nice, funny, but mixed up or moody during high school and not much a saint or a rogue or anything within any type real "in" crowds group, other then them knowing my name or face, and nothing of real in common. Appearing more in my own mind, like and in some ways a James Dean; but still it was just a small pebble in most other's streams, fighting all or any systems in my own quiet way until I couldn't hold in my screaming anger. Like all teenagers, Dean had spoken for me; but teenagers are all self-centered, yet feeling small down deep inside and feeling more like a toned-down James Dean without his Natalie Woods or brother's girl in East of Eden understanding me, then seeing Rebel without a Cause and East of Eden and then Giant two times in 1955.

After watching those movies and later reading his real-life story regarding his relationship with his father, and then looking at my father and seeing the lack of understanding between us, which makes us not get along at times, it was just like James Dean in his movies. Like most teens, after Dean's death, I wanted to become just like him. I rode my motorcycle; but I wanted to drive sports cars, desiring to become a real racer, becoming famous at something, and finding that maybe one understanding girl would come to care for me. You could find there were others like me who wanted to be like James Dean. These were the funny little pebbles who also watched Happy Days, liked the Fonz, and wanted to be a little like him or Dean more than anyone else in the cast.

My "not bad, but not good guy" gave mixed a representation or understanding within some pebble forms by typecasting my clothes. It was a warning because my wearing of leather jackets (one being blue suede and other black) over T-shirts with jeans, black loafers, or blue suede shoes had added to my badge of un-Goody-two-shoes type of guy and a rebel. On top of this, I got into some fights, mostly with authority figures, and been given "dummy shop classes" while my biggest interests, besides drawing, was hot rod. Then my later hanging out with some "odd artist" friends had put me on my way outside of the normal social mainstreams. My economical standards by living below the Foothill Boulevard and Huntington Drive neighborhood and within the surroundings of social standards with our general working-class type of guy that I hang out had painted me as a little of a "bad boy," but not really bad, with a few girls because only a few girls really got to know me in high school.

"Natalie Wood"

There was this one younger girl in one of my art classes, a rebel too, who was in some ways my Natalie Wood. Her name was Paulette. We were just friends, but the relationship lasted for many years with her feeling and acting out Rebel without a Cause in her own life. More or less, she have an older sister who did everything right, was very beautiful, and was a part of the "in" crowd of Goody Two-shoes throughout her school years and was just made that way, whereas Paulette wasn't.

Paulette looked a lot like Natalie Wood physically too, with her own beauty reflecting a real fire within her own rebel ways while always being compared with her sister and many others around her. She married one of my fellow younger friends who played on our same C football team and was in the same car club during and after our high school days. He's still into cars as much, or more, than I am; and we are still in contact too after we got married—he to Paulette and I to my first wife Jo Ann. We stayed in touch and all ended up living in Glendora with our kids growing up together, going to school together, and playing sports together too. His son also got into cars, like him, but have artistic talents like his mother. Our kids became friends for life too. And like Natalie, Paulette died young too and was always a rebel to the end. Funny thing, her two kids became rebels too.

At my tenth-year class reunion, one of my female classmates asked my then wife, "Who is your husband?" She had known my wife, who was an employee in the local bank where she did her banking in the same town where we all lived at that time. My wife told her my name, and then Lois said, "Oh!" And with that, my wife was taken aback, being very surprised by her reaction, and asked, "Did you know him?" Then Lois told my wife, "We thought he would be either dead or in jail by now." It became a joke between my wife and me because I am now an investigator on the side of the law.

It was funny going to our thirty-fifth-year class reunion and connecting with my present wife who had been married to John Hardin all those earlier years. We were classmates, and he was my friend from junior high and through high school. But they were now divorce as was I. It took one glance and a few dances for us to know what was about to happen, but of course this was after Jim Rood had told me to ask her to dance. During the night, sitting at the table with Jim Rood, he told her some of my past that she wasn't aware of during our school days, like my being stabbed in the local Golden Cage stripper bar. She asked, "You don't do those things anymore, do you?" Jim laughed, and I smiled with a no. She had known me, but she was very head over heels and blindly in love with Johnny during those high school years. She knew me more because of him being a car guy as well. He owned a 1940 Ford two-door sedan then, which Kathy says she had pushed as much as she rode in during those early years as it was always running out of gas because of his gas gauge off the level. We all thought cool cars had to be razed up in the rear during those days. After high school, they got married, had two children—a son and daughter—at their very early age right out of high school. He became the owner of a gas station, the Chevron Station, on Duarte Road in Arcadia. And then he decided he must go on to college in Redlands. His dad bought the station. His dad later moved to another station and ran the Chevron on Double Drive and Colorado in Arcadia before passing away from cancer. Many other car guys I had known and worked knew his father, who was known as JC, as one of the best human beings we've ever known. John, Kathy, and I had only seen each other in a few reunions before this; and he was and is doing well in real estate.

Kathy and I would have been like oil and water mixing together during our high school days, but now we both have move to that middle stream of life. It's in the stars, I joked to my neighbor that night before going to the reunion. Then I said, "There's a widow waiting for me there!" Little did I know? Even with my being a little late in arriving that night, it was for me, in many ways, not too late in our lives because something of great worth was found. She had lost her second husband in an accident not too long before this, and the maker of the stars had brought us together.

THIRTEEN

Rick and More Buddies

After Pee Wee and Dick had moved out with their girls, there was a newfound connection between me and Rick (Thomas) Orrell, who was from their class too, finding many other reasons besides his liking cars, music, and sports. It was very interesting that he had also come along with another friend of his who was in our class. His name was Mel Caudill; he played on the same B football team with him, but was there for only a short time in our class before his and our senior year ended because Mel's father was a military man, moving around a lot. Yet we still got to know each other really well in that short time.

Funny, after many years later and the completion of our own military service, our paths would cross again. We found we had been on parallel paths during those years of our military service from 1960 through 1965. It was in 1966 that we found each other again by working for the same employer at the same job location, but again for only a short time in our life's streams again.

Back to Rick, he lived in a small old house above Foothill Boulevard while most of our other buddies lived below in Huntington Drive. He played in high school football. But before his teenage years, he had bad asthma attracts, keeping him out of most sports until high school. Being an Italian and the only child, his mother wouldn't let him play much outside until a doctor told her sports could help him.

Now it was in sports where we met. He found his needed self-confidence, moving from that skinny kid on the beach of his youth and seeing himself on the back of comic books, and went way over the top. Which is what he does with everything from then on and after high school.

He started working out with weights, going to the gyms, eating healthy food, and later becoming a weight-lifting champion in world competitions during the sixties. He would also later work at what became Gold's Gym in Pasadena. Later, he talked two other ballplayers who were brothers from the next class down in the classes of '58 and '59 into it as well, Don and Gordon Wong, who played on our C and B football team. He

124

then convinces them of his beliefs and what bodybuilding can do. As bodybuilders, they both became runners-up in the Mr. World contests in New York. It was different from weight lifting, which Rick performed.

However, Don's family wanted him to take over and run their family restaurant in Duarte, which they lived behind with a large family. But after getting through college with his degree in business, this was not enough. He then changed direction after getting his BA. And I found him later one day at Pasadena City College, starting a new path in the medical field. Before that, Don had also been a member in our car club, the Intakes, during the late-fifties. But looking at him with his quiet manner, you wouldn't know there was always a fun-loving person underneath that smile. I've just learned of his death after he had become a very well liked doctor living in Arcadia with his family. For some reasons, his brother died at an earlier age too.

"Intakes" Don in his 57' Chevy Monrovia Day Parade

Back to Rick, like Pee Wee, he started out driving an old 1937 Chevy four-door sedan as his first car then moving up to a 1947 Ford two-door sedan by the end of his high school days; and then he found a little five-window deuce coupe with no fenders, chopped top, which looked like the America graffiti coupe with gray primer paint. That is, when it was running, we drove it to Carpenters, Bob's Big Boys, In-Out Burger and other drive-in restaurants around the area, looking for races.

However, there was one other racer, I think named Newton, with his full fender, chopped three-window deuce coupe that hung out at the drive-ins as well. He was crazier than most, always ready for fun or a race and was faster than anyone else around town, but we never met up with him when Rick was running.

The Real Rebel

Newton was older than most of us and had the fastest three-window deuce coupe around. During my freshman year, I had heard stories of him delivering milk for Alta Dena Dairy in the early hours before going to school and rumors of his drinking cheap white wine in lemonade cartons called Shaker Ups before or during school. It was only rumors, and we never knew for sure what he was thinking or drinking. He was very complicated and unpredictable, but always cool, never showing much emotion other than his own forms of fun. He was a real rebel without a cause.

One night while in Carpenters Drive-in, we noticed him with a girl sitting in his deuce. He was drinking coffee. Then came a bang from his door after he jumped out of his car, yelling and pulling open her door and then saying very loud, "You're all a like Sex, Sex, Sex." Well, it sounded like that to us. Then he pulled her out while opening the deuce's trunk. He stuffed her into it; now knowing she was a department store dummy. He backed out and drove off with her hand or foot sticking out the partly opened trunk. Everybody was watching and laughing in disbelief during his exit. But within only a short distance from the drive-in's driveway, the flashing red lights appeared. Then there was the fuzz, who maybe wanted just to check on his passenger or just to stop him because of his car. Who knows if they thought it was funny or not, but who would know in those days! However, we laughed about it for a few more days.

The Revivalist

On another Saturday night, our revivalist told us to meet him on Huntington Drive at the Old Monrovia Airport, which closed by 1955. There was a real tent revival happening there. When we gotten there, the revivalist told us, "Go inside, yelling you've seen the light of God and his son is among us." We laughed to ourselves, and then went inside the large tent. One of us went down one row. I and another guy went down the other one with ours arms out, reaching in the air and yelling while almost everyone was already into their own screaming response to the stage and others now on the floor, rolling wildly near the stage. They started screaming louder as we got completely in the lights nearing the front; but more were starting to take notice, us being white kids in an almost all-black crowd. The preacher stopped at that moment, now focusing on us; and then our revivalist was moving forward more into the light with his white bed sheet over his body with arms and hands out to his side, like one coming from his cross as seen in pictures. He was wearing a long blonde wig and walking very slowly.

Panicking, yelling, and moving forward with him as he came closer to the front lights, everyone came to see clearly, even in the dark, a small dark derby on his blonde wig. While he neared those front lights, everybody stopped in their tracks. We ran out as fast as we could through the side exist of the tent. We jumped into our cars and drove away with our tires screaming; and then the revivalist's car came passing us at over one hundred miles per hour. All we could see was dust flying high behind the mirror, and the headlight flying around in circles seen heading our way. Stepping all the way the gas pedal and not missing any of those speed shifts of racing we learned and not caring if there was any fuzz around, we knew we had to get the hell out of there. If caught, then that's where we would be headed. Meeting back at Carpenters and shaking from inside out, this was the only and last time we did anything crazy with the rebel. By my college days, Newton wasn't seen on the scene anymore and was believed to have gone into the service.

The Shooters

Much earlier in these times, once again on the farther east side of town on Huntington Drive, there was this liquor store called the Airport Liquor. It was where the local drunks could be seen. It had a major amount of black patronage because of its neighborhood, and they could be found there at any time of the day. This is where you could find someone to buy you a bottle of liquor for party nights. Police cars drove by, but unless there was a real call to stop fights, or any major problems, there was no reason stopping in that part of town. Our police department was all white in those days, and this was the "blackest" part of town just before crossing into Duarte. Duarte was, and is still, under the LA sheriff, a no-man's-land back then. It was known as Rock Town because of its being made up of mostly open rock areas with big rock queries with sand-and-gravel production. The lowest-income working-class neighborhoods still separate the races even more there then and now.

Earlier in these teen days, Rick with his old 1937 Chevy four-door and another guy's ole black 1941 Caddy four-door sedan drove up to the Airport Liquor after already dropping off another guy a few minutes earlier around the corner out of the light. He walked into the store; and coming back out a few minutes later, both cars drove up on each side, pinning him in between them because of its storewide driveway. We fired a starter's pistol with blanks toward his direction from within one car. The flashing fire was spitting aloud. Bang, pop-popping sounds bounced from the walls as he fell to the pavement. The other guy was with his dad's hats, raincoats; and another was holding a black machine gun (water gun), pointing at those stopping in their tracks with a few more shots into the air. We could see the onlookers looking from some spots in the store frontage. Our pigeon had fell, just like in the old movies. While two guys quickly threw him in the rear seat of the empty black sedan. The guy with the pistol fired into the air once again and yelled, "If any of you (#@#s*%) squeal, we'll be back for you!" Then they roared away with lights out, down and out the driveway into the road and around the corner into the darkness.

Again it was never reported as far as we knew, and we were all laughing about it afterward. However, during the whole time, our hearts where pumping with thoughts that maybe one of those guys out front may have had his own gun and fire for real while we drove away or maybe the police just would happen to driving down the street. This was the start of those bad-boy days—our ways in getting our kicks and not having any fear of traveling down this road again, but the world has now changed. Real guns are out there now.

Teen Racing Dreams

Rick, among his other notions, was a racer at heart too. We drove his ole 1937 Chevy with another guy's four-door sedan, a 1930 model-A two-door, to the end of Fish Canyon in Duarte during a rainy night. Neither car had much for tire treads, with their stocks gone, swaying side to side around the corners like old buggies. While the shocks on Rick's ole Chevy were so worn-out, you could make it jump up and down by stepping on and off the gas pedal and bringing it into a bunny hopping way before today's low riders had the equipment to do so. And it was good that we couldn't go too fast because of that.

Next, we stopped and got out near the dead-end part of the last street with nothing surrounding us for miles, other than cottontail rabbits and our old swimming hole a few hundred yards away where we also did a lot of skinny dipping in moonlight nights during the summer months. We all took our turns driving to the end, doing some with some amount of fear at slower speed, then hitting the brakes as hard as we could and then turning the wheel hard without losing it completely, but letting it spin around on the wet roadway. Round and round we would go, just like in the movies, and now the contest was on. Who could get the most spin around? However, it ended. Once on the second try, the model A went over on it side in what appeared to be in a very slow-motion manner just before it nearly completely stopped without any real amount of damage. We ran over, laughing and putting it back on its wheels. The fenders were those with old heavy metal and frame supports. It took two of us to pull them with a jack hand, making them far away enough from the wheels, and later pounded them back into shape. We also went at night to the Santa Anita Racetrack parking lots where there was gravel at that time and where we could do more of these spins there. We became very good at doing our controlling turns and spinouts. This gave us false confidence and racing dreams, but it proved to be useful later.

Dad's Racer

My dad owned a four-door 1941 Graham Hollywood; one of the first front-wheel passenger cars built in America with its factory supercharged blown-six engine and step-down unified body. My parents had gone out of town on this weekend. It was time for Rick and me to take this one German exchange student for a ride. He was always telling us, "We Germans drive faster and much better than you Americans." So it was time to prove him wrong and show what I had learned and could do with an American car! Picking them both up with the Graham, we drove to Chantry Flats into the mountains high above of Arcadia at night. It's all curves, changing from around two or three thousand feet above sea level within maybe twenty to twenty-five miles of distance. The car's gear shifter was also ahead of its time, being electric; and by putting it in one gear then pushing in the clutch, it would shift.

We started flying up the mountain with the road marker signs suggesting it as 25-mph zones for all else through the turns. But we were doing at 50 mph and never had any plan of slowing to 25 mph. making it to the top and turning around was easy; now we started going down with speed even much faster. The German was turning green in the reflection of the gauges of dash and holding on to his life with one hand on the dash and door, because there were no seat belts in those days. Rick had some trouble in his rear seat with his feet against the front seat that held him. About after the fifth curve, the Graham was now sideways and sliding a little more each time. But I stepped on the brakes and then on the gas pedal with my foot in a "heeling and toeing" action while slowing and then pulling into the turns. Thinking now, it was a work of art shifting down using the engine too. However, almost to the bottom now, I got way over my head with the brakes heating up under the front-end weight and me taking it too fast, about a mile from those last turns. We slid into the guardrail, just touching the outside driver's fenders, creasing them without much sound as we were looking over the side of the mountain and continuing at over forty miles per hour without stopping and the breaks softening. The guardrails just put a nice line down both fenders after checking them at my house that night. The student didn't say a word on his way home afterward and never told us again about his Germany's world-class racers, but he did say afterward, "You Americans are all crazy."

Then came my attempts to deal with the damage using the wrong hammer for the job, which was a small ball ping hammer. That metal was very heavy, and my hard-hitting attempts just resulted in the replacement of the previous damage with lines of dimples on both fenders in a much-worse state now. My dad would see this afterward, knowing who did it, but not discovering it for at least a whole week after it happened with the "shit hitting the fan." However, for that whole week before he found it, there was so much pain in my stomach with this became the longest of all weeks during my sixteen years of living. I was thinking, "I will never see seventeen." I was grounded for a whole month, and my car was also parked for that time with me walking the line, but never telling him the whole story of how it happened. Funny, Dad knew of my racing on the street, and it was all right because he did it too I guess. However, I never understood his reasoning. As a parent now, I guess, rolling stones don't travel far away from their daddy's stone or trees.

Dad & I built this car together in 1959

I hot lap it once, dad raced it and later this day there's photos showing dad standing with his head and shoulders showing only in the car, while looking at the crowd surrounding it, where the car can't be seen through the crowd

"Little Red Corvette"

Dad received his payoff money from his motorcycle accident late in 1957. At first we saw the local Monrovia Chevrolet dealer meeting him here on his way home, appearing in his work jeans, engineer boots, and motorcycle jacket, after work. Mom and I met him there after she'd seen and wanted that brand-new red convertible in the showroom window. You see that was in my mother's favorite color. The salesmen looked at my dad, thinking it wasn't worth their time helping those in my parents' class, just working class, and judging us just pebbles, because of the way my dad dressed and appeared. So I told Dad there's another dealer in Pasadena, near the college, where Don Nicholson had his Dyno tuning shop setup now, and maybe we could get a better deal there. There wasn't any big convertible though they did have a little red corvette with fuel injection, four-speed, Posi-trackion rear end and a hard top; and the whole family loved it at first sight. It had been originally ordered to be a backup race car for their dealership's sports car racing team, but because it was late in the year and was time for changing to the new coming models. It was up for sale. My dad paid $3,600 in cash that night. Dad and Mom were driving it home with me following in our old 1950 Chevy family convertible.

Within weeks, we brought it back and to Nicholson's Dyno personal tuning after having its factory oil changed and checked over with Dad putting on a pair of traction bars too. It was advertised at the time to have one horsepower per cubic inch with these fuel-injection models and 283 hp being something used then and now. This being the first "fuely" Nicholson had tuned, we guys went to Riverside drag strip with it the next weekend. First Dad, then Nicholson, and then I got my shot. I was the slowest pass; but recalling it, when that flag dropped, my foot was all the way there, tires burning, watching its tach. I tried to keep it straight, hitting the next gear then the next then the last one faster. But now I heard less of the engine roaring with each shift, and the tires sounded off each last time shorter. But it felt like I could just get out walking faster, for some reason, within that next few seconds; but it was still gaining more speed, over 100 mph. Then it was over. Through the lights, you could relax you body, but not your emotions, while slowing back down looking for that return road. God, that was a great feeling!

We had beaten new 1957 Thunderbirds with their new factory blowers, other Corvettes, or sports cars in our class at the end of the day; and we brought home the trophy. However, my parents drove everywhere in this car, crossing the country to see the races of Indianapolis, Dayton, and Arlington.

In one of these trips, Dad was driving home across Texas, making a stop for coffee. He had to move it behind the restaurant because the truckers inside informed him after hearing that the highway patrol was looking for a red corvette on their CB radios before they had stopped too. But they never did catch it or him. There were not many red corvettes in Texas then. My mom became the major driver. You would hear her coming home or anywhere around town seeing her little red corvette with its strange noise coming from that little engine under the hood. They sold it in the late 1970s when I had my kids and without enough monies for an old two-seater, but now I wish it was mine even more so. I had my few rides looking for girls in it too and did have some lucky encounters, at times driving it with my friends around and through drive-in restaurants during those college days and in one Monrovia Days parade with our car club. Its now worth, in any found condition over six figures. Those salesmen completely missed seeing my dad's worth, just another worthless stone. And just like many other occasions, his rough appearance and others not seeing beyond his unpolished rough rock appearance, brought pain throughout his life. There was much worth, wealth, and gold in this simple pebble stone, like there is in others of his time.

The Long Goodbyes

My cousin Ed's son, Little Ed, started driving quarter Midgets at age five or six; and he became ready to move up after filling their house with more trophies than any Little Leaguer have ever seen by age twelve. By twenty-four, he was becoming one of the fastest known top drivers in the big-time racing circles in Southern California. He was becoming well ahead of all the other drivers in points and on the circuit when he, then, paid the price. His dad, Ed, was just like his dad, Big Ed, always very supportive in building "the Best" and one of the fastest real-size Midget racecars during the 1970s until one event happened.

It happened one summer night on a Phoenix track with him going ahead overhead, flipping three times in the air after hitting another car that shifted sideways in front of him. He normally was always starting in the front-pole row, but there had been trouble with the car while he was on his qualifying laps before the race. He hit the other car at the end of the straightaway where they had hit their highest speeds on the start when it happened. But when his car did come to a stop, he was dead—just like James Dean—within a flash of time. It was like his head was on the end of a wipe, breaking his neck at the shoulders, and there was no sign of life, just like "the black number three" of our times. A young man's life was over within a flash, and he was the best of every thing you could like in any person, never saying goodbye.

He looked like Opie in The Andy Griffith Show; he had that freckled face with a small space between his front teeth during his youth, blonde hair, and those clean good looks that always melt hearts with his smile. Years earlier, his dad had done the same flipping while racing, wrecking on the Bonneville Salt Flats at over 260 miles per hour, breaking his back, very lucky to be alive afterward. His car had also flipped over and over many times, and when it came to rest, there was not a piece of body left on the car—his body and the engine being the only things attached to the frame.

Now this time, the first older stone had walked away; but his pebble didn't roll on any more, and his father still can't deal with his loss. He blamed himself for the problem with the car, but that's just part of the sport as we all know. The long goodbye is never over for the parents losing their child at any time.

Unforgiving

Like my cousin Ed, there was unforgiving and unforgotten bad days for my dad too. During one of our night races, an accident happened involving one of the other car's pit crewmen who ran out on the track without a flag. My dad didn't see him as he came running to help his driver. While Dad was coming out of the same corner at high speed, he hit and killed him. It wasn't my dad's fault, but he'd never forgive or forget that moment. It kept on repeating, flashing in his mind and dreams. That moment of the man's death, appearing and running for many years afterward, was unforgiving or unforgotten. It may have been a part of his later problems with drinking too.

Again much later, drinking or not, he was coming home late after another long day of racing with one of his pit crewman—a friend, a family man—who was driving my dad's truck, while Dad slept in the passenger's side. This guy fell asleep or was drunk or both. Anyway, they drove off the San Bernardino Freeway into the center divider area, rolling over one or two times and killing the driver. My dad was saved because he slid under the dash area upon impact, while neither had seat belts on and with the roof coming down to door level. My dad only had a few minor injuries. But this, too, brought further mental problems to his whole being and thinking. He was never able to completely forgive himself for either loss. He just moved on, like we all must do, trying to let it run out its course, without it holding us or killing us.

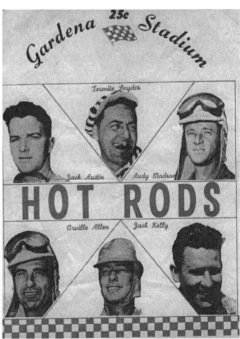

FOURTEEN

TV RACING MAKES LEGENDS

Dad is now one of those old legends in those "old racing days" with wrestling and roller derby during those 1950s TV shows in Southern California. Even much later in the 1960s' TV shows, because of those "red strips" on his cars, he would be seen on other shows too. And on one these shows, just at its beginning clips started, there came cars racing at you. This was on a daily local teenage show in the afternoon, and seeing dad's car with other jalopies racing at me started the excitement. The show was called Where the Action Is, with Paul Revere and the Raiders playing the show's theme. There he was with his car shown in two movies as well, one at the beginning of *The Killers* with Lee Marvin and Angie Dickinson at the races with them looking for someone in the pit area through the binoculars. There he was with his car and those "red strips." Another time, he and some other jalopies took a part in another TV show's storyline, the Pete and Gladys, show in December 1961. As Gladys got on the racetrack going backward, the jalopies were racing around the track.

I've also seen later a racing film made with Paul Newman doing its narrating in the early seventies about auto racing, and there again was my dad seen with those "red strips" racing with steam coming out front and trailing from the front hood while still racing around the track without stopping and without giving up the race. The film was named *Once Upon a Wheel* seen on the Racing Channel only last year.

My dad bought his first jalopy, a 1934 Ford five-window coupe racecar, from a guy whom my dad had went out with a few times in 1955. It had a hopped-up Flathead. But my dad said, "This guy can't drive without running into something every time we go out." Of course race fans and racers as jalopies now called the cars because they were old wrecked cars, bumping and pushing each other around the track in what appeared to be fun. My dad had raced Midgets on wooden and muddy racetracks way before this purchase in an off-and-on manner with motorcycles racing. We had an old four-cylinder engine, which I believed was from a 1938 Indian motorcycle, lying in the yard for many years before and after my teenager years. It was another project lying around. He was hoping to make another Midget car, but it never happened. He always had many types of other engines lying around at different times too. By the time, I had finished high school, there were always three or four extra 1933-34 Ford cars for parts with his other cars too. My dad went through three or four racecars during these times. He started painting his cars with the candy strips just before one of the Christmas racing events. His crew, which included me, went among the fans in the grandstands, throwing out candy canes into the crowd during intermission and repeating this almost every weekend from then on, wearing candy-stripped shirts Mom made for us all. So from then on, he was known as the Candy Stick Kid among the grandstand fans and the Sunday TV's fans of Southern California. He was well liked by Dick Lane of the TV station KTLA during this time, and he would get a lot of TV time with remarks from

Mr. Whoa Nellie! Himself. These promotions during events helped TV ratings and the racing association to become very poplar on TV's Sunday afternoon event, just like wrestling did for Saturday nights. By the time Dad had started racing his car in 1955 and until I was in college during 1958, we had raced around most of the Southern California tracks like Western Speedway in Culver City, Gardena Speedway, Huntington Beach, Saugus, San Bernardino, and then later at Ascot Speedway in Gardena next to Torrance and at the Riverside Raceway.

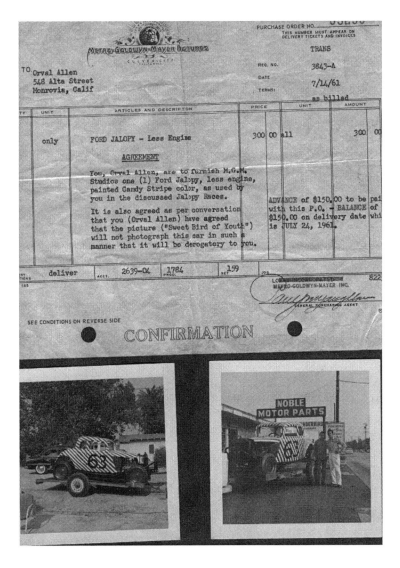

MGM contract
Photos of car completed for movie & I and dad

"Sweet Bird of Youth"

MGM had signed Dad, giving him a contract agreement to use parts of some previously obtained racing film with his car winning and leading a race. Part of this also said, we had to recreate that same car for the close-up shots, which we did only because I had more time during my college-ending days working on it after school. After the completion of the car, my dad found out then the star role was going to be shown doing drugs and heavy drinking during the beginning of the film, and with him driving my dad's car. My dad, plus the racing association, wouldn't allow themselves with that kind of image be shown to the public; and Dad was now thinking more of his own image with kids also.

Just being the Candy Stick Kid was like to him being the Lone Ranger in some ways. So no way was his car going to be used with the main actor's role and his candy strips to be seen in a bad light, therefore pulling out of the contract. The movie was made, and it was named Sweet Bird of Youth with Paul Newman in the starring role. They still paid him for the recreated car; however, it was originally my job to be in charge of the same car and moving it around while it the studio lot.

Well, as it turned out, because of my being available during the shooting of some of the scenes, they offered me a job as an extra in the political rally riot scene that for a few seconds was seen on the big screen. It ended up taking a few days in shooting, with me making some extra money plus a great lunch, meeting people working in the movies, and seeing how movies were made at the studio. This was July 1961, and this would not be the last time I appeared on the big screen.

Others Racers Around

Dad raced with many other local drivers, but the most notable during the 1960s was Parnelli Jones and Rodger Ward. Rodger owned a tire shop in Monrovia at that time too, and Parnelli got into the same business later. However, there was one kid originally from Kamas City by the name of Jim C. Penney, who still has speed and racing in his blood. He left California with a driving championship during the late sixties to race in Kansas. He was the grandson of J. C. Penney, and you'll now find his son Bobby with dreams of racing running in his blood too. Bobby is racing and learning the business of stock car racing in schools in the South and on Kansas's tracks during these present years like his dad.

My cousin Ed raced with and against and beat Mickey Thompson. He was a close friend of Art Chrisman and his brother during these early drag racing days. They all had the first record-breaking runs at just over the new mark of 150 mph during those days in the early fifties and sixties. During that time, they raced at the legendary Lions in Long Beach, Fullerton, Huntington Beach, Santa Anna, Pomona, Irwindale, Bakersfield, Riverside, and out of state on Bonneville. He became a member of the 200-mph club by setting a record over 200 mph in a single-engine streamliner during these days.

Also there was my association with Don Nicholson, who became known across the nation in 1961 as "Dyno" Don Nicholson and would continue throughout the years from the fifties to the seventies. Also during the seventies, Mickey Thompson was preparing on going for the Bonneville speed record and was having Nicholson work on his car at Don's shop in Monrovia, which was now south of Huntington Drive. I stopped by one afternoon and helped out by working on that car. This was the car with three Pontiac engines and ended up breaking the land speed record afterward. Mickey and I met a few other times before this and also through the years. Speed is a forever challenge against time and men. However, Mickey's death from another type of assault ended that all.

My Own Speed

The racing of my Ford during high school was just the beginning; later came my 1950 Olds, which wasn't your dad's olds. For a while, it ran three crabs from a 1957 C-2 on a 1953 engine with a built hydro four-speed automatic for fun on the street and track. Also during that time, building my 27-T Roadster while in my college years to beat my close friend Lloyd's roadster, never happened because of Uncle Sam. Again during my army years, because of Lloyd having one in college with a Hemi, I built a 1953 Studebaker; but I used a Pontiac 421 CI engine. After getting out of the army, then came owning my 1964 Chevelle and putting in a 396 Corvette engine for fun on the streets and in the drags again. I also later got my chances at driving on the round tracks with a modified hardtops 1940 Chevy car at Ascot Speedway and then driving hot laps in my dad's stock car at Riverside Raceway.

We built a 1966 Chevelle to race in the Big O in Ontario Raceway, but now putting in new 350 CI racing created engine from GM, we had made the mistake of running the crab. To learn, burning a hole in the top of its piston was like a cutting torch. That engine was later given to me by my dad and I hauled it around for over the next thirty years until three years ago. When after my rebuilding it and putting it in my now customized 1957 Chevy Bell Air two-door hardtop with all its new high-performance parts and twin-duel, four-barrel crabs, I with Kathy, Roger Albo with his wife showed up at our forty-fifth-year high school 1957 class reunion for some Old memories.

Jim Dean, Hairy, 57' Chevy & Kathy

Street Racing

We all raced along Route 66, known then as Huntington Drive, but River Grade Road in the Rock Town area of Irwindale was the favorite road for our then-big races before there was any drag strip built there in the late fifties. Just like in the movie Rebel without a Cause, we drove down to Irwindale with cars lining up to race, with some for pink slips, and others here just as followers. Most would just hear about it at drive-in restaurants. There would be cars lining the roadside's shoulders with their headlights shining on down the track to the finish markers; and because the road dropped down in this area, getting its name of River Grade Road, there were others placed as lookouts on the higher ground, looking for cops. Then with the OK by the flashing of headlights, it was time for the race to start. We would race around midnight, listening to rock-and-roll music most of the night while going back to the drive-ins afterward with our "highs" on just that night's smell of tires and of cars racing or thinking about what was needed to win in the next race.

Hot rod queens were girls without fear who would become our starters standing in the middle of the blacktop in the lights and dropping a hanky or just their outreached hands or arms to start the clutches burning. Some of them got rides with the racers before. After reaching the finish lines, a few were with the winners and a few were dreaming with their other girlfriends of riding with those winners of that night. Tires would be smoking, spinning with engines revving, gears making animal grinding noises before their fatal loss of teeth and the mixing of many still-unknown broken parts within our high emotion losses. There was always that squawk of rubber from those who weren't brave enough to race but wanted to be noticed. All our revving hearts were still racing on throughout many nights and telling of the stories, of what we thought we saw and heard that night. Myths and legendary stories started here.

Rick, with many others, had started in my yard working on his cars; and with that, he later went on to working part-time at a local speed garage owned by Don Nicholson, who was later known as Dyno Don, on Maple Boulevard in downtown Monrovia. Which reminds me of my friendship with Rick and helping him replace more-than-many transmissions in that 1947 Ford sedan because we reversed the shifting lever to the left side on his steering column. We now started up for first and then came down for second gear, which was faster; but if we missed it, would go into the reversed gear coming down. And well, let's say, "Bye, bye, gears." You would chance anything to get that racer's edge.

Big Pebbles

During the my time of helping others with their cars, there was another friend of Lloyd's and mine who was a very large person and has shown his big heart throughout his life. He was part of the class of 1955, friend with Reggie and the Van Gundy's too. Even then, he was large in size, over six feet tall and two hundred pounds. His name is Emil Nelson. One of my dad's favorite stories relates to his car and size. He brought his 1937 Ford two-door sedan over for some work on the engine, maybe putting it in, don't recall exactly. However when we finished, like Lloyd's Roadster, the gas pedal leakage didn't meet my dad's approval of being safe the way it was installed. Two crabs. My dad took his car keys out of his car and wouldn't let him drive it out of the driveway. This really angered him, to say the lease. There were some very loud words, and size didn't mean anything to my dad. So Emil retreated home, and in a short while, he returned with his dad for the car. His dad listens to my dad's side, but not completely understanding the leakage problem, but they both returned home that night without the car. Youth sometimes gets in a hurry, and sometime, they must learn that being safe is more important. But this may take just a little more time no matter how big you feel you are. We solved the problem the next day, and he got his keys back. And the word spread out regarding working on cars here. It may be a hot rod, but by god, it better leave safely.

Emil and I stayed friends throughout the years even during those many years of our being married men with families, as did Lloyd during the 1970s. There were parties at my house during my first marriage, with Lloyd and Sandy, Rich and Sue Bornt sharing the laughter. My family also went up staying with him in his Running Springs cabin, but now he has retired from his job in Standard Oil. Both he and his very beautiful wife have opened their big hearts and time by traveling and building homes through their church's origination for the needy across the nation until now. They are now semi retired, living in Apply Valley, California; and both are really true "big pebbles" making something extraordinary in their lives.

Lloyd Eggstaff

There was this other friend, who was a year behind me in high school, by the name of Lloyd Eggstaff. He was also another extraordinary pebble. He had and still has many fast cars. We would rideshare to Pasadena City College together after his graduation from high school. He was in good terms with Don Blair of Blair's Speed Shop in Pasadena. Don Blair built and raced everything, but mostly open-wheel cars like sprint cars and hot rods, making good deals with us for our or his speed parts while there came another connection for Lloyd by his marriage to Sandy after our college years because she was also a cousin to Don Nicholson. Both Lloyd and I were building cars during this time, my 1927 T and his 1923 T with a Buick nailhead V8 engine with a McCulloch blower attached to it. He finished his, but I never with mine. Also during this time, he had that cool and hot little red 1953 Studebaker two-door coupe with a hidden hemi V8 Chrysler engine that I'd mentioned before, plus later on owning a 1957 Chrysler 300-C convertible.

So one night, we were coming from college at PCC in his T Bucket on Colorado Boulevard in Pasadena. This black 1940 Ford coupe with a Chevy V8 engine came up beside us at a red light. The Forty revived his engine, kept looking at us; and Lloyd just reached out, hitting the switch for the blower belt to engage with now a new whole whizzing sound coming to a roar at our feet with my arms only inches from those large rear slick tires. The lights began changing with both cars' tires rolling slightly just before the real burning and smoking when gas is applied during the flickering changing of yellow for the cross traffic, then turning green for us.

The Forty crossed the intersection first, but our tires hadn't gotten their traction as yet; but then seeing the feeling of our front wheel razing up almost in eye level, we shot past the Forty in about another thirty feet through the intersection. But Lloyd's engine was still roaring, and I could see him trying to turn the ignition key off on the dash. It seemed like minutes, but he got it done just as we were coming to that next red light.

This was within just a few blocks and with other cars already crossing our path ahead of us. The T's all four wheels were howling, but the engine wasn't roaring any more; and we stopped just a few feet within the crosswalk. We just stared at each other for a moment with nothing coming out our mouths. By this time, the Forty had now stopped too, but there was a quick green light. And we watched him keep going like a dog with its tail down between his legs.

Then Lloyd spoke, "The gas pedal got stuck." We then jumped out, pulling it back down because it had turned over then jumping back in the car and starting it back up again. We drove on down the street very slowly within the speed limit to Bob's Big Boys drive-in a few miles farther. Getting there, we couldn't stop talking and laughing. Between us, we must have worn-out at least any double amount of guardian angels allowed for all others our age and many more than anyone else's during those times or the rest of our lives.

Lloyd's life continued on the edge within his chosen trade as well, becoming an elevator installer and repairman for Otis Elevators, working in those tall buildings of LA, Las Vegas, and in Alaska. He also pursued getting his private pilot's license and, during the 1970s, also tried talking me into going into the same line of work with him. He's now retired in Maui, Hawaii. But last month, I learned through Jim Rood that Lloyd fell off his roof in the rain, breaking his hip. And to think, after all those years, he would have learned something about heights. However, both of us pebbles have just kept ticking, like the Timex watches, but there is still lead in these two pebbles, with a little more in our right foot.

FIFTEEN

Don's Shop

We all found the local speed garage owned by Don Nicholson, later known as Dyno Don, on Maple Boulevard in downtown Monrovia. We all started hanging out there with other local racers by knowing each other's cars, last names, or faces. There were other cars around town in the making. Then came a "picking order" of what or who was fast or cool. We knew of the dandified dangers that were present because of Don's losing his brother in driving one of those first dragster rail-type car with a Lincoln V12 Flathead engine during this time. This reminder was always there, but we never thought in terms of its danger happening to you or us. Yet we were haunted, knowing death could come just around the corner with a lightning speed, just like James Dean, at anytime or highway.

At that time, the new Chevrolet and Chrysler engines were showing up with their newly built overhead V8 engine in 1955 from the factories, starting a major changeover from the Ford flathead engines, which had been king from 1932. They were brought to be replacements with these new-breathing engines within the racer circles and to start a new wave. We guys would do the "monkey wrench" work for Don, and he gave us deals on parts or for some of his work on our projects in return. But most of my many dealings with him would last throughout the coming years. Later in many other ways too, we would have connections though my fast cars or friends and with other racers too. We also had another speed shop and garage owner in Pasadena called Blair that we dealt with during these years, but more about that later. Don had started out driving circle track cars for Blair too before starting his own straight-line racer shop.

The Delivery

It was another Saturday afternoon at Don's speed shop when we took notice of a large wooden box, which had parts, delivered just a few days before for the shop. When the fun light came on, while one of the guys was lying down, we noticed that this box was just the right size to put someone "to rest" in. "Do you think it will work?" asked another after putting the plan together. We all started laughing just thinking about its possibilities. We loaded it in the rear of Don's delivery truck again with two in the front seat and two in the rear bed. We drove up to the front steps of the U.S. Post Office downtown Monrovia, getting there just before closing time. Stopping in front at the curb drop-off zone, we all got out, lifting the box out and walking quickly with the great weight of the container in each hands of all four now. We got past the first few set of steps. The sign was given with the last guy now stopping and lowering down his end of the box on the steps, which was also blocking some of the other surrounding people making their way toward the door. And this guy came complaining loudly, "We can't carry this box any farther." Now the other guys added, "Hurry, or we won't get it into today's mail." Now, among all those other busy people, these guys now dropped their end hard on the steps too. It fell to the steps, tipping over to one side with the top coming off halfway with a human rolling out with our red (ketchup) blood covering its head and his body rolling facedown onto the steps toward the feet of one woman with a small child.

Again people just stopped in their tracks. Some didn't know were to walk or what direction or how to react, while some others just turned around, going the other way. Finally the lady screamed seeing the body at her feet; this brought a second scream from the child. We hurried to the box, rolling the body back into its box, carrying its containers back to the truck as fast as we could, and driving away with people pointing in our direction. Some were still running in all directions. Getting to the garage was easy after getting past Library Park's main traffic light and through the traffic.

We got there and put him under the water hose, washing his head and face with red color running everywhere, while the rest of us broke the box into the trash container, adding boxes over it. Then it was now time to roll around, laughing, until we were crying while the city was closing down and rolling up its sidewalks for the night. Almost even greater for us, nothing was said in the local newspaper or no police coming around checking with Don about his truck license number or doing any follow-up. Only we knew this story and a few witnesses who were there that day. And we would never forget or like the Invasion of the Body Snatchers that was filmed in the city of Sierra Madre, or maybe the Night of the Living Dead, town B movies. But I guess, we never fooled anyone but ourselves, or maybe people thought it was just those crazy teenagers. Who knows again?

Bennie's Booze Enterprise

One of those guys we "hung out" with, but didn't go to school with, was a few years older than us both. He was not into cars, but we found out his dad had made, and ran, "bootleg beer" during the 1920s, so we got a copy of Dad's formula. At first, it was just going to be "makings" just for us guys, but then we found out it was done in "Dad's larger commercial amount formula." There was some downscaling done; therefore, we started by cooking it on Rick's mother's home stove, then moving it on into a rented old garage at the "Aztec Hotel" on Foothill Boulevard in Monrovia, and hiding our enterprise for something like $5 a month.

We put a low-hanging light bulb over the large crock jar, keeping the temperature even and the mixer working twenty-four hours a day, without us being there, other than when we were checking on its level and making sure it was "working." Once it had completed the chemical process under cheesecloth, it was ready for bottling. We found a capping machine in the Sears catalog, and we were now in business. We would sterilize the bottles and check the beer working until it was ready, which was a fine art. Also finding its bottom amount or longer brewing mixer was higher in alcohol percentage, and by adding more sugar, we would also make it stronger. We bottled it in quarts and sold it at 50¢ a bottle because it was too much trouble and better business with the smaller-type bottles. Now we had found gas money for our hot rods and their parts, plus enough booze for our close friends, while still making a little profit and ourselves.

However, one very hot day, while sitting in front of the high school in my car with two new cases of brew in the rear trunk and awaiting a few customers, there came a rude awaking sound. Most don't know this fact: beer is always working, and "it's alive" even after being bottled, but now I was finding this out at the wrong time because after one bottle let go, there came this chain reaction. So at first, I was thinking, "WHAT THE HELL HAD HAPPENED?" So I got out, walked around to the rear of my car, sniffed the air, looked under it, and then I saw foam finding its way out of my rear fenders and from the trunk floor holes. The beer was beginning to run out, flooding into the street. I saw by now the dark brown liquid, foaming and now forming a river running along beside my car's tires and into the gutter.

Profit was gone, and I knew there were some customers waiting, who were starting to walk over to see my car but now stopping in their tracks, and there was a crowd of others walking on the lawn coming toward the sidewalk and next to the street because school was now starting to let out. The customers weren't happy, as fear was taking over me, like seeing Halloween all over again. Back into the car, starting it and getting out of there as fast as possible without someone seeing exactly where this unusual river and smell were coming from or braking lose my tires. My car was a dead giveaway for weeks because of that strong smell known to most everyone. My washing and washing, which happened almost daily for weeks, with the added burden of trying to believe that no one would know but still recalling my encounter within the jail when I was twelve, had kept that fear alive and deeper within my troubled mind. Lucky for me, neither my dad nor my mom had gotten close enough to, or downwind of, my car, and using lots of "baking soda, plus pine tree" fresheners inside did help some. We became very nervous after that, and that had put the enterprise to rest. At least we were thinking;

why should we get shot in the back, or go to jail, like my uncle namesake Benjamin Allen and the other "outlaws" in the family tree?

Super Bike

Most of our plans started, like, at Nicholson's shop late at night, when we where tired of working and getting ready to go home. He would have gone home or still working, but his old 1940 Willy pickup, used by us for delivery and picking up parts, was always around, getting great gas mileage as part of this story.

On one of these nights, along came the guy who gave us his father's business beer formula with his small motorbike. He was here for a favor, requesting "a tune-up to get the best gas mileage ever." This was a request, when gas was only 25¢ a gallon, but he was always looking for favors without any exchange of money on his part. Now you don't bring something like that to guys who love speed, much greater than any better or "higher gas mileage." They just don't go together at all in that world, so it was his fault, as to what happened next. We once again came together like lighting rods, and this renewed and freshened our energies. We started by first stripping off the fenders and replacing the seat with an "old leather jacket" with old leather belts. This made the car lighter, and everyone knows, "the lighter, the better mileage," but that also makes it go faster.

Then painting blue and white flames on the black fuel tank from a spray can, just for "coolness" in appearance. Meanwhile, two others guys were working on the engine, including beginning to mill down the head for higher compression and enlarging ports a little with some "porting and relieving." Then the exhausted muffler was removed and replaced with a straight pipe that was formed into a funnel shape, giving it less restriction. Next, we mixed some high-test airplane fuel and started it up. Now came our "fine tuning" of the carburetor for its new fuel effusion with its changed spark plug. To our delight, real blue flames were now coming out to match its gas tank, with even louder, ear-breaking roars and shaking of its metal. We tested it around the block a few times, by turns, and had trouble holding it back in that now-quiet business area and closed-down part of town. We were told he was coming back to pick it up, wanting his newly improved motorbike, on the next day.

But before he did, we just had to have some fun that night with it. We loaded it up into the back of Don's little Willy truck, which only had a stock four-cylinder engine with two "big" guys standing in its rear bed holding the motorbike and us two smaller guys in the front seat. Then we were off, driving to Carpenters Drive-In because it just happened to be Saturday night, and we wanted to show off the new machine from Don's shop. The carhop's part of the lot was full, so we drove around to the back, where the employees parked. Rick put on his world war pilot's cap with goggles and a long white scarf around his neck. He started up the machine, while another guy ran up front with a green and checker flag in hand for the whole crowd, who were having their burgers and Cokes, not knowing the race pleasures about to come. Rick pushed it slowly to the front center lane, and then started it by pushing faster as he got between the two rows of parked cars in front, while carhops were busily delivering to their customers. There the flagman was waiting his moment, while we were closely following behind Rick in the truck. As we stopped on one side, watching for the green flag to come down, right in front of Rick, in plain view, everyone saw the blue flames awaking the surrounding crowd.

The carhops were very busy upon hearing that LOUD ROAR from the bike; then the bike started flying low with others in its path, with its blue flames, into the night, shining brighter in the overhead parking area lights and causing every person to stop in their tracks. Rick made two or three trips around the circuit circle of cars parked in the front rows, with the crowd now cheering. It was a great success, but then in the distance came a sound we all knew well, starting now to become even louder. "The Fuzz," someone yelled, whose station was only a very short few miles away in distance down on Huntington Drive, and they were on their way to save the day, but Rick couldn't hear us or see our arms flying in the air in all our attempts to stop him. So we went off in hot pursuit with the truck, coming along beside him, with him looking up in greater surprise as our largest guy in the rear bed reached down, and Rick let off the gas some while being swooped up with the bike in one motion while the others all joined in finding a place to grab hold of both, and both ended up on their laps.

We made it into the black back streets behind the restaurant and put our lights out. Everybody first lie down, as low as three guys and a small bike could do while pulling a canvas that partly covered the truck bed, whose occupants were trying to hold in their laughter. We had pulled into a double driveway behind a large Caddy with its tail fins taking up most of the driveway, and hid the small bike while pulling a canvas that partly covered the truck bed and its occupants in the darkest parts of the streets out of the streetlights. We waited in the bed and then climbed out, running into the bushes when we saw cars coming.

The police never found us, believing mostly that our other buddies came around the street first before the police started to check out the back streets and got us to our rides on Colorado Boulevard and then towing the truck back to the shop in Monrovia. After knowing it had to be back at the shop the next day, and the owner was retuning for his prize too. Now thinking about it, maybe the cops weren't looking for us at all. The next day we dropped the bike at its owner's house. He wasn't very happy, so we brought it back with the fenders and seat back on afterward. Shortly after that though, he sold it for more than he had paid for it because it became its own legend, which did make him happy again.

"But, Officer!"

During this time, I found a 1938 Ford two-door sedan for $15 in fair stock condition and bought it because my '41Ford had come apart after its engine broke the first time. One of my high school friends, Joe Bernard, whose last name started with B, was also the biggest bullshit ever and had always wanted to become a "big-time" race driver, boxer, or something just big. We'll just call him Joe B for all of these reasons. However, he did become a semipro boxer for a while, and then changed direction by moving to Moose Jaw, Canada, and getting his taste of becoming a mountain man.

He also became a master craftsman, building furniture with his own hand and building homes in Westport, California, but he is now living with no running water and no electricity, but he does have a telephone. He is kind of reclusive now, with no TV and just reading a lot. I don't really know where the Big B has gone.

Anyway back to the 1938 Ford: while I was gone out of town with my parents, Joe and another friend were fooling around with my '38 and breaking the windshield. So upon getting home I took it out and still continued to drive it around town. That was my reaction to what they'd done. Those early Ford windshields were built with crank handles and knops to push them out, letting the flow of fresh air in, and we called it "our forty-mile-an-hour air condition, because any slower than that, it wasn't much help in cooling off.

Anyway, after one of our home football games on Friday nights, we picked up four girls on our way home in the '38. There was a curfew in the city of Monrovia for teenagers after ten thirty at that time. There I was, driving with three other guys, including Joe, with two guys getting in the backseat to let the girls in, but now we were adding three more girls into the back, and they were sitting on the boys' laps, while one was up front with Joe and me because Joe always liked riding shotgun.

We all were now having a great time driving down Foothill Boulevard and on our way to dropping off two of the girls when a motorcycle cop flashed his reds, pulling us over for some reason. He got off his bike, with lights flashing, and walked up to my door, asking, "Where are you going, and where have you been?" So it was very quiet now, with everybody thinking, are we in some form of trouble because of the curfew? So during my explanation of the facts, the cop now put one boot on my running board while turning on his flashlight, with the light direct into everybody's faces as he was checking eyes, asking us our ages, and looking over our conditions, while I was still busy getting out my license. Then it happened: his elbow slipped from the hood, next to the door, and then through where the windshield should be, with him almost falling into the car over my dash. He then said in a very surprised manner, "Where the hell is your windshield, son?" Well, I replied in a very factual manner, "It fell out, but, Officer, I've got these goggles here to keep the bugs out of my eyes." I told him that they belonged to my dad, who used them while riding his motorcycle, and then I pulled them down from the top of my head over my eyes. He lost it and started laughing, trying to get his own composure back. He then told me, "Kid, get a windshield in this car. It's a requirement by law! And get this thing off the streets until you do." Then he continued with more, "Get these girls home before the curfew, and I better not see you driving around town without a windshield again." Upon telling Dad the next day, he found me another windshield in a junkyard, and Joe helped put it back in, and much later, I sold the car for $50, which was over the original $15 that I had bought it for, but this one story became something we all will never forget laughing about, and I would bet that police officer also repeated it many times to his friends.

"But, Officer!" II

There was one other time with Joe B, after one of our football games away from home, where teams had to fight side by side against all odds. This was our fight on the way home in another way, and in another guy's car this time. He was one of those very small guys, but wirier. He was from Puerto Rico, with a too-quick temper, which was driving us home from a Whittier football game. He was a cross-country track runner and was not a fighter. Here we were, driving with some of my other friends, one sitting next him and a girl this time in shotgun, while the rest of us rode in the backseat of his four-door old '47Chevrolet. Another friend, Butch, was sitting just behind the driver, with Joe B. sitting in the middle, and me on his right. Now, still being in hostile territory after the game played in this very unfriendly town and field, another car full of students supporting the other team started yelling at our driver next to us. With that, the car start moving forward, and the next thing we all knew, our driver pulled over to the side of the road. And we were stopping. To this day, I do not know what was said, and the question coming from my mouth at that time was, "What the hell are you doing?" However, by now it was too late. The other car had stopped only a few yards ahead of us, with all four doors now opening, the guys getting out and running toward us. We couldn't pull backward either into traffic now because of the bumper-to-bumper traffic holding us there.

This ill-tempered Puerto Rican had then locked his door, with the girl following on the other side in the front seat, but within that same moment, Butch's door was now flying open, and a guy was grabbing him with one hand and, with his other hand, punching him while trying to pull him out at that same time. But Joe grabbed this guy's arm and now started pulling this guy inside with Butch and all inside our car. Joe was winning that battle. Joe punched him from his middle seated passion, and Butch was getting enough room to fight back now. Seeing this, and another guy reaching toward my door, my timing for opening it was just right, and I did so as hard as I possibly could, with every amount of force found in me. The door went flying right into his incoming face, which was about level with the door top, to his surprise.

This guy went flying to the ground, with me following and jumping from behind that wide open door, which he would find imprinted on his face. I was flying toward him, landing on top of him with all my anger released, which had just started with our driver, who was now coming to the surface into this guy's face with both fists. Punching him with every angry muscle in every blow while both of us tried to get up off our knees, I then grabbed a hold of his head by the hair with both hands and got up on my one knee. And while he was still on his knees, I started banging his head into the car's steel wheel with its hubcap.

Again, just as I'm about to repeat this movement, I felt someone grabbing my shoulder from behind, stopping me for a moment, and holding me back now as I was turning with my right arm, ready to rear back and getting ready for this new focus. However, I then stopped in midair upon seeing this tall, statuesque figure there. I got ready for whoever this could be, thinking this was the next guy to be dealt with and coming up from behind me. There he was, tall as a statue, standing at least a foot taller than me, and I froze, and he was saying, "I don't think you better do that, son!" From the light of a passing car, I saw he was wearing a highway patrolman's uniform and had just seen what was happening and stopped too. Joe had made it out too by then and had been fighting another guy, outside with me, backing me up before the CHP had stopped us. Butch still had the other guy on the floor of the car and was now about to let him get out too. His guys helped my foe to his feet then, and they all walked back to their car, where another patrolman was checking out their car and talking with them. We got back into our car, saying many thanks in our low tones to the officer as he just stood there watching without any expiation as we drove away. It was my turn now, yelling again at that "Port O Rican," all the way home without giving him time to answer, "What's the matter with you? And why did you stop? And next time YOU'LL be left outside." "What if they had knives?" I asked finally.

The next day at school, it became talk around school, and during the next whole week's lunch too, and he was also in his "big man with his winner bright-shining spotlight" because of "the big fight" for our school. We all knew better—we might have been in deep trouble there. He knew he was no school hero, only a foolish small hot head, without thinking beyond his little bragging stance now, which only makes you feel "bigger" than you are, while in truth, it only really makes you appear much smaller.

You could always forgive Joe his "bullshit" because of his great personality and smile. Plus, he owned one of the nicest custom black 1940 Mercury convertibles that I'd ever seen, complete with a Carson top. I was always thinking I wish that were my car. And it turned out Pee Wee's older brother, Lawrence, owned it for a while after another one of our classmates bought it from Joe first and ran it into his back garage wall. Then seeing it parked wreaked at Pee Wee's house, I never saw it driven again. It was a big loss to the hot rod world. However, Joe B was always extraordinary, and his sister says that he's very happy in his life now. "All in all, he has done well." Having another extraordinary life.

SIXTEEN

"The Beat Goes On" with Attitudes

The winds and streams of time were moving many pebbles down the edges of danger, without a thought of what was around the next turn or possible next cliff dropping off into darkness and empty space. The Russians had just broken the darkness by putting Sputnik into orbit in 1957. There were now other new beats in space, around us, and growing within combining new waves of differences felt, heard, and seen in these new beats coming into the surrounding country and reaching me. A new age was coming faster at us on the horizon, and it was something we had not foreseen. Superman doesn't have a thing on most teenagers. We were made of steel in our minds, and we would never die. However, the news reported, there was a fourteen-year-old black boy from Chicago, who smiled, or said something that was considered wrong in "Money" Mississippi to a white woman had caused him to be found dead in a river. The country read about it, and this was a beginning of this new awakening about blacks and whites in the South, which was now starting a new movement in the whole country. But this was now seen by most in their hearts, with a new kind of striking awakening between the different minds and attitudes between both the North and the South. The country was rising and slowly growing in this mixture of both, and there was much more awareness. And eyes were forced to open.

Being alone most of the time, I became even more independent because my parents were busy with their lives, and now I myself was growing up more too. I guess I now traveled alone within my many broader circles of friends and class levels of younger and older people. I was trying to find myself, like all teenagers do, but now there was something newer and bigger on the horizon. There was now this new movement rising in America called the Beat Generation, which was becoming known throughout my world, and there were more of those other pebbles now. Some new younger thinkers, writers, and those who expressed the Beat attitudes started "the Beatniks. This mixing together of Beat with Sputnik brought on what was known as the non-conformers. My surrounding stones had a new language: "hip," "cool," "way out," and "you dig it" started with the black musicians in the 1930s and '40s. But they found a grounding usage and new beginning in taking an assertive hold within the white young "hip" crowds of the '50s. It had started in high school with my crazy crowd of older artist friends, with one of them living only a few blocks away at the end of my street. For some reason, we were all born with new type of IDs coming in high school, were now becoming known by our last names, or a nickname only. I was now reborn, known as Bennie, because Joe B, who loved using it for his own personal jokes, discovered my middle name Benjamin.

There were many other extraordinary found pebbles on the edges—like Garner, Cervenak, Lucas, Sullivan, and a fellow new rebel from Arcadia called Gilbert, later on in college, and yet still mixed together among these others like Rick. However, Garner was farther over the edge than any other of these artists found, say, farther than Cervenak and Ellis. These guys were from the class of 1955, 1956; and my first encounter with each one's talents, which began in high school, and my newfound self-confindance among these outsider types had been now discovered. We all loved making fun of the "in crowd" whether they are the so-called Beats, or the Goody Two-Shoes. We started hanging out at coffeehouses, where some had read Jack Kerouac's book On the Road, which had started the biggest underground movement among many thinkers at first. Then it became the "thing to do and to be seen at," like at the coffeehouse (I can't recall the name ours, something with a cat) on Huntington Drive in Arcadia, just past the railroad tracks bridge, and we all hung out there while Garner got involved with another in Monrovia, which was jazz and beer with an older crowd. Paul Burton's brother Bill, from the class of '54, owned it. He was always painting or drawing "those off-the-wall darkened things," while his hair got longer, and he was wearing looser and freer types of clothes, walking with JC sandals, and having much darker thinking while moving himself up into "the San Francisco scene" for a while. He would go there, coming back among us at different periods of times, and then disappearing forever. He was the only one who was really bohemian among us, but not a Beatnik. I don't know where that pebble sank or where it floated too.

Music

For Rick, he went deeper into playing his music after high school, with weight lifting, and started playing many different instruments. First came the saxophone, then there were some other woodwind instruments, and then he moved on into the electric guitar, leaving hot rods behind him. He had introduced me to a new world, listening to blues, jazz, and rock 'n' roll for hours, while he played alone too. He gotten deep into Charlie Bird, way before most "white" kid's had known this "bebop world of jazz," and could play his saxophone "way out there too."

But we would listen to the black rhyme and blues stations too as they became known during those earlier years of rock 'n' roll. First there came the doo-wop and blues groups played on LA stations. There was Art Laboe, in the afternoon and Hunter Hancock late at night, with a few others way late at night during the week. That is if you could find them, but you were supposed to be sleeping during these school nights. This was becoming more among the mainstream white teenagers every day as word had gotten out to what was "hip."

He, Dick, and I would drive late on the weekends to South Central Los Angeles, seeing Huggy Boy playing records behind a big window at the radio station, but later in the late '50s, there were more jazz clubs all around the local area, staying open well into the early morning hours.

The last time I saw Rick was while I was working in the 1970s and doing an insurance investigations job in an area known as the Artist Village part in the city of Sierra Madre, mostly known as the Canyon then. He was then wearing long hair, playing his electric guitar for a rock group, and traveling across the country doing "gigs." My learning about real passion, compassion, and determination came from Rick's view of life and music. There's a beat and music in us all.

My Music

At the age of twelve, there were other reasons for getting my newspaper route, besides the racer bike, and it was that I wanted to play slide guitar. My parents said, "Well, if you really want to, but you'll have to pay for the lessions yourself." And as stated in the contract, "If you finished one year of lessons, you get the guitar for free." However, after playing for about six or eight months, there was no free guitar because I had lost interest. However, I did learn some music, and something more about myself, besides learning things the hard way, and think you know better then parents. Again there was another small problem of being left-handed with this, and trying to learn by playing right-handed was slowing me down; then switching to playing left-handed wasn't working for me either. I guess there wasn't enough passion in me for music for me to overcome these bridges.

Loving music from hearing Ronnie's dad, the Piano Man, and his making it appear so easy, plus my being involved with Pee Wee's family, brought even more grand memories of closeness with my grandfather and my mother's love of music. There was always a love for music, and always I was trying to sing, but not very well. But I was having fun. My mother would take piano lessons during the 1960s; with the money she earned tailoring the teacher's clothes. She was doing both very well and was enjoying both the rest of her life.

While in high school, or even before, I never thought of joining any chorus groups, me not being a joiner or singer. However, a few times, just for fun, I joined with some group singing as backup with our own black doo-wop group of guys at the piano in the gym, after our PE classes, or later after a few football practices. This group consisted of

Bob Bartlett, Earl Collins, Fred Durden, Jesse Mency, Jesse Otis, and a couple others, and they were all black. I recall my joining in on Night Owl, during the chorus lines with my "hooting" doo-wop parts only, fitting into the middle background of two or three of them, where it was needed was fun. One day, a couple of them said, "You know, you have maybe some "soul" with little "country boy," but not knowing, if that was "cool" or "later man." However, much later, I learned they meant, "It was cool," and that "any SOUL" did not involve going to church.

Much later, there would be two other white guys in Southern California, but during the '60s, becoming known as blue-eyed soul." The Righteous Brothers sounding black, but I did not know if they were white or black with their singing style at first. Then I learned what these guys meant, and much later, I found out and learned that I could dance like the Godfather of Soul, James Brown, after watching some soul brothers in my army years.

We had a lot of good laughs and fun for no other reasons than just being friends in high school on their or my part. They did performances for the school noon dances, and everyone "dug it," but the social mainstream wasn't ready for their joining the grown-ups mainstream, or doing any performance for viewing other than at lunch with the kids. This was in 1956 and 1957, when the Hit Parade was white people singing on TV with Doris Day or Rosemary Clooney or Pat Boone doing cover records of Little Richard's Songs, and others, making changes for them in becoming white hits like "Dance with Me Henry" "taken off of Blacks "Work with Me Annie."

Later I learned that "soul is that basic feeling of deeper emotion found in your heart, and not your brain." White people think too much, always about what others will think, while trying to show their soul, except for us "country boys," who are telling sad stories, and that was my lesson about "white soul with a little country." Lately I've been learning more from those black blues singers like Ray Charles and others. Even Elvis learned this during and after growing up in the South to become the King of Rock 'n' Roll." Blues, being color blind, allows us to hear music through our souls, and the blind hearing it louder, making it clearer in their hearts like Ray Charles, either it is country or blues.

Another classmate, very much into music during the class of 1956, was Don Clarke, a standout in Concert Choir I, and way above the rest even then. And later on, he went on to becoming a member of the Four Preps, doing many recordings with them. Again my circle in life ran back much later in years, and to my surprise, I found him teaching music at my kids' high school. He became the head of the music department at Glendora High School. Also there were two other brothers, one older than me, Gregory or Greg Graeme, and his younger brother, Bob Graeme, a year behind me, whose mother was a singing teacher, and they both were very good too. Greg did go on with his singing, but Bob, who was also in our Intakes Car Club in the '50s and '60s wasn't as much into it. However, he, with some others guys besides myself, would fool around singing doo-wop songs at times, with a little help from a few beers, but he was always more of a loner too. I don't know if he ever went on with his music, but he had the talent. Music has always kept this pebble bouncing along my paths, or in my steam, maybe that's the Irish in me too. It's been said, "The bubbling brook would lose its song if you removed the rocks."

Newport, Jazz

The summer of 1957, while I was working at the Santa Anita Park race track with racehorses at age eighteen, opened a new world. So with some money saved up and after deciding my goal for the next summer of 1958, I said to myself after reading On the Road, "Why not go to the Newport Jazz Festival in RI?" So I put a few things together and talked with my parents, and in the summer of 1958, I started hitchhiking across America to the East Coast on Route 66, with only three weeks in August as my time limit. So I could get back for college. Once out of LA County, a "big rig" eighteen-wheeler truck picked me up, and within six hours, we were in Las Vegas. Then at another truck stop, I found another big rigger to Amarillo, and then came next a couple in an O'l Buick car to Oklahoma City in only three days. However, next came a very slow-driving old man, who talked and talked throughout our travel in the whole state of Missouri, but I was being so very tired by now, and sleep was an easy excuse for my not replying or listening to him with his stories of his youth. Next came another trucker, and we made good time through Indiana, Ohio, and Pennsylvania to Newburgh, New York, and making it right on time for the weekend into Newport, Rhode Island, from Providence. Next, upon finding a gas station, stripping, and taking a washbasin bath with a change of clothes, I found a "dinner" with eggs, a cup of coffee, and directions to the concert grounds on those last steps walking to the high school field.

I bought my tickets, then went inside and lay down in the cool grass next to a tree while watching every kind of person walk by in all directions and wishing that someday I could afford those VIP seats, or the yacht in the bay, but I made it there in good time, without much cost this time. Those sounds and getting to hear live the likes of Brubeck; Elli, the Duke; the Counts; and the Queen, Anita O'Day," with all the other mixed sounds coming from everywhere, knowing I was among cool people from everywhere made me very rich. My thinking about the "wild and cool" surrounded me and kept my tired mind, and I was just taking in everything during that moment, and doing so brought me more energy. Later, finding the stage and watching the performance kept me going with the help of my youth.

Wow, next I was setting in the grass and finding groups of young people near my age, we started talking at first about jazz while we waited for the performance to start. When they heard how far and how I had come just to be there, they shared their wine and some food with me. The nights were hot, but cool with these new friends, who asked me after one of the shows, "Why don't you come back and stop by, or stay with us in New York City on your way home." I learned that they where all in the advertising business in the city, having apartments in Manhattan. And then they continued saying, "You could have a drink, some rest, party, and travel on." Which sounded great, so I said, "OK, cool! What's your address?" That was my reply to one of the girls writing down her address on a match cover and drawing direction on another paper. The next few days after the last show, after sleeping on the ground for two nights with my coat as a pillow, I was on my way again.

I was finding my way to the train station in Providence again, which then took me to Grand Central Station. Next came the subway, and then I was coming out, looking up into that skyline of buildings with my mouth open like those "turkeys in the rain." The people came rushing into every direction, surrounding me, and I was finding it hard to find my place to just stand still out of the rush, and I looked up for a moment, trying not to have someone walking over me.

It was so overpowering, yet the feeling of enclosure within this busiest of energy started again coming from all these people around me and brought me renewed energy through all my senses, starting throughout my mental and physical being, because I was just there.

I found a taxi next, and I was on my way to that given address, which wasn't difficult to find. I rang the bell, and finding one of the girls home was beyond my dreams. "There's going to be a party tonight, and down the hall is the shower," she said, greeting me at the door. A real shower with a change clothes brought my mind and body back alive again for a short period, while my emotions were running wild with peaks and valleys. The party wasn't starting until almost nine at night, and it was only around five, but I couldn't get any sleep either after trying to do so for about an hour in her small bedroom. There was only one other room in this two-room apartment. Then two or three other people started showing up as we started placing and moving things out of the way, and it was like the whole world came there by midnight, with little room to breathe.

It was very sticky hot, despite the fact that I came from the West Cost with our "dry heat." But it was like something of a jungle heat, with no air to breathe. So I moved and found my way outside on the fire escape with some other five or six other people too. Now I was talking with them about my trip, with most of them putting down Californians, which caused me another type of heat, but after telling them I was an artist, they warmed up somewhat, with me cooling my own pride down some.

I'm not into putting down anyone, so to prove myself; I found some paper and pencil and started drawing cartoon caricature exaggerations of them all. Which made believers out of those watching me, and they also saw me having fun within those surroundings. They were now laughing too, so we all laughed together, as their noses or anything else got exaggerated, with some of their reflection growing on paper. However, I found that most of them were like the hostess—they were being very friendly, interesting, and engaging with me, while I thought about Gilbert, or other members of our group back home that may have acted the same way too. However, this was the real-life people now taking their parts in "the advertising world" in the center of that stage that was shaping our world. The whole vision in my head was like the party seen in Breakfast at Tiffany's, and it was not over until sunrise, with its caricatures tumbling.

I awakened around 10:00 a.m., with maybe two hours of sleep, while the others were still sleeping anywhere they could, but others were still talking, but they were now sitting down within small groups of twos or threes on the floor. The hostess was asleep under some coats in her bed, and we said our "Thank yous" and good-byes. Then I got my things together and found a passing taxi on the street and got to the Greyhound bus station. I found my seat for my long trip, eager to get back to California.

Off on my travels again, sleeping until Chicago, then Kansas City, and after each meal stops, I went back to sleep again until I got home, after rumbling along each day into the night for a total of three days more. From that day on, I knew the direction I wanted my life to go, and a new dream had found me. This pebble had traveled beyond any real world into a new plastic world that was exciting, and it was the beginning for a new vision.

Cervenak

Cervenak went on to Pasadena City College, where I would run into him with Lucas and some others, also at different times after my high school days. He was also a wild man with curly red hair and glasses. He was very intelligent, and most of his art was cartoonist at first. He went on to become a very well known author of children's books; he was writing and doing his illustrations.

I was reflecting on him during our time at PCC. One afternoon between classes, we were walking with a couple guys and Cervenak for a cup of coffee at Bob's Big Boy coffee shop across the street from the school. While we were waiting for the light to change, he asked, "Would you like to meet those two girls?" The girls were also waiting across from us on the other curbside, and they were outstanding-looking. I responded, "Ya," trying to keep my cool, but by this time, the light had changed, with us all now meeting in the middle of the intersection, face to face. And that's when Cervenak said loudly, "Virginal meet Bennie, Bennie meet Virginal!" This was just one of the many outrageous things he would do, but that was Cervenak, "Mr. Shock," bringing his own type of world into view.

Hot Kiss

Another time, four of us went to Hollywood on the weekend, and while there, we checked out this street book-and-newspaper stand just off Hollywood Boulevard and browsed through magazines late at night.

We normally went to Hollywood searching for jazz, coffeehouses, and girls, mostly. This night, having no money, which was most the times, Rick was looking through his body building magazines with Lucas looking over his shoulder, me at cars, and Cervenak was now looking at "girly" magazines, like Playboy, and others that they put those covers on now. However, standing beside him were two very "butch lesbians" girls, who where also looking at the girly magazines. He got even closer to the one next to him, and with a "KAWANG!" he grabs her, giving her a big kiss on her mouth while her face was turning redder than in any cartoon. She and the other one with her started swearing, and then they were swinging at him in rage. He just stood there, laughing at them, while the rest of us had put down our magazines, and while the owner was rushing over too, yelling for us to move on. You just didn't know what he was going to do next, Mr. Shock. Later on, he moved up to Northern California for further schooling, and you would never think of him writing children's books.

Gilbert

Garner and others would have parties with us sharing plenty of free-flowing wine, jazz, art, and poetry, or showing, or finding, and talking about the latest in books, arts, or films. Gilbert was the "thinker," besides having a very cool car, a three-window 1933 Ford coupe, full fender, in what is known as suede black primer paint now, with a "hot" flathead looking like the "California Kid" car that came later after his, appearing in shows during the '70s, from two other guys from Temple City, the next town over west of Arcadia. He occasionally hung out at Nicholson's too. He was what the guys of today are trying to copy in their dress and cars known as "Rat Rodders," because he wore cool clothes, but he liked his Zooter suit the best. But most of the time he wore bowling alley shirts. Mainly in his case, he worked at bowling alleys part-time, while working in machine shops as a mechanic while at the same time going to school.

He had a very greatly developed music collection too, and he mixed his taste for jazz, blues, and rock 'n' roll into his lifestyle. Also, he wore and really needed his large, really thick glasses like Buddy Holly's, but he gave off a sense of cool. He was interested in girls to some degree, but his focus was mostly on his education, and I felt those thick glasses may have covered any fear of rejection. There came more of a sense of "indifference look" in his expressions, and it was hard to know what was going on with him. His black hair, combed back straight, looked like what the "high shakers" of Wall Street in the '90s had. He was way ahead of any of most curves then and now. He had his ways and was always testing my IQ in thoughtful statements or questions or by suggesting that I readings about things that were for his or my thoughts regarding things like the deep philosophy of the likes of Aristotle and other Greek thinkers and other subjects. If you didn't pass his test, or didn't bring something new into play regarding thoughts or conversations, there wasn't time to be shared with you. He would also play with his dreams, making them in colors, and leaning toward escapism.

He lived in a somewhat more realistic world than all the rest of us because he was taking on responsibilities in covering most of the roots of his own actions. He lived in a very low-cost hotel room at the Aztec and supported himself. The Aztec was the same place where Rick and I made our brew, before knowing him, and we found him only because of his car. He, however, was the most distant, most disturbed, and disruptive in a slight, very quiet manner that I've ever known, and much deeper than us all. Also, he was my friend and mentor, but he was always saying, "No one has real friends. We only have people with whom we are acquainted during certain periods and spaces in our lives." I've always remembered that but was never really sure that was completely true in his ways, or meaning, but it has had some import of truth. However, in some way, he was right, but we all need someone to share our thoughts with throughout our lives, or we become lost.

Drive to Cool Down

Like the other car experiences, at one of those Garner parties, a few guys had earlier smuggled in a large basket type cover bottle they bought in TJ, which was about five gallons in size, filled with rum through the border of Tijuana, Mexico, under the rear floor of their car. Which in itself was something to celebrate, and again, it became free flowing, but for some reason, Gilbert wanted to leave after having more then he could handle, being too drunk to drive in my judgment. I tried to talk him out of driving, and for some reason, the next thing I knew, we were driving in his car toward Hollywood, but we didn't stop there either. So I guess I was too drunk too. We had already raced at over eighty miles per hour down the Pasadena Freeway, without a word said from him while getting there. We were crazy. Rum can do the worst things in its effect or something, or maybe there was some other reason bringing on his fieriness. I never did learn by the time this night was over. Now turning back toward Monrovia, at around 1:00 a.m., we were taking the San Bernardino freeways home in a somewhat reasonable manner, only stopping for a few traffic lights from the freeway going north, but for some reason gaining speed after each, until we had reached Holly Avenue going toward Arcadia.

Then we hit Duarte Road still going across Holly Avenue and now in Arcadia, at around three, with the car, and our bodies now flying at close to a hundred miles per hour again, but not knowing that the rear brake lines had been smashed down and broken on the rear end housing, while coming down in our big bounces of both sides during the crossing, and we were just a few blocks from Huntington Drive now. Gilbert put on his brakes to slow down after the bounce and for his right turn coming up there, but now he was saying, "NO BRAKES!" He was now shifting down gears, looking for some control and trying to make the engine give him some braking power, but now only sliding sideways around the corner with all four wheels and the running board crying on the pavement. Now, flatly without that rum alcohol clouding his mind, we would have seen, and knowing we could have just followed the street entrance going straight into the Santa Anita Park race track parking lot, with nothing to hit, and we just slowed down to a stop, shutting down the engine like what had happened in Pasadena with Lloyd.

NO, because of his attempting to make that turn, first we hit the driver's rear tire against the north curb, then crossing over to the opposite curb, we hit it with the passenger's rear tire, causing the car to turn toward the race track again, with its tires burning, while we went over the curb in the air with the nose of the car landing on a large rock in the middle of the center divider, between the highway going east and west. It wasn't over yet. The car now did a twisting sixty-degree spin on its front axe on top of this rock like a top running out of its spin. All this while Gilbert still had his foot full on the gas pedal, from the time of making that downshift.

The engine was doing everything it could, but now, the front wheel was under my seat with the engine still breathing and racing, trying with the rear wheel hollowing and pushing with no place to continue on to now. I yelled, "Shut it off!" Then it went completely silent, with headlight beams bent up into the sky and all that heat changing into cold darkness around us. Because of its copped top and, I'm guessing again, because we were just drunk enough, we had stayed in our seats with the door shut, with only a few small bumps on our heads from the car spinning on it nose like a kid's top. We had nothing broken. However, while climbing out with the lights still on and the doors opening from the front, I could see the wheel under me, and I knew the car was hurt and broken. He started walking around to my side, and I asked him, "Are you "OK?" And then I noticed he was without his glasses. He then stopped and now reached back into the seat and found them before shutting off the lights.

Our landing spot was only about two miles or more away from the police station, and this was the beginning place being cleared to build "the new chamber of commerce." We started looking the car over, finding the front lower running gear, fenders and bumper bent into twisted metal, but without any sign of any fire. We had come through this alive, without any type injury or burns. Those guardian angels kept me safe again, without Gilbert's believing, or any other convenience. However, we both agreed about being agnostic beforehand during our discussions.

We crossed the road, finding a crossing way over the drainage wash and throughout Arcadia Park to a pay telephone, next to the liquor store at the corner of Santa Anita Avenue on Huntington Drive. We called for help, hoping someone was still there, and found there was one friend still there whose father's owned the Owl Garage and Towing business in Monrovia. Then we waited about twenty minutes at the car, and to our amazement, the whole party showed up, arriving to see the car sitting in the middle of Huntington Drive's median like a dead animal. There were between five to six other cars here with a tow truck, and many people were still drinking or drunk, while the car was being hooked up like piece of meat, and we knew it was a dead friend going to a place of no return. It sat in the tow yard for months before Gilbert and the insurance company hauled it and took it to its final resting place. I don't know why or how we had gotten away without any police noticing or showing up with all those car lights and people surrounding us just down the highway from their station. The car went on to the tow garage, and I went on my way and got in my car while the sun was coming up. I was always thanking the gods or angels, neither of which Gilbert believed in, but I knew that he was sobbing and lost his cool because of the end to his ride, which did cause pain and anger, as I could see in his face for only a moment whenever we talked about it. He changed his direction by moving up into buying a 1954 Lincoln Capri two-door hardtop, with real leather seats and air-conditioning. This same car had also been among the big winner cars used in the Pan-Americana Mexican road races, but now it did better fit him anyway and was still "way cool." He moved on to college at Berkeley, getting a degree in chemistry. Last I know he was making drugs, hoping he found the right answers to his questions, before all things killed his mind or soul, and maybe some happiness without hell. It's easy getting lost along the way.

The Ones That Got Lost

Garner, being always out there, had bought a new Citroën (2CU) car, which was made in France with only two cylinders and, in my opinion, appeared to be made by cutting two pieces of metal into half circles for its side panels and with doors, adding bug-eyed headlights on both sides of its small "bonnet" hood with a canvas cover running over for a top. It bounded down the road and moved side to side like a toy made for the circus. However, it got the greatest gas mileage found in the States, and it was very cheap.

Among the younger guys hanging with us was Miller, a very bright guy whose father owned the Ford dealership in Monrovia, but his parents where separated or divorced, I believe, and Miller lived with his mother, who managed the Aztec Hotel while Gilbert lived there. However, that could have been the mother of one of the other guys too. Anyway, one day, with three other friends, Miller borrowed Gardner's car and drove somewhere in it, maybe to the beach. Anyway, on their way home late at night, while on the San Bernardino Freeway, the driver fell asleep behind the wheel like my dad's Pitman did, and they went off into the middle divider open area, down into an open space between the freeway lanes and dropped down on to the street below.

Miller was the only survivor, and he was in the hospital for months, recovering from most of his injuries, except for his head injuries. And afterward, for years later, he would be seen riding around town in his bicycle with only a quarter of his mental functions. Eventually he died at a very early age. "Bring in the Clowns!" It fits his moment in time—with that car and those forever losing their smile and wit. Funny, the others in that crowd of guys, like Lucas, Sullivan, and a couple of other guys, just stayed inside the circle for their short moments of time but went on to become very responsible and profitable, self-employed, or became what are known as "well-heeled" pebble forces as far as I know, except I've now learned Sullivan later succombed to alcoholism and commited suicide. Streams carry us into distances, where we get lost to our old friends and find new ones, or none at all. Only our memories don't get lost.

SEVENTEEN

High School Teachers

Most of the teachers in high school have a few favorite kids, and I had few favorite teachers. There was always my drawing in classes, except in my math or science classes. Which didn't give me much drawing time because I had to work on numbers, or research for answers in shapes, not words, or try to write or read my thoughts through writing. Drawing helped exclude those limited abilities of learning Basic English, spelling, and reading within these very difficult problem classes to me. It was easier to answer exercises using spoken words, but not so with written words. Therefore, placement in speech classes or shop classes was just enough for me to pass on into the next grades. It was all I was looking for, and that's what rebels do. Funny though, I never took any art classes until well into my junior year, with my only goal being that of becoming a pilot. I didn't know then that this couldn't happen, but I was always trying to be a very good student in most math subjects. Mr. Dunson was a great teacher of the sciences, but I had problems in his class too.

However, once we experimented with a pack of cigarettes drawing in its own smoke within this large closed water bottle, and while the water was being siphoned out, I could see the aftereffects in that bottle, with the cigarettes junk floating on top of the water, and that image worked well as a BIG DETERRENT TO SMOKING for me. I thought about what that must do inside your body, and the fact that I was still playing sports kept me from ever trying smoking. I didn't know though that being around my dad's second-hand smoke was just as bad. Then also much later, I found out that my eyes weren't 20/20, and this made me ditch the rest of my dreams. So those dreams and visions of becoming a jet pilot had gone up in smoke, and I lost my interest in the sciences too. The class of 1957 had its dreams, many going up in smoke for many as well, but others forced themselves into making changes, as I did within streams, but we continued.

Mrs. Clemmons was the art teacher, and after my first class, she had me too, because she was a very touchy person, getting me interested in her sexually because of her big breasts. However, I always still respected her because she did help me through some very trying times as well as with my art. In my first class, I won with my first still life

162

painting, which was placed in an exhibit at the Los Angeles County Fair, and recognized with a nice added Blue Ribbon, which did help. This gave me direction in claiming my inner soul, conquering my anger, and knowing art was a part of me, longing for expression. Opening to me was another vision or possible path.

I'm the model with Don Everett and Mrs. Clemmons checking his drawing

Mr. Morris was my speech teacher, who became the principal much later at Monrovia High, having a lot going for him, like being tough but fair with me or any others, and that's how we learned to respect him too. While you learn many things from books, or your experiences, there were other things that could be used in finding and building self-confidence during his teaching lessons, and it was the process going on within us in this class. He gave me hope within myself, made me believe in myself, and helped me have something of a moral belief. I learned that not all of the world or its teachers were against us here, although elsewhere others did make life hell for teenagers.

Another top teacher was Mr. Brubaker, our shop teacher in leather arts, whom everybody liked and who had very high standing among us all. His son also followed in his footsteps. He gave us respect to us, and we gave it to him. Then there was Mr. Hatch, one of the youngest teachers of the new class of teachers, whom all the girls would fall for as well. He looked somewhat like Tab Hunter, and he became the new basketball coach, and his new sports car gave him even greater appeal. There were others who were among the coaches too. Especially, above all other coaches, there was Mr. Dink Walker, our football coach for, first, our C team, and then varsity. Then there were some other teachers that would help us in rolling pebbles through our streams. They made even a bigger difference in my and in many other people's lives by giving us guidance through our many streams for good and bad times. The biggest thing brought to us was that being on a team; you could overcome against any odds and obstacles, if you work with all those members in your team, working within fellowship and execution. That means, "The battles can be won with teamwork."

Stewart's Folly

But then came "senior problems," with Mr. James Stewart—the teacher, not the actor. He didn't like the way I looked; he didn't like my drawing in his class, and he didn't like the way that I saw his class. Now, there were really "senior problems" happening here. It was all I could do to keep from laughing at this guy in his face, in his class. His books were better than any comic book, or those silly '50s TV shows about teenagers. But in fact, it wasn't funny after my first semester because he failed me at its very beginning during my senior year. So in order to graduate by state law, I had to complete this class, and I did take it over in the summer school of 1957. So who was the joke on then, you ask? However, I did get to go through the class prom and commencement in the end, but my mother had to come see him for a counseling about my "problems" because I failed in his class in that first semester. Then he was telling her, "That boy needs discipline, and you need to put him into the military service after graduation." She was so upset with me, and even madder at this guy afterward, she couldn't talk about their meeting for a week with my dad or me.

However, I did go on to junior college after high school, without needing, or getting, that military service discipline until much later, and it didn't work then, and it wasn't because of my "senior problems" or my failing his class. He did remind me so much of Mr. Peepers in that TV show. I'm sorry; it was easy to laugh at both. These were the teachers, who had some impact on my life, and others may have been there, but I'm sure my face or presence didn't have much impact on them either.

Pasadena City College

Being forced into summer school in order to finish my high school days, and then working with race horses during that summer shoveling horse shit, mixed with seeing my other dreams that never were and would never be, opened my mind to the real world. Plus, during that summer before, when I was seventeen, I was working for the Monrovia nursery in Azusa as a laborer with people who couldn't speak English, and working with them in the canning of plants in the hot sun, with oxen blood fertilizer baking to your lips and up your nostrils. It stuck to every place that was wet. While most of the day, I was having that feeling of being wet with sweat from the top of my head to my armpits down to my wet socks inside my shoes because of shoveling rocks and watering plants all day. My sweating, soaking shirt and pants now covered my every bone and muscle, which were crying out in pain. I found myself talking to my heart and head, saying, "This shit, I must find a way to become wealthy, or at least try." Then I thought about preparing and setting new goals. I thought the first steps must be toward college, or else I'd be buried in some shit pile. I saw and felt that this manual labor was in the bottom level as part of the shit pile of the world, and I understood that there had been NO ONE in the Allen clan who had ever gone to college. There were only a few who finished high school before me. It was my time, and it was the time for change. So I started college in mid-semester, majoring in art, business, and other subjects to enable furthering toward a four-year college education. It was just a junior at college, but it was my first step on the right road, and I was asking for the lowest in terms of costs from my parents and from myself. So next, I found a job at Arcadia's finer department store, in its new shopping center store called Nash's, where I worked full time as stock boy before the school's schedule had started, and then I continued part-time after school.

After getting to my first classes, I started seeing many other kids from Monrovia High, like Lonny from our class, and we got along well after being together on the same football team. Plus, I was also a friend with him during Pee Wee's days before his becoming yell leader. We had become closer friends during those later years at M-D, but now at PCC, we would share rides together again, with it working out for a while. But then we had some other commitments of our own and classes were becoming hurdles. He and I now found new friends, who moved us into new different directions, mostly because of his decision to pledge to a fraternity house and put himself through some "hell," but he made it through. I understood his wanting to become a part of that White Bucks and saddle shoes scene again. It was something he had always wanted at M-D, and it did work for him, and he became one of the three yell leaders during his senior year and got to that next higher level social standing. Once you place your feet on that next level, it's hard to turn back, and you want more movement to a higher level with those others that can help you claim higher standards. Then at college, it was not for me, but after he made it, we went to one of their parties, where there were girls and kegs of beer.

I'm sure some people find that fraternities give special opportunities to many, opening doors that fit their needs. I knew my feelings toward fitting IN, and I found it more fun being with my confederacy within "the car guys" outside of school, and I was more IN within the artist crowd at school. And that was my path or stream of choice.

My classes did start a whole new opening of a world of places and spaces, and I was thinking within a much wider range within those many changes in my whole thinking and my being, because that's what college does. This pebble was much smaller now, because it now found itself within a wider open ocean with so many more other things appearing to be very little, and yet bigger as well at the same time. But, finding myself within them, I was also becoming much larger within my own view of myself, the world, and I was seeing those rising bigger waves coming together, in front of me on the horizon. Yet bringing one of more small or larger sets that continued and followed like surfing, without seeing how much deeper below the surface their strength was razing into my thinking now and what I had become. Questions and things became larger within myself, just by my beginning to see larger things and more within myself in meeting that next new set of waves, which came on and hit me from any direction, because I was growing and learning now to ride with them. I was holding my head above and holding my place into continuing my understanding of my life's course. However, I still saw groups of students forming again together, again within some types of groups, and others not at all.

Again I found that I was now fitting in while maybe thinking or feeling, just maybe more wanting to join in with some others, but also knowing there were so many others, I would never have wanted to be a part of, and yet I was not completely sure either. The lines weren't clear here anymore, like in high school, and there were wider differences, yet there were also much more walls to find entrance doors into, and I was finding them. It was in many ways like in junior high school all over again too, yet now the players were playing like they were becoming or acting as if they were grown-ups now. Exposed to more smoking, drinking, the use of drugs, as well as the use of grown-up words, thinking of grown-up problems, and starting to get a taste of the beginning of their OWN new worlds. I've learned to laugh at watching pebbles dancing in the sun, or rain, and wind, but watching some washing into deeper drains, while the water was rising around them, brought sadness to my eyes and heart. Some of us make it, while others don't, becoming lost yet. This was higher and beyond any "senior problems."

Then there was SEX, with its highly visible sights during this time, with almost doubling of girls, the prettiest ones, everywhere, who came here hoping to become the next Rose Queen during the Rose Parade semester before the coming of New Year's Day. After January, however, there would be a big drop in this number of beauty queens at school. They had hopes of becoming "stars" from here and to ride on the top of that float on TV and the world. There were also the wild-artist type of girls, looking at these new waves of free love appearance underground, showing their free sprits, with no bras, and looking for that found freedom from their parents, before the '60s.

Sex was always on most young health boys or men's minds too, after seeing those changes from "the poodles to those shorter skirts" that now were surrounding us in double the amount during that first part of the school year. There was a great mix, and there were social levels with difference in age here too. Our own sexual drives were becoming stronger too, and that had to be controlled in this new social arena. The open mix of high school girls, because Pasadena High School was still on campus too, made things even more difficult. However, most of us were eighteen, and we were now finding there were some guys who had been in the Korean War and that they had seen people dying and had looked beyond just passing their class and given the GI Bill payments because of their grades, and they were competing in our same classes with us and wanting great grades, which would be another type of chance for them. It was bad enough, but occasionally, there would be "the little old lady from Pasadena" sitting next to you, older than the teachers, and they are there just to learning something, because they had lost that opportunity earlier in their streams too. All of them together with the vets were raising the middle grading level curves of our grades too. Because there was more here than at the four-year colleges, because it was cheaper there per unit, and also because most of the teachers were not there to spend just time like most do in high school. They really wanted you to learn something. For the most part, most of the "students" didn't want to know who you were and didn't care where you were going. That's just college! It's the first step of growing up and becoming a grown-up outside of those high school days or groups.

My College Classes

The most important class during this time was I, starting with my study of my own emotions, thinking, and who I was. This had started with my first art class in high school, and it was becoming more like looking into, but through a dark mirror reflection, and seeing behind your eyes. I was only seeing a part of myself because it's hard seeing that real you at any time during your life. You don't want to see yourself at first, but you keep turning around to see if there's more detail being revealed through yourself or your reflection with that fast small flash each time you look again and again. It made me think, and I was seeing that it was like the master doing that self-portrait, painting in poor lighting. How do you tell the truth, or see the real you? You could see more detail but don't understand what you are seeing. The problem wasn't seeing Van Gogh, or was it? Or could you be mad too? I was seeing within myself that there was this need, always trying for that further depth in need of further psychological analysis of one's self, and it would only come flying at you through your own incomplete understanding of anything, with only the application of your first class of Psychology I, but more could be found if you applied it to everybody surrounding you too, as well to yourself.

After seeing Tony Curtis in Houdini and practicing his self-hypnotism to accomplish those unbelievable feats, I started finding some extra funny skills within myself, like being double-jointed in my right hand and some other parts of my body, but most of all, using some forms of "self-hypnosis." I was just putting my vision in an "out of focus" form, and its usage of changing my state of mind, or physical capacities, into doing things. With this, I could put my hand over an open flame with no pain, and

I would be able to use this later in my life when I needed too. Also, it didn't help my thinking any easier after seeing *Lust For Life, and Moulin Rouge,* with those disturbed artists' stories reflecting in their troubled lives, and it wasn't easy being a part of those greatest moments of modern art times and stories, earlier at the movies, for me too. Most artists were or are mad with something, odd or out on the edges, doing wild things and fighting their ways into new visions. Beginning deeper reflections within man, or within nature's surrounding beauty, you find all around us are out of control too. Only social restrainers and families keep us in check. Sometimes there may appear to be order, but then comes complete disorder, without meaning and with new questioning. What was this path that I was now starting on? Where was my soul taking me, or was there one? There were more questions than answers, and that's college too.

There was a drawing I did for one of my classes, and for some reason, and it was a drawing of Russia's Rasputin, who was a religious mystic and faith healer. He was killed after they tried every means of killing a normal human being, and yet he just wouldn't die. In this drawing, after drawing his face out of my mind without any picture, I placed some Russian letters over his head and face for effect, but for some reason, after looking up what these letters meant at the library's Russian/English dictionary. I found a close form of what I had written in Russian, without knowing why, but these words and letters had fit into this madman's death and thinking. I told the teacher I'd looked it up first, before putting them in the drawing, but didn't, not wanting that to becoming upsetting or known to anyone else but myself. This wasn't high school anymore. Things where happening beyond the normal, and the answers weren't given you or found in books or came from parents, nor were they believable at times. It was your job to think and find answers. The pebble was becoming more extraordinary standing in a bigger stream by itself now.

My art and soul was growing each day, with each classes taken, and my art was put on display, sitting in the top half of almost every art class I was in, with grades of A or B+ except for my "lettering" class. Yet I still had those same old problems within any Basic English type of subjects. My first semester began in February 1958, and I received my associate of arts degree on June 17, 1960. I continued with my sports and gym classes, starting with swimming in 1958, and then later gymnastics that same year, until January 1959, and with boxing until June, then back for more gymnastics until 1960.

While taking boxing, I had tried out for the Golden Gloves, and thinking that because of my weight class, and because I had my advantage of a surprise by starting out fighting right-handed leading and then switching at any time to a left-handed stance, with a surprising hard-hitting left hand, I had this greater surprising advantage over most opponents. Until finally, during the trials, I faced this very tall black kid, with an arm reach of about six inches longer than mine, and this had become my surprise—him hitting me in the nose very hard within those first few seconds of that first round, and from then on, the inability to see him clearly with my watering eyes and blurred vision was something I couldn't overcome. It was over in three rounds because he had broken my nose again in that first round. My nose had already been broken, starting during football and in a few fights before in the neighborhood. After that first football time, my family doctor told me, "Don't worry about it, you'll never be a movie star." Then he put some tape across it, holding it in place, and told me to keep it on for a few days and it would be all right. The black kid went on to state finals, so I didn't feel too bad, but being an Irish kid, there was always a reason to fight, rather than any running or trying to talk my way out of corners. I never fixed that nose.

Speaking of other types of battles, in one of my design classes and in another drawing class, I found myself up against another type, in a battle with another interesting student at that time, who is now very well known throughout the world and has become one of the most impressive and best-dressed designers. He is among his own members in "Show Business and Other Dress Designers" for the TV shows business by the name of Bob MacKay. He had flair with his "artistry fellow followers" that came to surround him even then, but this was not my cup of tea, and I understand he went on to Chenard's or Otis Art School from PCC, and then on to studying under the wings of the Great Edith Head.

I was doing OK, designing the covers for the school plays, like one for Harvey, and summer and night school brochures. I won my share of Blue Ribbons for my ink drawings and other paintings in the college shows. My works were always in the school's art shows and won me a class at Art Center, which was in LA at that time before its move to Pasadena. It was a designer class for products, cars, and other things of the future. It made me believe in the dream, and this was how to get to New York, San Francisco, and bigger jobs in my field.

There were three teachers at college that had profound higher standards, with their higher capability as teachers and as mentors for students like me. One was Mr. Turnery in the art department, who had lived in Japan before the start of World War II. He studied under an art master for years before becoming a teacher. He gave us a taste for another world within art. I learned that just using some black brushstrokes with simple lines and shadows can make the mind's eye see beautiful images without needing more. The mind would do the rest. He told us his story while doing his studies there, and that has always lived within me. After studying for years under his master, the Master requested his presence for dining one evening.

Upon arriving, and as the ceremony began, he noticed it in one corner of the room, where there was always only one thing of beauty placed in the house, in that one special place upon every visit, but this time there was only a large long piece of rice paper with his Master's signature consisting of his "red Master's stamp" in the lower corner, like all of his works of art or paintings before. As his student, I knew ahead, and don't ask any questions, because it will be told "why" in time after lessons were learned and upon completion of their meals and drinks service. It was now becoming darker in the room, with small candles burning and with a full moon appearing outside the room. As the moon now rose higher, becoming brighter outside, and at that precise moment of time. The Master, sitting quietly, reached out and pulled a rope that was now moving and slid back a shingle in the roof, allowing the brightly shining moonlight to come through and down on that placed rice paper, revealing the images of a group of cherry blossoms' shadows on their branches from outside, now being exactly fashioned in perfect composition. It was being within its relationship with the master's red-orange signature with their new black, grays, and thin white images of natural beauty. This was a true Zen thing in art, thinking, and beauty. You must master each brushstroke, thinking and knowing those small amounts of shadows can express greater images without the mind and soul needing anymore to read. That's what a great teacher can show its students—teaching an artist what real beauty can reflect, or knowing what the master can bring to the student.

One other teacher—sorry to say I can't recall his name now, but from the first day of my just walking into his class while the rest was filing in, he came walking in and putting down his books, with some other items on his desk, but then bending over, he began standing on his head in front of the class on a chair. Then he said, "I'll stand on my head every day in order to make you learn this subject!" This was a biology class, and I was learning the subject thoroughly myself because of his own sparks felt by us, and what he brought into that class every day. He reminded me in his appearance of Red Skelton, with red hair and with that biggest of smiles that was always on his beaming face. Later, I also found out he was involved during his summers with filming the wildlife adventures that we all saw on our Sunday night TV sets during Walt Disney's nature shows and Disney movies. He did not hide from everyone or us. This was a great man because of his loves, and passions, and he enjoyed all life's secrets and gave them freely.

The third was Mr. Bukus, another art teacher, who was a commercial artist. He had filled others and me with his special fire for teaching and life. He was one of those straight talkers, and he believed in hard work. He helped me get my right direction and dreams together, helped me toward moving with my visions into the real commercial art world. Of course, going to New York City after my Newport jazz trip helped, and meeting those young people like this man in that world, I was hooked. He helped me get my class at the Art Center, giving references for my job, after graduation into "the business."

Collage Grad Photo

EIGHTEEN

Jobs, Big and Small

During my working day, I work as an exercise boy for more than one week or a few days; right after high school, this became my first real job. For me, those were great hours of my life, with possibilities of traveling around and seeing a whole new life; I was in a position of now opening my world wider with some special gifts, but then the pay was low with many other drawbacks for the future. This had awakened me. Things like watching your weight every day and getting up at 4:00 AM were very hard for a teenager, but again, by noon, you were through for the day. Hanging out with rich and poor guys while listening to old and young men's lessons that brought you to places like Del Mar was also great. Just going to the beach lying around and watching the girls kept it very interesting. There was always a lot of guys' stuff with laughing, telling stories every day with the job. Those horses were crazy high breeds, which could throw you off anytime, and you will not know when or where the next surprising moment of fast action will be, maybe just around your next curve of the track or at the stables any day.

These things made it scary, setting the blood rushing and hard on the nerves, causing you to be always in heads up and awake at all times with any of them being present, making you have very little sleep on top of it. Most of the time, you were just walking them, but they could still be spooked and become hard to control at times. We're talking about thousands of pounds of muscle and being controlled by a 110-pound boy. However, the lesson was you must learn to respect them and never think you have total control. That went the same way for wagering on them because they too had good, bad, and great days. Only fools believe that they know when that great day was about to happen or come. Was it the horse, or was it the jockey's day? Again it was fun work, and then there was the meeting of some of the most famous legendary giant jockeys like Shoemaker, Johnny Longdon, Vargas, and others—who each became very much part of its glamour too.

Later, I also came across one of my high school classmates here by the name of Jay Saladin, working with one of the stables and believing he has now became a horse trainer. He knew the job, because his family was already in the business for many years as well. However, there were always more losers than winners surrounding you in the business, but mostly there are those who were always looking for that big break and big money. It's always "over the rainbow with that next pot of gold," but one fall can stop the race or your hopes or worst. Next, after seeing that it was not for me, I found a new job in west Arcadia at Nash's Department Store in the new shopping center. I worked as a full-time stock boy; it was OK with them. And they let me work part-time there from 1958 until 1960. It was another learning experience. This was hard work too, but now learning how to use my skills with women and the public brought me to another place in my life.

I went part-time. Upon entering college, I also started to work on nights and weekends for another store within Nash's building. The place was S & H Green Stamp Redemption Center. I worked there after it was brought into the Nash's store, so I was working part-time for both as a stock boy from 1959 until 1960. It was funny. Donna's mother from those Pee Wee days in high school started working for S & H Green Stamp during the later part too. She was fun, and we had a great time together. Those circles of life kept flowing into my stream. Many years later I learned she married Lloyd's father, and Donna became Lloyd's stepsister. How funny is that? You just don't know where that next stream's turn will take you, but sadly, I learned she had died just last year.

Real Soul

During one of my summers on those times, I'll never forget that there were three black gentlemen, who worked as janitors for Nash's who had asked me if I could fill in for each one of them during their vacations. Sure, this would give me time in the very early part of the day, like with the horse tracks, before the stores open during the summer months. Also, I could work for another job too or go to the beach later in the day, giving me times to take up surfing at Huntington Beach as well.

This was my first experience of drinking a lot of black coffee. I need them. I was running on less sleep, even much less than with those days with the horses. Because I was full of my youthful energy then, I never needed coffee. But now, I need more help because some days I party until the sun came up. This coffee was Southern black coffee with a lot of chicory, and I poured a pound of sugar in each cup, and between these two, you'll find yourself running on high octane, burning the candle at both ends can be done. Between this, "no-dose" sleep wasn't found, but the mind would lose its place.

The most wonderful part for me, however, was their music; they gave me their roots and the beginning of all America's black music with interdiction to the blues, which is the mother of all black and white rock and roll and jazz. I loved theses guys for they're the friendship that I had found with them, for the talks. I loved listening to their talks about their differences in their ways of life, how they had been growing up within the South or South Chicago, and about their life there during their childhood. I also listened to younger men while running our brooms cleaning floors. One was showing me more of his very angry face, and the other was presenting his very mellowed soul with age while all three believed deeply in their god and their justice. I found Black's as a whole are loving people

There was no news or radio at that time in the morning; most of the time, other than my emptying baskets, pushing brooms or mops, I became aware of the silence. And I see the sun rising for a new type of awareness within my world, learning something about real soul and myself. My listening to some stations on a small radio brought me to tell them of my love for black music, mostly rhythm and blues, so they then brought in some of their old blues records, playing them while we worked our labors—giving us all the feeling of real souls, words, and beats. We were playing their small record players at full volume so we could hear it all over this large store. However, sometimes they let me sleep or rest on a table for a spell after having too much to drink while partying a night before showing up for work. Then still feeling this music in my heart, with the black coffee clearing my head, I made sure my work got finished before the store opened. I always made sure I finished my part of the work because of my respect for them. And I made sure I meet their standards for a good job. I ended up doing this for a couple of summers, always recalling the sounds of Lead Belly and Lightnin' Hopkins sounds mixing with birds. And the increasing traffic sounds outside in the world of our days ended while the sun was just coming up for most all others.

Small Jobs

During the next years, 1960 until 1961, I also worked part-time for Henshaw's Department Store, which was just up the street, during the Christmas sales. I was also one of their stock boys, and I was also assigned in the men's sales department. This place was within the same block with Nash's, making both of them the corner's largest stores in the area then. Then during that next year, I moved out and worked for Bullock's Department Store on Lake Ave. in Pasadena. It was a high-end new shopping center at the time. I first started at the wrapping section for Christmas presents, then again became a stock boy, and then assigned at men's wear sales. With this I was now moving up into the very high-class store environments and saw what it felt like having wealth. Now I changed my wardrobe from my blue jeans to my three-piece Moe Hair suites and neckties. But I still stayed with them both for one year because there also came an opportunity of parking cars for the Rose Parade Parking Lot on the Pasadena City Collage lots, on Colorado Blvd., during New Year's Day for a little extra money. I rode a neighbor's barrowed bicycle from Eaton's Restaurant on the edge of Arcadia and Pasadena, where I'd parked my own car. Then I rode to the parking lot at PCC. So after the parade was over, I rode back, passing all the cars stuck in traffic on my way back to my car, and then driving home was a lot more fun after laughing and singing songs of happiness for a new year.

My last year in college, I found another job at Crest Kiln Mfg. in Monrovia. I was employed in their shipping, which was creating the kilns for shipment and loading them for shipment on trucks, while I was still working for the other stores too. Therefore, I became a quick-change artist from work jeans and T-shirts, then changing them into cleaner clothes while driving on Huntington Drive next to Santa Anita Race Track and sometimes into clean pressed clothes while getting to my other store jobs. There were many times that I was driving with only one leg of my pants was worn. Most of the time I was driving only in my underwear shorts and hoping no one in larger trucks will drive up beside me and be surprised of what they will see. Then repeating this task on my way to my classes in college or art center in LA's west side was another challenge. There was a time that I was working three part-time jobs at the same time during the summer months or Christmas seasons.

By this time, when I finished school, it became a time to take a few months' off before looking for any new jobs in the commercial art-advertising field. But after I started working there, I was off to the races again, burning the candle at both ends again. Also, before that happened, one of my dad's friends had hired me one weekend to help clean a very high-class restaurant in south Pasadena. We washed down the walls and cleaned throughout the night, beginning at 2:30 AM. It took around ten hours until it was completed. I cleaned cigarette smoke from the bar area's ceiling, which was a great reminder of my lessons from Mr. Duncan's class and another reason to never smoke. These stained walls were dark brown, and after washing them, they became ivory white again.

However, my worst job came during this time too while working for a small fiberglass company in Arcadia. It was repairing or making small things using this new product, like the those little horses, cars, or spaceships that kids rode in front of the stores. However, we did one thing that was real cool. While I was building my 27-T roadster, we made a mold of my body, and my reward was receiving one free body, being the best part of this job. The owner started selling them, with 23-T bodies to other car guys, and shops too, by the time I quit.

The worst part was coming home every night with fiberglass dust in my clothes, skin, and up to my nose because of not wearing a good protection mask. My mother would wash my clothes that night while I was soaking in a bath for thirty or more minutes trying to stop the itching. I didn't know back then what this was doing to my lungs—no masks, plus being around my dad who was smoking, and adding also just living within LA's smog valley. My lungs were almost becoming like my dad's while he was also working for the shipyards, but we didn't know it at the time. It would affect me much later on in life, with the development of asthma at around age fifty.

NINETEEN

Stars in My Eyes

While working at Nash's, there was one lady working in the women's undergarments section, and she only lived a few blocks from the store. She had a son close to my age, finding out his name was John, the same name as the movie actor John Payne, but he was more like Montgomery Cliff-type kind of guy, being very moody and thin with a hidden dark side. We started hanging out together for a while. He had gone to Hollywood High before his family moved to Arcadia; he still had friends there too. So we would drive over to Sunset & Vine, hang out at the biggest music store, Wallace's Music City in Hollywood, California, get a few records of Elvis or someone; and then you could hear them before buying in a booth, and there would be other teenagers doing the same, like in shopping malls now. Then we would go cruising the Hollywood strip, meeting up with some of his old friends at drive-ins or coffee shops, just like what James Dean did when he was here making movies, and not knowing whom you will find in those places.

One night at a drive-in near the end of Hollywood on Sunset Drive called Scrivener's Drive-In, we spotted Ricky Nelson in his new Porsche, having a Coke, as we were cruising through looking for girls. We parked and walked over while I following John, and to my surprise, Ricky smiled that grin of his, and this was during the time when Ricky was just breaking into the records, making it big with his singing. John said hi, and sure enough, Ricky knew him, so we got in his car while talking for a while.

Ricky was a little cocky at first, doing things a little like what were seen on TV, but he was overdoing it just to see your reaction, very funny and close to his "TV Ricky" but very much more smarter. He was asking John what he was doing now; he asked him if he was doing any TV or movie things. John, looking elsewhere, responded, "Nothing lately." Guessing while talking later with him about that, he told me about his appearance in some earlier TV shows while at a much earlier age. John had been in some of the Spin and Marty TV show for Disney that was apart of the Mickey Mouse Club. Later also, I had met one of his other friends, who played either Spin or Marty, but I cannot recall his name now. Rick then invited to us to follow him to a party up in Beverly Hills at some guy's house. We said yah while getting out while two young girls were getting in with smiling faces. We followed Rick to his house first; as the girls stayed in the car, all three of us went around to the back gate, where the pool was. Rick then went over to the diving board, pulling up a rope with a six-pack of beer at the other end. Rick laughed and said his dad had put it there. We didn't ask any questions, just betting that Mom didn't know about this. We followed him around in the streets until we came upon parked cars on both sides in the street and in the driveway. We walked up to a wide open door, and there were so many people, you could only walk sideways through to the kitchen, where we all stopped. The music was out in the backyard with colored lights showing; there were even more people. No one paid much attention to us, but many stopped and talked to Ricky with his two companions. He reached out handing us both a beer and then kept moving on and talking with some others standing next to a bar outside. Molly Bee and Tommy Sands were talking with some people to our one side. I had seen and known Molly Bee from the Cliffy Stone show because my parents watch the show on Saturday nights. Sometimes, they would also go down to the El Monte Legion Stadium, dancing while the show was being broadcasted too. I had went down there a few times for rock and roll shows with the Art Laboe's Show, which was mostly composed of blacks entertainers, performing for us white or Spanish kids and younger crowd during that time. This was a great time for rock and roll, seeing those moving, jumping pebble, and listening to new music waves rolling in around us with the rest of the world awaiting its spread.

Molly Bee and Tommy Sands were becoming well known at the time through those teenage magazines, as were Ricky Nelson and others in this party too. Ricky Nelson was the first to be the MTV star because of he started it all with his singing performance on TV, and he sang his songs for teenagers. He was way before Dick Clark hit the nationwide screen too. While we were there, you could tell Tommy and Molly was having a big disagreement about something.

Tommy Sands later would go out with Nancy Sinatra too, and it was believed they had become engaged, but I think he was trying too hard in aligning himself with Frank. We mixed, danced, drank some more beer, and then started to leave; it was time to go home. We found Rick, and he told John, "Come down to the Laguna House at the beach this summer after Dad lets us have some time off from the show." John did get a call from him, and we did go down for one afternoon. I was surprised to see that the house was very much close in appearance to the TV house. I met Mrs. Nelson and David, but Mr. Nelson wasn't around. David was quite, and they both were just like on TV in some ways. We didn't see him after that, and again, I was saddened by his death many years later.

One other time, John, with one of his friends, and I went out. We picked up two girls, and in some rear parking lot up in the hills, John had sex with one of the girls on a blanket. I believed she was so drunk, she didn't know what was happening, but I wasn't really sure, but I felt he was taking complete advantage of her. We hadn't gotten her that way, but after that, I quit going anywhere with him, seeing that dark side.

The Hollywood scene was still something. I still continued with my cruising and hanging out on the strip in Hollywood. I went to places like Tiny Naylor's and some other drive-ins that were now becoming the places to hang out, but I started to wear three-piece suites and gone clubbing. One was Pandora's box, which was a mix of coffee house with music and high-priced food. It was located at Hollywood Blvd., La Brea, and Marshfield. So it was on this small triangle corner, which was very hard to find a place to park every time. Many years later, it was removed and replaced with a mansion for a prince and was painted pink. During this same time, there was a TV show titled 77 Sunset Strip, with Ed Burns a part of the cast playing as a parking car attendant. He so cool with Connie Stevens singing her hit song "Kooky Lend Me Your Comb." Later it turned out to be really Dean Martin's Club and with others also like Gene Krupa's Jazz Club and later in the 1960s "The Whiskey a Go Go" with a mix of other smaller places that were now becoming the places to go. Being an artist and working up a false ID for myself gave me experience of going to those clubs was the coolest thing to do during that time and years. And much later on, I also went to the Lighthouse in Long Beach for West Coast jazz. Just thinking about those guys who played in these place makes me know it was magic.

There was another jazz house on Colorado Blvd. across from the Academy movie theater in Pasadena, not far from PCC, plus later the Ice House, and it became more of a hometown crowd stage. We would hangout till 2:00 or 3:00 AM. It was cool West Coast jazz with cool chicks found there; we were always trying to feed a line. Sometimes, we were lucky on a blue moon night, but we were always trying. Gilbert and I had also gone to stage plays in Hollywood, like the Connection. It was a play about drugs and starred Gavin MacLeod way before the Mary Tyler Moore Show and other shows. Also, I saw A Taste of Honey performed before it was made into a movie. It was about a young white girl and a black man in a mixed relationship of love in an English view, and then I saw Sunrise at Monticello with Ralph Bellamy.

Plus, another one of my main interests was seeing those Ingram Bergman movies like The Virgin Spring and others, all being only subtle movies. Later came other movies like David and Lisa in small theaters in Hollywood and Boston. Times back then was filled with many waves and with new changing minds.

TWENTY

Venus and Other Temptations

My Venus appeared to me during my first year at PCC; it still had Pasadena High School on campus, and one day while I was sitting on the steps in the front area facing Colorado Blvd., I noticed a girl's reflection floating in the nearest fountain. It was like seeing Swan Lake with the swan coming alive; she was walking as if gliding on the water. She had the darkest of hair pulled up high into curls behind her face that showed her ears. She had a long, thin neck. Her skin was almost like ivory. She had the largest dark eyes, looking over a very thin nose, and chin of a Greek goddess. When she stepped forward, it was grace in motion, a natural model walk—shoulders back, head high, and hips being followed by her legs. Her arms were carrying a large bundle of books and papers.

She met another girl. She stopped, and she looked down. Slowly looked up at me with a warm smile. She kept talking to her friend, but kept her eyes looking deep into mine. The books slipped out of her grip, and papers were falling into the water. I rushed over and started retrieving papers from the water while she and her friend were trying to get the books back to her arms. She then said, "Thank you so much!" I said, "Sure, happy I could help, and my name's Carl. What's yours?" "Audrey, Audrey Heburn," was her response as she looked into my eyes. But blast it! Today this is just another name that's blanked out in my old mind. It doesn't matter now. She was an image in my mind, a dream. And I never saw anyone else like her until now that my own vision is blinding. After other encounters, I found out she was a senior at PHS (Pasadena High School) and was interested in arts too. I drove her and her girlfriend home after school one day; she lived in a small home just a few blocks below Colorado past Rosemead in the middle- and working-class area of Pasadena. It was just she and her mother; her mother was a nurse or something in the medical field with all kinds of different working hours. Her mom was a beautiful small Irish woman with a bubbling personality and hadn't been in America long, but her child was born here. I didn't know anything about Audrey's father either. The girlfriend was very plain in appearance; then I noticed she wore no makeup. She only lived a few houses away on the next block below and always found her only a short distance away from my Audrey.

Audrey and I started dating; she was like a flower opening to sunlight at first, but there were also moments of sadness too. She was Holly Golightly from "Breakfast at Tiffany's" with those mixers of morality and compassion. At times, she was the life of everything giving light, and then next she would look for a way out. Later again, I learned she had been dating another guy, and they had broken up just a few months before she had met me. He was talking about them getting married, and I guess other issues were involved too. I couldn't help myself; Sigmund Freud had to come in on his psychoanalysis coaching to save the dying swan. She began telling me about her relationship with her mixed feeling and all that she was dealing with deep in her heart. Well, I had to try fixing it for her. We became closer, but not the way my heart or my sex drive would have wanted. Then she invited me to her church, with her and her girlfriend. So OK, I'll go with her to church. Now, as a small boy, my mother had taken me to the Presbyterian Church on Foothill and Myrtle at the top of Monrovia. Stone faces were turning into smiles when people found my clothes stiff and unforgiving, which were enough to stop any kid in his tracks. Without all the other things going on, there was a man in black robes high in a tall box, telling me about my sins with the sounds booming around in this high block building as the older people falling asleep. Again, years later, I was going with some neighbor kids and their family to another church on Lemon Ave., off the main street in Monrovia, and it was much smaller in size. Here man turned clear water into red wine and then into red blood, sorry, not for me. Next, I went with Pee Wee and his family, mostly because of playing football and basketball with him in their church's league. They would talk me into coming to their church too, but I only went a few times; it was not for me. Then later during high school, Jim Rood and some other friends in the "in-crowd" talked me into going to Young Life meetings over different in-crowd peoples' homes. Well, this was all about girls, girls, and social climbing. I only went with them for a few times as well.

Therefore, now showing up in a suit for my Audrey on a Saturday night and picking up her girlfriend while her mother was working, we drove only a few miles or more down on Rosemead Blvd. in the county area that separated Pasadena before going into the surrounding cities. It was small, and over the corner, the crowd was getting in, with us making our way to some seats in the middle area. It began with people singing, just like in most, but then it swept into something more and louder. After seeing people in that tent revival with Newton, however, this was another level; a woman next to me started saying things and moving in ways I had never seen in my whole life. There were sounds, but not words, gibberish, and people were moving to the front with their bodies moving, as if they had lost control of their nervous systems. My eyes and mind couldn't believe what was going on. I was thinking, oh my God, these are aliens from outer space. The preacher moved among them, and this was becoming better than any of those church TV or a movie I've ever seen. WOW! My mind couldn't take it all in; we walked outside afterward. People were crying, and others were smiling while others were acting as if nothing happened.

Audrey told me they were speaking in tongues with God! I was now unable to say much, and what could I say? It's church. She said it was a Pentecostal church. However, it appeared to me to be a penitent way of worship. I knew her mother to be Irish and not a member of this church, or was she? Talking about mixed feelings and completely unclear in any understanding of how this could affect minds or souls, I was blank and speechless. Afterward, I did some studies about many religious beliefs for one of my college classes and a paper for my national current problems class. I then found my own mix of beliefs and asked if there was a GOD, making me lean more toward being agnostic during this period of time. Well, one day not much later after this, Audrey talked to me and told me she was going back to her old boyfriend, who was Pentecostal, and chooses not to wear makeup. I was very unhappy. Sigmund Freud was lost to another faith. My heart was broken. It was hard to repair.

A Helping Nurse

After that, one of my other friends, who were studying to become a doctor, was talking with some student nurses during break. He introduced me, and there was one with a great smile, with warmth in her and was very funny with a quick wit. She was a little older than the rest, and we started meeting days afterward, seeing each other within her small group at the same time for the next few weeks. It just happened that we only talked more between ourselves. She was from the Midwest, Ohio or Pennsylvania, coming out here to get out of the cold. She had been a nurse back there and was going to school to move up into a better job here. She was working at St Luke's in Pasadena on the edge of Sierra Madre. We went out for coffee and then for a dinner date. She was living with two other nurses near the hospital, and they all had different working-shift hours, and it was very hard finding time with school and work for our dates. So for our next date, she invited me over for dinner at her apartment. Her roommates were working or gone for the night. We had a nice French wine and dinner with everything so easy. Thinking back now, she was a mature woman. And I found myself feeling safe and warm from the wine and music. We move from a couch to the bedroom while listing to Johnny Mathis. She told me about being engaged before moving west, but that fell apart within the first year here, and then came my telling her about my of my Audrey experience too. It was comfortable; neither of us was looking for a commitment. Having so many things going on in our lives, it was not time for more.

Not too much longer, she had gotten a new job in the La Jolla Hospital in La Jolla near San Diego, and I helped her move down there. The telephone calls and the travels were becoming hard on both of us with our busy lifestyles. She was again rooming with two other nurses, and one weekend I brought my surfboard down there; we spent the day in the sun, surf, and lie on the sand. She was totally white; she spent most of her time under the umbrella while I mostly spent my time in the water and just come back to warm. I put down my board, and then I drag her on it. I hang on to her on the board as we paddled out for some waves to stay on the board. We laughed, as the water was very cold as it hit us. The farther we had gone out, the waves became calmer and smaller. We spent some time on the water, but she was uneasy, and a big wave came along, washing us both with a roar. We built a fire; and she had brought the wine, cheese, and bread again. The sun went down as we talked about her new job and piled more wood on the fire. Again I pulled her into the surf, and at first it was cold again, but we kept ducking under. Then when the shock was over, it became warmer with our bodies becoming used to the temperature with the air much colder. We ran out to our towels, the blanket, and laughed in the campfire. It was not *From Here to Eternity*, but close enough in the wrapping of two bodies. She had brought her radio with its new FM stations playing Montovonti as another type of wave was hitting the sand now. However, sex in the sand while trying to stay wrapped up in a blanket does leave a rubbed lasting memory afterward. I had trouble walking the next few days, and it wasn't like seen or reflected in movies. That was the last time I saw her; it ended just as easy as it had began. We had said good-bye on the phone with warmth. We both ended up nursing ourselves. The pebbles learned that there are ways to be close, the elements nearly together, and to be involved, being just joined together by a smile.

Dr. Wild

The student doctor that had introduced us was a guy from a year behind me in high school in the class of 1958. There was no one like him, just looking at him; he was part Steve Allen and part Clark Kent. He had this big smile with glasses like Buddy Holly with a funny hair and a last name of "Wild." No kidding, that was his real last name, but just thinking about it, his wanting to become a doctor with that name, the line came to mind—"Calling Dr. Wild." It was a great, pleasant surprise seeing him here at PCC, and as far, as I know, he and another guy, Don or Donald Wong, from my football team and same class of 1958 went on to become doctors. Also, one more thing funny, he was working part-time as an internist at Arcadia's Methodist Hospital Mental Ward. So like Superman, he could hold and restrain any of those wildest patients by going into his telephone booth, upon one or two who maybe getting loose in the ward. Believe me, it takes super powers to hold humans with their adrenaline flowing, and he just happened to be also another car nut too. I'd known him from our high school days through Lloyd and at Nicholson's speed shop in Monrovia as well.

He had this bitchin' black 1940 Ford coupe with a Chevy engine, and one weekend, we took it to TJ Mexico to have its interior done. We drove down, getting there around eight in the morning, and we were going from shop to shop, looking over some materials and workmanship. Comparing prices then was only secondary to workmanship, we thought as if we knew what we were doing. We left the car at the best-picked shop and were told it would be ready around three or four in the afternoon. We walked into downtown, found a place to eat, and had a few beers; but upon returning to the shop, we found out that the car wasn't done yet. Doc Wild was on the edge of now becoming wild, maybe Superman or worst, and I didn't know what was going to happen, thinking we may end up in jail or go home with the car half done. We went back to town with him cooling off, and in about another two hours, we returned with the car now done. He had it done in creamy white leather, plates with red trimming running around the edges. It looked good with him paying cash, and we went out of there around six o'clock. We got back late; he dropped me off while he had to go into work for his shift, but he needed sleep.

Well, about a month or so later, it rained with his car parked outside without any garage, and like all those old Fords, they always let water in somewhere. The next day, while drying out, he gave me a call, asking me to come over. "Ya, you're right," I confirmed. "It smell like shit, I'd say probably cow shit!" That asshole had put cow shit inside the interior somewhere. Victor found it and had that section redone in a shop in Arcadia for a double amount. We told everyone that if they were going to go down there, stayed with your car until it is done and never, never pissed off the shop until it's done. So this time, the Americano had gotten himself into some bullshit, but you know what? Dr. Wild laughed and laughed every time that story was told, and just like Steve Allen, he would just giggle and giggle some more about his own personal jokes being on him. He was a great guy with a great since of humor, and I bet he's a great doctor.

Oh, one other thing, another time, he took me over to the west side of Pasadena near the Arroyo to meet another one of his friends and see his '32 roadster. This car was one of the most beautiful cars I've ever seen; and of course, it was in black with red wheels, white walls, and stocked forty Ford hubcaps. This guy being, however, J. P. Morgan's grandson could have had any car he wanted but bought himself a classic hot rod. Dr. Wild knew people with wealth and good taste too, and you just didn't know who was in the next car at Bob's big boys in Pasadena or anywhere in their cars. It could be doctors, lawyers, or actors.

Bob and His Caddy

There was another guy named Bob. I met him at PCC too, and he was older with sores of money. He had this beautiful 1953 Caddy convertible, black with red interior, and he kept it in a garage with great care in Altadena. He was refined and had great taste in clothes. He lived in the area with the "ice cream" mansion and near where Frank Lloyd Wright's house was being built. We went to some jazz places in Hollywood and at the Pasadena playhouse. Then he made a play for me after some wine, but at first, I thought there's a mistake. I looked him in the eye and asked, "Are you making a play for me?" He looked back at me without moving, saying, and "What do you think?" Then I knew, I was right.

I knew what people thought of artists and actors, but thinking of what had just happened made me angry, and I told him, "You are mistaken about me." and I just couldn't understand his kind of feelings. "Get me back to my car," I told him. My car was at the PCC parking lot, and that was the last time we talked. Many years later after reading a book about James Dean's life and how, as a teenager, he took the wrong road and how he was used and then how he used another rich man into getting his way to the New York City life, it's easy to see how this could happen. James Dean was not gay, nor was I, but now I was upset with myself for not seeing him for what he was. All I did was move on. However in 1961, after I started working within Hollywood and going to parties through my job in these surroundings, I saw a lot of gay people up front or in closets. It then didn't mean anything to me; of course, most understood what they were. It was their cup of tea and not mine. Some weren't open, like today, but you knew.

Red White Heat

The year 1959 was a wild year, and again, my mind went blank scratching for her name or how we had met but I know it was at the PCC too. She had short dyed red hair, and everything about her was hot, you could feel the heat racing the moment she walked near; and when we did get together, the heat grew even stronger. She lived with her family in the Oaks of Arcadia, this area above Foothill Blvd. from Santa Anta Ave. to Michilinda Ave. across from Pasadena. During this period of time, homes in the area were worth over one million or more in value. I drove my parents' little red corvette to her house most of time, and her young brother thought that was cool. There was a pool just outside the den area in the rear part of the house to cool off. Her dad had an "out of site" stereo-audio equipment room, and he was gone a lot for business trips, and her mother was never home either. The younger brother had his own room, and toys were never around either. Soooo there was just us most of the time, playing Martin Denny with his birds in the tropical rain forests, bringing on a forecast of hot rain with romantic and erotic states of minds. We would play a game of who's going to give into the other's sexy moves first, with some added shots of tequila with lime mixer for more heat. She would put up her heat to white hot, and I could hold her off to a breaking point that became more difficult, knowing men are the weakest sex. However, I did give it all of my conscious effort listening to the mixer of Cal Tjader, Stan Getz, or other drumbeats that combined with the beating of my pulsating heart. We danced samba, then tango. We even were able to find ways into doing it in the small bucketseat with the top off of the little red Corvette.

However, one day it all came down around us. She said, "I've missed my period!" The heat was another type, and we waited another long twelve days with the pressing pressure looking for a miracle. The next step was a meeting with her parents, sitting down, and the mother went crazy, but her father was cool, telling us he would get me a job with his company. He was upset, but his manner of saying it was businesslike and kept things under control. Another week went by, and she called me over with everything going back to normal; she started to have her period.

She told her mother; then her father asked to speak with us both again. He told her he was sending her to Arizona to U. A. or she would have to go out and find a job to support herself in order to stay here, and I saw what everyone wanted. Well, we agreed, talking only for a short time, and we could still see each other on school breaks from Arizona, and we would be better off with his decision. To tell you the truth, I wasn't ready for a child or any responsibility yet. It slowly fell apart, and within the next year, she came back from Arizona with a new husband and a child on the way. Freud, what's your advice? Who was using whom? That Irish luck, or another force, but this pebble rolled away, hence avoiding that stream.

Cabinet Boy

Another guy from Arcadia came into my life, reminding me a lot of Pee Wee, but he was a year younger than I. He was attending school while working for his family's business. They owned a cabinet-manufacturing business and lived blocks from Arcadia High School. We went water-skiing in a boat owned by him at Bass Lake one summer, and there were other boy toys, like his new 1960 Pontiac hardtop with three crabs. It was fast. I was spending a lot of time at Carpenter's drive-in, looking and finding parties. We only hang out for about eight or more months because of an undesirable encounter one night, and on that night, while in Carpenter's customer parking lot, he had a need to mouth off to some Spanish guys from El Monte, where the family business was located. While we drove around to leave, after delaying another hour later, they had blocked our path. We tried to leave through the gas station at the next-door driveway, but it had closed for the night. They got out from the two cars, with three or four of them walking our way against only two of us this time. We tried shinning them on, but then one came up to my door; they weren't going away, and I wasn't waiting like that night after the football game. Using that same trick that had worked before in Whittier, my door hit him in the knees to his surprise, with him going down, and I kicked him in the chest while exiting our car, and he went down on his back. Two more were moving to my side now, and one had pulled a switchblade knife, so I now started backing up while pulling off my jacket and wrapped it around my right arm.

The others around were yelling in Spanish, and because we were close to the drive-in car service area, just across from us, some other kids started looking and yelling as they came running over to help. He lunged at me, cutting me on my right arm, but I stopped his hand using my arm wrapped the jacket. I hit him in the face with my left hand while he fell lunging forward. I had tripped him too, and sidestepping, he slammed into the car. It gave me a chance to pick up his knife while another guy hit me from the rear, and I turned, wrapped him up in my jacket too while pulling him forward, losing my jacket. Again, now the first one came rushing back at me after getting on his feet. By now, we were close to the big front window of the gas station, and he was trying to catch me sideways, but my turning threw him into the window first as I fell on top of him. This time the glass was falling and breaking everywhere; the sound of the breaking glass mixed with screaming alarm sound in my head during that moment. The alarm went off when someone pulled me off this guy. The cabinet boy had gotten back in his car, and I followed as the crowd was coming in from all directions now. Also, one attacker's car was gone now too. We drove out, not seeing where the guys went either, but they were gone.

Now, sitting inside the car, I again felt some stinging in my back; a mix of cold and warm liquid was running down my back. Then looking at my arm, I asked myself if this was the other guy's or my blood I saw. But I was more concerned about a small cut above my eye, which also stinging; I was trying to clear my vision. Cabinet Boy drove me to the emergency room at Arcadia Methodist Hospital while he didn't have a scratch anywhere. They sewed my wounds, and my mother came with the insurance papers and picked me up. My dad's insurance covered me while I was still living at home and going to school. My boy came by as I was mending, but after that, when I called, his mother was cold, and I was getting the feeling they didn't want him hanging out with someone of my class or getting their boy into trouble again. He found a girl shortly afterward, and I guessed things worked out for him. This would not be my last fight, or dangerous encounter, and my guardian angel was with me once again. I never heard anything from the authorities.

TWENTY-ONE

The Intakes Club
David McKinley

David was still in high school in his junior year, two years behind me, when we met. He was cool and had a 1951 Chevy coupe. He had no father living within the family either, just like Pee Wee, and I may be wrong, but I remembered him being dead. He had two sisters and maybe a younger little brother too, but there was always something of turmull here. David was taking on the responsibility of being the man of the house while his mother worked. However, he and his older sister had battles regarding that standing. His mother was cool while David was very serious about his family and life. In his short amount of time at Monrovia High, he had become class president, head yell leader, and president of the Intake's Car Club. But he was another "James Dean" type too with a lot of rebel in him, which made girls, with his good looks, and guys drawn to because of his rebel strengths. He had a dark side covered with smoking and drinking, with a lot of emotional troubles seen by those close to him. He was always trying to get his head straight, and we would have long talks. It sometimes helped to have someone to talk with when there is lots of stress, and I thought we had became very close, with me wearing that older brother hat. I'd known most of the other guys in the Car Club through high school, like football, or just hanging out.

While during my years within the club, I had designed the club's jacket's caricature and plaque, but the guy doing the plaques made changes to my drawing, and I became upset with the outcome. I liked mine much better, but in order to put in our club's name with Monrovia on there too, he cut down my drawing, and by doing so, he made it appear more into a cartoon type than that of my car drawing. No one knew this, but a few, that that drawing was my dream car, and I was building it in my backyard.

In February of 1959, Dad and I started building my 1927 roadster with its tube rails for a frame, Corvette engine with special heads that Nicholson built for me, three 97 crab intakes, plus built my own special headers, connecting a La Salle transmission and a '56 Chevy Posi rear end. We used the rear Model-A rear spring perch and welded on three point bars for the rear. I had built a custom body with fiberglass and steel. It had a tub front axel with 1939 Lincoln Continental brakes up with hairpin bars my dad made from stainless steel. I built things by hand, like the hand-formed windshield frame, my own backseats, and fitting a 1934 Ford dash with Stewart Warner instrument interior. A four-bar racing steering wheel with hanging peddles with hydraulic clutch. Then I built a head roll bar that went behind the seats for safety. Next, I cut down my T shell for a special radiator, with a model-T winged copper cap with a special red glass temperature made by my buddy Dick Dane topping that. It was coming together, with a custom rear body section with custom taillights and custom push bars.

27' "T" nearing construction in backyard

This was my dream car, and by January 1961, it was almost completed. The next step was setting it together. I had the front-end parts chromed now, and I bought the paint, a very dark root beer metallic found on the then new Olds while the interior was ready for a tan leather seat covering. I was getting everything ready to put it together, hopefully by Thanksgiving of 1961. But my world had started turning upside down, and I ended up selling it for parts. My dad bought the engine, putting it in his new racecar, which we built together during this time too. His car broke the track record with my engine while out the first time, but I wasn't around to see it. My dad and I were now starting to get along too. We were sharing our dreams, but another dream was lost and not completed for me. I never knew where the rest of the car went. The pebble was changing direction again with a new world seen on the horizon by 1962, but back to our club.

Larry Bonden Driving Float & Don Wong 57'Chevy

Day of Parade "Little Ed" and Doug Welch

Dad's Corvette/ David/ Larry Carroll/ me

I had been upset with the plaque result, but very happy with the club jacket's caricature. We did a Monrovia Day float in 1959, with my cousin's son, little Eddy, and another kid riding in their quarter-midgets as if they where racing on a track on the back of a large flatbed truck with a flagman, Doug Welch. The rest of the club guys, Denny Adkins and others, were watching from the back topside of the truck cab with Larry Bonden driving. I drove my dad's Corvette with David McKinley and Larry Carroll while Bob Zmrzell drove his own 1956 Vet with Marvin Handy, and Exstrom was driving up front, side by side with the truck float following behind Don Wong in his 1957 Red Chevy convertible. The great-looking girls Patti Canada and Janet Jones were in their bathing suits on the truck, and Judy Peck and Billie McDonald with Ron Thornton were surrounding Wong behind the two Corvettes. It couldn't get any better, and shortly afterward, David met Mary Ann, and she took over and became the love in his life; but before her, he and I were wild buddies, drinking, partying, and looking for girls while so were most of the other guys in the club. We did some good things too, not all "bad boy" things. He went on through school and married Mary Ann. Many, many, many years later, we ran into each other at the Standard Oil Building in LA, next to where I was working, and he was working for them; and that time he was already in a high executive level and was living in that same the Arcadia Oaks, where White Red Heat had lived. He had worked hard, finding his way through the darkness. Many of the other guys in the club crossed my life too much later, and who would have thought that they would all be doing very well now.

Parties and Drinking

One of my worst drinking experiences during those days with the Intake's; it happen one night. We, three or more guys, had gotten some beer, and I can't recall if it was Ronny Thornton or who, but it started with a six-pack or more. Ronny had troubles keeping his custom 1949 Ford coupe straight then too. We had drank all that beer, then found an old Wine-O to buy us some more, but he bought us a fifth of scotch whisky too, which we drank on top of the beer, with one more beer on top of that too. We were in my black Olds and found some people who knew there was a party in the lower section of Arcadia, in the LA county area. A big house with so many people, there must have been thirty or forty people inside and out. All young, in early twenties, good music, and I remember talking to two or three girls in the front yard, thinking I was cool and being funny doing my "James Dean" impersonation.

The next thing I knew, my eyes were looking up at the moon and stars, with Ivy surrounding my face on all sides because I had just fell over backward like in the cartoons, landing on my back surround by that Ivy, and the girls were thanking I was still being funny. However, this was not part of my act. I was trying to get back up to my feet, and nothing was working. The girls got some of the guys who were with me to help me to standing up and back into my car. Later, one of them drove me to their cars, and then he drove me to my house, but they couldn't get me out of my car. So they left me there because I was getting sick. The window was open; I threw up pizza, beer, and anything else that were in this mistaken, misapplied, misalliance mixing of drinks. This miserable human did this until nothing was coming up any longer. Then I was in a weakened state, overwhelmed of my condition of just lying there, until I fell asleep for a period of time, and then it started over again. This time it came up in the form of the famous "the dry heaves," with only the acids coming way down deep from my stomach. All were thrown out on the side of my car's black door. By this time, I now made my way out of my car onto our front lawn with its cold, wet grass, and I lay down. I tried to get as close to the edge of that wash without falling with my head hanging over. I was still lying on that wet, cold grass in the front yard next to my house, awaiting my fate. After my body did this thing of being totally out of control for a few more moments, I was able to make my way into the house, took off clothes, and found my bed covering myself with warmth, trying to stop the shaking of my body and now looking forward to sleep.

The next morning, still was very sick; I was hearing a load of sounds inside my head, and it added to the shaking all over my body, from ears to toes; a cotton filled my open mouth. My dad had made me get up in order to wash off the side and seat of my car. The acid had burned off the paint on my door and later required a new repainting. From this, I now learned you don't mix scotch whisky with anything, and I was not able to stand the smell or thoughts of drinking beer for at least two or three months afterward. However, like everyone does when you're young, your mind forgets those bad things for the good; and in time, I took those returning steps back to partying, drinking, being funny for the girls, or playing James Dean again.

The La Salle

During this same time, Dad was working on a project for aerojet at Edwards Air Force Base, and they were developing explosive bolts for the separation of the rockets' sections in the space program. On one of his weekend home, he told me about seeing this 1938 La Salle coupe for sale for seventy-five dollars. It was in the desert town close to an area called Red Mountain. Well, to me, the transmission was worth that much for my roadster. We went back up to check it out, and after finding it in good shape, it ran; the trans was also shifting good, so I bought it for the asking price. It was an opera coupe with small rear seats that folded down from the side, which is cool, and it has a flat-head V-8 engine that ran quite like a big cat, with the exhaust manifolds coming from the top of the heads, seen as a first for me. There wasn't any rust and the paint wasn't bad either, and I loved the front grill that looked like a knight's big shield. La Salle made the cheaper model below the Cadillac's cars, with the same body and engines. Buick also used this same body too. I now thought it's not bad, pretty cool even. I drove it for some distance and got a ways down the highway, but still being in the high desert, the water pump belt broke. When I heard it, I saw the engine temperature starting to rise, so I stopped, and Dad too, who was still following me. I lifted the hood and pulled out the old belt to know its size, and away we went looking for some place with maybe a belt or some close to get it fixed.

We came upon an old rocked face a gas station with glass gas pumps that where eight feet tall with glass measuring marks standing guard at its entrance. There wasn't much else around for miles, so stopping, I went inside, and there was this old fellow working on a car inside the garage. I'd asked him, "Do you have any water pump belts this size?" He then asked, "What kind of car?" I was thinking, this is 1959, and this is a 1938 car that isn't made or seen anymore, but maybe he'll know the car. I said, "It is a 1938 La Salle." He then raced his eyes and started looking up along the wall, where there were belts hanging on hooks all along the top part of the walls and then took a long pole, reached up, and pulled two or three down together. Turning to me with one in his hand, he said, "Here ya are, sonny." Sure enough, it said "Cadi & La Salle" with the years for my car, matching in size and close in length to the old one in my hand. "How much?" I asked and got a reply of, "Three dollars." We drove back laughing, put it on, and then drove home without any further problems.

One more story about this car, I cut its front springs, dropping it lower and taking off the front bumper, giving it a great rake and cool hotrod look with a long hood. I drove it while working on my Olds and also drove it just for fun. One last time, while driving on River-Grade Road, I was drag racing it with another car because of its top end, but the old engine gave up its bearings and had to be towed home. Then I sold it for seventy-five dollars to a guy, who put in an Olds late-model V-8 engine in it, keeping that very low and cool beast flying down the road.

There was also another friend during this time with a cool car, a 1926 model T doctor's coupe, full fender, black with a Chevy V-8 engine, all chromed out, and on a rake too. It was like being inside a fishbowl, looking out all that glass. He, with his father, who was a fireman in Arcadia, had worked on it, making a perfect ride; and it was of a show car quality. He and I drove it to the beach during Easter break once, after the La Salle couldn't go, and cruised Newport Beach. On one occasion, we went to a party on the island, and we were among all the beautiful young people. There was the owner of the house, the actor Denver Pyle, with his white beard, laughing and checking out the young things in their bikinis right out of The Dukes of Hazard show before it was thought about being made. Dirty O'l man, was my thoughts at the time. I watched him while he was having a great time at his party and enjoying the scenery. We found that it was a great time for all who were there.

TWENTY-TWO

The Beginning of a New Nation and Dreams

The fifties was fabulous; and the sixties was a time of the un-established, un-denied freedoms and mixed social changes for the baby boomers. The year 1960 was the beginning of another great change in my life and this nation. I got my degree and thought that this was the end of my schooling, I thought for a while anyway. There were also the changes being formed within the country from having a new presidential change from IKE, the father figure who took care of America, to now a new frontier with a new young president, JFK. The president asked, "Ask not what your country can do for you, but ask what you can do for your country." Also, there were new issues throughout the fabric of social society, on race issues and with another type race strong in need of a leadership on the world's stage again communism. This New Frontier in space enabled this nation to put a man on the moon, and Camelot now became a higher level of culture awareness toward a new nation. I found myself starting on life's path toward finding a job, and I turned twenty-one, a man in life's stream.

Now I was working as an artist because of Mr. Bukus taught the real adverting class, and he gave me a connection with an ad agency in the edge of Hollywood on La Cienega Blvd. and Mel Rose. We did ads for large new housing sales, and my job was doing what is known as "paste ups," and I was occasionally adding some drawings. It was a good starting point. We would find a customer, put together ideas, show conceived concepts with drawings and pictures at the beginning of the week; and by Thursday, it had to be completed for printing in the newspapers in for the Sunday edition.

There were martini lunches, long working hours, sometimes running in the next day. There were tight deadlines, and there were many changes for our finished works after the customer submitted and requested new changes at the last minute. However, we partied hard, mixing business and pleasure too. Then I enjoyed a quite time, being only for one or two days, before it all started over again. I made more money than I'd ever thought of in my life, but I was losing weight and getting ulcers on this fast track plastic world or streams.

Speaking of tracks, one day while standing on a corner next to work, this D class Jag came flying around the corner, just as I was about to step off the curb, attempting to cross the street. It almost hit me as it breaks, and wheels were all attempting to stop, but not the car or its driver; but then, also turning and facing me, I saw that it was Steve McQueen. He yelled, "Sorry!" Now I heard this clearly coming out of his lips with his wheels continually flying down the street off into the distance. That was the way everything was surrounding me then, things flying all around me at the speed of sound. My dad had informed me, "It's time to pay rent since you're now working." So after paying for a few months at home, I found my own apartment in Arcadia on Huntington Drive, and I had been thinking of finding a place closer to work, but I would lose my roots. While in my college days before this and while I was working for the department stores, I had readied myself for this day by buying dishes and other items, knowing and wanting it's coming someday.

The apartment was small, but now it was my own place, but the pebble was now heading into a storm, without knowing how big or long it would last and without knowing what was to become my way in much larger upheavals for the nation and me. I'd narrowed my thinking and direction to work, enjoying my newfound dream foundation and views in this new stream.

Sylvia

At one of the parties, Sylvia and I had met; she had worked in New York City doing some modeling, and she was working at some other jobs with her step dad and mother in a local newspaper business at this time. Her dad was an editor, and they had moved to California from Kansas City for a new job opening. They lived in Arcadia, very close to the racetrack, like my apartment location now too.

However, her mother had a new baby a little later during this time, being one of those "oops" while also having a younger teenage daughter as well. The family had move around a lot because of his occupation, and the whole family was in a state of "on the go" most of the time. So Sylvia would also do a lot of babysitting. Later after dating and deciding a commitment to each other, we thought we found love; she then told me of having only one kidney and therefore cannot have any children of her own. It wasn't important then, and with the near miss, it was somewhat a relief too.

She had red hair, green eyes, creamy skin with freckles, tall around five feet seven inches with breasts larger then most models, which made it very hard for her to find work in that field. She was clever, intelligent, and sexy, had a mixture of being another Holly Golightly too, and reflected a mix of very good New Yorker's taste. We would share this taste for the finer things, but as the song goes from Pal Joey, the lady is a tramp. She was a mixture of all my previous two girlfriends before her; it was always an up-and-down relationship too. At times, it was all because of my own faults, and other times, because of her problems. "We were in love!" We were lovers, but it was hard to find that steady ground with these ups and downs in this emotional relationship being mixed with this new lifestyle; it drained us both.

Then the events of times stepped in and changed everything on our streams, but before that, I had found my job in August before meeting her in September of 1960. We started making plans to run away and ride this shooting star through the heavens within our heat and hearts. It had started with me giving her one of my paintings from my high school drawing classes. It was a cubistic oil painting of a monk outside of a Montessori, and this was the first time I gave away any of my art or soul. By December 1961, we're going out together over a year; there were so many opportunities before me, like Nicholson running his 409 Chevy and asking me to join his racing team. Then the added demands of spending time with Dad and my goal to finish my dream car were pulling me apart, and I was now even getting even thinner. Then there was my dream job, working as a artist with a lot of hardworking hours, drinking at parties, and that traveling to Hollywood taking an exhausting amount of passion that may have not be have enough, but there were other possibilities now, seen within the connection found within the art field too, and also during this time, her parents were having financial troubles. After giving her my high school ring, we believed we had true love so I bought her an engagement ring; we had the usual lovers' quarrel, but still we found support during our own pains or troubles by just sharing our deep love together; it was new for both of us. My life was riding along the edge, and it was becoming harder to balance it all, not seeing what was coming over the horizon until it came in the mail. The next new big wave would change my life's stream again forever.

TWENTY-THREE

Uncle Sam's Army
"Greetings"

It was December, and just before Christmas in 1961, the mail came with "greetings" from Uncle Sam, requesting my presence. I was to report for a physical in LA before the New Year. So I drove to downtown LA. I found this old departmentstore building with lines on the floor that had been there for many years, and many years later I would return working here in this very same building. Again you followed, you undressed, and you waited, and then followed the next guy from the next step to the next. You found yourself among others, who came in all colors, sizes, and shapes in this state of disbelief. At the end, I found out that if I hadn't eaten a big breakfast that day, this wouldn't have become a life-changing situation. I weighted only 113 pounds on that day, but if I were only 110 pounds, I would have been passed over until the next time. I was given until January of 1962 to get myself ready for a new life. Many were signing up for marines or navy or air force for their choice, but for longer terms. But telling Sylvia and my parents was the start of an emotional roller coaster. There were a few guys that I'd known in college who earned their degrees in liberal arts, but who were now in training as draftees and carry machine guns around for mortal combat for the rest of their time in the army.

So I went down to the recruiter's office to talk, and seeing what could be done, he told me, "Sign up for three years, and you can pick a job, and that would become an honored contract that would be a guaranty." It was only one more year, and at least, I could get something back, something that I could use afterward. Then I talked it over with Sylvia. I then returned to sign up for administration personnel to specialize in office duties and out of harm's way. No one was happier than them both, my mother and Sylvia. Sylvia and I had talked about marriage too, but so many things were in the mix during this short time, like working for our goals, so we waited. All my dreams were put on hold; I given notice for my job, which they would have to hold for me because of the draft status. And next, I also gave notice regarding my apartment, and I was ready to move back with my parents. Now I sold my cars and reported on January 10, 1962, downtown at the induction center with my parents and Sylvia, saying a hard good-bye.

Boot Camp

I now reported to the U.S. Army in Los Angeles, and my family went along with me to the Old Union Station for the train trip to Fort Ord. We got to Salinas by morning, and they placed us on a bus for the rest of the trip to Monterey, and then on to Fort Ord as the sun came up. We got there, and the cattle started moving from one stop to the next pin, with every amount of mixed feelings building within, but without much seen on our faces. There's nothing in our souls, damned, but dazed, with soon to be uncovered, shaved heads, after getting feed. The word becomes "hurry up and wait" while you're in the army, and this becomes a way of life. Just do it, no questions, your life will become open, and you'll be better for it. You'll be pulled out of your skin, and then put back in, becoming reshaped, organized, and trained in the army's ways. The result is no one knows that lost identity of yours from before—of who you were in the past. I looked into that new pebble in the mirror or to any possibility of others' personal position surrounding me and standing with me. The birds pick you apart, and they hope to make you grab your own shot at becoming a part of their hell. To me it was hell. You are to become a killing machine, a shining little soldier, within some amount of pride within yourself for what you are about to achieve.

The process began like this: after getting all your clothes, you are assigned to your squad, platoon, and ours was C company. Now a chain of command begins with your new drill sergeant, who is in charge of training, marching, manual of arms, becoming your mother's replacement for control of your every move within your life. His first question was, "Who has had any military training or experience?" You will learn much later to NEVER EVER GIVE VOLUNTARY, ANY VALUABLE OR VOCAL INFORMATION, and THAT CAN BE USED TO MAKE YOU THEIR VOLUNTEER.

I made my first mistake by raising my hand. I was then asked, "What kind of military experience?" I replied, "I was in the Civil Air Patrol and did marching and drills." In a flash, I was now assigned as assistant squad leader with a temporary armband to join in with the said "squad leader"—he received his too, and we put this simple symbol of authority around our arms. The other guy had ROTC training. Again, back to being second in the line to somebody, we were assigned to a building, where we took all of our belongings. We were then given this little card, with these "rules" to memorize, which reminded us we are in the army and its control.

The next morning at four, we were awoken and rushed outside. Names were called. "ALLEN," and I replied, "YES, SIR," with the echoing sound repeated down the line. This was REVELRY, this was REVEILLE, and then on to further processing with shots put in our arms, butts, and food in bellies. Then they had all the new recruits assembled, and the upper level command gave us the welcome and pep talk; and then the drill sergeants began their thing. Lucky for us, our sergeant was white and could speak enough English that you could understand most of the words coming from his mouth, with half your brain out of action. His assistant was a corporal, who had been busted down in rank for drinking, and you could tell he has found a home in the army. Now he was trying to get back to this ladder in the chain of command, but you could smell without looking that he was a loser in life. All the others, I couldn't understand half the words coming out of their mouths or brains, and if this was possible. These people were in the lowest end of my, or any other, species. However, our sergeant was young, and he just got married, living in a basic housing with his family.

Many of the other white sergeants were mostly from the South and couldn't understand them with their slow draws, but we did have a large group of new recruits from Texas. Who could, I guessed, understood them. I would say, "Bear'ee Hill (Berry Hill), how come's, I'd can'n talk like yaw and you' a cann'nt talk like us'en?" Then there were black sergeants from the South, or some other islands, with a small amount of mixed Spanish sergeants, from Porto Rico, plus others from the Philippines, who became sergeants from former wars, before I began high school. None of which, most humans could understand. I just want you to understand, it wasn't race, it wasn't color, it wasn't education; and you just couldn't understand any damned thing said. There was also one Scottish recruit. He moved up and became the commander of us temporary squad leaders and became the recruit most likely to become "head of the class" at the end of training, which he did to no one's surprise. He was also hard to understand, but he had good reason. He was from a foreign country that speaks the "mother English" language but was again on a rebellion, upstarts tongue, and he would remind you, "I'm a' not a bloody Englishman."

However, we quickly learned there were two young Italian neighborhood buddy recruits in our barracks, who were known as "Hold Over's" to be recycled again. They hadn't passed the requirements to be further assigned on, or were awaiting assignment for retraining or discharged. They stayed in the sergeant's room at the end of our barracks. They were assholes and thought they were wise guys, only without a godfather or family here. They always walked on our polished wood floors and messed around with the men in our squad. "Wising off," and I'm sure that's why they became "hold overs."

One day, I placed newspapers on both the sides of the floor in order for us to walk on without leaving marks on the floor before our inspection the next day. Our two "friends" walked right down the middle to their rooms from the La Tureens, and I had just asked them very nicely on their way not to do that. They just laughed and went on their way, saying, "What yaw going to do about it?" My reply was, "Let's discuss this outside later. I'll meet you outside anytime after inspection is over, and I'll be happy to show you." So the next day, they came walking up from the PX after inspection, and there was no one else around besides me. We started talking with me explaining, "Just stay out of our way, and everything will be cool, until you're reassigned out of here." Well then, the biggest asshole said, "Look, we'll do whatever, whenever we want, and you can't stop us." With that, he gave his friend his bag and reached into his pocket, pulled out a roll of nickels in his right hand, and the other guy backed up. The talk was over, so I pulled out my handkerchief and wrapped it around my right hand too. He rushed at me, swung with his right hand at my face. My first reaction, which I got from my boxing training, was to duck and step aside, and it was effective. Now following with the connection of my right hand to his jaw, I added a well-found upper cut while he passed by. Then came my left to his right eye, stopping his foolish forward motion. I continued with my right to the midsection and followed with my knee to his face until he stopped from going any further and went down. Next came my boot to his midsection again while he was now down on his back trying to find his breath, and then I looked up, over my shoulder, just as the other guy turned and ran. They found the asshole in the dirt with his roll of nickels, now bent in half with his head and feet sticking out the same direction, like an envelope, with his butt stuffed under the barrack floor and supports, which was about two to three feet in height, easy for this position, as he was stuck and unable to get out from under there after another kick to his middle section, after he tried to rise up again the first time. While I heard faint sounds of him, crying like a pig below our building, I turned and left him to find the rest of my squad.

Later, a sergeant platoon leader found me, telling me to report to the "sergeant of the day" office. Following orders, reporting to the small office at the end of our barracks row, "the pigs" were here waiting until the door opened. It was our drill sergeant, whom was our own staff sergeant for my platoon, and it just happen to be "the sergeant of the day" on duty that day, waiting for me. After going through the military salutes, he asked me what happened, so I told him and the platoon leader my side of the story.

The next day, the two "Hold Over's" were gone, but I wasn't, to leave the platoon area for a week or go to the PX. Not knowing if this was for my protection or punishment, but I got the feeling he and the other sergeants were very happy about the turn of events. My boxing training and reactions were better than the assholes' mouths, which needed training too.

My squad did well with our next inspections, and like my dad's little happening of a "wrong turn" before, the word had gotten out among others in my platoon, don't passé with me. They learned and knew there was an "extraordinary pebble" presented by action and not just words and my gaining respect among the other small pebbles for a while.

My other mistake regarding volunteering came as we were out in a combat training area, learning to crawl in the dirt, under barbwire, with live machine gun rounds going overhead. They asked if anyone had an artist talent? So again my hand went up. This time now, it ended up at the end of a ladder with a paintbrush repainting a sign, marking the troop entrance into this range area. At least, I wasn't down in the dirt crawling, trying to keep my head down, trying to keep my ass down or shot off, and making sure my heels were down or being shot off, but I did have paint everywhere.

Fort Ord—what a "wonderful place"! The army always places its training camps in the most likely of all "Hell Hole places" found in our nation. It was cold, wet, foggy, and rainy in most of the fort while there was hot sunshine on the other side in the city of Carmel or other parts outside the camp. It was mostly sand, with more mud, wet sand, and with a mix of a lot more unpleasant existing conditions, including the constant mixing and changing of weather. The fog that surrounds you at night or early morning in every direction would be gone once the sun was out with its burning rays of sunshine. You had another problem too if you got sunburned, which could happen because most of the time, outside of the fort, the sun would be shining and warm, surrounding you from those dark clouds which are hanging over the fort most of the time. So you were always fighting off colds or some more serious pneumonia or mentalities medical problems too. Which is why the fort was closed down for a period, much later during the sixties. Near the last of my first six weeks, I had gotten sick too, but I was not going to miss training by going to "sick call" or become a "hold over," starting hell all over again. The sunburn would get you a court marshal section and that was easy punishment.

Real Shooters

One day on the firing range, while it was raining, we were in our rain gear—which consisted of a "poncho," covering only from your shoulders to your knees, keeping more water in, then out, with the metal helmets covering your head and water running down your neck. Now, I never liked "peas or pea soup." However that day, I was wet to the skin and in most places, where it makes life most miserable, and in your boots. It now was the best tasting and best thing ever to warm your bones on that day and ever since then too. I've loved it ever since that day. Oh, what the mind can do; and now, I went into each shooting position, first started with the standing, then sitting, and then with the worst coming, getting down into your shooting prone position. First down on your knees with cold water starting to take over your body heat in your lower sections, then into your elbows, as the sand surrounds them, giving way to the weight of your body, with water rushing into filling those lower spots. The water was running off the helmet front and back; it went running down the neck's back and into the front of your nose and around your chin with drips running into the sand, disappearing.

I learned early, at around ten, that my eyesight was better in my left eye for aiming, and therefore, I had to use the opposite to normal position again like in school and in my life. The problem was with the hot shell casing that came out on my right side in front of my face and at my arm, burning me. The first thing to do is to put the clip in, then put your thumb in that old M1 to release a round into the chamber; if you're lucky again, it slams close without any part of your thump. They gave the order, "Ready on the Firing Line." You look for the right target in your lane because many of these guys would shoot at yours, an easy mistake too. It was easy for some to get mixed up in this nervous state, and then because of the rain, water was in the "Peep Sight" now. So you would have to blow it out, clear your vision, and line up the target. The next order was "Comments Firing," taking off the safety while trying to hold it from moving up, then down, then sideways, with the sound of others pulling their triggers in your ears, with the steel helmets—all of these was affecting your concentration. You could not think of the cold water running down your pants, your legs, toward your waste, without your arms moving; and the puddle under your stomach is getting bigger. Stay only on that "damn target," take your aim and fire. Then with the order "clear," you roll over to one side with your weapon, making sure it's pointed down range at all times; and a sergeant checks for unspent rounds. Given the clear signal, you are now standing up with water running into your boots and getting ready for another trip to see what you've hit. The next poor guys turn behind you, and then you get to retrieve your target. There were many found moments; we would all duck, as your skin would get the chills, from some fool having pulled off a round in the wrong direction, or the wrong timing without following the orders given. You—not giving much confidence in these fellow soldiers—would think and hope that guy would never be in combat with you. We would spend most of the day in the rain and sand with my thoughts returning to the movie *Sergeant York*, with his sharp shooting, as a Kentuckian, wetting his sight with his thumb and shooting turkeys. Also these men in World War I were in that muddy cold war and all the others of each following War II or Korea. Then receiving the awarded "sharpshooter" marksmanship with this weapon and others later with the M14, M16, and a few handguns, which came much later because of my inter controls found in college. But the cleaning and the care for that weapon was what would keep you alive in combat. You would learn to break it down, put it back together with your eyes closed, but some had trouble keeping both focus.

"Sad Shack"

We had a "Sad Shack" in our C Company. He was tall, very thin, with a very large hooked nose that kept his glasses—which was always halfway down most of the time—from falling down; and his beard would be a stubble by noon with very white skin, and his Adam's apple appeared to stand out almost, as far, like his nose. His helmet liner and helmet was not adjusted right, and if he ran, it would make its way down over his eyes, with him bouncing along like Ichabod Crane riding a horse through the woods in the story of Sleepy Hollow. He ran into trees when going through ours drills of attacks because his helmet moved up or down over his eyes. The sergeant told him to "call that tree to attention" before runing, so he could run around it. He got a laugh.

In one of our many war game days, we were out on maneuvers, with the squads walking along both sides of the road. A small airplane passed over, dropping "flower" bombs on us. We all dove off down the side of the road for cover, and the yell went out, "Find cover, hit the dirt," as the plane turning for a returned run. Well, "Sad Shack" had jumped, falling down the side, and ended up rolling into a string of barbwire. He was warped up, yelled for help by the time the plane made its last pass, and everybody else was back on the road. He had to be cut lose, with cuts everywhere on his body. I really felt sorry for him most of the time. The drill sergeants were on his back most of the time because he was "Sad Shack."

Once he got dirt in the barrel of his gun, which resulted with him given extra duties of digging holes and then filling them back up after our meals at night. He stayed with it, making through to graduation—he was not a "hold over" either. I found myself laughing at the army most of the time; it was this surrounding of large cartoons, and by using this, it lightens up our situation. This was the only way to make it through in most of my army times and during this period of hard times. I also recall the many song hits of the day going though my head, day or night, like the "Duke of Earl" and "Soldier Boy," which was played and put a smile on my face as well.

Food for Young Bodies

They would give you "K' Rations" while out in the field. The food helped to control your nervous times because you would be hungry most of the time, and there were always cigarettes with chewing gum. I picked the gum, but most of the others made the easy choice for the smokes. Most of the guys started at eighteen, which at the time was cool, but now most of these guys have paid the price with their health now. There were always "smoke breaks" between and during classes. THANK YOU USA MILITARY! And to the tobacco company that got their young bodies hooked. The Indians also got their revenge with the white men for taking their lands and breaking those promises for all these many years too by smoking the "peace pipe."

Of course, I took drinking of beer to numb my thinking and brain, but most of the time, with the need for much more sleep, it kept you in a state of "la-la land" anyway. This is all about, of course, keeping with your companionship and your fellow comrades too. The beer tasted watered down (3/2 beer), and there was talk of them feeding you "Salt Peter" to keep your sex drive down too, which was never confirmed if any of this was true, but I wouldn't be surprise. The mess hall food was something more than only for the stomach but not for the taste.

You would stand in line after running in the morning and afternoon with a metal tray while food was thrown in large lumps on it, and you rushed in, sat down eating, and then rushed out, so as the next line of men could eat too. No talking just hopping up and dump the tray with leftovers in the garbage cans on your way out. You would at least get once at KP (Kitchen Patrol) peeling potatoes, serving those lumps, cleaning pots and pans and—if you're lucky—our favorite "cleaning out the grease traps." You could always make trips to the PX for hamburgers and other items, except during those first two weeks, but I did put on weight, eating anything placed in front of me after that. For many years afterward, my kids would use me to see if things were eatable in the refrigerator as their gage.

Monterey and Carmel

If I can recall correctly, after the first four weeks, you could have visitors and get a weekend pass off the fort. My mom and dad brought Sylvia up for that weekend. They had drove, which is around a five- or six-hour drive, and when they came on base and found me, I was just like a small puppy with the owner coming home with my heart pounding its way out my chest. The next became even more out of control afterward, with breaking out with the hives and red spots from nervousness all over my body. First we went to look for something to eat and then to a motel along the beach going into town. My parents needed some rest from the long drive, and I needed Silvia. She made my body and mind travel far away from the army by just being there with her. Like escaping from a bad dream or touching a lost memory. It felt like it had been years. We took a shower, and then I put on some "civvies" clothes, followed with a walk on the sand along the surf with the cold wind coming off the waves in our faces. We talked and then kissed as the big red ball skunk into the waves while staying closer together, trying to keep each other warm, not wanting to part again.

Then back with my parents, we went to dinner on Cannery Row with Steinback whispering his stories with each build we had passed. I still had time to read the book at night before they came up between cleaning toilets. The next day we walked in Carmel and its shops with the sun out, but it was still cold in the wind. We sat on the beach with the clowns of clouds that covered the sun quickly. Knowing, I would be left empty for another four weeks until seeing my family again, I would cover my face with my own clown's smile. That afternoon, back on the base, there was sadness while I tried to keep a happy face with those clowns surrounding, laughing at us all. This moment within our good-byes was building even larger inside, but I felt a fresher mixed of emotions as they drove away. Then again, in the Mess Hall, I felt hating the army even more while I sat and ate that dried-up chicken, which had been heated and set in pans since lunch. Only a few hungry solders were around, being it was Sunday, so you could now take your time. Then to the PX for a few beers with some buddies, after walking from the mess hall, before returning back to that building with nothing except waxed floors, beds, footlockers, a few sleeping comrades, and a time to write a letter.

The next four weeks of training was more training on how to kill the enemy of the U.S. Government and the continual writing to Sylvia and my parents. I stated, "I'm alright and really enjoying myself" in letters while I hated every minute of it, but still, I laugh at this crazy army's world.

Now I became sick physically with a flu during the last few weeks, but still the mind was pushing the body through, not wanting to become one of those being recycled "Hold Over's." My parents and Sylvia came up at the end of that last week of Boot Camp for graduation. One step was completed, and I felt more with some joy, now being much warmer this time, over that last visiting day. We all felt the sunshine, looking forward to my reassignment for the next eight weeks of training as clerk, but still I stayed here at Fort Ord and then moved on into that final next step of the army administration schooling to follow.

Army Clerk

I was moved to a new company but again started out as "assistant squad leader." So here again, I started a new phase into a new world of all the things that I didn't do well, during all my former educational years. We started with typing and bookkeeping classes, and before it was over, I could type forty-five words per minute. However, this was just copying words. There were problems seeing the first letters in the words on some sentences, with my old problems writing letters in my youth and grammar usage. The using of English grammar and my spelling were the biggest problems, but the rest of the other things evolved were the things that could be thought a monkey to perform and seeing some performing this. But because of my legal contract with the army, they felt it was something that we must deal with before sending me on for more training. They made an appointment with an army psychoanalyst after many attempts on trying to talk me out of continuing on this "job training." He began testing me in all kinds of areas, and the test showed "an above normal IQ" in many areas; and now, he believed the problem was with the way my brain was seeing things because he found I was seeing things in reverse, and transposed. It was what he called "dyslexic." This was something that was now known and found to have effects on much large groups of people in the world through new studies. Being left-handed and this moved me into a part of a very elite distinguished group of people. Now, we knew what had been my problems in school with English, reading, grammar, and rebellion. He told me there were studies and many new ways of dealing with this problem now, and even more were now being developed. So once a week, I began attending a session with him on how to deal with this. The army agreed to keep my contract agreement and me going on with my training. Now being able to meet all the requirements and meeting the army's level of passing, I knew now why I was that Extra Extraordinary Pebble.

TWENTY-FOUR

The Next Move

Writing Sylvia and my parents about only my good news, I then received the worse news in return, putting my world upside down again. Sylvia's parents were moving back to Kansas City in a few months, and she was thinking of moving with them. She had lost her job now, and needing their support, she couldn't stay in California or with me, being in the army and without knowing where the army would be sending me. This too was a big problem for both of us to deal with now. Being a private E2 only, with an eighty-five dollar and eighty cents per monthly paycheck and maybe adding another fifty-five dollars and twenty cents for dependents, Sylvia would not make it, and I had to agree with her. Money was short, and I could only go home on pass every few weeks. So I flown down the week before she left; my parents picked me up at the Los Angeles airport, but before this, I had to take a bus to San Jose and then fly from there to Los Angeles for twenty-five dollar space available. It was cheap then, and it would take one hour from there to Los Angeles, but it took my dad over one hour in traveling from Monrovia by car to the airport. When I knew this, I called them just before taking off. And sometimes there was a line at the bus stop on base, but some other times, you could find a share ride with someone else on the fort on your luckiest of days.

Sylvia and I spent the time with less talking and more loving each moment we had together now. We rode around town in my parents "Little Red Corvette," sleeping together in my old single bed and in my old room before we left in our own new unknown directions or streams again. It was a long ride to the airport with my dad because Sylvia couldn't handle goodbyes, and there were only two seats in the Corvette. But now sleeping on the plane, then there I was riding back on the bus to the base from the airport, thinking about our destiny. Then on to the P X for a few beers with more of that dried up chicken in the mess hall again, with despair and anger building.

There was only a few weeks left of this training, and then it happened again. I guess we all were under the pressure. Anyway, the squad leaders had been to a meeting, and they came back just when we all were lining up to go somewhere else. So I, with the other assistant squad leader next to our line, broke it off too, and then we ran into the back of our lines. We ran into each other face-to-face when we turned the corner. Our books and papers with notes flew into the air followed by fists flying, as the papers hit the ground. He and I had problems before, as did some of the others in our squads. Then both lines were now fighting, with the sergeants running towards us; but then, they just stopped, just stood there and watched for a few minutes before they did something. Then one of them came running with a "fire bucket" full of water from a nearby building and another one followed him, and then they threw water on us all. We stopped, stood there all in shock, wet, and then we started laughing. There were only few bloody lips and noses with dirty shirts, pants covered with sand and mud. There was no punishment given out or any further problems with us all graduating as "clerks," looking forward to not being armed only with anything besides a typewriter for most of the army time left.

Photo at Racing Assoc. Award Dinner
Sylvia & her sister/dad &mom/Albert & wife/Uncle Ed Sr. & Aunt Lemoyne
Before she moved

Racing Trophy

Sylvia moved and wrote weekly; she was happy about finding work with her family. She now was in a great house with horses, her other great love, on few acres. She was very happy now, busy with it all, but our future was becoming thinner with each passing day. One letter said, "Let's see where time takes us, and we will always have the days of the past."

The next weekend, I went home again for the "Racing Awards" dinner with a new date because dad was up for an award. But just within a few weeks before that, while I was down working in the "pits" on my dad's car, the "trophy girl," whom was a striking young belly dancer at one of those clubs on the Sunset strip in Hollywood, came over; and I learned that her name was Gloria while we talked. Then she came back over after the end of the races again while we loaded up the car. So knowing that I would be back in a few weeks for that dinner, I asked her if she would go with me to the dinner. "You could meet some people whom could maybe of help to your career and mix with some of the big shots too of other tracks while having dinner with me." She said yes and gave me her telephone number. "I'll be waiting your Call."

When I got home, I made the call with her. She gave me directions to her house in Monterey Park. Upon finding it, I knocked on the door, and her family greeted me—that consisted of two brothers, with her mother. She was Syrian; her father had left their family many years ago and went back to the mother country. While waiting for her, the two brothers pointed to two large daggers on the wall and told me, "If any Syrian women lose her virginity before marriage, the man will lose his working parts too while she will lose her family." At that moment, I was not sure whether they were joking with me or not, but I took them at their word.

Awards Dinner with Gloria
Standing me and Mr. Hal Noble (Sponsor)
Cousin Juanita "Pee Wee" & George/mom & dad/Gloria & Mrs. Noble

We had a great time at the dinner and went out for a few other times after that. On one occasion, she was working that night, and we made it into a dinner date afterward. She wanted to perform her dance for me, so they placed me at a front table and gave me that personal VIP treatment—just for me. But later we had moved to the rear table in a darken section, ate especially middle-eastern foods like grape leaves with lamb, used only our fingers, sharing, staring, and laughing. We always kissed goodnight, but that's as far as I was brave enough to go.

Gloria

Later, she got a job in Las Vegas after I had been transferred to my next base. She wrote me two other letters, telling me how she was doing. I still responded, but we both knew there were always new orders coming further down in the future, moving us both on—that's the army's way, and it's the same for show business pebbles too. It was fun telling my army buddies about dating a belly dancer, but it was really just two pebbles dreaming and enjoying each other during the moments and being friends.

Fort Benjamin Harrison

On May 1962, I was assigned to Fort Benjamin Harrison, Indianapolis, Indiana. For what I thought it was going to be my last schooling period at the "Adjutant General's School for the U.S. Army," the next stop. Of course, it is a president's name, but it's funny also for me, the thought that I would be sent to a fort, with my middle name and my uncle's too, which was the financial center for all the service—it hit a funny bone. It had now been almost five months in this damn army. I looked forward to move on and finish this school-training thing. We traveled by train, took two and half days of doing nothing, except looking out the window and sleeping. I did get to see more of the country from a different view than before, but there were other guys, who were on their way to Germany because it was the beginning of the building of The Wall between the East and West. I had gotten off only with a few others guys while these guys just continued on their way into a land divided by guns and fences.

While the wall was being build, some time later, two of these guys that I have known from boot camp did write me, not having anyone else to write, telling me about there being shots back and forth with real bullets flying from both sides and people were dying, trying to cross over the wall. These people were trying to run for freedom, with some dying, only within a few feet, before reaching freedom, within sight of these young soldiers and not being able to help in any way, trying to stay "cool" following orders. This was a real war, not a "cold war," but it had begun with the Berlin division and airlift after that. It was now in the hands of a new president.

It was hard to believe as we had gotten off the train and walked next into a bar in the middle of Indianapolis, finding everyone in there buying us drinks, just because we were in our uniforms, treating us like someone special while we waited for our bus from the fort. This was not the way people treated us in Monterey or Carmel or California. There, we were treated below dirt and looked upon as the lowest form of humans. There was larger than life "war memorials" everywhere in the city, and you then had sensed we had traveled back into another world where these people remembered the sacrifice of soldiers, whom had waged in war for everyone's freedom. It gave you a different view of being in the service.

When we got to the Fort, we found it to be an open-gate fort, with large brick buildings, appearing to be more like a university or college. It was not only army, but there were also all the other services station here for "Adjutant General's school and payroll records." This is where all the pay records are processed, the "services bank." However, like being at a University, there were dances with girls from town coming here to cheer up us lonely soldiers. Whole families would come on to the fort during weekends to invite us soldier for Sunday dinner. I'd never seen "fireflies" before dancing around in the night to the music during our summer dances. These girls where fireflies, not moths, under the very watchful eyes of all, during these occasional social gatherings, and they couldn't be captured or touched.

This was June through July, very steamy hot and sticky with an occasionally spill of rain appearing out of nowhere. Many times, you would see the climate changed coming in very quickly with dark clouds on the horizon, and once while at a lake, I saw clouds turning into a twister. People jumped in their cars and hoped they went in the right direction away from it. My insides felt those same clouds, and I became more out of control with many twisters deep within me. I found myself, when off base, drinking a quart of the local Black Label beer and having pizza with my "buddies." One occasion, I found myself the next morning waking on top of my wall locker, next to my bunk bed, not knowing how in the world I had gotten there. The twister must have dropped me there overnight, and the letters from Sylvia were fewer and further away.

Being the army and coming from the West Coast, our uniforms were these heavy "dark-green dress," an issued wardrobe upon our arrival, but now here, we wore the khaki uniforms with so much starch you couldn't move without feeling like a robot or the "tin man" in Oz. We now had them "fitted," and that was considered to be sharp and looking good. However, it was very "hot and sticky" here; therefore, you would be wet in all the wrong places within minutes after taking a shower. We would line up outside praying for rain from the "rain gods," and then it would happen. We then looked like wet dogs or cats but felt so much more refreshed while our uniforms would turn into rankled washrags until our starch set again, and we "Californian have learned, home was still the best."

I am now doing very well in my classes; most of the training was in math, payroll records, and accounting. The results ended in the upper half of our class at graduation, with an ever-increasing ability to drink more beer as well. One of the last things in Indianapolis that I did was take a ride around the "brickyard" in a VW Bus, and then I got a card stating, "You have completed a lap around the Indianapolis Speedway." Cool, I got one of my dreams, even if it was in a VW, and much slower.

A New Direction

As I thought it would happen again, I was now ready for my new reassignment, but then the "devil" jumped out of the cake and laughed. Those test back at Fort Ord showed something else besides being "dyslexic." The army had now completed "its" contract with me by giving my requested job training and getting that extra one year of my life. However, that test had also shown me, being a loner, with the ability to think outside the box, smarter than that average bear and with a greater amount of abnormal dark sides present in mind for self-preservation, being an extraordinary pebble again. As the sergeant had put it during my interview for reassignment, he said, "Frankly, you have what is, and what most would be called in some strong ways, a criminal mind, figuring all the angles, and the army wants to put that to its use." He continued, "You go outside the box!" At first, I thought he was joking with me, but then he continued again, "We are sending you to A. S. A, the Army Security Agency School, for further training." I thought, "Now what?" How does having a criminal mind fit within army security? What the hell will I be doing?

TWENTY-FIVE

Fort Deven

On June 27, 1962, my new assignment was now to Fort Deven, which is next to the town of Ayr Massachusetts, off Interstate Highway 2 and 2A, not far from New Hampshire and close to Lowell and north of Worcester and west of Boston. We had our own small airport for small aircraft, and we also controlled all of the army reserves for the New England States, which include New York State, being the largest number. Most of the base was, however, ASA with the other parts support units, and this had been also a training camp during WWII. If I'm right, I recalled reading it has been now closed down now for many years and was made into a golf club and course. This is the area near Lexington but closer to Concord, where the Minute Men had fired the "first shot heard around the world," having the Minute Man Standing Statue, which is only sixteen to eighteen miles away from the fort. The very beginning of the America Army and its fight for freedom and independence was started here.

So my duffel bag was packed, and I went on to the train again for a few hours to Massachusetts nearing the end of summer. Then again to a bus but much smaller one this time, driving me on to another fort through many very small towns. The fort was small too, with maple trees and brick buildings again but a completely different feeling. I was placed in a building with smaller rooms, with fewer men during any other training, after reporting to my new CO. I was to report to duty and training the next day, after being escorted on a tour. The next day, he informed me, "You'll be trained in only specialty classes, having a mixture of the classes and not within any group, and only a few will be getting the same training as you, and there will be no longer in a squad or group but just a company." He didn't say it, but I knew he meant to say, "You will be with other misfits." Your training will be checking information, checking safe numbers, checking on personnel records for potential security clearances leaks at your next assignments. You will also work in the areas of your previous training, in "personnel clerk" assignment during and after completion of these classes. You'll understand more, as the training is completed. You're moving into a new MOS (Military Occupation Status) of number 520." But I found it was never changed from my number 716.30 in or on any of my records after completion of my classes. They told me it was because my full training and classes in that MOS weren't completed, but I knew again, the army was pulling something. I was told not to tell anyone unless there was clearance given. This was only to be known by a few, and a password was given to me for that person's clearance.

Army Buddies

The guys in my building were mixes of what you would call "odd balls." So I guess, that's why I was here too. Again, I found out much later in life two guys from my high school class had went through here as well, after talking with them at our thirty-five class reunion. I believed then and now, the army puts you were they need a body, where if it fits well and if not, well, it has to learn to fit. However, later in my life, I found other people in this field were special, with special talents and being "extraordinary."

Daniel

Daniel became my closest friend; he was gay with a funny little walk, after Bob, and with all the others seen during my college days and business dealings, no big deal. He also tried putting a move on me, but he found, he was wrong also. He was from Pittsburgh, Pa., being a court recorder before the army. He also had a new car, a 1962 Studabaker Lark four door, which we drove all over the New England states.

However just before being transferred overseas in my last days here, we drove it off base to a movie on a Sunday afternoon. It was raining when we went into the movies, but upon coming out at the end of the show, the streets and roads had turned to heavy ice, with the town roads now being salted, but once on the Fort, nothing had been done. It was Sunday, no need, as far as the army was concerned. On base, we dropped off two other guys at the hospital, which was down the road. We turned around attempting to drive back up the hill, with the car sliding into the snow-covered bank and ice about another half mile up the road. So Daniel said, "You get behind the steering wheel and try rocking the car back and forth between reverse and forward, and I'll get some ash out of the trunk to put under the back wheels." I had the door open while he was opening the trunk in the rear of the car. Then we both heard this large truck coming down the hill; it was a two and half-ton truck, known in the army as a "Duce and Half," and it was coming faster while the driver tried putting on his brakes, which was the natural thing to do, but the wrong thing to do on ice. The wheels were now stopped and sliding, but it was still going faster than before—he was totally out of control now. It was coming right at us. Daniel jumped over the side into the snow, but I, wearing my dress shoes with their leather soles, placing one foot on nothing but ice, took only a few seconds deciding which direction was the least likely for injury—should I stay in the car or jump for it. I jumped toward the driver's rear wheel and landed on my butt on that hard icy spot, just as the truck hit the other side of the car, just in front of the other rear tire; and it kept going, pushing both and ending up in the snow bank. I now became a hockey puck traveling on the ice, burning my hands and butt down about fifty or sixty feet on the road over ice and rocks along the way. The truck had hit the gas tank, spilling gas, and flames started under the rear part of the car, leaving the front end of the car and truck deep into the snow bank, where they had found their way to a stop. The driver jumped out, and both started looking for me in the car, but by then, I stood up yelling, "I'm down here!" My angel did another great job without much pain, but poor Daniel's car was totaled. I wrote a letter to his insurance company, explaining how it happened for his behalf. He got another car after my transfer, but I had used up another one of my cat's life and knew another bell had rung for a guardian angel's wings.

Before that, he had brought me to his parents' home for Thanksgiving, giving me chance to see Pittsburgh with its black Amish Carriages and horses traveling down the roads in their own time clocks and farms along the road. There they wore black and white clothes in their own past Quaker beliefs, but in the present world that hasn't changed for hundreds of years. It was something to see, with their painted barns' signs in trying to keep evil away while the rest of the world was rushing around stepping on each other. Then we traveled into the city with all three rivers mixing around those tall buildings and hills, knowing the roots of this country pebbles could still be seen. The rich and poor still shining gloriously surrounding this city with its roots of steel.

It was funny many years after our army days, Daniel moved to Hollywood, California, where we had lunch together, laughing about the past and setting in the bright sunlight, without those "steelworkers'" minds surroundings us or him anymore. "Gay Pebbles" where breaking out into the open visions of the rest of our world during the seventies, but there are still misunderstanding on igneous ignorance groups, using them to divide our country and blinding minds to the facts that most of these Gay Pebbles are extraordinary too. The "trap-door spiders" are attacking our children every day and should be seen in a more harming way in our world than "gays." If you believe in heaven, the Bible, then you know predators come from hell, not born.

Music Preacher

There was also this black sergeant. He was older, and again I have forgotten, which area he was from, but I believed it was New Orleans. He played alto saxophone and had played in traveling bands but now started his own religious church, among his army duties. He was smoother than silk, talked in a simple meaner, with good looks, and finding many women giving him money and their cars while I believed his religion was for his only betterment and own worldly goods. However, he was cool sharing his wine, music, and thinking with us nonbelievers within his own room because he knew how to obtain that too, but I never knew what his job was within the army. It wasn't preaching, but on Sundays, he did preach to his followers off base somewhere, whether it is being a women's bedroom or some form of church.

One night, it was very hot and sticky to sleep in those old buildings that didn't cool down; one of the guys moved his bed outside our room, trying to catch some cooler breeze, sleeping in the end laundry room. But in the middle of the night, someone jumped on him, pinned him down, and then pulled off his shorts and tried to sexually assault him. Breaking free, he came running into our room yelling, "Someone tried raping me," screaming like crazy after fighting the predator off. The preacher came rushing in taking control of situation; he tried to calm down the hysterical young man with some of us nonbelievers seeing his shorts ripped. The preacher took him to his room, took notes, and wrote down what the kid could recall while the rest of us went back to bed, without sleep. They reported it in the morning, but no one ever found out, what exactly happen, or who did this. This guy had trouble sleeping from then on, and then he was moved to another quarters. No one ever slept out of that room again; the preacher was more than a tax write-off exemption after that. He showed compassion and showed that words can clam down man's hysterical minds.

The Minute Men

Because it was the end of summer, there were many army reserve units from the New England states doing their summer training here. While many others were training in Rochester, New York, during the winter, the coldest part of the year and condition to see how tough they are too. So they would become a part of our buildings for two or three weeks too. Among them, there were two Italian guys and two Jewish guys that I became friends with during this time.

One of the Italians was named Sonny, he was from Brooklyn, very stocky in build with the greatest smile that was at all time coming from within him. He was a fireman in New York City with us, staying in touch after my army years. He moved to Long Island, with me kidding him about those tall New York buildings burning and maybe falling on him. Today, it's not funny, I don't know if he was on the job during 9/11, but I hope he was retired by then. I did stop spending some time with him before going home after my overseas duty days and more about that later.

The other Italian, let's say, looked like that stereotypic "wise guy" with "shark skin" suits, not much to say, with his Brooklyn accent. He had told me, "I'm an insurance man on the docks for a living." Sonny would laugh. During one of their training days on the shooting range, he showed us one of his targets from shooting handheld submachine gun known as a "grease gun," all well within the center rings, and both would pay with cash from a roll of bills, but that's an Italian way in the city.

With this same group were also two Jewish guys; one was like Sonny, just an all-around great guy with a good head on his shoulders. However, the other was always on "stage," making jokes with that almost Lenny Bruce humor and view of things. He was thin with glasses and shorter than most, which gave him that "I must make myself important, looking for that center of attention and trying to find that "bigger" than I am spot in the group," but even he was great to have around because he was funny at times. There were the outings for pizza, playing a few games of that funny "English or New England Bowling," with its funny little balls and pins and drinking Black Label beer while looking for girls and any kind of action, but mostly with a lot of guy talk for fun. Then we stopped at those all-night dinners for coffee or something to eat before hitting the rack in the early AM's on Sundays or during the week with heavy heads rising. This was like playing soldier during the day and hanging out with the boy's club at night. Not all these young minutemen could know what was possible over the horizon and the rest of the world. It would have been a shot heard around and changing the world again for us all, but it didn't happen.

The Cuba Storm

They returned to their normal lives in October 1962, not knowing how close the world came to the brink of atomic warfare. We, however at Fort Deven, were put on alert; and setting the wheels in motion, for recalling together, these minutemen's records were to be readied for their deployment to Florida first. It was like a forest fire, starting very small and then becoming an almost uncontrollable blaze while everyone was in action and hoping it was only a drill with lots of roomers. President Kennedy started on the first and then on until the fifteen of October, playing "poker" with Khrushchev for control of our part of the world, just sixty miles off the cost of the USA.

Only a few of us at the time knew how close we came to this position and of a possibility with full use of all their and "our all-out" world-ending force. The newspapers and reporting agencies at the end of it reported the final pulling back by the Russians on November 1. It could have been the beginning of war and the end of mankind. Later came the Bay of Pigs with the continuing problems of Castro and another Cuba storm, with his continuous hold of power over his people because of so much support by the Russia our mistakes and the agreement reach with Kennedy afterward. Robert Kennedy continued the fight, but only Castro would live on into our today's world, with the two brothers dying at the hands of an assassin.

Boston

Meanwhile, it was enjoyable being there mostly in the fall season of New England with the changing of the leaves and seasons and with our many trips on the weekends into towns like Lowell with its French and Italian pockets; and there was the Boston commands, wherein you could always see sailors on the lower side while you walked to Beacon street with the old brick buildings and read graveyard stones full of history. Seeing the North Church gave you so much history while walking the "freedom walk" with John Hancock's shop and others and seeing that part of the America's beginning. It was also a great fun riding the MTA while singing the Kingston Trio's song—"He'll never return, No, he'll never return from beneath the streets of Boston"—around the Boston area. I'd never returned to that time and place again. You could travel on those "roundabouts," with cars coming to you in all directions into a small circle, like racecars. Then they would disappear into their own direction, and finding their own way out was great training for what was to come. Then a more peaceful feeling came from watching couples on the Charles River lying in the grass while bringing me into Cambridge and searching for youthful people.

Those were the surroundings I missed; they reminded me that there was still youth burning within this artist's soul and thinking of Sylvia. Watching young girls find their way into becoming women was only a part of my search too. Going to this small found Movie Theater near the college that shows Ingram Bergman's or Italian movies with English subtitles relit my artist memories too and feed my soul again. Near it, located downstairs, was a small bar, where I could order a Manhattan in a small jar and filled my glass twice, which was my practice before or after the movies; and it was easy finding deep talks with students or sometimes drawing them in my mind or on paper napkins, knowing someday my army world would end while I continue my inner search for some reasons of my trials and laughing at it all.

The Studebaker

The local newspaper had a 1953 two-door Studebaker Champion for sale like Lloyd's. It had a six cylinder and three-speed stick shift painted in that factory "pea green" with a cream white top. After I saw it, I bought it for a reasonable price. However within a few weeks, I'd blown the engine by driving on the "turnpike" too hard for that little "six." So I checked in the local junkyard and found this new totaled, wrecked 1962 Pontiac Catalina with its 421 CI engine, with a four-barrel crab. Rated at 390 HP and having a four-speed transmission, my inter temptation took over for "a sleeper."

I bought all the running gear for three hundred and fifty dollars. Next, I found, by ordering through Honest Charlie's catalog, all the motor and trans mounts I could get in order to just bolt it all in, without much trouble. Working in the Auto Pool area, with some guys cutting the driveline, bigger radiator, and some others interested in helping, it was back together within one month. It already had 4-11 gears in the rear end with Posi-Tracking that was made by GM matching yoke, but it needed traction bars, and it would "jump and fly like a Cheetah," down those small town roads.

After I got everything worked out, and while I drove through town one day, this new 1962 Corvette drove up beside me at the last stop signal in town. With it came a big grinning face, which looked at my little Studebaker. Because you could hear my pipes that weren't stock, it also had Smithy's mufflers ordered from Honest Charlie's stopping under the car. He raced his engine a couple on times, and I followed with short revving while the signal was still red. Then the light changed to green, and he put his foot into the floor, and his tires responded.

He was now halfway across the intersection while I eased my foot down with some attempt on controlling my tires. After getting to the other side, my tires were still making howling sound but getting traction, and my Cheetah came next to him, coming closer for the kill. Quickly I shifted into second gear, and the Stude's front end jumped with its smooth flat hood raising and carburetor sucking all the air they could pull in. Now finding another gear, I was now about ten or more feet ahead of him. The speedometer showed the needle hitting 110 mph because that's as far as it could go while it bounced wildly, but he was still trying. I found that final fourth gear with the tires sounding off again and now found him back in my rearview mirrors. I let off the gas until he came up beside me shaking his head in disbelieve. He yelled, "What do have in there?" I just smiled back, pulling away again with the Cheetah smiling too.

This was in November, and by the beginning of January came another new military order, another new duties station. So the Stude was up for sale in the newspaper again, notice posted on post. That following weekend, still not knowing how he knew, the Corvette came looking for me again but bought it and told me, "No one in town is going to have a faster car than me." He paid eight hundred dollars, and maybe he got satisfaction, but I had my fun days in the New England in the fall months showing them what Southern California car builders did. "It's all about hidden speed. It's Hot Rods!" Making sleepers with nothing showing on its outside appearance, only showing that killer Cheetah unordinary.

New Plan

However, before these orders came, I found another soldier in California at Fort Macarthur—with the same MOS and amount of time in the service from the East Coast (New York)—wanting to come home too. I had put in for my Christmas leave of two weeks during December but was not approved until my going home in January. My plan was to contact him then, see if we could work out trading duties stations while put in requests that would still need approval from our company commanders. I also received my promotion to private first class on Sept. 18, 1962, with the cards already being dealt.

TWENTY-SIX

The Long Trip Home

They gave me fourteen days leave after receiving my new orders for overseas duty in January 1963. Trying to save money, my plan was to take any military space available flights home. I started with a flight from Fort Deven in our two-seated mail plane to Andrews AFB in Washington DC in Maryland while I knew there were more flights out of here than in any other on the East Cost. Next came one going west to SAC Command at Wright Patterson in Dayton Ohio the same day on jet. This was the land of the B-52 Bombers, hopefully many other flights, but the weather turned bad with very few aircraft coming or going. So slept there in the airport for a day, waiting the weather to improve. Then the next day came a chance on a DC-3, an old World War II two-engine cargo plane flying on to its Reservist Station in Texas. As long, as it's going west, I would sign on. I walked out to the plane when the crew told me, "You'll have to sit in the cargo seat area on the side until we reach our flying altitude around three thousand feet, and then you can come forward into our cabinet with the heat." Well, there was snow on the ground when we took off, and I was flying just dressed in my "army greens" with no overcoat, carrying a small traveling bag because you can't fly space available without wearing your uniform. Hell, I was going home to California with its sunshine, but I did bring my gloves and wore those rayon dress socks and shoes. My feet felt the coldest, with my teeth next on my list at this point, and one of the crew gave me a blanket as the engines warmed up for takeoff. It was quick taking off, but a very long cold, for five or ten minutes, got to our flying altitude with a lot of bumps around once we were up there—it's because of the weather. So I stayed belted down for another ten minutes before one of them came back and got me out that flying rear refrigerator. When I was already with them, it was warm, and I was given a hot cup of coffee. These guys were just Air Force Reservist who got their flying time requirements before they went back to their families and civvies jobs and Air Force pay.

Kansas City

We were over Missouri a few miles away from Kansas City when there was trouble with one of the only two engines, which started to lose oil pressure. One went back and looked out through a small side window; he yelled there was oil coming down the side of it but in very small amounts, as they shut it down. They said, "We'll have to sit down in Kansas City." So I went back to my seat in the cargo area again. It still wasn't colder than Massachusetts where it had been a few days twenty degrees below. Now I thought, these planes made it through the worst of conditions, more than any other planes during the past wars, just please do it again. I closed my eyes and covered my cold ears while I waited for our plane to touch down, but our landing was without any kind of fanfare or big things or a lot of people or seeing any ready fire trucks as we touched down; it made me feel better. After getting off strip, they said, it would be a few hours before they would know what the plane's status was. So I went into the pilot's part of the hanger while they talked and looked at the airplane with a reservist mechanic. Then, still talking, they pulled it into the hanger taking the cover off the engine. I began thinking—Kansas City, Sylvia here.

Then I looked for a telephone book and started to look for Sylvia's parents' telephone number and found it. So now with bigger butterflies I placed the call, and then Sylvia answered. I unable to say anything for a moment, and then I said, "It's me." She asked, "Where are you?" I told her, "I'm in Kansas City at the airport." With that, she started talking so fast I couldn't keep her words clearly in my mind or gets a word in with any reasonable response. "I'll be there in twenty minutes to pick you up, which hanger?" Now, many things went through my mind. My heart was beating at an uncontrollable rate after I hung up. I then turned to one of the reservist and said, "I won't be going any further with you, sir, but thanks a lot." They laughed, and I got a feeling that they thought my response made them think, he's "chickening out" because of what happened. I did not tell them they had uncannily delivered me into some dream. I began to think maybe I'm dead, without knowing it yet.

It was about half an hour later when she showed up with her sister; they had trouble getting into this part of the airport. She got out and ran toward me, placed her arms around me, kissed me, and cried at the same time. It was her dream too, and now she couldn't speak, but her sister said, "Hi." Sylvia wouldn't let go of me. She then asked, "How long do you have?" I replied with the number of days total but added it also would depend on my next available departure flight from here to home. She said, "Okay, let's go to our house. You can stay the night, and find you another flight home early tomorrow." By that time, we got to her parents house, everybody was home and everybody was happy seeing me again. They told me how good I looked now. The baby was now walking around, with Sylvia's sister, and her mother started dinner. Sylvia and I went for a walk around their yard with its barn and horses, and it was easy to see why she loved it here. We talked and kissed while only looking into each other's eyes, looking deeper into each other's souls. It was again unbelievable to be this close again. We slept together, but because I had little sleep for two days, my mind could only want to sleep. However, as hard as I tried, my mind wouldn't let go long enough of this moment to give me any sleep yet. We both told each other how much we missed each other and loved each other still. The next day, I found a flight to Kelly AFB in San Antonio, Texas, on another transport jet, after taking a shower and having something to eat before leaving. She dropped me off, and I got there just as they were fueling up the plane, and I had to get on board without much else than another kiss with the words I love you coming from her lips, then walked away.

Texas to Home

It took another day until I found another flight from San Antonio; this was going to Kirtland AFB in Albuquerque, New Mexico, and by the time we got there, it was snowing again. They hadn't had snow there in years. So they had to use farm or road equipment to clean the runways of the snow. The airplane landed with a sliding funny motion feeling under my seat, the same as if I was driving in icy conditions in New York Turn Pike once. Next came my last flight to Nellis AFB outside Las Vegas, Nevada, but once I got there, I put out my thumb, knowing how close I was to home now.

Along came a guy whom had been driving for days cross country, and this guy started driving at eighty to ninety mile per hour the whole way past the city. His driving was worst than the airplane rides, but I was almost home and did not care. It was hot so no more need of gloves or coats, just a much-needed shower. We got into West Covina; he dropped me off at a San Bernardino freeway exit in Covina where I called home. My mother came finding me at some restaurant, where I used the telephone booth. It had taken longer by airplane than when I had "hitched hiked" in 1958. The winter and my being able to see my Sylvia made it worth it all.

Home

It took a few days catching up on my sleep and eating those home-cooked meals. Dad and I went around town to see friends, and he let me drive the "little Red Corvette" a few more good times. We talked with some of the neighbors and the cop's family across the street. I found out the FBI had been talking with my neighbors, asking about my youth and friends a few months back, checking my background. I laughed because this neighbor was the one whom had put me in jail when I was a kid. We had an "after Christmas" dinner at my Aunt Lemoin's and got to see most of the family again. My cousin, who had bought my olds, had to give me a last ride in it too. Within one moment of talking with my parents, I told them about Sylvia, and they told me they would write her. A few months later, she moved back to California and lived with them for a while. Also, I did get a hold of that guy at Fort MacArthur. He was ready to give it a try, but it was too late when I had gotten back to Deven. Again it wasn't to be in the cards for either of us.

TWENTY-SEVEN

Leaving Home Behind

At Ft. Deven, again the joker had jumped up playing his hand while gone on leave. My plan of returning to California for a duty station with Sylvia was not to be. I was informed that my next reassignment would be overseas, and if I turned this down, maybe the next one would be to Korea. Later, after I talked with some other sergeants, that also had been decreed that as being good duty too, I found that mine would be better. I was going to Paris, France, at SHAPE Headquarters. That's Supreme Headquarters Allied Powers Europe, the Command center for all NATO, stationed outside Paris, near Versailles.

The special orders were cut on January 16, 1963, with my travel orders set. So this time, I was flying by paid airlines from home to Ft. Devens; and on February 25, after my fourteen days of leave, I returned directly to McGuire AFB in New Jersey on February 26. It was a chartered flight from there with our arrival on the 27 at the Paris Airport. We were bused to downtown Paris from the international airport. While we were waiting for another bus from SHAPE, by the Arc de Triumph, another new dream pathway and passage was unfolding for this extraordinary pebble into the middle of a French Stream.

The French Stream

This was now a new French stream in more than one way. Together with this long air trip and many cups of coffee, I looked for a bathroom once we got in town, and I saw a sign, down some steps off the street. When I saw a man's sign on the door, I made a dash to the urinal. Just as I was relieving myself, there came old woman in my view, right next to me, out of nowhere. She was very close, and I thought, "Is she checking me out, or what?" Then, she started wiping down everything next to me with an old rage. When she finished, I got the hell out of there, but later I learned she was just only "cleaning," looking for a tip from me for her small efforts. Later after being in France for a while, I looked around town and saw these small water poles with small screen surrounding the outside cover at about shoulder to knee high on the streets wherein you could pee in the open air as long you did it with your back to all. Many times traveling, you would see people from both sexes, by the side of the road, with their backs to you, taking care of their needs. In all the dance clubs, there was also the "everybody" restrooms. Both boys and girls in one room with separate stalls, no mindsets like us "American hanging on to our old little mind of thinking," as we have then and now. No one thought about it, like some beaches with clothes, IT'S European.

SHAPE

We got to SHAPE in about an hour as we drove along a river through small towns outside of Paris. We came upon some larger bunches of trees and then up a small hill until we saw the circle of flags with the NATO flag in the center that was unexpected while we're at the top. We drove up to the front doors of the main buildings and then crossed on some large fields and find our quarters after we got off the bus. We had two to three guys in each room with our own bathrooms—this being a very small unit of mixed personnel, mostly army and some air force and navy together. Females had their own quarters. Our supreme commander was a five-star U.S. Army General named, L. L. Lemnitzer, commander of all the fourteen countries forces under NATO at that time, and he had small units of personnel from each, except for noncommissioned officers from Turkey. Something about, "If they pulled out their knives, they would have to draw blood."

Many Chinese and North Koreans had found this lesson true while they were next to their fellow solder whom was now just leaning over in a foxhole next to them. When they checked if he was asleep, they found that their buddy wasn't ever going to wake up again because his throat was cut in the silence of the night. The Turk's were well known for doing this during the Korean War, and they were the most feared and scary of all the UN troops during that conflict.

226

The U.S. personnel had their own mess hall, but there was also a main cafeteria, where all the countries would eat and drink. The officers had their clubs too including the noncommissioned officers, starting at sergeant and above with their own club as well. But after the day' work, most of the Americans' lowers noncommissioned would drink their beer from cans, building their primitive pyramids on their table with the empties. The Brit's would sing songs at their tables while the Germans would drink and sing their songs, which became louder than all others.

Then sometimes, from somewhere, someone would throw a can or bottle, knocking down the Yank's towering efforts and bringing out "all hell" in the hall. The "frogs" drinking their wine would run the other way or hide under tables if there was no place for retreat while the Germans would stand back "cheering on" the sports. They, the Germans, would have liked to join in, but if they were found to be a part of any kind of trouble, they would be "shipped out" the next day. No one ever got hurt or got really mad; they just liked letting out their steamed up emotions and energy. You would also find the Canadians or others jumping in with the losing side. Most of the time, it would be blamed on some hidden shadow and ghost hiding from the Great Wars of the past. I would just say it was just man's instincts to prove his manhood.

TO: SP4 C. B. Allen:

As a memento of your contribution toward winning the SACEUR Trophy in 1964.

L. L. LEMNITZER
General, U.S. Army
Supreme Allied Commander Europe

So the officers oriented a sports trophy competition called the "saceur," among all the countries, which ran throughout most of the summer months with the United States always winning it. In 1964, being on this team and now being in the best shape of my life, I competed on the swim team while I tried playing on our soccer team too. Later in my married life after the service, my children would receive some things that I had learned from my poor experience, and I passed them on while I coached them now in this sport to prepare them for a higher-level experience. Most Americans, or youth before coming here, had never played this in our schools because the Americans played something called "kickball" only, and everyone else had played it since they learned to walk. So they just played with us, but we did have other advantage in speed, size, and within every other sports. Because you see, General Lemnitzer loved "our American football," and we had some fourteen or more "sheet counters" on our personnel rolls during that fall season. His football team would travel to all the other U.S. military bases, and this was at a very higher level, like that of a collegiate to semipro in standard and events with the players of this game available to him. They would fly the whole team on his personal aircraft at times, and they were among some of the best players found throughout all of Europe, including officers among them too. The quarterback was from the Air Force Academy with others from navy or army academies or colleges recruits. The first thing I was asked upon arrival was, "What sports do you perform?" S-Supreme, H-Headquarters, A-Allied, P-Powers, E-Europe (SHAPE) was the word with us winning it all for the general or else. This war could not be lost; however, there were some who played for higher sakes. This was still the "sixties," and here, the race didn't mean as much as it did back home or at other camps with field leveler.

Being Black

This was a time with many issues now in play for our nation and us. However race and civil rights were at the top and now were at the forefront under current stream levels. We all were becoming more awakened to the race problems over here and in America. There was a civil rights war going on, and it had been growing larger during these years. You see, because of all those black people who were prominent in sports, entertainment, and education, there was more earthshaking and awaking because most blacks were gaining a better level of understanding through and from the whites throughout most of the nation and the world. It was a time for more equality, civil rights were on the news, and the nation had to start making changes. It was a time when Martin Luther King Jr. was becoming a force to making these changes, with the help of a growing amount of white leaders too. Whites and blacks were pushing for more changes in the Old South, mainly at first because of its still Old Crow ways; and there were more black football and baseball players, like in our "Sheet Counters," among us, changing views too. The black issue was in play and had started for most of us during this time, before even the Ike and Kennedy years. It was a time for blacks hopes and dreams to be raised by Dr. King, while many others joined the marching now, and while he brought the greatest pushing force in this nation for these dreams, they were in the foremost vantage point of the rest of our people too. The Kennedy's were also drawn into the picture, whether they wanted or not. Pebbles were becoming stars, by the thousands, in marching for a new future, because Blacks had dreams too, far too long suppressed.

The company clerk was a great guy from San Jose, California, who'd played for San Jose State, and was also black. He ran a smooth company, knowing how it was done, and who to get things done with, besides being a great football player. Since both of us were from California, it started us on some form of our common ground, and yet neither of us knew what it was really like to be "Black" in places like on the East Coast, or what life was like in the South or in the ghetto of South Central LA. The marches were going on while the fight between both sides was becoming stronger in our nation in those days. It didn't hit us, like most around us, until the march to Washington, DC, by thousands, with Dr. King's Lincoln Memorial speech, "I have a dream" on August 28, 1963, bringing the nation and world closer to his vision, which we all could see like a rising tide.

Eight-Ball

One day, going into the recreation hall while some black guys were playing pool (Eight-Ball), I started talking with a few of them, but then one addressed me with a real affected attitude and a posturing glare because I was white. Now, judging most people by the way they treated me, I couldn't understand his problem since we had never met or spoken before. The rest didn't say a word to me until later. Talking later with my fellow Californian, he told me this guy was from "Phili" (Philadelphia, Pennsylvania) and there was no "mixing" of races there in his neighborhood. He and others had overwhelming reasons for hating whites and used their attitudes and postures to gain respect in their neighborhoods, either black or white. Funny, that hasn't changed, but now white youths are trying to become "blacks" like them. Anyway, I later gained his respect, and we came to a point of understanding because of the way I treated him and our relationship on the playing field and in sports.

One of the other football players was of mixed race, his mother being Russian and his father being black. Besides him being built and looking like Adonis, he also played for our general's team, and being very good, he also played rugby for a French pro team, earning an amount of francs larger than what most got, on the side, and driving a new XKE Jaguar, which showed he had a lot of class. He was also someone to know because he worked within the Special Service Unit too, with so many inside and outside connections. So one day he gave out the word that a French movie studio needed some movie extras. "American-looking guys," needing some extra francs, see him, so I became interested.

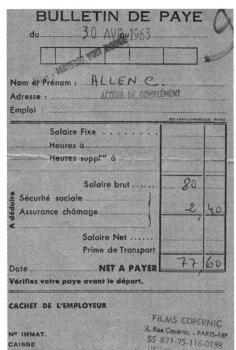

Another Movie Extra

"You'll have to take leave, and get paid by the day," so signing up, I took two days of my leave at one of France's largest studios, called Films Copernic, and the movie was about a famous French detective called Mairgret. The movie was called in French *Mairgret Voit Rouge*, or English *Marigret Sees Red*. The story was about some "American Mafia" hit man team trying to kill a government witness while trying to take over a French gang's operation. So they needed some American-looking extras in their film to make it into an "American Paris Bar." I got used in two different scenes: One while in the bar's background, where the lights go out with shooting and then the lights come back on with two French bosses dead while Marigret was there during it all. The other, I was faking bowling in another bar, with me coming at the camera or someone getting another few seconds of full screen, for a sum of 77.60 new francs per day, that being around four francs per one dollar during that time, so that's $38.88 dollars per day. Seeing the movie later, I was up here for maybe three or more seconds per scene, and having a great time with free lunch and extra pay on leave. However, this was April 1963, and there was also another gentleman with a cane, a walking stick that had a silver wolf's head on it, and he was also on the movie set and motioned me over after watching me for a while. He asked, "Do you ride a horse?" I replied, "Yes, I was born in Cheyenne, Wyoming, and did some riding on my uncle's ranch, plus working with horses at Santa Anita and Del Mar horse race tracks in California for one summer." Then he asked about guns, and I told him again, "Wee"(yes); but he wasn't French, he was Italian. He then explained he was making a Western movie in Spain starting in a few months, and there would be a young American actor star in it. He would like me to come down, do some work with him, and be in his movie, but after checking back at our command, I couldn't get the time off, not enough leave time available—it would have taken a few weeks or more. So I called his office, telling them, "Thanks, but no thanks. Just can't get the time off." The army came first, and there went another missed opportunity. You see this was his first "spaghetti western" movie called *Fistful of Dollars.*

Unexpected Death

There was another U.S. military base only a few miles away called Camp des Loges, which had only U.S. Army personnel and some citizens. It was mostly a transportation and supplies unit, but had an EM (Enlisted Men's) Club for us lower-level soldiers, with live performance music on almost every Saturday's nights. However, it was a mixer of "white" rednecks, good ole boys, and Black working-class guys, whereas at SHAPE, it was mostly officers with only a small amount of enlisted men and women, with higher education skills or special "jock jobs. After meeting a young French girl working as a clerk during our working hours over there, I decided one Saturday night, with two other guys, "Let's go check it out," looking for some fun, dancing, drinks, and girls. We heard there were always some military women with a mixer of some French and Spanish girls around too. The Spanish girls really liked our "Black soldiers" because of a lot of reasons, which don't needed to be covered, but because of this, there would be problems, and on this night it got way out of hand. While standing up next to the bar, drinking a beer, fighting erupted at the other end.

The bartender rushed to pick up the phone for the Military Police (MPs) because of some previous problems, and within a flash, two of them came in through the back door. They found they were right now in the middle of the fighting. Just then, one of the Black fighters broke his beer bottle on a white guy's head and came at one of the MPs with his bottle. The MP reacted by pulling his Colt .45, yelling, "Halt right there!" pointing his finger with his left hand, with his gun in his right hand pointed at the Black's forehead, but with so much yelling going on at the same time, only I was close enough to hear him. The black guy didn't stop. Next came a flash, with a loud POW, with his weapon firing one shot. The bullet hit the black guy between the eyes; he stopped and at the same time went flying backwards, with the back of his head and a mix of brains covering the wall behind him, as he flew with his feet in front of him, and stopped with his head against the wall, not moving again. There was no sound now, nothing said, and time had stopped. It was like a stop motion camera had taken a picture of the whole thing in my mind, and my first thought was "Get out of here now," and so I turned, making my exit, slipping out the same back door the MPs had came in, exiting into the dark. Within seconds, the other two guys appeared, chasing after me toward our car while looking over our shoulders. We never went back there for anything again. Afterward, there came many troubling nights for me, maybe because of the LA Park with this replaying, but from many attempts to keep this out of my head too. There were repeating bad dreams for many nights, with me waking and thinking I heard the shot again. Death was easily found in France, like in the South.

Later in the summer of 1963, I took a vacation to Cannes and Nice, in southern France, for just a week in the sun. My "Black Irish" skin was darkened to a dark brown, close to black, except for my blue eyes, while traveling with a guy called Montana, who was whiter than whitewashed skin. I spent the whole week in shorts or a bathing suit until our returning to our company clerk's watch and our signing back in with him, saying, "Man, you're going to have to ride in the back of the bus with us if you go back statewide like that, and those blue eyes won't move you up front!" Sports help to level the playing field for most of us, but for the blacks the healing sometimes never comes. It's still burned deep into us all, whatever our skin color is. I, too, have lived in and come from "the back of the bus."

TWENTY-EIGHT

France in the Nineteen Sixties

Charles de Gaulle, an ex-general of WWII, who was disliked by America and the English military alike during and after the war, now governed France. However, he disliked us even more. The Kennedy's did improve our relationship with him and our standing with France, during their short time in the White House, but he and the French were always trying to bring back the glory of France. The daily newspapers and cartoons were always about the days when France controlled most of Europe during the Napoleonic Wars. After my leaving France in 1965, he also kicked out The NATO Headquarters (SHAPE), and it was moved to Brussels, Belgium. France still had some colonies in the world and was still fighting wars while I was stationed there, and one war was with Algeria in North Africa. They had ruled them for almost one hundred and fifty years. The Algerians continued fighting for their independence with the use of terrorism and demoralization in both France and Algeria, during those beginning years of my duty in France. I believe Algeria did get its independence in June or July of 1963, shortly after I had arrived, but it was enough time for me to see the effects of terrorism on both countries and their peoples. Also during this time, off in the shadows, was being waged another war that they couldn't win, and that became true of any wars they fought on their own after the Napoleonic Wars. They also lost the Vietnam War, before our leaders decided we should get engaged in it too and win, but who could have known that was to become our first and biggest lost war too. Now there's the Middle East, and we didn't listen to them either about their lessons.

The Arc de Triomphe

The Arc de Triomphe was built to celebrate France's returning victories during the Napoleonic Wars. But upon one of my first visits to Paris, the Algerians were demonstrating with a parade, marching down the Champs-Élysées from the Arc de Triomphe. We American servicemen were told to stay away from that area on that weekend. There were thousands of people, with the police trying everything possible to break up the demonstrators. Then they started arresting everyone, putting them in police vans with red and blue lights flashing with their sirens screaming loud high beeps with lower beeps everywhere. I was trying to make my way to the Left Bank, really trying to get away from this massive crowd but then learning this was where the "big jail" was located. Now, going the wrong way, I saw they weren't putting them into jail, saw the police pushing women and children with men or anyone else into the nearby Seine River. These were Arab people dressed in robes that consisted of heavy clothes, and not many, I believed, could swim. It was just like throwing trash in the river. They didn't need them going through any courts or jails. Besides, there were too many of them, and they didn't have any rights. It was like seeing the Black marchers in the South. This was Judgment and Justice all in one act for the French. That's when I learned they weren't people anymore, just looked upon as a lower form, lower than dogs in the streets. While I had known there had been many French killed by the Algerians during those years before and after, I had also known this had not been covered much by America's vision or press. However, for many reasons, the Algerians and Vietnamese did get their independence after fighting for many years while the French gave up their control because they couldn't win.

On July fourteenth, like our fourth, is France's Independence Day, called Bastille Day, and this is the day the people stormed the Bastille jail, bring about its destruction, and the day commemorated as the beginning of the French Revolution. There was a large parade, composed of all military, parading in front of their president, Charles de Gaulle, with giant flag hanging from the Arc de Triomphe and along the Champs-Élysées. However, the police on the travel routes covered it with men and their machine guns because of the many attempts on de Gaulle's life.

There was also an Elite Special Police Force, these guys dressed in black leather helmets, jackets, pants, and boots, mostly riding motorcycles, which they had to learn to lay-down at high speeds. They were much crazier then my own twelve-year-old experience and trained professionals with protection among other things, just to prove their selves with enough skills and courage to make it in this group of the elite. They all had heavy weapons, and when de Gaulle went anywhere, they blocked the freeways, streets, and bridges for miles. This police force would be seen coming and going to our headquarters for many reasons, giving you an idea why, during my time, with the rest of the US forces in France, we would on occasion sleep with our M-14 rifles by our beds, and security was very high. If the Algerians could have gotten them, everyone would've paid the price of hell, I was learning about France's homeland security policy then.

"Pig Alley" (Pigalle)

In the hills of Paris, overlooking the city is the area well known around the whole world as Pig Alley, where the Moulin Rouge and other places of entertainments exist. Men have come to this area for many centuries and many reasons, but most of all, this is where the women sell their bodies from doorways and in clubs. This is the red-light

234

district, with the discarded and disaffirmed. Therefore, there are also many gendarmes' police walking or standing around. They are known to have business connections with the ladies of the night just like in the movie, *Irma la Deuce* with Shirley Maclaine and Jack Lemmon in 1963.

The GI soldiers couldn't afford the clubs or ladies for the most part, but it was great fun, watching the gentlemen working out the prices, and make disappearances for their short, or long, rides. Also the gendarmes would walk down the alleys or streets with the ladies, disappearing or talking over their nightly business. You see, most of the ladies had to have their medical cards, showing their medical condition for doing their line of work, but many didn't too, and they could or would be arrested unless they paid their fee to the police. The earlier GIs of World War I or II brought home postcards, but some had many things you didn't want to bring home after seeing Paris. GIs came here to explore things not seen on bus tours, or at home, and there was a place for us to hang out too.

There was one bar, called An American Bar, where the GIs did hang out, and whose clientele was made up of 75-80 percent GIs most of the time. They made the best American chili, and you could get it at any time of the day or night. So one night, while walking from this American bar, its name was something "Blue?" But I can't recall its full name now, but it had this big night scenes with little lights showing the Brooklyn Bridge. Anyway. It was around two or three in the AM near The Moulin Rouge, down one the many side streets, and I wasn't afraid to walk anywhere, being a young U.S. "killer" soldier, and sometimes walking all night with another soldier without having a place to sleep while waiting to get transportation back to SHAPE on one of our buses or by some other means. Back to that night walking on this dark street, I was looking to find a metro line, (the subway line) back to downtown for our bus stop. Then, from a dark opening, on the darkened part of the street, without much of any streetlights or any lighting in this part of the block, I heard a door behind me open, just after I had walked by. My instinct told me to stop and turn around to check it out, but just as I was turning, a man ran into me, almost knocking me down because of the uneven sidewalk. He only got another ten or twelve feet in front of me when across the street ahead of both us came a gendarme stepping into the light, pulling back his blue-and-red cape, and with that came fire, the sound of his grease gun, a machine gun, with a short burst of bullets hitting the running man passing him. He went into an odd flipping dive, landing on the cobblestone street, and rolling over his shoulder and sideways at the same time. With this, my reaction to myself was, "Hell, hit the sidewalk." Now there was enough light on him from my position, where I had landed belly down on the sidewalk, that I could see he was "Arab" with only half his face in the light, and his clothes indicating a possible, or reasonable, surmise that he was Algerian. I didn't move as the gendarme walked over to the man and kicked him over on his backside. He was twisted from the hips down, with his eyes just staring up, his blood running down the street next to the curb and mixing with draining water coming from the streets above ours. I got up very slowly, walking into the lit side of the street, repeating low at first, and then louder, "American military, I'm American!" Now with my hands showing high, I pulled my wallet, standing closer. He looked at my ID while motioning me to continue my walk up the street into a much brighter glow of lights from a few cars driving away down the main crossing street. No one else was around or cared, there was no responded to the gunfire or sounds in this early morning night. The gendarme never said a word—"Stop" or "Halt"—to the running man. It was like he knew that man would be coming from there, and it was his duty to kill him. I knew the Arab was dead, with no reason for me to remain there. My body began shaking from the cold air and reacting to what my eyes had seen, and my mind couldn't accept it. Death in France was always close by, no matter how peaceful it appeared or how quiet the night was. From then on, I didn't travel by myself in dark alleys or places off the main streets without lots of other people walking or driving around at night except in a car. However, driving a car in the countryside was not safe, not because of the crazy drivers, but because of the crazy French police.

The Fontainebleau Exist

At another time, one of the staff sergeants at SHAPE was requested from upper levels to do a follow-up on a French killing of a whole American family in a small town near Fontainebleau, another American military base. I went along, helping with his reports and taking photos of the site for our government. It appeared an air force sergeant and his family was traveling on a road that had been set up for a roadblock for searching for arms, something to do with terrorism. The French security police had set up their road block with a strip of nails on boards across the road with signs to stop traffic, etc. However, there was police set up on both sides of the road along the higher points of these small hills and off the road. The stupid bastards had set up all this in a blind spot hidden around the backside of the curved part of the road and down out of sight for the U.S. serviceman's view. It happen to be dusk, with other poor mixtures of visual conditions, and then came the American's car around the corner, too fast and unable to stop in time. They hit the spikes, blowing the tires, awaking the police on the upper road positions, who then opened fire on the car from both sides of the road, thinking the sound of tires blowing was gunfire or shots fired. The car was a small European four-door with bullet holes covering every inch from end to end. I saw the interior with broken glass mixed with blood, and then I saw the body photos taken by both their and our investigating teams from the military police in the file, just a man and his wife with two small children becoming part of a war. The French had offered and gave their regrets, but took no blame for the deaths. The staff sergeant and I returned with this information we had found and reported it for further upper levels to deal with. However, I don't think either side took any further action or made any response. You could only hope, "I'll be luckier," not becoming one of these stupid mistakes.

The cars in Europe are very small because gas prices even then were five dollars a galleon or more. Also, they were not made to be safe, just thin metals, except for Volvos, maybe some English, and Germany's cars. France was one step away from being the number one in having the craziest of all drivers that I've known, and their cars using only yellow headlights for driving at night came next in being a big problem. These headlights cut down the distance you could see at night, except where there were a lot of other lights, like mostly in city-lit areas. These kinds of lights cut down the glare from the oncoming headlights, which was good, but it meant in the area out of Paris you were in trouble. Also, most highways were three-lane roads with the passing lane in the center lane, so the French would play chicken with the oncoming cars heading at each other while using the lane and trying to pass other cars, seeing who would give in first, and in their roundabout this was in play too. When in roundabout, you raced around while the cars to your right had the right of way coming in, except if he gave in to you—now you had his right of way, if you didn't give or hesitate either. It was like driving on a real racetrack, seeing how close you could get, without hitting the other car or putting on your brakes, giving away the right of way coming from the next street into the circle too. When they did have a wreck, most of the time the speeds were down, but when speed was high, there was always death from impact, and it would take a long time getting medical treatment. The guys I knew in Monrovia paid the price for driving one of these French cars before I ever came here.

I bought a 1959 Simca two-door hardtop, which was a good car—anything from the fifties was good—but they were known to have heating problems with their engines, mostly during the summer months or on long big uphill grinding. It was fun to drive, easy parking, good on gas mileage, with the front seats lying down backwards all the way, like our old Nash Ramblers in the States. I enjoyed that feature the most—it made it great for dates or sleeping anywhere.

I drove it all over Europe, and this helped in giving my parents an up-close experience when they came over in my last year by driving them in it through Belgium, Germany, the Alps, Italy, France, Spain, and back to Paris without any troubles from my little French friend. However, another one just like it gave me problems before my leaving for home.

The Race

Horns were used a lot, but not in Paris, which was like being in the middle of a circus, without the need for more distractions. Therefore, "When in Rome, do as the Romans do!" when it came to driving, as if all of us were in an auto race all the time. However, there were occasions for the real thing. So in France I had to go to the world-famous twenty-four-hour du Mans (Le Mans) in June 1964 with two other army buddies, and before that, we went to the Monaco's Grand Prix in May 1964. Now both were well worth the experience, but also having Ford breaking into this world of European racing was a mark in history for us fans. They didn't defy or defeat Ferrari and Porsche until 1966 with the GT40, but in 1964 they were on their way, and at Monaco's Grand Prix, I witnessed Cooper, McLaren, and Lotus from Great Britain run away with their light cars on the twisting turns and streets of Monaco before coming to America's "Brick Yard." As an American, it was more special seeing, feeling, and hearing these cars running all-out around you on the track, day and night. It caused the "speed genes" of any male to rise. Then years later, seeing Steve Mc Queen's *Le Mans* and James Gardner's *Grand Prix* movies, pulled me back there, feeling and dreaming of these times with my buddies while we shared French bread with white cheese (Like Laughing Cows), Italian wine (Chianti), and German "hot dogs" without much sleep in my car, and sleeping in our bags provided by the U.S. Army at these events. As for the girls, they were from every part of the world, and a camera would get you an introduction, then a little rock & roll music background and dancing would create the stage for "having a lot of Fun." Sometimes you would just get lucky, before those now-popular NASCAR stock car races of today came along.

After the race was over, there were thousands of cars and drivers turning into race drivers on their way home. Once you had gotten some miles away from the track and out of the slower-moving traffic, you would see the third-lane highways turning into a chicken's run, with drivers chancing their crossing into that passing lane, with no place to get back in their lane for miles, wondering if there was another fool or drunk now heading at you. Most would speed up, trying to get back to safety within inches. The drivers with too much wine, or false spurts of courage, would bring impatience into harm's way, affecting those around them as well. We saw repeated flashing lights with people, and cars off to the side of the road, with damage or death to both. These cars were unable to protect those with blind stupidity, there or here, French or any kind of other human. They were no longer thinking, or reasonable, humans with cars or guns.

Just before leaving France, with the money I'd saved up, I bought a new VW Square Back Station Wagon, light blue in color, to drive home from New York. My buddy, Mike, had bought the same car in a different color, but shipped his to California while we drove mine back cross-country. However, two months before leaving, I was driving through Bois de Boulogne entering Paris and got hit in the side by one of those crazy French drivers. Now it had to be fixed before even being shipped. I'd already driven over two and half years without an accident, but because of this accident, it meant I couldn't leave the country until my insurance company paid this crazy French driver. Also, I looked at a 1963 XKE Jag coupe and the James Bond Austin Martin DB and a Facel Vega with the stock Chrys Hemi engine too, before buy this car, and had test-driven each before leaving Europe. There were just too many problems in bring back any one of these cars to the States. One of the guys I knew did buy a new Porsche from the factory on two different occasions and shipped them home. He was a rich kid, having no problems with the money, driving them in Europe and then making a good profit from their sales after shipping them into the States. If you had a rank above E-4, the service would ship it back for free. Now I wish I had bought one of them too. Oh well! Most streams pass us by, and we see what we think could have been in our rearview mirrors.

TWENTY-NINE

Changing Streams With Buddies

"Dear John"

Upon my coming to France, Sylvia and I wrote every week, making plans and awaiting that possibility of her coming over. From the raising now from PFC (Private First Class) E-3 in my pay at Fort Deven and also now receiving overseas pay, I was able to save some money, and it wouldn't be long until getting E-4 (Specialist Four) grade. That happened in October 1963, and if we had gotten married, there were also other added allowances with a little higher pay to live on with off base in housing added on. She had been living with my parents with no rent, plus sharing food costs, therefore giving her spare money to save too while finding a good-paying job again. Also, on the weekends she was going to the races with my parents, this also being cheap entertainment cost too. However, there was some doubt if she wanted to come to Paris after I wrote her about the terrorist problems with the Algerians and French during those earlier months.

This went on for around six months, and then she wrote me out of the blue, having moved out of my parent's house, and now being on her own. A month later, I got my "Dear John" letter, to say good-bye forever, without any reason. She had met another guy at the races, and they had been seeing each other for about two months, and that's one of the reasons she had move out from my parents' house. She gave my ring that I had bought her back to my mother to keep. Then they got married, moving to Orange County. She now had her horses, and I wrote her back, wanting her to always be happy and wishing this is right for her. It just wasn't in our cards. So like in the song, "When your sweetheart sends you a letter of good-bye, you just go ahead and cry."

Years later, after getting out of the army and coming home, I found out her marriage didn't last too many years, and she was now divorced. But by then I had moved on too. I found this out after my mother had talked to her on the telephone one day after my getting home. We then talked by telephone once more, and then she was lost again. My mother told me, after they had talked before this, Sylvia discovered she now had multiple sclerosis, (MS), and this was on one of the reasons for her marriage not lasting.

He couldn't handle her disease. Never finding out when she was given her diagnosis about her dealt hand was a big question in my heart and mind.

Many years later, after my children were born and I was living with my family in Glendora, there was an article in the local newspaper about a woman in the next town over from Glendora, which is San Dimas, who had a few private horses and worked at a riding stable there. This woman had MS and was in charge of a teaching program for children with disabilities who were learning to ride horse at that stable. There, sitting in a wheelchair with a smiling photo, sat Sylvia with a different last name, helping a blind child on a horse, with many big smiles surrounding them both. Never contacting her, I was so happy for her now. She had found her place. She couldn't ever have children of her own, but now she had her love of them with her love of horses, mending together both in her stream, which meant much more than anything else in this world, and this pebble was in her place of the stream of being extraordinary. My children by now had become more important into my life, more than anything found in the world too. Streams run away and then return to cross or close, but not together ever again in this world—or do they?

Over There Friends

There are arrival points in your life you must work with, live with, and play with, but you're not really friends with until you feel they and you share some common grounds. The same can be said of any relationships of any source, but the army makes some relationships more important by our being put together in events, which place us far away from our home and families. I'm a lone wolf in nature to some extent, but have always liked being with people. I watch people and gain my own insights into their inner appearance and stories, attempting to know what and who they really are. Many of my friends during this time gave me support, while we gave each other some support felt or seen by just being there. The steams of life shifts the sands and pebbles into smaller collective groups against larger groups by merely standing closer together against anything, but we have no control over it at the end. However, just being together as comrades does help.

Minister

My room was only a short distance inside from the entrance to our barracks, letting me easily see many comings and goings of human's pebbles with their stories just outside my door or inside my room. For some reason, my longest roommates became two different chaplain assistants. The first was a funny little guy from the South, and what's more, he was a Southern Baptist, and before the army he had been doing his studies to become a minister with the Good Book. He believed its exact wording must be followed literally, and on top of this, he was very young, just married before going overseas, and would only have sex with his wife as a weekly reward, which now had brought on an unexpected crisis now. His deep belief in religion and his natural sex drive were affecting him physically to great extremes. The confining constraints boxing in his thinking about anything that could relieve this sexual problem, besides his being with his wife, had started with some trouble sleeping, then evolved into a larger problem of just walking about or sitting, and this now had affected his carrying out his church duties. It now had became a health problem too, and he had to go seek medical attention, with some embarrassing results.

One afternoon I came back from lunch to our room, finding him sitting with his pants down with the seat down on the head, with a bag of ice between his legs. He literally had a bad case of what is known as "blue balls," as we used to call it, and the doctor had informed him this wasn't normal. Therefore, he needed to take this into his own hands for some form of relief, if you know what I mean. Of course, I did see "them" being really blue, especially lying on the ice in a very extra-large swollen condition. The problem went away, so God must have brought some answer for his prayers. We all had our fun reminding him of the flesh and its "sinful surroundings." He was returned to his wife at stateside after about a year because he was only a two-year draftee, and not having the quality of a "Sixty Minute Man," as the song goes, if you know what I mean.

Priest

After awhile, the next chaplain's assistant shipped into our room, being another man studying for the cloth before Uncle Sam's invitation, and was roomed with me from experience—I guess they thought these guys were not the type to be placed in with the other jocks. This one was a good-looking guy, quiet type, who was on his way to becoming a Catholic priest within the Jesuit order before coming into the service. There was something reflecting a whole lot different between these two "Godly" guys. This was a thinker, a reasoning person of conviction, but having humane deeper feelings toward the troubled world of today. He had already been changed enough in his thinking, knowing he didn't want to be married to the church for the rest of his life now. So one night, we took him to Paris, giving him a few drinks, which is OK with a Catholic, but we also added a paid short trip up those stairs into the worldly sins found there, with a very bewitching young woman employed in the club. Like in the Rolling Stones rock group's song, "She blew my mind," after his tasting the honey-covered apple, with the snakes whispering sinfully from the tree found in the Garden of Eden, he was now truly amongst us other sinners. He was just another guy like us, a sinner with no saintly standings with gods or Man, being just a man. He and I went on a few double dates with some young French and English women, found through the downtown USO club, but he was again moved on to another station by his superior The priest, by my thinking, had became clay, and no longer wanted a priest's celibate life.

Tony

Down the hall in another room was Anthony, or Tony, who was in the air force and was very much like my friend Sonny from New York City. He was very Italian, with curly black hair, good-looking, with that Italian charm with the girls. He was from a small town, I believe it was Lowell, Massachusetts. That is one of towns I loved going to with those guys for pizza and beer during my time in Massachusetts. This was a town with both Italian and French pasty shops, mixed with a few pasties dancers at a few restaurants, and Italian wines. It was a fun place, with large sections of Italian and French people and their food mixed together in old neighborhoods. This was my experience before going to Europe, and Tony was one of those "straight shooter"-type guys, but of course he did sing a lot of Frank Sinatra and Dean Martin songs. He wasn't stationed here very long either, but brought another type of family experience to France.

One of his grandfathers had died during his time here, so he had to take some emergency family leave, flying back to Boston for the funeral. He was gone for a few days, returning with his family story of the funeral. Tony's dad was a Boston police officer, with many of his other uncles being either policemen or firemen as well, but there was another side of his family too, just like mine. Some of his cousins and uncles on the other side were also "wise guys," with one, as a matter of fact, being his real "godfather," who also was a real "godfather" to him and was "family" too. So therefore, Tony told us how on one side of the church sat his dad and the "good guys," and the "bad guys" sat on the other side without ever saying one word to each other throughout the whole service, entering and exiting on that note. They just nodded their heads in respect to each other as they passed by their row leaving the church. Then Tony told us the FBI had been in the back row, watching everyone on both sides, and that's why no one was able to exchange a word. They did the same at the gravesite, but at the private gathering afterwards at the family dining hall for the wake, some formal greetings were exchanged. Tony was a good guy and wanted to become a cop like his dad after completion of his service. These streams make funny mixers for us pebbles in life.

Warrant Officer

One of my other longest roomies was an army brat from a military family with short flat top blonde haircut and stocky-built body. He liked jazz, and in many ways reminded of Rick Orrel from high school in his build, self-confidence, and focus on achievement. He worked as a personnel specialist too, but he wanted more. He wanted to become an officer, therefore he did go on to becoming a warrant officer after passing and completing his training as a helicopter pilot. So we would spend time doing physical sit-ups, and hours studying for his entrance tests. It took around one year, but he made it, and I got a letter afterward announcing the completion of his dream, but not knowing if he became one of our Vietnam losses. I always wondered, years later, if he became one of its many lost causes or if he weathered that storm. He had an angel face with a devil smile at times, and I was able to learned karate with him and some deeper understanding of these military types of thinking, as an individual and in their beliefs. He would defend the benefits he saw with health care and other things found in staying within this army. It's become better now, but this was not the life for this pebble to believe or follow.

"Montana"

Now here was a paradox of contrary common in belief. He lived and grew up on a ranch in Montana, but to look at him and to listen about his ideas of the world, you would've never believed it. He had the roundest of faces, with red cheeks, and hair getting a little thin on top. He liked to eat, making him a little round around the middle too. There must have been some muscles under there because he told stories of piling hay in barns and working harder then most of us in our "civic life." He did love his "Big Sky Country" and was going to return there after the army. Contrary and contradictory was his being very smart, with a great control of expressing language and vocabulary skills higher than the average soldier's or cowboys. He was working for a general here, and his previous duty was at the Pentagon. He was there during the Bay of Pigs invasion and told me the truth regarding the mistakes made by the Pentagon and by Kennedy. I knew he wrote letters for the general and staff in his office, yet he never wanted to become an officer. He was quit, and just another extraordinary pebble, but much taller than most surrounding him. He was a good friend and the one whose car I borrowed to go with the Mike and girls to southern Spain on my last trip.

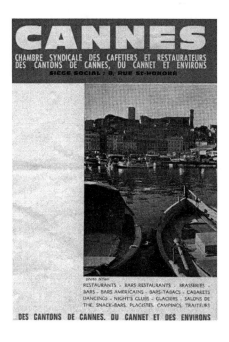

244

Prior to that trip, though, we went together to Nice in the south of France during the film festival in my car. His general, who he worked for, had given him a name and address there, so we had a place to stay. You see the general had known this woman during World War II as The Liberator for her and France. He advised "Montana" to bring a bottle of Black Label Johnny Walker to her from him, and as a result, we were treated like we had just liberated France again. Our flat was only a street away from the water, with a balcony overlooking the sea, enjoying our rear five-stories-up-room vision of the sun. We stayed seven days, enjoying the other visions, watched the girls in the polka dot bikinis on the beaches too. We walked with movie stars and Montana caught Jane Mansfield with his camera coming out of the water with a towel wrapped around her head in her polka dot bikini.

Little did anyone know at the time that she would lose it at the back of a truck only a few years later? One other thing coming from American, seeing everybody changing clothes on the beach was a very wide eye-opening event, and topless girls water-skiing behind speedboats also became even more unbelievable for an artist and cowboy. When my parents came over, we had to stop here, and my dad with his eight-millimeter movie camera got his own keepsake travel film footage too. There's more to their trip, but we'll cover that later. Montana was a great friend, with a great head on his shoulders, who had gotten drafted, and therefore, was only in the service again for a short period of time. I lost touch with him, and it's hard to believe him returning to a rancher's life, but I guess that's the art of his paradox.

Mike del Pilar

Mike del Pilar was Hawaiian-Filipino, coming from a large family with many brothers and sisters. He was of a darker skin than most, thin, black hair, medium build and height, but very good-looking in his own cute way. He had a great smile, with straight teeth that he took convincing time with, and they shined very white. He was born under the sign of the fish, and myself being a crab, we got along well, with us becoming better buddies. He entered into the army in San Francisco, California, but was born in Hawaii. He loved surfing, playing, and doing anything for fun, but was at his best shooting pool. Later, after getting out of the service, he would hustle at pool halls, which helped pay for his college education with assistance of the GI Bill. Now for the reason he joined the army, it involved his love story, which was in reverse to mine because while he was living and attending junior college in San Francisco, he fell in love with a Japanese girl, and it became somewhat a Shakespearean story because her family was also from Hawaii, and in Hawaii, the Filipinos are looked down upon by all the other races there, considered the lowest form of humans on the steps of social life. Her family (the father) was against their romance and had them end any further contact, but as we all know, being either Shakespearean drama or French novels, it continued in bringing the Fates and their works to an unlucky ending. She was given in a traditional marriage to another Japanese family for business and was never to see him again. So, heartbroken, he joined the Army, and these pebbles were cast into faraway streams, feeling the sweeping force of the currents.

He went on to the Army Language School at the Presidio of San Francisco, learning French and speaking Spanish. The Spanish came from his family Philippines history and his great-grandfather was known to be a great and famous general in the Philippines from that war with Spain, with a statue of him in the center of a plaza there, after fighting and winning against the Spanish during the Philippine Revolution. So this had also brought issues from his family regarding that love, and the Japanese lost again.

So besides his many assignments as interpreter at SHAPE, we were roommates and became buddies, traveling to Spain and other countries. We also ended up getting out of the service together and continuing our many years connected. After the army, we traveled across this big country in my VW station wagon to the West Coast, and he had his "Playboy Key," which let us hit every Playboy Club along our way. More of that trip will follow in time, but let me say that he was asked to become a part of my family, with his family also showing my parents their Hawaii, which most don't ever see. I've not seen or heard from him for many years now; he had gotten married and divorced, had a little girl, who is now a woman, I'm sure, and he was losing his hair and having those hair "plugs" replacements done in the last photo. He was last known to be living on a houseboat near San Francisco Bay. This pebble was also extraordinary.

Terry Westagard

Terry was from Phoenix, Arizona, Scottsdale to be exact, and friends with everyone. He was thin, laughed a lot, but appeared to be too serous at times. He was always telling us—the company clerk, Mike, and I, all from California—always trying to sell us that Arizona is far better than California. We would kid him about no beaches in Arizona, and he would reply with "It only takes one good earthquake to fix that," and we all would laugh. I don't recall for sure, but I do remember him having a girl at home too.

Terry's father was a liquor salesman and district distributor back home in Arizona, and he returned home and joined the business. So knowing all these thing, one day he asked Mike and me if we'd go with him for dinner with a couple of French girls at their apartment in Paris. I can't recall now if Mike went or couldn't go, but I said, "Sure." Then he told us these French girls were the daughters of the "Hennessey Cognac" family, and we were impressed. Not only because of their social status, but you see Cognac was cheap in France at this time, and my drinking it at a price that was around, or less than, a dollar a shot on our nights out on the town had given me another incentive to go. You see, with a liter of German beer starting our evening on the town, continuing with that good "high" with a few Cognac shots for the rest of the evening while at the disco clubs, it became my drink of choice and cost.

It all started because his father had the occasion, back before Terry was in the service, to host the Hennessey family during one of their visit to Arizona, and Terry had met them on their trip there. Therefore the two daughters, being around his age and having a great time with him, wanted to show their gratitude with a dinner for him and his friends at their apartment in Paris. We arrived at their apartment, just off the Champs Élysées, and were met at the door by the concierge, who told us which floor to get off at using the old elevator and its iron gate. One of them met us outside the door, and it was a very nice apartment inside. They both were very thin, and had a just so-so looking French model look. To my surprise, they spoke Queen's English very well, but appeared to be very down-to-earth in many ways and manners. Dinner was now ready, and after standing for a while, talking and drinking wine, we started the meal with more wine, half-shelled shellfish, fruits, and bread. You see, the French have their salad last, and as the meal went on with conversation, I learned their English was from them going to private schools in England and now having boyfriends from, I believe, one from England and the other from a Scandinavian or German part of Europe. There were many little surprises, talking about America and Europe at length. I think we learned more from them than they did from us, but that's the French way.

The French have their own views, but I did enjoy a great meal, ending with a great glass of Cognac, and was again surprised by an invitation to their Cognac country villa sometime later for a weekend day.

I had learned a lot about how the French taxation systems works too. You'd see houses with modest appearance outside, or in a decaying appearance similar to that seen all over France, but then going inside you would find it became a palace because if they would improve the outside, the taxes would then go up. So you would see very little improvement from the outside. However, the government was spending millions by starting the cleaning up of Paris during my time there, with a lot of sandblasting of the outside buildings and statues for tourism. It had become a dirty city, resulting from too many cars and burning of coal for heating.

Pebbles and people in big cities rush around like in fast-moving streams, sometimes not very friendly, bumping along with running water or flying freely in the air everywhere within fountains, but it's "The City of Lights," with its nights flashing lights' reflections in those waters everywhere, or by the river. But almost every day there was its cleaning by receiving a few new raindrops for short periods of time, as a part of its rebirth, and always with its people cleaning the sidewalks in the early morning with brooms swiping the dirt away. The smell of things like good food, the perfume of flowers, like the people trying to cover themselves and all other things that turned your stomach were throughout the city too. This does bring to one a great feeling of being alive mixed with that moment, under a tree out of the rain or under an umbrella with your body close to a female and sharing that feeling of warmth against the rain or cold. These are the reasons most say Paris is a city like no others, seeing the city with artist's paintings and written poems of feelings in the air of present or past loves.

This dinner, with the rest of my experiences, brought me into being of a mind, and a small step closer, with them, yet a better love of our country too. The GIs would always talk about returning home to "the round doorknobs, and girls with no hairy armpits or legs." Terry had returned home first, but he did give Mike and me a few more connections for our trip home after being in the service of our country. We return the favor by taking him to the just newly opened Playboy Club in Phoenix while on our returning trip home, and I must now also thank him for pointing me in the right direction to where I live now in Arizona since retirement in 1999. He was right about Arizona's having some things better than California for us older citizens, but over all, I wish it had a beach and ocean.

"W. C. Fields"

One last story of fun with one of my army sergeants found again within my room. He was in his middle life travels, he was a drunk, lost his rank may times, and was stuck in the service forever. Every night and day, you'd find him drinking either during lunch in the cafeteria or at the EM club on base. Most U.S. servicemen didn't spend much time off base, other than to go to the PX for many reasons, which just happened to be a few short miles down the road, and everything was provided close to base for us. He had that "W. C. Fields" big red nose, round face, with those small blood vessels in the cheeks, and, most of the time, his bloodshot small slit eyes. He was overweight and had the same manners of speech as the famous actor, which he played up for us younger soldiers: "Ah yes, someone put some lemonade in my lemonade!"

One night he had gotten all cleaned up and went to Paris, of course it was "Pig Alley." The next day, I saw him in the cafeteria, drinking, but hadn't changed his clothes yet. I asked, "How did it go?" "Well," he said, "I'll never trust another woman or those French again," and he continued with telling me his story. He found a bar, had a few drinks, and a very nice-looking woman sat down at his table, wanting him to buy her a drink. He started buying her those watered-down drinks, which was part of her job, and everything was going well, and the next thing he knew, they were upstairs in her room with a bottle. He had undressed and was waiting for her to join him from the bathroom. She came out with a very sexy violet French robe, and he smelled sweet violet perfume in the air. She dropped the robe and had on a long sexy violet slip covering her. She did things to him that awoke things drunks don't feel very often in their conditions. Then, it happens, he reached down and found something between his partner's legs that was not acceptable. "What The Hell Is This?" he exclaimed in shock and jumped out of bed, grabbing his pants and running for the door. "It was a THING!" The devil had diabolically changed his dream into a nightmare. So now our W. C. said, "You can't trust children, animals, and any form of woman." And he never went to Paris again.

"One more, Bartender"

There was a time at the end of first summer when our company funds for our recreation activities had built up into a large surplus of money. Therefore a vote was taken in favor of hosting a large dinner party at the Enlisted Men's Club with free, drinks, steaks, and music. Yes! Therefore I had a need for a new suit of clothes, which was followed by going to the PX and finding me a new light-blue "Palm Beach" suit, looking "so cool." Way before Miami Vice. I arrived with two other roommates after the party had begun, and I hadn't had a good mixed martini since Boston. So I gave the order to the bartender, "Two doubles, please," receiving one in each hand—and why not, it was free. Also on to the table with my buddies, there were free bottles of red and white wines. Now this was a five-course dinner, starting with clams in their shells, with a mixer of shellfish in a creamy-white French sauce, also starting with a glass of white wine for dinner. We were underway. Followed with the main course of a filet mignon steak wrapped in bacon strips, a large baked potato with everything on top, and asparagus in cream sauce, with a bottle of Burgundy wine to wash it down. We now finished with chocolate mousse, with a smaller glass of warm Cognac. Why not? After another round of two-handed double martinis, I was feeling like a king and had gone to heaven on a magic carpet. Now walking over to the bar, making the order again for "two more double martinis, please," and drinking them before service had been no big deal in my past life, but now, sitting here, was I "OK"?

At first I talked with some people since my speech sounded somewhat normal, but for some reason not just right. Suddenly, I fell off the barstool with no found form of support or framework to prevent this mishap. Climbing back up and trying to find my center wasn't working, and with that, I exclaimed. "Bartender! Another round of the same!"

He was looking at me with disbelief. "You've had enough," he poured out, as if he knew my condition. I exclaimed, "I'm Irish, We CAN hold our drinks," and with that, I slipped down to the floor once again. The bartender waved my buddies over, and they helped me into a cab with a lift under each arm. There appeared to be a semantic problem with my legs too. The taxicab driver dropped me off at the barracks entrance, and the army is always ready with a night desk duty soldier for these needs, paying my fare and walking me into my room. Beyond and above the duties is that service found in the helping of our fellow solders in need, and when my roommates came back to the room, they found me with my hands embracing around the "head" and trying to get that needed taste of water, like a trusty dog, the only available source of water found at this level or of my capability to reach. They helped with a glass of some found water and helped me take off that now-multicolored marked charcoal-blue suit that was never the same.

With the next day being a working day, I arose from bed with that oversized pounding head and blurred vision and attempted to get dressed after a short shower. The hardest part became putting on socks and shoes, after finding the front of my underwear and pants. I made it to the exit fully dressed, and then making another mistake, I stopped for that "COLD DRINKING FOUNTAIN WATER," and just feeling that refreshing cold liquid on my lips and replacing that funny feeling in my stormy stomach with drinking as much as possible with my teeth repelling the cold water, at first was so much relief. But by the time I reached the other side of the field, with our offices, for work, I found I was drunk all over again. I walked in smelling of gin and vermouth, with a twist of lime on my breath. I was sent back to my room, ordered to report to "Sick Call" for a day off duty. They were quite understanding, but laughing, and the new suit was sent for cleaning but still had some faded marks on the knees. Thinking about martinis again, or any form of mixed drinks, was something our minds overcame with time, and then thinking later at some other point of our youthful body ability to recover is very remarkable.

Art Students

One day while in the recreation hall, I found something about an art club and classes posted on the billboard. After contacting Martine, the person on the notice, who was in charge of the many recreation activities here, I found to my surprise she was French. Very thin, tall, in her mid-thirties, long hair that was wrapped high on her head, with a very feminine appearance. We started talking about the class. Her English was heavy with French, but she was very interested in my past schooling as an art student, for some reason, while we talked. At first she wasn't sure, but during our coffee she gave me a pencil and a sheet of sketch paper, so I started sketching her. After a close likeness, she said, "OK, we need a teacher for our class, but first there would be a needed approval from those in the class. Which consist of mostly officers wife's, and they are a mixer of different levels in their abilities and standards." She had at first tried to teach the class herself, but as luck does at times, I fell out of the sky and fit the bill. She informed me all my art supplies would be free, and there was a small amount in her budget for my time.

After the first class, we had about five or six students of all levels and ages, mostly officers' wives looking for something to do with their time. Then after asking them to vote on which medium they would like to try, the response was mixed. So we started them off with just some basic drawing instructions to see what they could do. Two were into oil painting, so I started painting with them and used my Irish insight on the rest. It was a night class for two or three hours that met once a week for the first month, then with a few more coming every other week after that first month. This did get me back into my painting, and finishing five oil paintings before it was over. Like cream on top, Martine found a small art studio for students near the Left Bank that helped me to sell three of my painting, then I gave one to Martine, and the last one ended up in the hands of my last girlfriend before leaving Paris.

Martine's apartment was within a few blocks of the Left Bank. We would meet on occasion at a small cafe on a corner, where students would have coffee or wine before going to their classes at the university halls within the Sorbonne just off St. Germane Avenue on the weekends. She talked me into taking the army's class in conversational French on our base during my working hours. Using both tools of my art and a little amount of French in seeing Paris gave me insight on being an American student. And my friendship with Martine and being in the army gave me a new view of Paris life. However, because of my still being a rebel, my duties station was changed, and new characters became added.

Captain "Major" Yeary

Following a change of my duties from personnel to the supply section warehouse clerk for the USA Supplies Section for SHAPE, I had now become one the sheet counters in some sense. It was one of those things I'll go into later. I had learned the mess cooks and supply sergeants were the persons who you need to know in order to make "life the best you could" while you're in the services. At first there was a Lieutenant Colonel in command of this section, who later retired. He had been very reasonable man, like "Colonel Potter" in the TV show M*A*S*H—which we all would enjoy seeing for years later on TV—and just as pleasant to work for. Then came his replacement, Captain Yeary, who was somewhat like another "Frank Burns" character in that show. He was stocky, early thinning hair for a very young man, and, you could tell, working harder than it was necessary to get through army life.

You could see the conflict between "Hawkeye," our sergeant major, much older and wiser, running the unit, and "Frank Burns," unrealized vision for the sergeant major, who spoke French and had been stationed many years in France with his very nice French national wife. He would build harmony by drinking wine with our French workers at breaks and lunch and understanding the French and U.S. Army ways. He later would retire in France. There was a cast of others, but Captain Yeary was very special in trying to make his new command control known. Just like the TV show, it was fun watching each one of these characters in this sitcom playing on a daily run, but not always. It was closer to the Barney Miller police comedy also at times too.

One sergeant, being "Old Army," with his potbelly gut, was worried about many things, which included passing the new level of physical annual test to just stay in the army. His workday started with coffee, snack, reading the newspaper, and then taking papers out of his In-Basket, then another cup of coffee. Then pulling open his top drawer, looking into it for five or ten minutes, closing it, and then moving some papers around before repeating down to the next drawer. By now, it would be lunchtime, off to the PX for an hour (eating, I think), and then back attempting to stay awake for the rest of his afternoon. Then on to more opening and closing drawers, stamping some papers, and moving them into the Out-Basket ending his hard working day. He didn't like me much, finding I'd do things to him or things while he was sleeping or ask him things that would fly way over his head, or through any mind he had. There were a lot of things he should have been worried about, but being a simple mind, he wasn't capable of much.

Captain Yeary was looking for ways to trim out "the waste and fat" in his command, but there was something else. After awhile, we found out Captain Yeary was in fact the brother to a well-known higher-ranking officer, who he was proud of but very envious of, by the name of Lee Majors. You see at that time his brother was now in movies and on the TV show, Big Valley, receiving help from Barbara Stanwyck after injuries while playing college football. Now we all know where he went from there, like The Six Million Dollar Man, Fall Guy, and Farrah Fawcett in the seventies. His agent was also James Dean's, who had found Lee and they had other things in common, which was a similar youth for both. Lee's father died before he was born, and Dean's father had left him too, with both youngster mothers dying when they were very young. His father's brother had adopted him after his parents' death, and he didn't know this until much later in life now, like James Dean—his aunt and uncle raised him too. Both excelled in sports and then became actors. Lee didn't have the acting skill or degree of standing or problems of Dean, but did rise above the ones he had. So I'm guessing our Captain Yeary never did make it beyond his own level, other than in the military, or to that next level up in his stream as his brother Harvey Lee Yeary or "Lee Majors" did. So Captain Yeary would be always outranked.

The Lost Captain

While talking about captains—in my job upon arrival, I was assigned to the personnel section and handling files because there was the movement within personnel between NATO bases. There appeared another young army captain rubbing everyone the wrong way, making many enemies with most of the enlisted men, which happened to include myself. You can see from my former background and thinking toward those thinking they are above us pebbles that they should tread lightly where they step, and when finding themselves among us poor little pebbles, they might be in for a fall. Now part of our mission and duties was the handling of payroll documents while doing their traveling or on temporary duty station assignment. The captain received an assignment to travel for a couple of months to Italy on what is known as TDY (Temporary Duty). Therefore, in order to get paid, among other things, his files are sent to his new assignment for most of the time there, and the officer carries them most of the time. However, because of the nature of this guy, "It's best, and I feel everything should be done to make it simpler for me, just send them. It's too much trouble carrying all those files."

So his files and paperwork was made ready, but it just so happened his payroll folder was shipped to Korea while the rest were sent to his assignment in Italy. Just how could this big mistake be made? How could that happen to such a nice guy? Without his payroll papers, it was necessary to draw money from slips in different amounts, as needed, which started many accounting problems, with a lot of paperwork for him. He didn't find this out until the end of the month. However, my initials were found on his payroll folder after it was returned. Therefore I took the fall. However, it was not my doing totally, and it may have been an effort of many. I didn't care because my new job was much easier and had more perks. Also, my real job regarded security checks through the personnel files, and information was slow and uninteresting. I had the highest of all Top Secret designations and was ordered to report to a much higher-ranking ASA officer, who was assigned directly above me during this time. There were many restrictions on my travels, like no traveling to Berlin, Germany, or any Eastern Bloc countries. I could fly to Berlin, but no ground travel since it was surrounded by East Germany, but I enjoyed my traveling throughout the rest of Europe, which became my duty during later army days.

Dreams Do Come True

Everywhere you travel in France, while walking around, there would be two young women with one young man. I found, first of all, this being a majority Catholic country—like most of them in Europe, like Spain and others—women are to be escorted. Therefore, the company of two women was something you would believe and dream of as a possibility, being a young man, and dreaming what it would be like having two women together in bed was always there. With the schoolgirls, you could understand their being just two friends together, but as women still doing this, it was quite interesting from a man's point of view regarding the possibilities with three. There was always an appearance of a playful interaction between all three seen everywhere.

One of the sergeants working with me was young, married, having two young children, and living off base. Bob had been in the army for a few years and now had his family overseas with him. He made a lot of trips for business to Camp des Loges, where there was a young woman working in the office of the supply depot warehouse. They would play games of flirting on the telephone and while we were in her office too. It was just fun interplay, and harmless as far as I could see. Men are men, and for some reason, this happens with many married men, who without a lot of playing-around experience before marriage, become confident and now start to flirt with any women for sport. I've seen this happen a lot, even now.

He had arranged to have her come to his house and baby-sit one night because he had plans on taking his wife out for a special occasion. She was in her early twenties, thin, dark hair and eyes. She was nice looking, but very plain, not much with makeup, and dressed very plain too. We had talked on a few occasions, when I accompanied Bob to Camp Des Loges. She had said yes, or French oui, to Bob about the babysitting job, except she wanted her girlfriend to baby-sit with her too. Therefore, since I knew her, Bob asked me if I too would come over as their chaperone to "accompany" them, helping with they're English with the kids and anything to make them comfortable.

Upon my arrival, I met her girl friend while Bob and his wife got ready. However, she didn't speak much English and was maybe another five or six years older than me, thin, and also not much in awaking my interest at first. Bob had told me, "There's some wine, Jack Daniel's, and records, so have some fun, and we'll be late." His youngest was all ready for bed. After feeding him his bottle and then putting him in bed, one was down. Now we were free except for his young daughter being around, who was four or five years old, and she played with her new friends. The girls had fun with her, and I did my "James Dean" thing too. Then, she was in bed by nine o'clock, after much protesting, showing off, and repeated trips for anything she could think of by request. She finely gave it up, and it was "OUR" time.

Now we were free except for his young daughter's getting up a few more times, but I had now poured some wine for the girls and some Jack Daniel's on ice for me and put on the music, which was soft at first, keeping the children asleep. At first, it was difficult not being able to speak a lot of French, and so there wasn't a lot of talking, so I started dancing with the youngest, who didn't know how to. The older did, and she was helping the other learn to dance in French while all three of us started out with the fox trot, with a one, two, three, and step. I would lead with the older one and the younger with our hands together and them following. Then some rock 'n roll steps with a mixer of the twist, which was becoming big in France by now. They finished their wine, and I had another tall one. The younger one was feeling her wine, now loosened up and able to dance a little better, while the older one was dancing with both us, and then the girls together while I poured the older one some Jack Daniel's too. We changed off dancing as the music got slower. Bob had shown them to his extra bedroom before leaving, and the older one disappeared into it, changing into a long loose nightgown while the younger and I were dancing. The younger was more bashful, but did go into the bedroom, changing into a much shorter nightgown. They started fooling around, pulling on my pants. I had not known this was going to become a pj party. We laughed and were having trouble standing, and then next fell on the carpet floor. All three of us piled up, as if playing football. I went for attempting to kiss with the bottom one and was kissed by the top one on my ear at the same time. Therefore we turned over now, with both laughing and kissing me while the other finished undressing me to my shorts. Off into the bedroom, where we stayed the rest of the night, and into this small bouncing bed with all three of us turning sideways in order for us to find space without falling on the floor.

Ah yes, this was heaven! The younger was not as active, but I felt it was my duty to keep both women interested, and I found the older knew much more, completing our transaction within time. They both would rest in between, and I however never did get much sleep—but at twenty-four, there wasn't need for much sleep.

Bob and his wife came home during the very early hours of the next day, finding my clothes on the floor, and they peeked in while I waved from my middle ground before they closed the door, and then I heard them checking on their two babies. Then, I heard faint laughter coming from their room as the older moved on top of me one more time. The next day, my head and every part of my body was asking for some form of relief as I got up finding my clothes. The girls stayed in bed as I exited the front door while everyone else was asleep. My dream, which only all other men throughout the ages had dreamt of within our hidden lust, had come true. I now knew another much more deeper-meaning French phrase, "Ah Mei Toue" while the girls had a small taste of American whiskey. Bob and I would laugh a lot about this evening while the younger woman would turn a shade of burnished pink the first few times after seeing me looking with a smile at her face, and would move her eyes down. Then she would quickly look up with that sparkle in those dark eyes for just a moment, with a slight smile in return. She did continue babysitting for Bob and his wife, but I was never again needed to chaperone or escort either woman again, as if it was all my fault, not Jack Daniel's or their wine's responsibility. HOWEVER, BIG THANKS TO SERGEANT BOB AND FRENCH WOMEN!

The Nightclub

The continuing hidden secrets mankind finds and uses repeatedly throughout history are in those hidden places that are about his military finds, and the Nightclub was one of those places. The Christians used it for hiding from the Roman legions and were the first known to use it for protection. It is in a hill hidden a few miles outside Versailles, within many underground catacombs. The Germans found it in World War II and enlarged it to hold a division of Panzer tanks from any air attacks. All had tried keeping the underground dripping water from their iron machines; and by now, we had moved in there, with modern-times electronic improvements, with higher improvements in all levels of protection as well. The Germans were now a part of that much-improved nightclub, with all of Europe on our screens with small lights for military, our checkmate games. This all started because the Romans had ordered the construction of limestone quarries, digging deep into the hills surrounding Paris, which now honeycomb the hills nearby. This nightclub was for our command, and that gave you the feeling you were going into the bowels of the earth, ready for man's hell from atomic warfare.

Now being part of the US Army supply command section, there were many trips made with deliveries of supply and equipment trucks into this place, doing my escort duties again. I would have to be a part of the supervision over the French workers making deliveries and the unloading of supplies, entering through those large gates and doors into this "movie set." It was very highly lit with busy people everywhere, shadows with security personnel, and many kinds of buildings still under construction everywhere, and with many areas completely sealed off. When we finished with our delivery, we would be expelled back into sunlight, seeing the natural world. US money was being poured into this underground command center, and its many problems during the whole time, I was there. Upon my leaving the army, it was finished, and later NATO was kicked out of its nightclub. The French received it with the opening of many bottles of wine and black hearts, or is it still there now?

The President Has Been Shot!

It was a quiet evening, and most of us were just lying around on that twenty-second day of November in 1963. Then it speared throughout the mess hall and into the whole headquarters. "The president has been shot in Texas!" You could hear loud radios thought thin walls, and word that he was dead had not been announced yet. He had given his "Itch Bin ein Berliner" (I am a Berliner) speech in Berlin, Germany, on June 26, 1963; and there was a feeling among many here, after the completion of his first thousand days in office, the world was becoming united against the Soviet Bloc. There was much hope with this new president, but now lost with disbelief.

Late into the night, TVs and radios became louder, and at higher levels, than ever before, as if no one could hear the facts all the way into their head into making them believe he was dead, and now Mr. Johnson was the new president. It was as if hornets were lost on the whole headquarters. It was moved quickly to red alert mode, designed to warn us of danger or trespassers. Not knowing if the Soviet Union or Cuba had been responsible for this, action was quickly put into motion with the most of the high command being sent to the Nightclub. Now again, the world was setting with "its time clock" moving very slowly to the edge, where reasonable men must control the world's future over a crazy man's action.

We were transferred to those underground rooms with large screens showing lights of many colors on maps and many red buttons that could release "hell" upon earth, without most of the world knowing what happened to them. This storm would be coming from man's bowels of hell, burning the earth, while we're saved down deep into this mountain's belly. A few days passed and the alert was removed. We returned to our jobs and lives as the nation and the world wept with a million of tears, watching his wife, children, family, and nation carry on, what was necessary to move forward into a new different future page. The whole world's oceans were still the same, but many pebbles had been moved into new streams.

USO

Thanks to all the previous wars with the French as host, GIs have been using the USO, with its hostess of young women to keep our behavior and spirits at a higher level than that in "Pig Alley." The first time was with my chaplain assistant's friends. We had found a mixture of young women of all ages and countries. So with some dancing, drinking Cokes and coffee, and talking, you may find someone who liked you and who was willing or inquisitive enough to meet you afterward, which wasn't a part of their normal duties or a part of the USO. However, you found these girls were here for their many own reasons. The Spanish girls liked the black boys because of the Moor's connection, which started from the eighth-century invasion and occupation of Spain. Plus Black Man spent more money on them, treating them with much high signs of regard and having the same taste in bottoms with Spanish men. The English like us because we spoke English, but more than that, they liked the idea of maybe going to the States someday too. There was not many French, but there were some Germans and Scandinavians trying out their English too. Many were from UNESCO or some other form of United Nation organization found in Paris.

My first connection was with two Irish lassies, and trying to date each one for a short time as well was the "priest." Then came a very young English girl, whom I spent some time with in October 1963 with her parents in their small township south of London, England. That was my first time hearing the Beatles at her dance club on records, with girls dancing with each other, yelling "I Want to Hold Your Hand," played by the club's disc jockey. I never saw anything like it before, except for Elvis, and found I wasn't very sharp on them at first; their were yelling or screaming most of their songs, such as "She Loves You." Their hair and clothes just didn't do a thing for me while I was being more into the Beach Boys, who were now becoming more known within us California kids. However, between these two groups, they both changed music forever, becoming bigger than anything seen before for England or California's view in their own styles, with their own state of mind for the world's youth of the day. Having always my liking in telling the girls about Southern California and surfing, which fit Mike and my images, they didn't understand "hot rods," as a part of that only American scene; but California boys appeared more interesting and masculine than most European men. So that did sell with some girls.

However, getting my first razor haircut by a woman in Paris was fresh; there was no more cuts like the old barbershop with short hair or white sidewalls cut for us GIs either, which made you so noticeable to everyone as American. Way back in high school, my ducktails, waterfalls, and bleaching of hair during spring break, for the summer months, and blaming it on the beach or pool, was cool even with European girls. So for now, that Beach Boy look would do, with my hair getting a little extra help at times over here too, which the girls did like, reflecting that American Beach Boy look. The army wouldn't allow too long or mop-top styles of hair at all yet.

Patricia

Later on, Patricia, with her roommate Vanessa, and I met at the USO one night. They both worked for UNESCO, speaking French, and we hit it off. There was something about her that attracted me. She was not that pretty, with a long nose and large ankles, but her perplexing personality had attracted me to her more than her physical appearance. She spoke the Queen's English and had class and loved to dance, and so did Vanessa. Vanessa was going with another American serviceman boyfriend too, and his name was Ray. We got along very well too, and after getting out of the army, we kept in touch until the nineteen eighties. The girls roomed together, so we spent a lot of time together in their apartment, and we boys slept over after a time. We could get the girls things through the US PX for all four of us that worked to bring us all together.

Patricia had a failed relationship with a Portuguese boyfriend before we met and was still thinking of his charms in comparison to mine. She also spoke some Portuguese, but she was also a good Catholic girl, taking this American boy to church with her when she could. We were in a mixed-up relationship most of the time. Yet we traveled together with many things holding us together and enjoyed each other for my last year in Europe. I was in love with her and our relationship. After leaving Europe, and service, I was thinking about going to work for the State Department within the Foreign Service; after seeing and knowing some friends, I had some contacts with the American embassy during my time in Paris. This would have brought me back into that world, with maybe Patricia, and I would still continue our relationship, but that wasn't to happen.

We wrote letters for another year after my departure from that world, then after going into another year, her world and mine started changing. I met my first wife-to-be in that first year, but we didn't get married until 1968 in Monrovia. That next year, 1969, Patricia called me and was now in the USA—in California. She did believe Mike and me about that California-dreaming life. She and some of her friends stayed with us for a few days, before moving on to school at the University of Berkeley. After graduation, she went on to work for the state of California in a very high office position. She also found a man who was black, like in the play A Taste of Honey, and I'm sure it had a great impact on her and her family in England. However, during Patricia's visit, my ex-mother-in-law was living across the street from us and had called my then wife while she was at work, playing with her mind, knowing that Patricia was my ex-girlfriend, and telling my wife that the curtains were still closed. She was joking with my wife, but my wife wasn't buying it anyway because it was even funnier that Patricia and my wife really had gotten along; they liked each other, as does my present wife with her. We received Christmas cards for a few years, with notes on how her life was going, but more about us pebbles later.

THIRTY

My Parents' European Trip

My dad worked for Aerojet General, who had put together their group vacations for their employees in 1964. With me being stationed in Europe, this gave them a great opportunity to be with me for a short visit and travel to the Old World. This was one of those many tours were if you know which day it is, you know what country you're in. They started by landing in London on September 22 for the first day and being in Amsterdam, Netherlands, for the next day. Now with Europe smaller and half in size to the United States, with my owning a car, they flew from Amsterdam to Paris the next day, connecting with me at their hotel but again later reconnecting with their tour there on October 10, after being personally driven by their son during all those same middle days of enjoying sightseeing and traveling to the same countries.

After picking them up in Paris, we began our own small tour of Europe in my small French Simca auto instead of the bus. We drove to Verdun, had a nice French dinner with wine, and stayed the night at a nice small inn because they still had flight jet lag. From our hotel, you could still see and feel the battles of World War I in large mounts of earth surrounding the countryside, as people rode their bicycles with loaves bread in their baskets down the small roads. Our next countries to visit were Belgium and Luxembourg all within that same day. We enjoyed these two small countries of mixed history and people tied to all three countries of France, Holland, and Germany. We felt that great emotional touch upon seeing those grounds of white markers as far as you see at Hamm, Luxembourg, with its tributes to General Patton and all those fallen solders of World War II, feeling the effect of that greatest-turning conflict nearby on all. This was where Europe was saved from the Third Reich with the help of one of the Allen clan, fighting for his country, his own survival, and at the same time becoming a victim, because my cousin Buddy had been a part of it, airborne, and never been the same.

The next day entering into southern Germany with the Oktoberfest, which was happening in Munchen or Munich, as we of the English countries call it, we joined in starting with some German food, ordering Wiener schnitzel for my parents and something of "beef" for myself. My "beef" arrived just lying there on the plate in some form of a great white cow's tongue, with steam rising before my wide-open eyes. Everyone's reaction to my expression had brought on laughter with my surprise. My dad's enjoyment was heightened because just before this, I had bragged about my college German, but now having to order something else and paying for both with my embarrassment had brought him a repeatable story to share with all his friends. We moved on into the festive Oktoberfest streets and halls drinking a few liters of beer with that great fun having already begun as we joined in with the singing and polka bands. There was also milk chocolate with ribbons and large pretzels for the kids, and my mother. Also there was smoked fish with many other mixtures of great-smelling things surrounding our sensory senses flooded with people of all ages sitting, standing, singing, with that great mixture of dashing moving waitresses, filled with their full-of-life souls, rosy cheeks full of joy, and bringing more beer pitchers. They were carrying six or seven full-liter mugs of beer with bubbles only spilling very little through delivery, as if sailors walking their ship upon the open sea of Oktoberfest were under way. It was time to be a part of this trip, easily joining in the many raising of these mugs of this festival, within these great halls and crowds. It was easy to see, how and why, this was one of my and my dad's favorite times.

However, next he and I shared the bottle of aspirins as I was trying to stay focused on my driving now that we're on the autobahn, with cars passing us without any speed limits, and most of them at or over hundred miles per hour flying by us into the mountain heights into the Bavaria castles area. On the way, we did stop in a small village to have lunch, renewing our craving with a small beer and something to eat; there were some locals in a garden setting. We found through talking with them that day. They said, "You Americans are the greatest friends Germany knows!" We asked why. After knowing the effects of World War II with its death and destruction on them, they told us after the first war, the French and English took everything they had, leaving them with nothing except despair in a vision of slow death through starvation, while most believed their country would never recover again. "So because of that hatred and the German will, we raised higher than any other country around us did or could at that time. That was why Hitler was able to control our souls with his evil; but America has helped rebuild our country with Truman's help, the Marshall Plan, and Monroe Doctrine, keeping the Russians from taking over our lives. Also with your help during the Berlin Airlift, and now with your strong resent president Kennedy's Berlin speech [assassination months later], this had brought our two countries closer together."

Visiting the royal palaces of Ludwig II of Bavaria was like visiting the real Sleeping Beauty's castle, with Wagner's operas coming to mind and soul. These palaces were surrounded with terraces and magnificent fountains looking down at surrounding Alpine Villages, which brought on a peace of mind, only to find the man was crazy. It would be easy to exit into this scenery, and I would find myself returning to this area again during a winter with Patricia for one of our last vacation trips.

Then came our moving farther and higher into the Alpines of Innsbruck, Austria, seeing all its beauty the next day, and staying overnight with sightseeing for only one day. From there we drove through the mountains to Verona, Italy. There were roses found on the edge of the Alpines with small streets, only wide enough for a single small car, and its hidden gardens unseen behind walls. Most don't know this is where the star-crossed lovers' tomb lies and the story began with Juliet surrounded by roses in a courtyard. William Shakespeare's story is believed to started from within these walls and now findings its forever imparted here, because this town is where the greatest of all love stories was began and told because of these two young lovers' struggle within their families. Then we continued to Genoa, where we stayed the night, had dinner, and slept. My dad had a reaction to the water or food along the way. My mom got her turn the next day as we were traveling along the edge of the mountains to the sea.

Our next stop was Cannes, where I'd been a visitor before, and Mom was still not well, so she stayed in the hotel room. Dad had recovered, and we drove along the beach with his Super 8 movie camera, where he started filming the girls changing into their bikinis or back into their normal daily clothes with only the usage of a small beach towel for coverage, with no place to change while on the beach. They would place the bikini top over their bra, unhook it, pull it out from under the top bikini cloth, like a magician pulling a tablecloth, and then again, covered with the towel, they would remove their other undergarments then pull or tie the replacement item without showing anything that was not or should be seen. Others were lying with tops down or water-skiing by the shoreline without much other than our minds racing from one direction to the next and eyes getting great visions. This openness gave him a shortening state of being speechless, open mouth, and some disbelief. He did tell all of this to my mother when we had gotten back, but there was more later. Mom stayed in that night too while her two boys went out for some drink on the town.

There was one bar where my buddy Montana and I had found on our previous trip. Being a very small striptease club, and being a weeknight, we found it had only a few patrons that night with us becoming the only ones. The girls were slowly performing their dances, and they would approach us, asking us to buy them a drink, as part of their nightly duties, but as it gotten late, they asked my dad what was he drinking. One of the girls was also working as the bartender, and she asked me in French what was that drink called that my dad was drinking. So Dad and I with mixed English, hands, and a little French told her first you start with a tall glass of ice, followed with one-third vodka or gin, a small amount of lime or lemonade juice, then finish it off with white soda water to the top, adding a cherry with a mint leaf on top, but they didn't have any mint leafs, only cherries. "That's what is called a Tom Collins," we told them. She made the first one, and then we helped improve each one because each girl had to have one too. We had three or four, and my dad was the center of delight for the entire crowd of ladies. It was close to 4:00 am before we found our way back to the hotel with my mom still asleep. My dad had found another thing besides movies on his trip that had been very successful only to him with its special moment for telling a new myth to his buddies now.

The next day, we traveled north through small villages at high speeds and sometimes on the sidewalks because the streets were so narrow with small cars parked there, having only room for carts during the earlier century, when they were first built. It was my pleasure giving my dad many white-knuckled rides and finding my revenge for all those rides he gave me as a child in the mountainous curves on the edges of many roads in California, with me sliding around in the backseat of our 1950 Chevy convertible with the top down. We stopped within the wine country and had some fine wine with French bread and Laughing Cow cheese, along the road under some large shady trees halfway to Paris. Then on to Paris, where they connected with their group again and saw the Lido Nightclub, the opera house, the Eiffel Tower, the Sacre-Coeur de Montmartre, and the Notre Dame.

Also on one occasion, we ate at the Renault Restaurant on the Champs-Elysees one afternoon, sitting in booth seats made to appear to be old cars. Then for my mother, through my special services connection, I got her an invitation to sit in for a small showing of Christian Dior line of clothes with models. The last stop was to SHAPE, meeting my fellow army buddies, and afterward we had a real T-bone steak dinner at the PX on its once-a-month dining night before returning to their hotel and home. They made many more trips to other places in the world, but this one was the most special for all three of us to recall.

THIRTY-ONE

The Other Job

Before my parents came in September 1964, I had traveled to Naples, Italy, and Athens, Greece, all on "leave" for three days through the months before March 1964; and later during July 1964, I traveled to Belgium, Netherlands, Holland, Germany, Sweden, Norway, and Denmark. All were NATO countries; with my extra baggage, I carried a briefcase attached to my wrist or folder with documents or papers on these "leaves."

These trips were more than incidental to various military stations with highly classified, top-security documents, mostly wearing my military but occasionally civilian clothing too. This was a part of my new "other job" assignment staged by the Army Security Agency. There were times I was issued a sidearm for protection and companionship. The first issued was a very old Colt .45, very heavy, and fired like an old cannon, with its carriage flying loosely and recoiling after firing, which was not good in repeating firing, plus it made me walk very heavy on my right side under my armpit. The arms supply sergeant found a cool nine-millimeter Browning from WWII that was lighter and fit my body in a very convincing manner.

During these days, this gave me a wider and greater chance of seeing the sights of other countries paid for by the US taxpayers' money while staying in nice assigned hotels and with meals. I could imagine myself being no more than a non-dangerous James Bond, without a number or license to kill, just laughing at myself, thinking about comparison. I was just a messenger boy. Only once on a train did the hair on the back of my neck rise up, after two men had noticed the handcuffed case to my wrist and began whispering to each other and then disappearing. Maybe they thought I was carrying jewelry items because of our traveling through Switzerland, but afterward I locked myself in my room until departure time had come at the next station.

However, I was never able to tell anyone about my travels other than traveling on "leave." It consisted of only picking-up and dropping-off point, never knowing what was delivered or when there would be another next trip, but always ending at a military site assignment. I was just given a briefcase or an envelope with travel papers from within official security SHAPE officers, listing the delivery location and date of arrival only. I learned many unknown facts to most of the world and most others related to places like Southeast Asia duties. I put two and two together on my own, knowing it was time to leave the service, after already extending my tour of duties for six months more, above and beyond my volunteered time of three years of duties at the beginning, starting as just a draftee. At first it was great playing Bond, but then stories of other things, and knowing things, started to encompass a possibility of much greater dangerous duties in my mind and other things seen coming on the horizon. It was time to get out; there was Vietnam on my list of places to see.

England Holidays

My first "leave" trip was in 1963 to England with Patricia and her parents for the Christmas holidays. They live in the storybook town of Nottingham not far from Sherwood Forest, which doesn't have many trees any longer. Her father was a part of the upper middle class in his sixties with a heart or some form of illness when Patricia was born. Her mother had been his nurse before their getting married, and she was much younger than him. She had been taking care of him for some time for health reason, but then they became lovers, with Patricia coming along later, being their only pampered child, who was now twenty-one, when we met. Patricia was flying solo and speaking the Queen's English and learning in a private school to speak also two or three other languages, and this is how she got into her present employment with UNESCO with her friend Vanessa.

Her mother was very pleasing to me, with a "Hello, nice to meet you," in a very understanding way; and her father had trouble getting up until I made my way in with the suitcases and then just dismissed me as another young man from the colonies after our handshake. However, Christmas and Boxer's Day were full of surprises and very enjoyable for a colonist who didn't know the English holidays. This family was Catholic, and we went to midnight mass with my knees crying out "enough" after continuing at it for over an hour. It was less of the commercializing Saint Nick's holiday, but more faith-driven celebration, as it should be for them, as well for the French. We returned to their home for our meal and warmed wines with the opening of presents.

The difference with their teas, by having cookies as biscuits with many other types of English foods, was interesting, like "kidneys and things," which brought on some more colonist moments. As for Boxer's Day, there were more presents added because the upper class started giving "boxes" to the peasant class, like giving to the postman or employees or friends, but doubling the fun now after Christmas for all. That's where it originated, but now you just give and receive more presents on the following weekend; therefore, there is more commercialism than us over in the colonies. It was very nice of her family and her to have me with them while I was thinking of our family with turkeys and pumpkin pies. Patricia and I returned to her parents' home for our next Christmas in 1964, but we would make other trips to other places during our time together, for over one and half years.

A Scotch New Year

But there was another trip to finish this holiday, by traveling from Nottingham to Edinburgh, Scotland, after Christmas, by train on "leave" during the New Year holidays to an air force base; and this was my first "leave" trip with me now becoming nervous. This turned out to be one of my most, above all, enjoyable trips for NATO. It was one day before New Year's Eve when I arrived at my hotel that night. So the next day, I walked and did the usual sightseeing to the castle while shopping and buying a sweater; and just after high tea at the hotel, while sitting with some students, they told me about the "the happening" and where to go on New Year's. It was under a large town clock in a plaza, and now I put on my new suit then found my way to that plaza, where the merriment had already began, as I was walking through the crowd and finding those students. They gave me a medium-size water glass with some clear form of white Scotch whisky that was so smooth. I was never a scotch drinker, which made me hesitant to drink more. Then we formed into a large circle of joyful crowd, with singers growing louder and larger, as time moved closer to midnight. Bottles of whisky appeared and being passed from one person to another, filling your own held glass, and then passing the bottles on to the next person beside you, with it continuing on, with new ones coming around to replace the one from that unknown beginning. Somewhere there were clapping hands and singing; we brought our arms over our shoulders with attempts to jug the bounding glasses around and drink some too as we began snaking around under that large clock. Then with more joy, it stuck twelve o'clock, with people now moving on down the streets toward the surrounding houses. Many of the doors were already open, with some of the people carrying bags of coal.

All shared in to say, "Let this coal warm your house for the coming year!" Then we heard someone from inside saying in response, "Warm yah selves," sharing more drink for the fellow followers of temporary guess. By now, being a drinker of large amounts before, and while in the army, I was now in a lost world; but I held my drink, as that could be expected. However, after now being in our fourth or five house, my legs and my head required much-needed assistance; and there were those who helped me continue with the arms-over-shoulder method.

Somewhere along my travels, I was usually able to know north, south, east, or west or streets; but this was way beyond my abilities now. The party was slowing down. As I was with that last house of the evening, I now asked for someone to please call me a taxi, thanking everyone by starting with the boys with a large handshake, followed with a "Cheers," then kissing girls repeating my last "Happy New Year's." Now I found myself outside in the early-morning fog, attempting to find some straight thinking, some focus of my vision, finding the waiting taxicab with its lights in the dim light of dawn. The driver then asked for my hotel name, and we started driving to my hotel. Upon pulling up to the hotel, I began fumbling through my pockets looking for my wallet, but there was no wallet to be found. He smiled and then laughed with an uneasy manner. "OK, Yank," he said after showing him my key to the hotel, "here's what we'll do." He wrote down his name with his cabbie number on a small piece of paper. Then he told me to pay him upon finding my wallet, knowing I was lost, and then he told me that he himself had been in many worse places than this on many a New Year's Day. Then he gave me some money, telling me how to take the public transportation, which was a bus, and writing the address on the other side of the paper, where I had been picked up. Then off he went back into the fog, as if he was my own guardian angel.

On finding the bus stop, my head was now beginning to work with some limited clarity. It was a New Year and my first day with some fog clearing around me, but it became colder while I was standing awaiting the first-run bus. Being there by myself, the bus arrived with only the bus on the wrong side of the street, but I gave him the address upon my stepping on board; he knew the street block and would make sure to stop. The driver smiled and stopped at the nearest corner of the street, being somewhat my known last stop, where the taxi found me. I found the number given me, and knocking at the door came the joyfully received "Happy New Year" before I said anything. I was then told my wallet had been found and turned in to the local walking police officer, who was passing by just after my departure. So again, I found my way walking the short distance to the station after receiving more directions.

Now, I found myself informing the constable at the desk of my story; he checked, and there was my lost wallet with my ID and with its money, but before this, I was thinking, No way, there wouldn't be any money, but I was wrong again. All of the money was intact, and again I asked, "Would you call me a taxi, and if possible, the same cabbie on this small paper." About five minutes later, he showed at the station, laughing with that special smile; and we returned to my hotel. Giving him his requested fare, plus the money he had advanced, and adding a large tip, I wished him a "very, very happy New Year," and he replied, "May God be with you."

The next day around noon, after some coffee, I made my way back to that address again by using that same public bus number; and I found a very nice, attractive young lady in her early twenties, standing there at the door, answering my ring of the bell, who now recalled me being there earlier in a different state. I said, "Good afternoon, could I reward the person who found and returned my wallet?" She informed me it was she, and no reward was expected or necessary. We talked for a while, and then she told me the celebration was to continue on for another two days and nights. She offered an invitation to join her with some of her friends again that tonight. I replied with a sure yes, but I told her she must go out for dinner with me first, and she said OK.

Then I returned to the hotel and freshened up with a shower, changed into my wool suit from my advertising days, and returned around five. We went to dinner, a reward for her kindness; and now seeing her clearly with new eyes, there was more there than my eyes could see. We then met up with her friends at a dance club. Ordering drinks with me paying for the first round, they then told me about the white scotch, now knowing it could only be found and sold in Scotland. Then of course it had a story too, along with its great taste. It had something to do with Scottish myth. I found out that like the Irish, the Scott's like their stories tall and hard to believe; there's some drinking done along with these tales into helping it to become more believable, and it always becomes easier to love the myth. We all told more stories, laughing a lot in between some dancing and drinking until another possible past midnight had come, and then there was just the two of us, now ending alone at her apartment. Like white lightning from the USA, this scotch hit me with a force of walloping my judgment. However, before drinking this scotch the night before, I did recall my long ago other occasion of dealing with this witches' brew. I recalled in my early twenties I drank a scotch, and as a result, I threw up in my car. My stomach acids removed the paint in my poor black old car. Surprisingly this scotch had no hangover, this time or the next day.

I awoke in her bed, with her already gone to work; my suit was now clean, hanging in the bedroom doorway, but I now recalled that somewhere before this, both of us had done some rolling around on her rug and the removal of clothes before we could make it into her bed in the dark. She was gone now, there was a very nice note on her pillow laying beside me, telling me where there were some breakfast rolls with tea and enjoying the encounter very much, but she hated goodbyes like Sylvia. I knew it was that, but I always remember that honesty and this place will always have a very special place in my heart or soul. So I got dressed and closed her apartment door and again found my way back to the hotel. I got the briefcase, which was safely kept in the hotel safe, onward to my "leave" assignment. I recalled our night before and she told me about a boyfriend in the US Air Force, but they were no longer together. It was hard for her to move on, but our encounter had helped her in some way with that, she said while we were talking over our drinks with pebbles washing into new directions.

I never told Patricia about her, but I told her all about the lost wallet and its recovery with the greatest people that I had ever met. She wasn't real found of the Scots, but she also was a person who lost or misplaced things a lot. We never know which angels or stream any of us little pebble may find in our travels. The way people treat you is much more important than the places you see or visit because this becomes so much more a part of you and that place stays in your heart and memories.

Luxembourg

I met two nice German girls again through the USO before Patricia, Montana, and I had traveled to Luxembourg over Easter in March 1964. Luxembourg was a mixture of German, French, and Belgian people coming all in one of Europe's smallest country, less than five hours away, and we loved it. It was something of another Switzerland in northern Europe for most its neighbors. Just getting away from the army and our jobs was always needed, but combining that with two delightful women made it even better. We drank, ate, and viewed the renewed wildflowers coming into bloom for spring while at that time, Patricia was still in her on-and-off thing with her boyfriend. So dating others was OK with both of us then, but after returning from that trip, things started changing.

We did not know if it was April in Paris that brought us under its spell of bringing us together like other young couples, but this time we found shelter standing under trees through the raining clouds, raining days, and finding some sunshine, and a closeness of together for each other now.

Summer Traveling

On July 1964, we embarked on another trip to Germany for a pleasurable leave, combining a "job leave" without the briefcase. Patricia's roommate's boyfriend, Ray or Raymond, had some time and a very small four-door French Renault Dolphin called a car. So all four of us got into this box of a car, being even smaller than mine, and we started driving toward Munchen. This was a sort of getting-to-know-you event for us guys, with the two girls being friends and roommates already, but now all of us were together with more interaction. He and I bonded and got along well, which became the beginning of us staying in touch for many years after our getting out of the service. Funny, he became an IRS investigator accountant in Chicago; he was married, but not with Vanessa. That just didn't work out after their togetherness in their life's streams

English, it was a must. Upon leaving Germany's port on the ferry, my crossing began during the midday with smoky cars and surrounding people from around the world. Therefore, riding out on the top deck watching our busy departure, I found myself standing next to a small redhead young woman, who was laughing at the people, waving goodbye. She was around twenty with green eyes and freckled face, wearing a white sailor's hat holding her hair against the wind. We started talking; she was with her parents on their way back to their home outside of Copenhagen from a few days in Germany. Having no idea how or why, we had started talking about the difference between the American and the Danish sex behaviors. I will never know. Then I thought she must be a student when she said, "Why do you Americans have so many sex hang-ups, looking down on our free Danish beliefs in our having sex before marriage or anyone else that just wants to enjoy it for themselves?" Continuing, she said, "My parents had sex without being married, which is why I'm here." So what could I say? I then told her, "I'm not like most Americans. I see nothing wrong with sex, and also I am an artist with my own found enlightenment and beliefs formed before going into the army." I added, "You can't say that about me," and then continued, "I'm a free thinker."

Next I told her, "There is what is called the beat and hippy movements in America now, starting throughout California before my leaving there, and there is also now the love-inns in California, which is where I'm from. It started with young people changing the ways sex is seen now. But not so for most of Americans' thinking."

Her parents came up while we were talking; her father told me to call him Red with a red beard, and her mother had green eyes with a very flashing smile as they introduced themselves. It was easy to see the Viking spirit standing there. After a while, I learned from our discussion that there was a very high tax imposed on the Danes for bringing liquor into Denmark from Germany for Vikings. They could only bring in one or two duty-free bottles, and then they asked if it was possible for me to buy them two more and take them through customs for them. So at first I was kidding. I laughed and said sure, but they had to share a drink with me afterward. They didn't understand the joke, but they did invite me to their house for dinner. After they gave me the money, I walked downstairs to the store. I bought the bottles that they requested just before the ferry left.

Now the ferry departed, and I told them it's OK, but I did not have any transportation. I gave them their bottles down further the street, feeling like maybe Uncle Benny, but I asked them where I could find a bus or train station. They pointed to the signs, with me saying, "That's fine, and goodbye." I turned to leave on my way, thinking about where would I find directions to a student hospice. They stopped me after a few steps. "No, no," they said. "Please, we would like you to come see our house and have a dinner. We know our daughter likes you very much," as their daughter smiled. They must have discussed this while I was buying the liquor.

after Paris. She was very self-centered and most of the time was using him, mo: what she wanted, but he was in love with her at the time. Love makes you forge own wants and values at times. She used everybody, which included Patricia of the time as well, but Patricia would fight back too. It was a so-so time at fir. Frankfurt, but by that time, we had gotten past many soft walls and into Munich partly because of how closely we sat with being packed in that small car and all girls' clothes taking up some space; we overcame most of the problems with laught seeing this like an English vacation comedy movie of the time. We did have some goo German beer, weather, and mixture of enjoyable food with shared laughter over som jokes about the French soldiers' trucks passing us, leaving Germany in their convoys, appearing in their "tue sweet" (very fast) manner, as if they were practicing the process of "how fast" they could retreat back into their French homeland, which was repeated and learned very well in all their previous wars. They still believed even then that the Germans would rise up against them again, but really I guess, they just wanted to get home in a hurry.

The French soldiers' families start receiving monies from the state for their male child during his early childhood until and after entering the service, but most don't save any; therefore, these guys don't have much when their time comes to report for duty. Now grown up and in the army, these guys' uniforms are unkempt and find themselves without any money to spend on needs or wants to be there. Not like the Germans, who had pride and discipline, which has always been reflected, and why they were still a major force, greater than France. You could also see in their cities and houses along the borders the difference between the two countries, which reflected a complete change in aptitudes and attitudes.

The German houses' widows would be seen with clean bedding hanging out and for airing out every day. Its people cleaned the streets with water and brooms. Everywhere you looked in the city, the streets were all clean with pride and neat for the newly started days. The French were overly taxed for their houses' outward appearance, so they would hide their pride inside, out of sight, unless you received an invitation into their home. The state paid for most of the cleaning of the streets or street toilets. For the most part, you would know if life was poor or great for them by looking at them and not their houses. It was more by their clothing and personal appearance that would determine what their status was. The threesome "musketeers" of Patricia, Vanessa, and Ray had to get back to Paris while my own "job leave" had to be completed, and they left me off in Frankfurt.

After completing this assignment, I boarded a train to Denmark for just a little longer of my own pleasure, continuing on for another unforgettable journey. I had heard so much about Copenhagen with its jazz clubs, famous Tivoli Gardens, and Hans Christian Andersen's Little Mermaid; and with all its real-life beauties everywhere speaking

We walked to their car, placing my travel bag next to me, and then we traveled our way down the streets, canals, and small crossing bridges with bicyclists going everywhere and them talking a little English, but my mind wasn't following the conversation. We arrived on a small street with small colorful painted house and doors in a row. We got out while the father parked the car in their rear garage, and the mother went around to meet him. I waited at the front door with Ingra, giving her a name to the best of my recollection now. Red came out the front door with his wife, as Ingra, his only child, stood with me. She then took my hand as we walked in with her becoming my guide. I did not know who was the child that was being led, but I just felt some comfort and warmth as we entered. I have always loved Danish furnishings; it's so clean looking with its rich woods, yet so plain. He opened one of the bottles that I had purchased for them and filled glasses for all. He said something in Danish, a toast, "Many gifts of health and happiness find you," and then he tried to explain it in English.

Ingra showed me the rest of the house and then their backyard, where there was a sauna, a hot steam house, with a tub next to it, outside on a decking. "We'll go in there after dinner, you like?" I only replied by nodding my head yes and smiling. We had some type of white fish, greens, and white wine with a Danish pastry, topped off with chocolate liquor topping. There was jazz playing in the next room; the father knew most of America's greatest hits, having many of them on old 78s and newer 33s records. This was a Danish dream or maybe just a fantasy.

After dinner, Ingra brought me one of her dad's robes, telling me it was time for the sauna and showing me to her bathroom to change, where I came out in my army boxers under the robe. Her father had poured me another drink, and then he went off toward his bedroom, where his wife was awaiting him to change. By then, Ingra came forth wrapped in a towel as we walked outside, with her mother and father following; the long day was coming to an end with the drink and steam weakening my whole being. Inside the father poured water on heated rocks, and they all laughed at my boxers as I disrobed with the mother giving me a large towel to cover my American pride. Then Ingra pulled out some eucalyptus leafs out of some place near the door, telling me to lie down on the side bench; and when doing so, she began hitting my back with the eucalyptus leafs. Her touch was soft at first, which became stronger with each release. My mind was going off into the rising steam and thinking, what have you got yourself into? But it did smell and feel good after the mind accepted it. We all were sweating when Red poured on some more water, just about before my going into total meltdown, and then Ingra again took my hand, and we went outside where their tub was waiting. Climbing the steps into the small overhang around it, she said, "Jump," and so we both did at the same time with her second announcement, with my heart and blood running to the warmest possible place it could rush toward, which was my head, because the water was cold, really cold, even in July. She showed me to the steps, and we got out while we both laughed like small children running through the sprinklers during a hot day at home. Only we didn't have a thing on; picking up our towels, she pulled me close, wrapping the towel around us both. We kissed while her parents were still in the sauna. She laughed again, and we ran into the house with telltale of wet dripping following behind us and then up some stairs to her room. We left the towels on the floor and jumped into her bed, getting very warm again, feeling some leftover steam heat, drink, and then everything completely falling off on the floor, with no need of anything, other than our bodies. The next morning she went downstairs, getting my clothes from the bathroom, while her mother was brewing some very needed strong Danish coffee. We got dressed and came down, hearing her mother giggling with those big smiling green eyes. I lost my boxers somewhere and picked up my small travel bag while Red told me, "Thank you very much," as we were getting into the car that was already park out front because everyone had to go to work, and Ingra rushed giving me a picture of her with that white sailor hat with their address before leaving.

Just last year, I threw away my little black book with their address but did keep her picture with those long-ago memories. I told them all on my farewell, "Health and happiness had found me," while I was thinking, you must be the luckiest guy that was walking on earth that day. These people showed me unconditional love, with me saying, "Thank you again." Then as Red drove me to town and then dropped me off on his way to work, his last words were "Hope to see you again!" We did write a few letters back and forth until I got out of the army in another world.

The first thing to do was finding a student hospice and put my name on the list for that night. It was nothing like the luck that had brought me to the night before; there were just beds and boxes for your items, and it gave me that appearance of being back into the army barracks again. Then off I went sightseeing, first with the Little Mermaid on her rock looking out at the harbor and then finding Tivoli Gardens. I spent the whole day there; it was the first real Disneyland with its gardens, yet it was more like an amusement park too, with boating, theatres, and restaurants. The night fell with brilliant illumination of colors in the park, and I got back before they closed the doors to the hospice. Just before this, I went into a few of those step-down clubs with jazz, but short on money, I was only able to buy one drink.

It was a good thing; I had bought a return trip on the ferry back to Germany, but I hadn't saved for the train. I was expecting to meet someone here into giving me a ride back to Paris, but he hadn't shown. I wrote a postcard to my mother from there the next day, telling her I was out of money. I'll just have to hitchhike again back to Paris, as if she could do something for me from home in one day. Mothers are the first you think of in times of need. Also I put on the card "Ha-ha," but it was true. I only had about five dollars left to get back on.

After getting off the ferry dock in Germany, I then checked my map for the main highways to Paris from there, it was out to the highways, and in a short time, and I found my back facing the highway. A nice young German couple picked me up, speaking some English, and we traveled on to Hamburg for a short period, but that's as far as they were going, but they pointed me to my next route, which was like most of the rivers, the roads just followed along each other very closely through Germany. Next came along a middle-age man in his Mercedes-Benz; he didn't talk much but drove very fast, so now I just watched the landscape changing more into farmland as we arrived in Hanover, and from there he's headed toward the crossing rivers that led into East Germany, the German Democratic Republic. So he let me out, and as for me, I must continue going west while it was getting dark. I did not want to get lost ending up somewhere I wasn't allowed to go near. I tried a little longer; however, no one wanted to stop in the dark picking up a rider.

Most people were eating, drinking, or getting ready for bed. I began thinking more about that too, but I only had an apple and a bottle of water. I sat down along the side of the road. It was time to begin looking around at fields with piles of hay, and with each passing auto, there came that cold gust of winds reminding how tired I had become. I put on my jacket and then recalled my summer in my uncle's ranch in Wyoming and how the heat would come from the center of the stacks. I started looking for some being sighted a way from any houses. Then I got up, hopped over a small wooden rail into the next field, found a nice large stack, and pulled myself while tunneling into its side for my bed. Then I pulled more to cover most of my body from the cold mist that was rising outside because of the surrounding small canals of water. It was quite warm while I looked up at the few stars in the dark sky from my hole and found sleep.

I awoke to the sounds of the rousing roster, who was calling for the world to start taking notice of the sun rising; it was time to get moving again. After refilling my sleeping hole and pulling the straw from my clothes, I started looking around to find a direction back to the highway, and then I jumped back over the fence. It was only a short time again, and another old man driving a Mercedes-Benz truck to Cologne came along. He didn't speak much English at all, and my German was very limited too; however, we bounded along the highway with the same ups and downs, like a father and son would without much to say. We stopped with him buying me a beer at a cafe just before noon with my stomach complaining loudly. We arrived in Cologne in the late afternoon, with me saying, "Good'ne Tag," in the middle of the town, which is near the center of a university. Spotting a small Hofbrauhaus with real food and beer, I spent my last five dollars; and while eating and slowly drinking my beer, a group of young male students came in having a very "universe of discourse" discussion over many things in life. One asked me, "Are you American?" While laughing, I replied, "California, American!" Then they all laughed. With that, they asked me to join them as they ordered another round of beer for all. Next, they wanted to know, "Are you a student?" I again replied,

"We all are students of life, studying our surroundings, while also studying you, during my travels back to France!" Then further into our conversation, I told them, "I'm in the US Army on my way back to Paris, and I ran out of money along the way, so I'm now hitchhiking back." This got us all into the next American discourse regarding the coming presidential election. They had liked Kennedy but weren't sure about Johnson. Then one spoke of Goldwater and said, "We had someone like him and his beliefs." I asked, "Who is he?" I expected someone further back in Germany's history. He replied, "Adolf Hitler." So next I told him that Goldwater may speak like an old Western cowboy but so far, he hadn't killed anyone, none that I knew of yet, and Johnson is from Texas where Kennedy was shot and killed, and they also hanged blacks or Mexicans there.

Then another said, "I can give you a lift to Luxembourg." I responded with "Oh, great! That would be very helpful." While thanking him, I started rising up again readying for another adventurous moment of furthering this travel and ending this soon. Upon making my position politically and now standing up, it may be time to leave. Now feeling the beer and a cause for looking around for a place of deposit, the guy offering the ride and another quiet guy with him led me to that place, and all three of us exited together. Finding and getting into his older Auto Union, a three-cylinder car, we started for the highway. Then he began telling me about the great Auto Union racecars of the past, and this brought thoughts of the past drive I'd given to that German exchange student while in high school and my driving down the mountain with my dad's old Hollywood Graham car. Also again we were "flying" while my eyes watched the speed on the speedometer hitting 90 and 110, but I thought that's closer to ten to fifteen miles per hour. I hoped that he's not drunk too much and knew what he's doing. There wasn't much talk as we arrived in Luxembourg within a few hours in darkness.

I gave them my thanks for everything as they dropped me off at a train station, but from there with a few French francs left, I called SHAPE and found my army buddy Montana; he came within a few hours and gave me a ride the rest of the way home. It was a great summer; my life was further enriched with others' respect while I found their and my eyes being opened to wider surrounding views.

THIRTY-TWO

Last Trips

During the month of February 1965, since its Patricia's birthday, we planned another trip with her roommate Vanessa and Vanessa's boyfriend Ray to Munich, Germany, again. After our enjoyable time there in July, along with my time there with my parents in October, while still reflecting on these all, always being great times because of its people, and of course the beer, it was worth another last visit. At that time the US armed forces gave great deal on a special hotel and ski package, not too far from Hitler's Eagle's Nest in Berchtesgaden.

This time we drove in my car, but after running into a snowstorm with drifts flying on the autobahn, we stopped for the night before getting to Berchtesgaden. The next morning the car's motor was frozen; it wouldn't turn over because of the cold it had gotten. The antifreeze was OK, but I guess either the battery or the starter couldn't turn it over. It had stopped snowing now, and the hotel manager called the police in order for them to give us some assistance, but they showed up in a Volkswagen, "the people's car," in black and white. We laughed at first; however, right away they hooked it to my car and then pulled the car around the parking lot. The old Simca resisted at first, but after another pull, it became very resilient and was running again. We all jumped in while the engine was still running, but there wasn't much heat coming out through the heater for a while. We waved goodbye to the officers and the hotel manager with our "thank you" and "Dunka, Alf Vetter's Sane." They unhooked the car, and back on the autobahn we went, which was cleared now too. This was after being in Munich for only one day and one night, but now we were on our way to the Alps driving very carefully on the icy roads, which had been cleared most of the way without the need for chains.

We arrived just as it was getting dark, which happened earlier in the mountains, and this was a very nice hotel just for the US military with its own nightclub and great food. We got our rooms then our meal. Then Patricia and I walked outside into the night; we felt some very lightly kissing of snowflakes on our faces, and we saw around us only some small moonlight reflecting the crystals of mounds and piling around the pine trees. We also heard small sounds of snow falling from the trees. The girls wanted to go dancing, and we returned to our rooms to shower and change. The drinks were cheap, and there was a floorshow with a band for entertainment. Then before going to bed, we arranged for tickets for the ski lift and some skiing for the next day. Ray and I were the only ones who had experienced skiing before, but we all went to the beginners' slope at first. I hadn't had much experience either, just some in Big Bear, California, but I was still learning. I forgot how much it had cost, but it was like only few dollars for the skis and maybe five for one day's lift tickets. They gave the military big breaks on everything.

The girls' clothes were not much for skiing, so we spent a lot of time at the lodge next to the fire with good German schnapps to warm up our bodies from the inside. The next day, we had to leave again because we all had to be back in France, but I'll never forget these fairyland surroundings. It was no big wonder this was Hitler's favorite place to be, but now it was the Americans' reward to its military.

The Last European Trip

Just before leaving for the States in June 1965, Mike, and Patricia's another girlfriend Valerie, Patricia, and I took a trip to Spain. My new car was being repaired after my accident in Paris and being readied for shipment; so we were forced to borrow Montana's car, which was another Simca just like mine, except it was red and ran very hot most of the time. We put in for five days of leave, and so did the girls for a vacation; we planned of maybe driving all the way to Portugal. Patricia once had this Portuguese boyfriend; she learned to speak some Portuguese from him, and she wanted to see the country. Mike spoke some Spanish. I only knew some from my high school class, which I had earned only a D grade.

We left early on that first day, with swimsuits in our suitcases, and looking forward to finding some summer sun, seeing both girls being very English with white skin. While comparing Mike's very dark and my being black Irish in a more moral tone, there wasn't any middle-color areas. We drove one whole day to Bordeaux and stopped for the night, where they were having a middle-age fair. We enjoyed our short stay there but made the coast by the next day. Mike and I had heard about some great surfing in that area of the coast, and therefore we went to see the Bay of Biscay, but it was cold and still being the Atlantic Ocean, we did not see any waves or surfers, it was disappointing.

We crossed over to Spain's Basque province sometime in the afternoon or later. We stopped in a small village, found a small cafe for something to eat and drink, and then noticed this was a quiet town with very little movement on the streets. As we went in, the owner told Mike in Spanish, "Sorry, we have a very large party coming for lunch," but there was no other cafe or anything open around, and it would be a very long time before the next town. We had forgotten it was Sunday, and everything was closed. The girls were now hungry and hadn't eaten much that morning anyway, so Mike went to work on the owner. Just then a bus drove up, filled with only men, Basque men. They had gone to the bullfights in another city and were returning for their Sunday lunch, but lucky for us the owner went over to talk to those in charge and returned with a great big smile, speaking Spanish to Mike, "If you and the women don't mind, you can eat with these men." He added that they would be happy to share their food with us, but there was one condition: we must perform something entertaining for them, as they will for us. Now we all had been aware of their separatist movement seen in the newspapers, but the girls being very hungry did agree but said they had to keep their clothes on, and we all laughed.

We followed the men as they went into a large rear room with tables set up in a large horseshoe shape. The waiters set us at the end of the last table, making room, and began bringing large plates of food out. At the head table, there was a popping, which made us jump, as corks from champagne bottles began flying in the air and with cheers surrounding us. They were laughing and telling stories in their own language as we all sat down and then started eating. They poured us wines for each course of the meal while making toasts to honor their events, friends, families, and just revealing their great expressions of happiness with each rising of their glasses as we all got a little higher. We were honoring their hospitality, with our eagerness to raze our glasses high too while drinking down those continuously filled glass with the growing moment.

We didn't know what they were saying as long as it wasn't something to get us put in prison or killed. In the same manner, we didn't know what we were eating, except it was very good. The Basque raised sheep; therefore, it must have been something of mutton, with a lot of cheese dishes too. These guys had knives on their belts yet all in their Sunday best dress, which brought thoughts to mind regarding their present long, fight to free themselves from Spain now.

With the eating slowing, the entertainment started with the main leading gentleman at the head table singing and then telling a joke with all laughing, followed with some others playing guitars; but then one who only had one arm got up and showed his violin. He then placed the instrument under his chin and started bowing it with his one arm, but not very well, so he then started plucking it while playing a very lively tune. He was dancing around as our eyes changed our focus to the whole picture, where he had a beret hanging from the front of his trousers, and it was bouncing with the beat of his playing, but he stopped dancing with it still bouncing. At first the girls didn't notice it, then it hit them with a great gasp. He then lost the beret, and there was this very small thing sticking out from his pants. All of the men started laughing very loudly, watching our reactions, which turned into a loud roar because the girls couldn't believe their eyes, with mouths wide open; he then just stopped. You could now see his trick because before his performance, he had pulled one of his arms out of his long-sleeved shirt and then had run it down his pants before picking up his violin, and now his index finger was sticking out of his pants cover with his beret. No one was going to top that, but now our turn came to entertain them. So we all four steadied ourselves, trying to get to our feet, and we all had agreed earlier to sing. We started singing the Beatles' "She Loves You" in a very off-key attempt, with them all laughing, but we were thinking they enjoyed our condition more than our song. And with this, we thanked them all by shaking their hands and smiling, making our way past them trying to find our way out. The meal was free, and it was something again none of us would ever forget. As it happened, no one was able to drive. Luckily there were still two rooms available upstairs, which just happened to be about the price of the meals. So we stayed the night, finding these rooms were about the size of an average American's bathroom. So Patricia slept on the single bed while I slept on the floor with the help of a large downy comforter wrapped around me. This was not the time for romanticism, or any of these thoughts; just laying the head down without feeling the room spinning was a challenge, and we all took our turns stumbling to the bathroom before that undertaking.

The next day, we all had very, very large hangover, with trouble seeing more than a few feet away, with a pounding head that was trying to lift the top of our heads. We had some fresh bread with strong black Spanish coffee provided, before each showered at the end of the hall. Now being Monday, the streets were busy again with people, bicycles, and a few cars. We again said our thank-you to the owner as we got in the car with the sun rising and chickens running down the side street with us heading south.

Our next stop was in Zaragoza with its mountains surrounding us; we had bypassed Madrid and Portugal due to our time limits. So on to Barcelona, with the Costa Brava towns and ending up in Tarragona. However, the car had gotten hot because of the mountains and heat, which we were here for, but the French car wasn't. It had burned some valves, now running only on two cylinders.

We brought sleeping bags with us, and there were cabanas overlooking the beach that you could rent, so we stayed above the beaches in a very nice campground. We would walk down the cliff sides to the beach, drink wine, and eat some bread with cheese and fruit, taking in the sun. The girls had their bikinis while coating their bodies in oil and getting their golden tans, while Mike and I just got darker. We would drive to town for dinner eating biotic shrimp and lobster stew at a street cafe and then to nightclubs with flamenco dancers in their red and black flashing bodies blinding with high stepping shoes and sexy moves. The sun takes energy from you, but the dancing with some wine would bring a young person alive, finding fire within the soul. Mike and Valerie were only friends, but Patricia and I knew we were in the last part of our relationship, knowing I was about to return to the States. So this too was becoming more a very mixture of emotions and passage with trying moments of passion.

Patricia and Valerie

We spent three days there; the last two was with my taking the engine apart with only a limited number of tools in the trunk. Then using a pair of Patricia's nylon stockings and some grease from the front-wheel roller bearings, I began the very long process of regrinding the valves by hand, using the fine sand obtain by using the stockings, using the fine mixture and the grease compound. However, I did find a garage selling a new head gasket while everybody else was finding ways to get back to Paris. It would be impossible for me to leave Montana's car there, so for me it was working with a flashlight into the night. The three of them returned by train while I was putting the car back together, and the next day, it came together. It ran a little rough, but on all four cylinders again, and now I was so thankful for the things my dad had taught me in that shade tree schoolyard. Next I called my friend Montana; after talking with the company clerk, asking for two more days of extra leave just in case, and waiting for an OK from the captain, I started my way back. Now I was very careful while driving back during the night for most of the way until I got into the cooler parts in France. The car made it with time to spare, and Montana was very pleased to get his car back. He wasn't able to tell the difference in the way it ran now compared to its sound before, as I told him what happened and that it was the best I could do in that short time. He being an old farmer boy started laughing, just thinking about me working with just the basic tools and making it all the way back. We took it down to the car shop, and another friend took it apart to finish the repairs, with me giving him some money and thanks. My new car was fixed now also and on its way for delivery to Brooklyn, New York, USA, and I was next.

Going Home on the Army's Sea

As the results of my hearing more about involvement in South Asia and my unwillingness to stay in the army came, besides the fact that Mike was getting out at this time too, it was time to go home. We both got our orders to depart by train from Paris to Bremerhaven, Germany, which started this unforgettable trip on my birthday on June 25, 1965. No more first-class traveling; this was surface travel on an old troopship named the USNS Rose, which was scheduled for arrival around July 3, into Brooklyn, New York, USA, but as it was, we got there on July 22.

It was cold, foggy, and with that mass rushing around in confusion and standing in lines when we got to Bremerhaven, which neither of us had seen for the past two years. Once upon the ship, we were assigned to decks with a bed; there were no going-away parties. Some of these guys had been in trouble their whole time in the army and wasn't going home any easier. Mike got assigned right away to the captain's cook so he could get the best of the food, but I bet it was partly because of his being a Filipino, a discrimination seen by the world. I wasn't that smart because when it came to eating, it was from the ship's deepest hole for the rest and myself. He did get me a piece of cake that night and other goodies when in need.

The command service crew put up what was a fair KP role for the rest of us, but nobody was showing up. "Hell!" It was said, "We're going home, and the army can't control us anymore," this being a major feeling among this mob. At first they were serving food, but next we found ourselves in the North Seas passing along Northern Ireland, with the ship rising up then dropping ten or more feet with each wave. Now I understood more why I was told to pick the top bunk bed and its advantages, like when that feeling hit you, it was up to those down below to find their shield, but my guys below never received any unexpected showers from me, but most of the ship did. However, the motion was more from the top too, but holding it down came by learning another lesson: by watching the sea through a small porthole or on deck finding that some point of leveling. Up on deck, there were times also that the waves broke over the bow on to the deck and the ship rolled sideways at the same time, but you get your sea legs or lie flat in bed riding this like in a cement mixer. This only lasted two or three days, and we were back to that KP duty problem rising with more wanting to eat now but still not wanting service duties.

First they tried no meals, but the guys just ate from the vending machines or what they had saved and stored away from previous meals. Mike brought me some of his extra feast when he came off duty, and this went on for a few more days, but the captain had enough, stopped the ship, and completely shut down everything, with him coming on the speaker announcing, "This ship isn't moving until you show up for KP duty. We don't care."

Now everybody wanted to go home and get off this ship. It was now a very sticky hot Fourth of July. Some needed showers and clean clothes; it's worse than any team locker rooms of my past. The ship was now moving further south, but very slowly, and nobody was having fun in these past ten days. You got the feeling the ship captain held all the cards. So starting at the top with my last name starting in A, I reported into the hole and began my service. Upon reporting, they told us it should be only one full day of duties with these many guys on board. Well, there was some bad As, Bs, and Cs mixed in there because after each meal, the service metal trays were somehow finding their way out of the garbage hole with the garbage. Their reason now appeared to be "No trays, no cleaning problems," but this made other problems that these guys with below ABC thinking didn't foresee. Therefore at the next meal, without or only half the trays available now, people had to wait while these growing smaller number of trays had to be cleaned, bringing a doubling amount of their repeated washing, and everyone was now forced into washing even faster and more often. Those involved were not rocket scientists, and reflecting only perceptual little brain pebbles in their heads, no wonder they were losers.

We made it near Brooklyn's harbor, but we stayed only within a few miles offshore seeing the bright lights reflecting and our viewing into that night before our docking, so no one would jump ship until morning. It had been twenty-seven days at sea. We docked; again there was that same old rushing around, followed by standing and waiting in lines, but now a miracle appeared, with everyone being cooperative and following orders just like their first months of boot camp. We got our papers then the inspection of our bags and turning in our heavy coats or whatever equipment the army still wanted. There were also found guns and stuff that you couldn't believe that was being recovered from some of these guys, and then there was another ship coming in at the same time, doubling like the lost trays. So it was now, "Get the hell out of here!" That became the orders of the day.

Both Mike and I had started our service in California, so with our leave pay came another bonus with us getting paid by the miles from New York to California. The first thing we did was picking up my car, which had been shipped to Brooklyn many days before us. Mike had bought the same car in a different color, but it was shipped home to San Francisco. Now I changed clothes, got something to eat, gassed up the car, and then found a pay phone.

Home

We first called our home and families, and then I called my friend Sonny of New York City. He said, "Come on over," with his friendly New York, Brooklyn, and Italian voice. There were no "computerized street-finding maps" in those days, so he gave us direction, and the routes to his house in Long Island, which took some time and a lot of dines with us both trying to map his directions, while Mike wrote and I repeated his words until we thought we had it somewhat clear. We got in the car laughing, saying, "We are free!" So on July 22, 1965, after three years, six months, and five days, we knew there would still be a reporting for inactive reservists duty until January 17, 1968, hanging over our heads. Because of both of our MOS, we could have been called back in for service or war.

New York, New York

After many tolls, and a few wrong-way streets, we found Bayside, and when we got there, Sonny had already request his wife and daughter stay with her parents for a few days, while "us boys" played. He showed us our room to put down our bags, but then it was off to his "Club Members" pal's bar. We walked in getting a better greeting, then that "Cheers" show that appeared later on TV, and we shook hands with every guy in the place. We were also offered anything on the house, which even included our pick of two Puerto Rico girls, whose purpose there was to give free oral sex if anyone or we would like, but neither of us needed or thought of these needs. We were just happy being in the land of round doorknobs; besides that, they were in need of a bag over their heads or maybe two, while thinking they must do this for drinks. We had our own "club" to share with Sonny as well. Before leaving, Mike had bought his "Playboy Key" with thoughts of us first going to the London Club, which we didn't get to before leaving, but the next night in New York, we took Sonny there. All three of us dressed now in our finest suits, with our thin ties. After an hour shaving, showering, and clone, we were ready for our night on the town. I drove while Sonny gave me directions between lights, and we laughed like teenagers before gaining our "cool cat" composure appearance, as the elevator raced us into a different world with the "hips" of people. We showed the key going through into everyman's dream. It was "top class" in the upper town part of New York with its "bunnies" appearing everywhere trying to please your wish and looking for big spenders. This was better than witnessing the Easter Bunny, just watching them making deliveries with us grown guys acting like "cool" kids. How did those bunny suits lift and stay in place, causing our minds to be unable but trying to fit it all in, without losing one's visual scanning of the curve traveling from ear tops to heels? Right away, Mike wanted to shoot pool, while the bunnies got us drinks, then another one racked up the table with her joining in as the four player of eight ball. Later, came our finding a fine meal with filet mignons steaks wrapped with bacon, being at what was an unbelievably low price. The boys had an unforgettable time with great food and drinks, being surrounded by those Playboy pages, which came alive without us finding the centerfold. So Mike and I found a new continuing mission: to hit and experience as many clubs as possible on the map that we could find in going home across America.

The following day Mike and I went to Rockefeller Center, first seeing Sandpiper, with Elizabeth Taylor and Richard Burton, followed with the "The Rockets Dancers" performance. The next day, we all went to the World's Fair, "It's a Small World," and seeing the presentation of the new Ford Mustangs. Now still having my SHAPE plates on the car, we parked it on the street and laughed at the parking ticket on it, when we came back out, because these were diplomatic immunity plates, so the laugh was on them all. So being limited with our funds and time, we crowded in just two days this great city sights and sounds, with Sonny asking me, "What's your favorite Italian food?" I answered, "Lasagna," recalling my last time ordering it at one of our eateries in New England, with him always saying, "None of these come close to Momma's cooking." Those were always his remarks. It's been over two years without some "good Italian cooking."

Sonny & Mike at NY World Fair

Now finding out, he had called his mother, asking her to cook dinner for his special guest. Now remembering this was July with temps running over one hundred in both degrees and humanity. We drove to his old neighborhood in Brooklyn, parking in front of an old brownstone apartment building with kids playing in water from the fire hydrant in the late afternoon on Sunday. Clad in white shirts, army undershirts, and sport coats with ties, we were met by Sonny's parents. As their door opened, their hearts of gold and smiles melted us before we felt the other heat in a three-room apartment with no air-conditioning, held against fans running from both directions. "Mamma" had been cooking all day in this heat, because this is what she has done for her family and friends for all of her life. Now we knew where Sonny obtained that brightness, other than his name in beginning. His father first said, "What's da mat'r wit yuz boys?" "Taks thos ties an shirts off. Yuz can't eatz Italian food lik's thats." We were already wet in all parts of our bodies cover from necks down under our clothing, and so with the pouring of the first glasses of real Chianti wine making us even warmer, we stated disrobing, but not yet confident setting there in our T-shirts before starting this congenial meal. The windows were open with the long table sitting as close as possible to it, and we sat with Sonny, Papa, and his mother placing the food on the table. As we said grace, a small breeze came grazing our senses and filling the air with many smells of the best Italian meal of my life, and Mike had to drive us afterwards to Sonny's house. It wasn't so much the drink as it was becoming easily lost, so there was a few wrong turns before Mike found our way back to the house.

The next day, we were on our way west. Sonny's family was returning to their home, and that was the last time I saw sonny's smiling face. We wrote Christmas cards, and I'd found during the following years that he had some family in San Pedro, California, but I never was given another chance to return his unforgettable friendship. I hope now he wasn't near those towers and was retired on that September day, but knowing him, he would have been there with his heart giving it his all.

Washington DC

Our next stop was Washington DC for many reasons, the first being that it was the next closest place where we knew someone whom we may be able to stay with for free and knew the city. The second was that we heard it was a place with over ten times the number of women to men, and the third being it was the capital. Our friend Terry Westigard's female cousin was working and living here with a couple other single girls, and he told us to get in touch with her on our way home. We have gotten into town, giving her a call. She met us just like Terry said; she was good-looking but had some great roommates, plus we were welcomed to stay there. Then after they all had gotten home from work, we went out for something to eat, and then all of us where off to the disco clubs in Old Town. We bought them drinks while taking in the numbers of so many other young women there, and Mike started dancing with our escorts two at a time, while I was having girls coming up asking me to dance too. Of course these were mostly fast dances, and the girls had to work the next day, so we had to get back around midnight, and after driving from New York, plus adding the dancing, their coach or rug on the floor with a few pillows made it easy to find sleep. The next day Mike and I got up having coffee with the girls, and they told us where to find the cereal before rushing off to work.

We did the "monument visiting" to all the free places, like Jefferson, Lincoln, and Arlington with its rolls of white crosses and Kennedy's flame while standing in silence with our long salutes, and at the statue of the marines raising the flag on Iwo Jima. These three places will always hold that place in your mind with mixed thoughts of what happen in history, but more, how all these men had changed so many lives. After another day on our feet, and after the girls gotten home, we all went out for pizza and beer in my VW station wagon. Again, we laughed a lot, driving around seeing Washington at night and then back to their place for talk and three bottles of wine until midnight again. Then again with the morning shining, it was off again with a big thanks.

Playboy Clubs

After crossing the Potomac, we were ready to concur any part of the rest of our trip by hitting only cities with Playboy Clubs. However, we visited Daniel in Pittsburgh, Pennsylvania, first and stayed only one day before moving on. So next it was on to Cincinnati, Ohio, and then Indianapolis, Indiana, where again we stayed with some people whom I had known at the time while being stationed there. We pasted up the heart of Playboy land and its first one in Chicago, but we found one of the best was the next one in Kansas City. There was no disappointment at any, and we both where like kids eating so much candy; after a while you can become filled, then sick, plus you knew the bunnies were untouchable. The last one was in Phoenix before getting home, but a breakthrough came there for Mike. One of the bunnies in Phoenix was being transferred to the opening of the newest club in San Francisco, Mike's backyard. So he gave her his home telephone number, and when he did get home, she did call. So this bunny was shown her new pin—that's what the clubs were called—and Mike had used the right carrot. They saw each other for a few months before his moving down to Southern California later. However, we both had hit the Hollywood club a few times, much later, and it was on its way down, or we were no longer seeing things through those same eyes as of before.

Cheyenne Days

After Kansas City and moving west, we were now into the last week of July with Cheyenne being our next stop. There are no Playboy Clubs here; however, this is play-cowboy time, with cowgirls running wild all over town. The last weekend of July is the famous "Frontier Days" rodeo, known as "The Big Daddy" of them all. We arrived at my aunt Nellie's house, and she met us with open arms. Frank and maybe Paul were still living with my grandfather Carl, but there was more room at my aunt's, and Frank was involved with a girlfriend, while we wild army boys were looking for cowgirls.

We went to the rodeo in the day, while Mike had never seen anything like it, with Cowboys and horses flying in the air with dirt blowing in your eyes with hundreds in the stands. The chuck wagon races with cowboys racing around trying to get things in the wagons and themselves in, while the driver is racing with the others going around the barrels to the finish, just causes you to stand to your feet. Then cowboys tried to ride bulls as big as cars flying in the air with crazy clowns working like bullfighters running with big floppy feet, while Indianans with their teepees waited outside the stadium to sell a reflection of their gone life too.

However, night came with a whole new bread of cowboys and girls. The whole city of Cheyenne was closed off from car travel at night, so all the drunks can walk from bar to bar without getting hit by a drunk behind the wheel. Some of the bars' entrances had beer cans flattened and running from the street across their floors without anyone losing their footing. All those cowboy boots and cattle moving through kept the cans flat while just adding more, because cowboys are used to walking through piles on the range. But most were from those two places close by, those called places of higher learning, Universities of Wyoming and Colorado, and these wild students mixed with real cowboys and cowgirls on the loose, but who cared less who you are? Cowboy hats and boots give you the license to "yep it up," drinking as much beer as could be bought or drunk.

We found one bar full of young women with rock and roll music louder than the "shit-kicking" music down the street. We found a beer and some girls who wanted to dance, and we commenced dancing. Next looking over, I saw Mike found one "Long Tall Sally," almost two feet taller than this Hawaiian, so he got up on a chair and started dancing with her holding on to the chair. It was like seeing Mickey Rooney dancing with Ava Gardner, with his head heavy into her breast with ears almost lost. Now as the place started clearing out, Mike came over and started telling me he was going home with her. I then asked, "Mike, where does she live?" His response, after going over and asking her the same question, was "Laramie." Then I had to advise him, "Mike, do you know how far that is from Cheyenne?" Then I asked, "How are you going to get back to my aunt's house from there?" He didn't know; then I dropped another on him. "Mike, that's over fifty miles away, and you'll have to get a Greyhound bus back. We're not in the city, this country, big country." He reluctantly went home with me with a broken heart, but they had a very long time in one dark corner, where he sat on her lap kissing their goodbye. It was Monday again, time to move on with my aunt Nellie feeding us a big country breakfast with ham, biscuits, eggs, and coffee.

New Mexico

Normally I drove most of the way, but we were driving just out of Colorado dropping down just out of the mountains, and I was getting sleepy. So Mike said he would drive since it was mostly just open plains, knowing and thinking he couldn't get lost, which he had done into the past. The backseat folded down, and having our sleeping bags from the army in the back, so claiming over into the backseat, I fell asleep on them. Well somewhere before Santa Fe, Mike woke me up and told me, "We are just about out of gas, and I don't think it would be a problem finding a station but we had passed one a few many miles back." We went on maybe ten or twenty miles more, and the car quit. There wasn't a house or anything along the way after his wakening me up, and there wasn't anything near in sight either. He had no idea, how far back he had seen that last gas station he had passed, and we didn't have a can or anything to put it in either.

I was mad, upset, but holding back anything that I may possible say. He was a city boy, and it was my fault too. Anyway, I got out putting my finger out into the wind like many other previous occasions. A few trucks went by, looking at those funny license plates, but not stopping. Then came along this old forties four-door Dodge covered with dirt, slowing down and then stopping forty or more feet past us, and I ran up saying how happy I was he had stopped. His face was filled with the weather of time, and there was no way of telling his age or race, and it could have been God, but he asked, "What's your problem, young man?" I told him we ran out of gas, but we had money; however, my friend just didn't understand the distances around here from place to place. He said, "Jump in," and I opened the door finding there was only an old tractor seat, which he was sitting in, and then he said, "Have you ever ridden a horse?" Noticing now that there was an old saddle sitting on some hay, I stepped in and sat down on it, while he let out the clutch and I tried to stay in the saddle. The muffler was broken, and it was pretty noisy as we drove away, so he couldn't hear me talking as I said a few words, but he wasn't much of a talker either. It was around another twenty miles, and there was an old gas station with a few cars out back and front. We stopped, and I tried giving him some money, but he refused it, driving off in the dust just as the rain started with the wind blowing harder too. He disappeared with the road, as I ran up into the small building with people standing around talking about the weather but stopping while looking me over. Then the guy next to the cash register asked, "What can we do for you?" And I told him our problem. He reached down, getting a gas can telling me it'll be three dollars for the can, walking out in the rain filling the can, and then coming back in giving me some change from my five. Another guy overhearing my story, who later had told me about him being in the army too a ways back, said he would give me a ride back to the car; he was going that way anyway. He appeared to be part Indian and didn't talk much either. Then as we drove up, I could see Mike was in the backseat asleep, and the rain had stopped. As I thanked the traveler, he just smiled and wouldn't take any money either. I poured in the gas as Mike woke up with the sun turning this big sky country red to purple.

We both then started laughing when we got back to the station, getting back my deposit on the can, hoping we wouldn't need it again, while the attendant filled up the car, then seeing this was one of the highest prices paid on the trip, yet never close to any Europe's prices of over five dollars a gallon, which takes 3.7854 liters to make a gallon for them. But I drove most of the time from then on. We hit Santa Fee to have something to eat, and it was still a small town with the artist just beginning to find its beauty. We slept in the rear of the car in the sleeping bags, because there wasn't any motel vacancy.

Phoenix, Arizona

We drove to Phoenix, finding it very hot in this car, which was built in Germany without any need to have air-conditioning. The first thing we did was call Terry Westagard, who was married living in Scottsdale, where he had grow up, and was following in his father's footsteps in business now. He welcomed us into his home with open arms, with that Western hospitality, and he insisted we stay with him, traveling a long ways in time and country just getting here, but we now knew that feeling of being closer to home. There was a restaurant or place he wanted us to go, and it had to be with him. So we let him drive this time, driving on a paved road for a while, until we hit a smaller dirt road on the north side of town. He insisted that we wear an "old tie" before leaving. We drove up, seeing it was something out of the O' West, a part of a working ranch. There were a few small buildings with an outside barbeque fired up with smells of mesquite wood burning coals reflecting meat in rows among the smoke on this long three- or four-foot grill. The smell again was making our mouth water as we walked up to outside bar, and Terry put our names on the list. Now there were cowboys and a gunfight show going on, while we jumped with the firing of shots and men falling to the ground. Terry said these guys also worked on this working ranch, but he thought the meat came from Nebraska now. We got our drinks and watched the show before going into the dinning room and sitting down. Two waiters came over, grabbed both our ties, and, using a pair of large scissors in their other hands, whacked them off. After getting over the shock, they told us, "No one wears a tie here," and they took them with our names to hang on the ceiling, with the hundred or more hanging there. There was T-bone steaks, ranch beans, salad, and fresh bread. We were stuffed and had a few more drinks outside watching the coals in the fire and the stars covering the sky. It was at the base of a peak named Pinnacle Peak, and that was how it got its name: Pinnacle Pete's. My wife and I went there just a few years ago, and houses surrounded it and it just isn't the same now. They had other locations in California now, with one still in San Dimas, where one of my daughter's boyfriends used to work; therefore, we always got a great steak there too and it is still one of the best.

Therefore, the next night, we took Terry to the just-opened Playboy Club in the top of a very high building downtown overlooking the surrounding city of Phoenix, where we treated him to its eye candy, adding another nice meal. Mike met one of the bunnies, which was about to be transferred to their new San Francisco club, which was not open as yet. When he got home, she did call him and he showed her this city with his own hospitality. So he was in a dream for a while, until she got her feet wet, finding the money class, which she was looking for from the start, not needing Mike's views anymore.

Terry enjoyed himself but was more into just being with "O'l Army" buddies again and those old stories of our togetherness in Paris. He had also talked with the girls in Washington DC after we had left them, so we all laughed about our time spent with them too. It was now time to take our leave the next morning, before that heat and the sun came up. This was our last journey junction until my getting home, but there would be a little longer one with Mike later on in his quest. The stream changes again, but these people will meet again.

THIRTY-THREE

Home Again

We found Monrovia had made some changes too, but before our arrival in California, within those two weeks prior to our arrival; there was "The Watts Riot" in Los Angeles. It started with the arrest of a black man by a white policeman, then his brother, and then his mother, all-getting caught up in the arrest. Now adding to this came a new exposure with news reporting, with the usage of a live helicopter reporting on TV, which came into everybody's living rooms, bringing further division within the committees. It showed these deeper problems existing in South Central, and the gathering into building a firestorm, and explosion in LA streets by race. It resulted in the expending of their own business and homes in this area, with "The Man's" business ownership keeping them down. The fruits of that whole black-and-white anger issue had been pent up for centuries and smoldered between the police and people in property here, and had brought on that spark of burning everything. Its expansion was seen by the nation and the world, which began on August 11, continuing five days further until the National Guard troops were called up to stop the riot, using rifles and jeeps with machine guns which men mounted, driving the street to take control by the twentieth of August.

There was a fear felt throughout the suburbs and cities everywhere, including Monrovia and Duarte. A year later, "The Black Panther Party of Self-Defense" was formed in Oakland. These issues are still there, and there is little improvement because of the rich white politicians and black activism using these public images against each other inside and out, standing with or against the poor black inner cities. So again over and over it raises, Rodney King or O. J. Simpson giving away to these great crisis cresting into flames, gathering again.

Mike stayed a few days with my family before returning home, but upon his homecoming, he found that home and his dreams had changed too. There was no room for him within his large family all living in one house, and he knew it was time for him to choose new paths too. Within a few months, he was back to Monrovia again. He stayed with my parents and me for another few months, until finding an apartment and getting his feet wet, also returning as a student in college again. His skills learned in the army with his pool stick, added to his GI Bill money, kept him afloat. He bought a Honda 350cc motorcycle after selling his VW Squareback in San Francisco, and we had fun ridding that "Little Honda," like the song goes, just having fun, fun, and with us riding against the winds into the night.

For me, I was in a limbo state bordering between my feelings still for Patricia, who was having troubles getting into the States, getting a work vista or student permit. Along with that came my weighing of all the different paths to be chosen, like going into the Foreign Service or back into art or advertising. Those three and half years had brought many lasting effects and brought about many changes within myself. I had been involved with the embassy and a few people I'd found there, like the marines and others servicing in lesser roles. Those people were living the good life, plus putting away money earned there for service overseas and getting extra benefits too. On one occasion, I worked directly with the cooks and servicing personnel at NATO. General Lemnitzer's house parties a few times, mixing with these embassy staff, who had brought a new view into opening my eyes to new possibilities. Just the traveling and playing in that secret travel world a little appealed to me, but I knew that to do so, I would need to apply at the foreign service school in Maryland to be accepted. I now had some contacts, but it would be another three or four months before that could happen, also getting mixed feelings about leaving California again. I knew that once in the Foreign Service, I would be stationed at the bottom feeding countries and lands before being placed in places like Paris or London, and that would take some time, years. Besides still in the back of my mind was that little-known South Asian section of the world which had American advisors taking more active roles in it's fighting and killing, which we now know would only get bigger.

I had also tried a telephone number given to me for recruitment into the Central Intelligence Agency, who requested me to just leave my home number. Funny, they wanted public accountants and mathematicians in their first recording, but later I was contacted by a real human voice stating they were very interested in my past military record and jobs after giving them my clearance. I then gave them my military number, and next came another call to meet with someone after they would check out my records, but this left many unanswered questions in my mind about what they knew about my "jobs or tours." This next meeting never occurred, and I never saw any further need in contacting them again.

Finding Work

Next, I tried contacting my former employer at the ad agency company by telephone, then finding they were no longer in business. Another one had bought up their agency, while the people that I had known had moved on to other cities out of LA. Besides that, I wasn't crazy about that lifestyle anyway, or anymore, but did believe maybe there was somewhere for my drawing experiences. But without any references, it would be very difficult finding work again in this field. Besides, I was living with my parents and still had some money from the military, but they both were on the clock now and starting to run short. I've always had troubles with making up my mind about things, and more so now, after being in the military, where they didn't want you to think but just follow orders, which had became too easy.

In a few months after going through the newspaper want ads, I found a job in Pasadena with an investigation business which had advertised for people with administrative experience, calling itself "Retail Credit Company" then, and known now as Equifax. The foundation had started out in Atlanta, Georgia, just being a group of retailers who were selling and giving informational reports about people they did business and their standing among their local community. They became national, and then worldwide, known for these reports, which are used for scale importance in helping insurance companies with risking factors, medical, and any other background valuable secrets, and open service checking information. They changed their name, now known as Equifax, which is more known among the credit rating reporting firms now because of so much basic credit rating reporting.

After testing and the interviewed, I began training first in their investigation units and was told I would have to work my way up into their management programs, which was a joke, but I did find my military ASA training had put me a few steps ahead of others within many areas. After a few days, a funny thing happened; I was now finding these strings in time and connections began happening in my life because there he was, Mel Caudill from high school. My circle of people, places, and chances of meeting up again had begun. Again, because he just started working here in this same year, getting out of the military over a year ago though, and spending one year in Europe, after getting out of the military, he had then married a girl from the Netherlands before their they returned to the States. He also had military duties within NATO, dealing with microwave computation also, if I recall. They were expecting a baby, and this company carried a very good insurance coverage, since most of our work came from and for them. Mel only worked here for a short period of time, moving on, just like he did in high school, and had other bigger dreams besides this job, used to moving along. I lost track of him after that, and he hadn't shown at any class reunions. I'm sure high school was not important to his life now, but I would like to find him again.

There were other very close relationships and bonding among us who had work here during the seventies. My two bosses above me were from the Deep South, as was the company, and we had also become very close friends besides the many other fellow employees too during my time working for this company. We had become truly almost like family members to all and me, being apart of my family. My first wife, with our children, and the other children, all grew up together, doing family-type events at our company, or doing our own family picnics, pool parties, and camping trips together.

The guys all played poker once every few months, and starting while families get together would only play for pennies as cheap entertainment on the weekends, but the guys also after work would go to the horse races at Santa Anita during its seasons, with some out drinking on occasions, but this was like Gilbert had said. "Friends" stay for periods in time only, and all of us are moving on to new directions like during the 1980s, except for just a few.

There were some unforgettable characters working there at different times too. Once again appearing was another Rick, but from West Virginia, a country boy, with a city wife from California. Their two children were born around the same time with our three. He had been in Vietnam, seeing a lot of ground fighting with his fellow soldiers dying in rice paddies, which affected his views, and he came home with some loss of hearing. He had also lost faith in our government, with many ghosts reappearing from battles still waging in his own confederate raising anger at the world, and trying to find some kind of peace now. His mother worked within a prison in West Virginia, with him making runs back home a few times a year, and doing so in two or three day runs each way, like cannonball runs or Smokey in seeing his family, but also bring back some real moonshine in his Black 1974 Trans Am Firebird. We all would party with his specially prepared punch using Welch's grape juices and blackjack gum melting before our eyes for effect, and maybe some taste. The partying women, after drinking it, would begin playing on the kid's swings, teeter-totters, and merry-go-rounds next to their condo's "party" building, without stopping their giggling and laughter like small children, but would pay the devil's price the next day.

He had one of the highest tested IQs found within his company's testing history, and later started his own very successful business with two partners from ideas seen and found from within our company. He was young, with his wife working in the "heart stress control" medical field, but she couldn't protect him from his own overeating, drinking and stress. He died of a heart attack after finding what he believe was the answer to a great life, with it ending way too early with only a daughter, owning fast cars and a nice home in the exclusive Lake Arrowhead, California, area. He was always a mountain boy at heart, with me kidding him about walking with one leg shorter on flat ground, because of his growing up in the hills of West Virginia, but really it was a gift from Vietnam, if you looked closely.

He loved fast cars, first having a dark green 1967 Mustang at first like "Bullet," which I'd helped him work on, and this began our driving rivalry. At one of these times, with my father owning a cabin in Big Bear, and my owning a 1968 Olds Tornado, its battery had died in the cold up there, causing me to leave it there one weekend. So the next weekend, the two of us went back up with a replacement in his then Trans Am. He asked me if I would like to drive it. "OK," I replied with a big grin, and then we got in and buckled up before starting up the hill.

By the time we found "The Highway of the Rim of the World," my lead foot was into it, finding and getting the feeling for the car's stance with it becoming a part of me and being far greater than that bad driving night in my youth with my dad's Hollywood Graham, and also a much better driving machine than my Simca in Europe, because of so much more power. He sat swaying and pushed into his bucket seat, but not like the German student, not showing any fear on his face. So we went faster and faster, with each curve, until our laughing became out of control with the slowing down as we reached the small road crossing over the dam going into the town of Big Bear. We put in my new battery, and the race was on again, with me in the lead going back down the hill. We both now had our 455 CI engines, mine front-wheel drive, and his rear with less weight, but he was very pleased when getting past me in those last curves before hitting the freeway. At the time of his death, his pride ride was owning a black Porsche 928, which he called "Wolf" in German, and I drove it once too, giving him this time a shorter ride on the newly open 210 FWY before his death. I drank my last toast with a shot of Johnnie Walker Black Label to my "Jonnie Rebel Red-Neck Racer Buddy," enjoying my mellow memento of him, and joined by many others after his passing, that became a burning, great big loss in all our minds and hearts, like good whiskey does, and will stay evermore, only a reminder of what could have been.

Rick and his wife rode many times with my wife and me in our Tornado, traveling to Las Vegas for our company-bowling tournament, which became our annual event of fun without kids. On one of these occasions, another couple in the Tornado also joined us. I started by adjusting and searching for my own electric seat and mirror settings before going out the driveway, followed by getting under way with the completion of setting the cruise control on the freeway. It was like sitting in our own private jet plane before takeoff and now in flight, because my wife drove this car most of the time, but it was now in my world of power and speed.

I drove our 1966 "1600 Fairlady" Datsun Roadster to work, which is still parked in my yard but not running for the past thirty years, and my kids still recall us all driving to the beach with its top down. Anyway back to this Las Vegas trip, during that time, once you reached the border between California and Nevada, there weren't any further speed limits existing on the Nevada side highway then, just your judgment of safety. So I'd put the pedal down resetting the cruise control to over 100 mph. This car was the same chassis that was under the Cadillac Eldorado, so we were flying down the highway with the ease of power, grace, and control of a large bronze Panther, and the brakes weren't ever applied, until we hit the city limits of Vegas. But now as we stopped at our hotel, the new male passenger upon getting out of his backseat, got down kissing ground. He was just joking, but his wife was not laughing, while the rest of us all were laughing, and the fun would begin again.

Some of this fun involved another of our companies employee, by the name of Carl too, who worked at another of our office in Southern California part-time. However, you see, Carl was black, and we enjoyed telling everyone at these bowling tournaments, "This is my COUSIN," while keeping our own very straight faces, while some were unsure whether it was true, but still getting a mixture of looks with unbelieving faces becoming part of the joke as a result too. Most of them are of a very conservative group and company, yet it may not have been true; he and I may have been of some mixture in our close beginnings, like him having some Caribbean connection, and me "black Irish." Besides that, there may have been an Irish mixture in that part of the new world too. There are a lot of Allen's, and we all are "cousins" anyway. We all are in some ways connected to man's beginning in Africa, and some further back than others.

He went on working part-time and gaining more business with the starting of his own investigation company, and later asking me on occasion, during our later encounters at the Los Angeles County Court or record building, while laughing about those years, if I'd like to work with him, joining him in doing some investigation jobs in the Caribbean. It sounded fun, but with a wife, kids, and good job, I would tell him, "Send me a postcard."

Speaking of the meeting in the Los Angeles County buildings, there was one other couple and their two kids that became very close family to my family, by the name of Chuck and Marjean. They also went to all the Las Vegas trips and enjoyed having a great time. Chuck was a very gifted singer and enjoyed giving his performance of "O'l Man River," with real heart and soul, which was his most often sung performance whenever and wherever he could find a few places, like at his local bar or at our company parties; but his laughter would make everyone feel good just laughing with him. Marjean didn't enjoy any spotlights or getting her hair wet at our pool parties, as I found out one afternoon, but they had two very beautiful children. Their daughter, who walked on her toes from youth, is a ballerina, embracing everybody surrounding her with love and grace, and now lives in Las Vegas. Their son is John or Johnny, as known to us, whom I would also encounter in those same halls of the county, after working his way from Explorer Scout in the West Covina Police Department to becoming a Los Angeles County sheriff. Later I saw him working his way up the ranks in the office of assistant to the sheriff himself, but now he is retired from injury.

There was another black married couple that the rest of us became very close with as well. The company was very much into sport competition activities besides our bowling, and the other big one was basketball. So within all the offices there came a need for better jocks, just like seen at SHAPE. Bosses recruited most during their job interviews, and that would always come up. "Do you play any sports?" Sometimes offices would hire part-time jock ringer for a season sport.

So John was someone needed for many reasons, besides the showing of the company's new racial ratio employees standard needed, and encouragement was brought on and imposed during those earlier years, but it became a plus with adding some athletic skills to all. John and his wife came from their ministry families, where it was preached to have some fears about being exposed to the many surrounding worldly temptations from us uncontrolled sinners, freer-living and freewheeling bunch of guys. At first neither could dance, because they did not have any exposure to that kind of music other than church music or any other surrounding infectious influence. It became my job to influence, but I'd also found an eager and willing soul to join rock 'n' roll soul music and become another "brother" joining my "Blue Eye Soul" joy at our parties. He could play basketball much better than I, but even with my efforts in teaching him to dance, he and his wife just didn't have any rhythm. They did get better at it with time. You have to find rhythm with your soul to become a good dancer, and I could out dance him still. He didn't stay too long with the company.

He and his wife later moved to Glendora, and my wife would see them around town for a few years, after I had left the company full-time as well. I still worked part-time for a while there, but was now working full-time for the county of Los Angeles, and also going back to college, using my GI Bill money for a few years, but there was a big difference in my grades and efforts this time around, as I now majored more in business and accounting. It was funny; besides being back to working three jobs again, I now had a family but had support from a loving wife. It later did pay off as I moved up into become a supervisor and then head claims investigator with the county's auditor-controller.

There also came a time during my supervisor duties when two black employees working under me claimed racial bias on my part, filing actions against me and the county. One was a woman, and the other was a chief from Nigeria with a college degree; however, after outside review and interviews with my black boss and other fellow black workers, it was found in my favor and to be the opposite. I also had two or three other Spanish workers working for me, plus all of my documentation done during their employment had disproved their action, and it was no contest in the end.

Also, during my "just being an investigator" working with a retail company during those early years, there also came another fellow investigator, who was my supervisor at the time and who also went to work for the county the same time I did, who became the head supervisor investigator for the county counsel's office. He died of cancer at an early age, and will always be remember as a friend. After that, there were two more who came into the county from that company, and I had hired one of them. She was black and a woman who went on after my retirement became supervisor in my old section after me.

In the later years, while I was still working part-time for RCC, it became Equifax, but it made many new changes into what its business is now. Again also during that time, there was one very multipliable talented fellow investigator working part-time then who played flamingo guitar in the local dinner clubs but was also very odd and strange. He pictured himself another "James Bond" and married a young virgin woman, but did not sleep with her on their wedding night, maybe just another Tinny Tim in some ways, but he was a fine investigator other than that.

I became very aware of the conclusion: "Any investigator who is good is like an artist and is usually an oddball in comparison to the normal world." You have to be different, and for whatever reason, whether that army's testing had given it to me, or I had found it, or having any truth, or maybe it was its own random choosing, I don't know, but it did put me in a place to find and I ended up with these guys on the outside edges, well outside most others in our way of thinking, and we are really a very extraordinary group of people.

THIRTY-FOUR

Dad winning in Car he built in 1962

New Racing Groups

Are you always fully aware of how lucky you are? Maybe with the coming of old age now, yes, but finding there have been some amazing people in your life who have been guiding forces and inspirations on your path is always easy in hindsight. In fact, some of the most difficult ones have taught you the most. My dad was one of those very difficult teachers, beside myself, and my mother was one of those amazing great persons who balanced all things out for others and myself. My dad was still racing at the time of my coming home from the service, and he wanted us to pick it back up where we had been before my leaving. It was very easy getting back into building cars, but I had grown some, now thinking about making a living and where my future was going. He now had a new crew of guys; while he was also helping some other new young guys into racing that were living down at the end of our street. But racing had now changed too. Crowds, TV and Southern Stock Car racing was making money more of a factor. Most of these new guys were all my age, living together in an old rented house with some others who where still in the air force at Vandenberg Air Force Base, coming down on the weekends to party, and lending a hand at the races too.

NATIONAL SPEED SPORT NEWS

Penny Slugs Ascot Claim Car Rivals

By JOHN BERG and DAVID VODDEN

GARDENA, Calif. — It was like duck soup for Jim Penney September 27 as he drove to victory in the CAR 23 by claiming stock car feature at Ascot Park.

The real race was for second and third spots, with Leon Garrett coming in inches ahead of Chuck Becker, Jr., who took third when Bill Whitworth was forced out with a blown radiator with four laps to go.

Willie Kimbro wheeled his way to win the semi main, as he took the lead from Bob Stone at the midway point. Heats were taken by Johnny Jones, Jerry Mysenzahl, Willis Hartman, and Kimbro, while Chuck Becker, Jr. won the trophy dash and Miki Ross the girls' race.

1964 JIM PENNEY AT ASCOT PARK IN GARDENA CALIF.

There was a very mixed group with J's (JC) or Jim Penney, who was the driver and owner of a claimer and figure 8 Chevy coupe with the others just fooling around and doing the pit crew thing. Dad would help with Jim's much-needed major repair works to his car or other needs. Upon my coming home, there had been a crash, or pushing into the walls with Jim's car, and he lost his front end on this occasion, while learning the art of coming back next weekend and driving again. Jim had tried keeping my dad out of some disagreement with some of the other drivers on occasions too. Gary, or "Big Gary" or "Opps," as he was known—because of many reasons, mostly because his size would break things—was the mechanic working on both Jim Penney and my dad's cars. He also was learning to put things back together of course. He continued working with my dad after Jim moved back to Kansas City, who also continued his racing there. I filled in working more and more with Dad in the following years.

There was three guys renting the house at first, but there would be others beside the original guys paying the rent at different times. They would come and go in short times, because of being released from the air force. One of them was Dick, or Richard, who was one of these guys still in the service for a while when I first got home. His home was in the Sacramento area originally, but he had ended up marrying Carroll, the sister of another guy named Gene, known as "Crazy Gene," who was also hanging out at their house, who had a very fast 1965 Mustang and was interested in cars too, but more so in drag racing like me. After Dick and Carroll's marriage, Dick became a draftsman, working for Aerojet General in Azusa, where Dad's buddy Albert was working and was my dad's employer too, but at another location. Dick and Carroll started a family within a few years and moved to Spoken, Washington, working for General Electric's atomic plant. But before them moving, they became family too with my parents, my first wife and children, along with one of my wife's best friends, and me. During these times, there were many people coming and going, sharing of those helping hands on the racecars. Work became an exchanging pit pass on race days by these guys, and many of my dad's friends working on his cars at home in the garage. As time went on, most of the air force guys would get out and return to their families, places, homes, or future dreams, and not racing.

One other reason the air force guys came down was mostly because the house became "the party house" like in Animal House with girls, drinking, shared food with fun times, and fast loud cars. But there was more; guys found a place to forget the service and maybe find a girl for a short or lifetime dance. However, for J's and Gary, it was a passing period, as it was for us all. These two guys learned about racing from my dad, and he became their dad in turn. My mom and dad took them in as their sons, as they did with many others before and after, giving them someone they felt they could talk with and share their problems with too.

My parents also had a mountain cabin in Big Bear, California, and this mixture of groups would go up for the weekends, sleeping in their small one-room living room, lying side by side in any available space, listening to my dad while still asleep in his one bedroom, talking in his sleep to Gary, while Gary, also still asleep, responded to my dad from the living room. We all shared stories, playing poker or cards or checkers and drinking beer or root beer floats, pie, and ice cream in front of a big wood-burning fireplace. Most of the trips were during the summer, used for enlarging the cabin, but we did have winter fun too. It became two stories, with three bedrooms, two bathrooms, and attached two-car garage house, by the time my mother divorced my dad. Once Gary and I had almost fell off that new second-story roof while we were in the process doing the roofing. Years later, my cousin Eddy would buy it from my dad and finish it before he sold it too.

Animal House

The animal house's roof was falling in, and its plumbing was always having problems. I think some of the girls looked for points while cleaning the kitchen a few times to be noticed by the guys, except for when the dishes got too high, but it had a deep yard and wide driveway to park a lot of cars. Jim Penney had a great red 1960 two-door hardtop Bel Air Chevy, which got washed and cared for, as if it was the queen of the house. His racecar was number 160, red, but I am not able to tell you the year, because of the many changes to the front end or body because of damage. It was either a 1939 or 1940 Chevy coupe with an almost stock small block V-8 for power they had gotten from junkyards. But to watch Jim drive was like he was out for a Sunday drive, with the other cars flying in all directions, and he just continued his drive to win. In figure 8 racing, you have a center of the 8 on a big hump, where you didn't want to meet another car coming across the intersection at the same time as yourself. Before or just upon my coming home, Jim had one of those meetings, and my dad was with Gary, helping Jim get his car back together to race again, when I first met Gary and Jim.

Gary & Dad at Racing Awards

Jim was another very complex, competitive, and complicated "Young James Dean" in the form of a shy country boy. Jim worked every day at his job, but like Jim or "James" Dean, he was always looking for excitement and danger. At the parties, he was very much a loner drinking his cheap red mountain wine from a large galleon bottle. He had that hidden smile too, saying, "I know something you don't," and tried going to bed early before every race day, always. Then there was Jill, his girlfriend, who had been part of the Pasadena Rose Parade Princess event, having full sight on the JC Penney

Company future and using her beauty with some brains in the use of the tender trap as well. However, after his family made a visit to California, seeing the house and how he was living and with Jill on the horizon, changes were made, and he returned to Missouri without her by his side. But before he left, he was crowned Champion Driver for his racing class in points, and he took home a large trophy for Gary and himself. He continued racing in Missouri and operating a used car lot for a living. Sometimes people find their way back to streams that were known as family or home first, but racing is hard to get out of your blood.

Gary is a very large man in many ways, but in many ways still a small child liking and looking for approval too. He stood around 6'10", and I told him, when I was teaching him to water-ski, because of his feet size, "You don't need any skis, your feet are large enough without any need of them." We'd laugh with him taking off his needed glasses to see, but showing that inner determination until he got it right with a bright smile. He had a heart that was bigger than his understanding of the damages that come with that physicality. Whether tightening down bolts or using his strength sometimes, breaking things off, not knowing how strong he was, or lifting whole rear ends out of cars when required, you knew his heart was out there trying. There were many great things with big rewards in this, but there were many, many "Opps" to recover from at times too. He worked harder and longer, with more energy than us all, and had an intrusive learning of why, what, and how things work within any projects he undertook, and he still does. His height, his need for glasses, and his size make it very much a danger to all surrounding him in his dancing moves, but he loves to dance, and does very well for a happy giant. Just give him some room.

After J's left, he became my dad's shadow at our house with most of his time away from his job. He worked night shifts at Day N Night company in La Puente and drove a nice black 1962 Ford Galaxy 500, which became another "Opps" story. Later, he took the 352 CI engine and trans, with a lot of its running gear from his wrecked car, putting them into an O'l 1956 Ford panel truck, that had been a GE repair truck, painted gray and dark blue, fading with age. We would go down the Harbor Freeway hauling the racecar on a car trailer, and when changing lanes the truck appeared like an O'l stagecoach bouncing up and down while going sideways because of its poor shocks without us rolling over. There was many things that worked or didn't, not being important, and they weren't pretty, but they were something he made with his hands.

His parents were divorced, with his mother having a drinking problem and his father's abandonment of him and his sister for most of their life. He was sent to a privilege school because both parents had money, but no heart or understanding for a cumbering large growing son. Like in many stories, he came away hurt, more than with anger, and was always a better person than both his parents. He had had many setbacks, but there have been angels watching both men, Jim and Gary.

For myself, I recall one of they're parties at the Animal House, where I was no angel because there was one guy who had gotten under my skin and was still in the air force again. He was one of those very loud types in playing himself up or thinking or just being a wannabe cowboy, maybe from Texas, always wearing his cowboy hat. My thinking was this guy had never seen either ends of a horse or cow and was just big talk.

One night, I had drank just enough to go into one of my own James Dean nights, and that drunk cowboy's hat just happened to somehow slip into the open fireplace, going up in flames like his childish actions and mine. He was too drunk to know what happened, while I just continued drinking, looking for a girl to dance with and hiding my adjusted smile from the glowing fireplace.

One of those other third party persons in the mix of things was a small Italian guy, Danny, and his wife Cheryl, who were married before my coming home also. Cheryl was the younger sister of a girl from our class of 1957 whom I'd known both for many years, the sister more because of high school, and I also knew her sister's husband, who was in our class too. That couple is Judy (Pierce) and Jim Tubbs. However, for both Danny and Cheryl, they are both under 5'3 or 5'4", made for each other, and my dad used to call them his "Little Ones" without any disrespect to either. Gary would get down on his knees to dance with Cheryl at our parties while the Credence Clearwater Revival songs played on those more than any other longest of all cut performance. Danny was also in the National Guard with J's, and both had been called up during the South Center, LA, and Watts Riots before my getting home. Danny is another car nut, having so many classic cars in the past and present years, more than mine, and it would take too long listing them all. However, he owes one thing now, and the last time Dad and I visited with them, I just had to have a picture of both him and my dad standing next to myself on his black Mustang motorcycle, just like the one of my youth. He is a perfectionist in all his work and takes care with all, which reflects his former job, but he is now retired from American Airlines as a mechanic, living off Mayflower in what is now Arcadia (but still called the "Mayflower Village"). They are only blocks away from where my first wife and I bought our first house. They are grandparents now and have free trips once a year flying wherever they like, with maybe only old age stopping their travels now. They are still very close to J's, visiting him, his wife, and the son had now taken up racing like his dad. There're others close to Jim, but I guess my parent was among the top five for him and Gary.

THIRTY-FIVE

Dance Partners

First I must explain that during the time of my coming home, Patricia was still in my heart and mind for those first six or more months while we were separated by countries and oceans. But there were also my other thoughts back to Sylvia, only a short distance away living in Orange County too. So going to any parties and dancing was just fun, but there were some elements eliminating these ties with both of them in my heart and head. There also happened to be some easy dance partners, who fit into any young man's dark side for easy sex, for sex only, and there were only a few cleaner than freshwater spring's girls at these parties. For the dark side, there were two sisters with their one close friend that stayed together at these parties, liking the English group, the Animals, of rock 'n' roll fame during this period of time, and they reflected their taste in men as well. It was very easy getting anyone of the three in some form of sex foreplay, but not going all the way. "They were easy," as is it's said, with that kind of appearance for most guys. Therefore, finding myself with one of them for a short period of time was easy too, spending some time in the back of my VW Squareback, and its rear seat folded down with a light blue hairy carpet over a form rubber padding with its matching pillows was easy too. Later at another time, we found ourselves in her bed, resulting in my having to rush out because her to-be-wed boyfriend was on his way over, which does give you a picture of our relationship. I don't think they ever married either. These girls were all working girls, having varying hours with the telephone company as operators, so it was easy finding congenial times for others get together.

Also, one of their roommates was another girl named Donna, whom Gary was involved with in a more one-on-one relationship, which was a little more pure and innocent. But they all had that motive, like Jill had, of looking for a man, looking for someone to support them and make life easier at any cost. Later Donna and Gary did get married, and she worked with these other three at the telephone company in Baldwin Park still until having their first child. Donna and Gary started together as two children, out of control of themselves, their finances, and their emotions, and ended having two children, a son, John Allen, and daughter. But after years of trying to grow up, and with Gary spending most of his days or nights working at his job or on Dad's race cars, Donna couldn't take it any longer and ran off with another man who paid attention to her needs.

So then Gary was left with the raising of two children on his own, and they had some problems too. With some irony, shortly after Donna left him, his mother died, leaving him gas and oil wells in Texas with some easy money coming in after their divorce, but he had the need to file bankruptcy with Donna earlier during the marriage. Years later, she tried coming back to him and the children, but once he became wounded, the mind overcame the heart. He had found another tall woman, Barbara, who's almost as tall as he was and had a big heart like his, whom he met at the Tall or Tree Top's Dance Social Club. She had loved, and cared for him and his children with all of her soul. She was the best thing that had ever come into his life and his children's too; however, there's also room now for Donna and her husband in all their hearts now. They, too, all enjoy being grandparents now and are readying for retirement.

There was another just-married young couple at the time I came home too. Their names were Bill and Sue, and they also came to these parties, and a few times Sue brought two of her O'l school girlfriends joining among us "Old wolves." One was Lynn, who had always brought her French-Irish energy and burning fire for life alone to dance at any parties. The other was their best friend too, named Jo Ann, who was always much quieter in her own behavior, and much more reserved in stance with her own reservation of manner around others than both her friends. Yet all being very young then, with their fresh appearance, they did not make much of an impression on me, other than both having healthy chests and freckled faces just out of high school.

Lynn had black curly hair and blue eyes reflecting her sparks of wanting to have fun, and she said clearly what she was thinking. She was shorter, but much more interesting. And she had her sights on marrying, which she did much later on, with her long traveled school sweetheart, who is one of the best guys I've ever known, by the name of Art. He is easygoing, with a deep respect for others and himself, and become, what you would expect from people like him. First he was a sailor in the navy, then he married Lynn, following with college, and then he became a fireman. Still later he joined the Coast Guard and became a house builder, and most of all was always a perfect fitting partner for Lynn's ambitions, while giving balance, as father of their three great children, two of which are twins. Lynn went on working throughout college after their marriage and got involved in real estate sales after they moved to Oregon, getting away from family because her mother was attempting to control their lives and had her own ambitions too. They have changed many streams in Oregon, living along the rivers with green forest and watching salmon swimming. Art and I had teamed up once to catch one salmon from the river with our bare hands. We had also exchanged our boats on another vacation one summer at a lake in California, where I taught his kids to water-ski behind mine, and he taught me the art of sailing. As for Bill and Sue, they were married shortly after high school and at the time had a 1963 Chevy, but Sue gained weight, and they gotten into station wagon living shortly after the birth of their first child, Billie. Next came their daughter, and from then on, it was always a battle for Sue to control her weight and emotions. They became very close friends with Dick and Carroll during this time too, later moving together into the same area while also working in the similar fields as Dick within Westinghouse or another company in the Spokane, Washington, area. But before moving from California, they had lived in San Dimas and then Glendora, California, for a few years, where my kids had mostly now grown up for over twenty years. We lived only a few blocks apart from them, while they lived there at first, and they had became one of our reasons for moving there. They too, before moving away, had been apart of the crew of people going to my parents' Big Bear Cabin. We all had swimming parties together on the Fourth of July at their house or others during the beginning of our married years. Bill was tall and with glasses too, but not as tall as Gary, and had some interest in cars and camping, but he felt himself as not quite a member of "The Guys Club," while always trying too hard to fit in. Sue was more the controlling force, as was Carroll, so this brought them all closer in some way and yet at odds at times too, even after moving to Washington. Jo Ann keeps in touch with Sue and Bill, but I don't know what happened with Dick and Carroll.

Now that leads me to Jo Ann, a new dance partner who, I must say too, wasn't much impressed with me either, but she needed someone to go with her to their senior high school prom dance or some dance, as I recall. Anyway, that's the reason given by Bill, Sue, and Lynn for them asking me the question if I'd think about going with her, and that same reason also given to Jo Ann about going with me. So thinking we should get to know each other a little beforehand, I asked her on a date, then we went out a few times, but funny I don't recall ever going to the prom or dance with her now. However, we did enjoy our dates, and it was a turning point for both of us. She was breaking up with her guy, and Patricia was becoming someone who appeared not really trying hard enough to become apart of my life. As seen from my view, time went on and our letters became fewer. Jo Ann and I learned more about each other, and there was now a growing closeness, respect, and concern for each other, and we saw a growing liking for the other person. We both had mixed feelings; she was young with that attractive innocence seen in those deer brown eyes, without any protection but wanting to get away from the controls of her parents, yet not pushing them away either. It was hard for "the rebel pebble" having to play by the parents' rules, and in doing so, I did it only out of respect for her, with some understanding and appeasing needed. For her, she still had feelings for her other guy, but that relationship was on thin ice and only pending more because of their many problems. I was someone older than her, whom her parents didn't like, and she was looking for someone she could lean on with some understanding of her situation, while I was trying not to repeat my mistakes made during my college days with "my Audrey" experience and that choice made with the other guy. But I could feel it was coming on.

She was a good Catholic girl, like Patricia, who had gone to Annunciation Catholic Church and also attended there in the lower grades with both Lynn and Sue throughout all of their grammar school days. They had that stark experience with those nuns as teachers gave guidance and guilt had its effect on all three of them in different ways.

She had been covered, protected while yet yearning and wanting to be released into her own streams after high school. All three went to public high school at what was then known as Monrovia-Duarte High School. One story she likes to tell about Lynn during high school is when Lynn lost her underwear getting off their school bus on their way home one afternoon. She never looked down and just continued walking away while the bus drove away too. What makes this even funnier is that much later in life, Jo Ann, while working at the Glendora's main branch of the Bank of America, had the same experience happen while she was taking care of a customer at the counter. Her underwear slipped and fell down to her ankles, and she kicked them slowly to the side unnoticed, until they could be retrieved later without anyone noticing. Her fellow workers couldn't stop laughing.

There is so much in her being a different type of person now compared to then, and anyone's first impressions of who Jo Ann St. George was when we first met would be different to now. Yet we all can change directions from our youth because as we meet those many different streams in our life, we make changes in others and ourselves too. We can't find who we are until we are released to do so for ourselves. Those people and those around her have traveled streams, influencing that little girl's world into becoming the woman she is now with a much greater sense of who she is. And the love she gives to all those who knew and surrounded her is stills the bigger part of her life. The world is a better place with her for many people and for me more than she had known. Who knows how the heart and mind find love? But let us always be grateful.

Jo's Love and Family

Jo Ann was involved with a boy. I think his name was Rubin, who was believed to be half Apache Indian and had just gone into the U.S. Marine Corps before we had met, but it had became an off-and-on relationship still during that time of my first meeting her.

Her father, Gerald St. George, was an LA police detective who was a very large and tall man that had that John Wayne real-life role type down well, which was also fitting with him not showing much emotion most of the time. Having a dry sense of humor and being in the navy during WWII reflected that type of man of his time with not much needed to be said. Always smoking and drinking too much, he also loved fishing, hunting, and being alone a lot as though he was isolated in his own "club." Her mother, Betty, was another short-tempered Irish whose maiden name is O'Reilly, which is now maybe shortened in America as Reilly. While being a very strong-willed person who was known for her sharp tongue and for sharing what she was thinking without much reservation, she had a soft side too. Their mixed German shepherd dog was also named Reilly. She worked all her life at the Monrovia branch of Bank of America until retiring and wasn't very happy with life most of the time. For any young suitor, seeing their daughter was like climbing into O'l King Arthur's court with a much-needed amount of armor for protection, and there was not ever that much into a real welcomed feeling into the "round table." As I learned much later, Rubin had climates and walls to clear in climbing besides his own standing within his own race. Just meeting others' standards and her parents' during this period of time was a challenge, but then being born into an environment of protective parents with strong Catholic beliefs made it even harder to overcome. Jo Ann had many tears and conflicts with both her parents over Rubin and me. Later, I also found my own close friend Mike's appearance, like his long hair and skin color was a problem for her father, just like Rubin. And I'm sure this too was apparent to Rubin during their time together, but most fathers are overprotective of their firstborn daughters. Then there were my parents whom her parents didn't have much approval for as well because of many reasons, more being that my dad's appearance and coarse actions.

After moving from Duarte, which was becoming darker, the St. Georges now lived in the Mayflower Village area of Monrovia with a large den, a fireplace, and a pool in the backyard. There was also Jo Ann's younger sister, Cathy, who was still in high school when we met; and their parents had less control over her than Jo Ann. It's also funny that one of my other classmates, Robin Ririe, used to baby-sit both of them while they all lived in Duarte before they moved to Monrovia; and he too later became a LA police officer, who is now retired.

On the other hand, their next-door neighbor on Fairgreen at that address at one time was Lesley Van Hilton, who had been friends with Cathy before she had ran away from home, away from her family into drugs and who later became one of Charles Manson's "Family," a convicted killer. Lesley had been a different pebble there and in high school too, but pebbles can find black holes to be drawn into without any control. Pointing out streams to cross for pebbles can change in ways that they will never return to again.

There was one time when Jo Ann, Cathy, and I went for a day at the beach. Jo Ann stayed on the beach while Cathy and I went for a swim. There was a heavy riptide, and we both were being pulled out farther while I became cold and lost my strength trying to fight the tide, and I was getting cramps in my legs. I told Cathy that I was in trouble, but she thought it was a joke because it was easy for her since she had just taken a class in life guarding, swimming every day and in better shape than me. Now she was thinking I was fooling around with her, but I wasn't. She swims away from me toward the shore as I was fighting the pain and riptide. I guess she didn't learn that part of being a lifeguard. Again, one of my angels was helping as I found a large rock underwater to rest upon for a moment before continuing and then making it to shore—completely exhausted, unable to move, lying there for a half hour or more until being able to speak. Then she felt bad knowing I wasn't kidding around. Jo Ann became aware of what happened only after my getting angry with Cathy after I finally caught my breath, and then she was angry. But Cathy was always irresponsible and self-centered compare with Jo Ann. She always saw Jo Ann as her parents' favorite, never doing anything wrong in their eyes. It was Cathy who was always getting into trouble and who always hated her father's smoking and drinking habits, speaking up from time to time as she condemns her parents' behaviors to their faces during those earlier years while still under their control, whether she was in trouble or not. Cathy was always more like her father, and Jo Ann was closer to her mother. Now many years later, she is repeating those same hated behaviors that she also loudly condemned. Jo Ann didn't confront her father, and not until much later did she confront her mother's problems. We all have our own weakness and pay for them in ways that we are blind to. Cathy has always been angry at the world for whatever has been dealt into her stream.

Their father, years later, had retired, giving him more time to drink and smoke, drawing himself further in a world of only watching TV and sleeping during daylight hours then being awake mostly during nights, in part because of his last assignment of working shifts at the city jail. For whatever reason, one day, he went into the backyard checking on his pool water; and while on the way back, he was stopped in his tracks by a massive heart attack and died before he could hit the ground as the examining doctor told us later.

Betty came home from work and did not know he was in the dark backyard, so she went into her routine of changing from her work clothes and then sitting down to watch TV; but after an hour or so while awaiting him to return (because sometimes he would go down the street visiting with some close neighbors), she then became concerned. She called around, and no one had seen him; yet knowing his car was in the driveway when she came home around six, she then went out in the backyard after turning on the lights and found him lying there, cold in the walkway and wet grass. He had been gone for sometime before her getting home, but she didn't know. Because there was no doctor present at death, he was taken to the county coroner's office. But because of my connection with some friends working in that investigation section, there was no autopsy performed on him following Betty's request through my efforts. Therefore, the time of death was unknown, but the cause was known, and he was under the care of a heart specialist. The wizard's poison finds its way into the king's heart even with the protection of the knight's armor. Before this, he enjoyed his greatest loves by spending time with his first granddaughters and grandsons, and he also did some fishing. He and I had became closer by my approbation of his dry, slow hidden humor, sharing a few fishing trips and our rivalry over who had the biggest fish. One of his favorites was that I had helped the biggest fish that indeed was bigger than mine get away from him all because of my messing up the usage of the fishing net. I never learned much regarding his life before our sharing in this short time other than him being a sailor in the navy during World War II as well as being an LA policeman, and that something gave him a cross to carry hidden in his soul. This had became only a part of that passing on of his St. George shield with a few guns, and this continued a genetic pool to his grandchildren more than any memories.

Years later, Jo Ann and I were at a group reading with friends located at a church in Orange County where a woman psychic was giving personal short readings with mostly questions about what the future will be for each of us. And then Jo Ann asked, "How is my father doing?"

Without any hesitation, she responded, "Your father is with his brother and at peace." Only we knew his brother had died within a year before his passing. Two of our friends, Don and his wife, were told they would be taking a trip to Asia. This would be their moment for a lifetime; and they found out within a few months, because of his business, that this trip was available through his work. And they took it together, but shortly after this, they learned he had cancer and only lived a few more years. So is there an existence of other dimensions where family is still with us after crossing over like the John Edwards's psychic people claim? Are they the angels, or do they help because of our family's request of the need of their presence for us? Or maybe they are our unseen dancing partners? Jo Ann and I became dance partners for more than twenty-four years, but more about that later in my story.

Finding My Loves

After giving Patricia my Supremes record of "Baby Love" with those words and another song by them with the lyrics "Why can't you let me go and you keep holding on," it became clear these songs were becoming more fitting both within my relationship and Jo Ann in hers. Then more so, as time went on with Jo Ann, she became my baby love, and it became harder for both of us to let go of our previous loves. She was taking baby steps away from her Rubin and her parents, and for me, I was becoming more interested in her and slipping away from Patricia. So next came my Catholic classes as part of our agreement to allow our children to be raised Catholic and for our marriage, after asking her to marry me, and to observe Catholic practices.

We got married in their church after many battles with her parents in that same annunciation church, off of Longdon Avenue and Peck Road, which was only a few blocks from her parents' house. It was so much a part of her old schooling, and she now started another kind of schooling in her stream. As it turned out, our first house just happened to be across the street from her parents' on Fairgreen; and our first child, Shannon, would go to public school only a few blocks from her mother's school. Also, it just happened that one of the teachers there would be Jim Rood's wife, Lynn Rood; and this was her first teacher's job too. Parts just keep moving together and then fall apart.

We also had a dairy farm at the end of our block, which was owned and operated by Altadena Dairy, while, at the same time, one of the owners lived just a few houses from us on the same side of the street. They had their own two daughters who occasionally babysat our children and went on vacations with us too while doing the babysitting, camping, and getting in some water-skiing. We didn't move to Glendora until all three children were born mainly because this house, now with three kids, only had two bedrooms and one bathroom—it was time for growing or moving. So we moved. We still had our parties and made many good friends on this street before moving, but with Jo Ann's parents having a pool, we had to have a house with one too; and having grandparents just across street brought many other good times and memories for us all. But after Jo Ann's dad died, her mother moved to Glendora too for many reasons. She was always close, creating some problems and yet having many blessing at the same time; but she brought too much weight on our marriage at times along with many other things as well, as life does with family.

Second Dance

Walking into my thirty-fifth class reunion, I discovered it was only a small get-together of fellow students gathering at the old swimming pool building in the Monrovia Recreation Park where I'd spent a lot of my summers during my youth growing up. Now finding another dance partnership. The pool building—with the help my friend's wife, Mrs. (Lynn) Rood,—was now turned into The Historical Monrovia building and a gathering place to witness Monrovia's past history. I was late getting there but just in time to find a table with those other single guys from my class, and having just time for something to eat.

Funny thing was we started talking about our years in the military, and then I found out that two at the table had been in the army during the early 1960s, like me, and were stationed at Fort Devens, Massachusetts, for training in the ASA (Army Security Agency) school. These two guys were also members of the same science club in junior high with me, and maybe that's why we're single—just kidding. However, after eating and talking, it was time to move on with the reunion as our Oldie songs from the fifties began playing. These guys weren't into music much, then or now; so walking over to join Jim Rood, his wife, and some of the committee members at their table, it was time to check out what's going on. And after we had talked for a few moments, Jim asked me, "Why don't you go over and ask Kathy to dance?"

Now I had known Kathy very little in high school, only through a few meetings with her while talking with her husband-to-be, John Hardin, because they were a "thing" during that time. I also knew them from our previous reunions after they had been married, but we had talked very little on any occasion. She was sitting and talking with some of our black classmates, whom I'd known too; but I didn't know she was divorced now, like me, and didn't know she was now also widow after the death of her second husband, Jim. I'd joked with my neighbor about meeting a rich widow at my reunion while driving away on my way there that night, and I also did not know Jim Rood had been at her second marriage and her first too until talking afterward. Kathy had danced a few with some of our black female classmates as single women or girls do before I went over, and I did not know at the time that she had noticed me upon my arrival too, asking, "Who is that?" Then she recalled my name after being told by one of the girls at her table. Again, she only recalled me as friends with John in high school after someone told her my name.

The reunion was called "Back to the Future 1957" after the movie's theme, and the members of the reunion committee were dressed in fifties' costumes, dancing to the oldies. So I asked her to dance, which started something old but also a new dance partnership too. Upon the close of the reunion, I had Kathy's telephone number, and Paul Burton with his wife took our picture together as we where leaving that night. It was easy to see in that photo that we had found our spark of something special, or I should say, it found us. Paul sent us that photo, and his wife had said they knew we had found love. After that, we went on our first date, meeting in Redlands Park with a Fireman's Muster competition; the smoke was visible from any distance. Then we were onto our next date at a street dance in Glendora with Kathy losing her car keys somewhere there. So I had to use my old "skills" opening her car door, getting her extra keys from the glove box so she could go home. Each night, we fanned the flames and stars together with talk and thoughts of things we shared now.

Kathy and I at 35th Reunion

On our next date, we went to Redlands again to watch her grandson, John, the fourth in the family now, play soccer and to meet her son, John, known as Jay, with his family. She had told me beforehand, "My son doesn't talk much. But on the other hand, my daughter, Kelly, will never shut up." Then we found our daughters shared the same name, but the differences in the spelling of Kellie for my daughter, which brought on us both laughing. During the game, her son, often called as Jay because of all the Johns in the family, and I found it very easy finding talking points away from the rest of the family. He started talking; and we found a lot of subjects like sports, etc., to talk about. Afterward, Kathy told me, "I've never seen my son talk so much in my whole life!" After Kathy said yes to my question about "giving me an income tax ride-off" by marrying me many months later before the next years ends, we got married by my close friend and minister in his church in Glendora, just around the corner from my house.

Her son had asked her before this with his dry sense of humor, "Are you sure? This guy is left-handed, dyslexic, and has asthma! Oh well, maybe that will work." All our close families were there, but our best man was who else but Jim Rood. We went on our honeymoon on a cruise to Mexico, and we danced a new year as new dance partners for life again. How extraordinary is that?

THIRTY-SIX

Mike Returns and New Buddies

Now back to the year of 1965, Mike returned within a few months to Monrovia and started college at Pasadena Junior City College while moving into an apartment on Duarte Road near Mayflower. He found some guys to move in with after a few months, and this started further connections, bringing in another mixture of guys to Gary's house parties, Dad's racing, and hanging out at my parents' house too. They too became a part of the group, helping at the Big Bear Cabin; and they were, as Gilbert said, "friends for those moments of time."

Me Left & Jo Ann, mom &dad, and Bill & Twin at Big Bear Cabin

Bill's Carousel

There was Bill Dillon who slept at times on the floor; and you would walk in there, finding him asleep, but his eyes were wide open. On my first occasion of coming across this, we shook him and checked his breathing, thinking he was dead for a few moments before he awoke. He did many things that were odd; but he was the most loveable character and, as my granddad would say, "Wasn't worth the powder to blow him up."

Bill was like in the musical *Carousel* tragedy, but he hasn't died yet, always appearing happy with life. He always made hard choices without taking the responsibility after making some wrong ones, yet this troubled him deeply. He and Gary lived together in another run-down house on Mayflower after Jim's moved. This was before Gary married Donna too, and during that time, there were topless dancers bars springing up around the area. Not knowing the exact details, but Bill started dating, or whatever you would call it, one of twin sisters, one topless dancer, and the other, an office worker. It was like seeing both sides of one person, somewhat like Mr. Hyde and Dr. Jekyll, side by side with these two girls. One wild with short skirts and the other side looking like a teacher with glasses in proper dressing appearance. Bill had a baby out of wedlock with one. I believe it wasn't the topless dancer, and I don't think they ever got married.

Before I had gotten married, he and Mike had motorcycles; and we would go riding, with Bill having a few beers or many. But on this one occasion, I was riding on the back of Bill's bike, and we went sideways after hitting some water on Duarte Road at Pick Road, next to my old Santa Fe school. We were up and then down, crossing up and then back down again, before gaining total control, like my dad on his ride of my Mustang, but continuing like nothing had happened. We were very lucky again with angels or "whatever" because there was no other traffic on the street as we used both sides of the whole doublewide street in that area to find a straight line.

On another occasion, Mike and Bill decided to hop on a freight train going north for a weekend because it was easy to do while they traveled through our area. The tracks were only a few blocks away from the apartments, and on the spur of the moment, away they went. The car they hopped into got closed in Pasadena and wouldn't be opened back up as the train gained speed traveling up the coast of California. The train finely stopped in Santa Barbara, and the door opened with trained dicks finding them hiding among some boxes, coming out cold, hungry, and needing water. They were arrested, and some of our friends went up to get them out of jail after a couple of days following that weekend's adventure. Many years later, Bill moved to Glendora, finding me; and we would laugh about those times along with many other things we've done in our youth. He was part of my wedding party too with Gary and another good friend, Don, as my best man; but Jo Ann's parents wouldn't let me have Mike as my best man. They were paying for the wedding, so I didn't have much say. However, Mike did become the godfather of my firstborn; and for Bill, he is not married with two ex-wives, two children, and many grandchildren, living alone still in Glendora in a small house across from a very beautiful park with no carousel but many of dreams of days gone by. He sent me a Christmas card saying he's thinking about moving back to Texas maybe where his exes are.

Other New Pebbles

Also, there was Don, another roommate with Bill, Mike, and a fourth guy named Dave. Don and Dave were from Ohio, I believe somewhere around Akron because Dave worked for a tire manufactory testing tires in LA's smog and checking its effect on the sidewalls. Don was an electrician and later started his own electric contractor business. Don was very good looking with wavy black hair, looking very much like Dean Martin but a little shorter. He also had a very dry sense of humor and enjoyed watching people then made remarks that made you laugh regarding those observations. Jo Ann sold her 1956 two-door Olds hardtop to Don's sister after we had gotten married and after she had moved out from Ohio. Later, she moved into the community of the Sierra Madre Canyon where Rick Orrell was also living and with all the artists, hippies, and actors. However, Don always had his refined air about him yet was little of a blue-collar type guy like Dean O but always being a big brother having Toluene for his sister and for his friend, Dave, who came out of the closet much later, admitting to being gay. Dave was always a nice guy, giving me tires for my cars to run and be tested on the highways while helping Bill and Mike if they had gotten short of cash or anything else they may have needed. However, Dave developed a major drinking problem after all of us moved on with our own lives; and the last time I saw him, after many years, most of his teeth were gone, not taking care of himself. He is now living and working as the manager of the same Aztec Hotel where Rick and I brew our beer; but it still was, at that time, a very low-class drunk's bar. It too has now become a very respectful place, being something of becoming somewhat a place of pride for Monrovians as part of its history. Dave couldn't handle being alone and also gay, and he lost his way without a will to fight anything in his stream.

Don and Valerie's Little Angel

Years later, Don found and married Valerie, which brought together another beautiful couple; of course, she is a very beautiful person in her soul as well as in her appearance. They believed in their own fairy tales, and they now live in a very beautiful two-story house in a very beautiful neighborhood near the mountains in the city of San Dimas next door to Glendora too. For Don, he did well with his business and had the American dream with three beautiful children. However, they paid a very heavy price for living on the edge of that mountain one day. Don was home and the kids where playing out front on skateboards; and their youngest son, Ryan, got on his older brother's board and was lying down on it, which he had been told not to ever do many times.

There came the sound of car brakes and tires, breaking the children's laughter at the nearby street corner, just at the end of the block and just three or four houses down. Don rushed outside seeing the woman driver crying with her stopped car in the street, and there was Ryan lying to one side with the skateboard. Don ran down, picking him up in his arms and holding him as Valerie came running to them. "Call 911, SOMEONE CALL 911!" he kept yelling, but life was leaving his little boy's body while he held him in his arms; and before any help could come for them, he was gone. It wasn't the woman's fault; Ryan was lying down on the board racing down the street as she turned on to Their Street without seeing him in any way during her right turn. Then it was too late for them now. Valerie has her very religious beliefs and even years later continues saying things about Ryan as if he's still with her every day, not wanting him to be forgotten, knowing every day that she does live with that pain and lost. She will never forget the gift she and Don had for a while. I think Don felt the lost just as deep, but like most men, he has been better at dealing with it on the outside. The last time we were together again was just a few years ago; he was helping me with some pool electrical problems before my selling of the house in Glendora. He still continues his humor and holding on to both of today and yesterday's life's streams without any walls. Our trials continue, no matter how beautiful or faithful or tightly we try holding on. Finding those most precious as our beloved and loved pebbles can only be kept in our hearts or souls, not our arms or hands.

Mike's Return

Back to those years in the sixties with Mike, he finished junior college here, then returned to Northern California for more schooling, then found a wife and had a daughter; but last we spoke, he had gotten divorce too. He lived with one of his brothers for a while in New Mexico, which is funny when thinking about our trip, and then back up to the South San Francisco Bay area, living on a docked houseboat that he was repairing and planned on staying there for a while. I think about getting in touch with him every once in a while, but he's moved again. However, one of these days, our paths will cross again I'm sure. Before my parents had gotten divorced, they had taken a trip to Hawaii with his family showing them one of their greatest vacations before their spitting up. Also, he became my oldest daughter's godfather. She also went to Honolulu for her high school's graduation but did not meet his family because we had lost contact of Mike by then. Hopefully, he will see her child someday too. Also, my youngest child arrived, whose name is Michael, better known as Mike. Maybe someday, who knows, pebbles may find their paths passing together from the past and present that will bring them closer as well.

Mike's Brother, His daughter, and Mike in New Mexico

THIRTY-SEVEN

Angel Traffic Jam

Regressing back a little upon my returning from the service, without a job for a while and living at home with my parents in my old bedroom again, racing moved into the forefront of my energy and again was surrounding me, and Dad had the usual three or four race cars in the yard just sitting there. However, one being a 1954 two-door Ford in a banged-up condition, he was racing almost every Sunday. In a promising progressive state was a clean 1957 two-door Ford, which Gary and I started working on. It later became one of my dad's best-looking and faster-running stock cars. We raced it at Riverside Raceway on the road course and then on the half-mile tracks before getting an offer that he couldn't refuse.

Then he found a 1959 Ford hardtop, which was one of his worst, but he raced it and then sold it too after wrecking it during the first time out. He also had another old racecar, an old prime red 1940 Chevy Coupe with a small block 265 CI V8 in it. Dad said it had "heating" problems, so taking on that challenge between looking for a job and still waiting on word after applying for an appointment with the Foreign Service school, I started working on it, finding its problem. However, within weeks, I started working for a retail credit company because of my need for money toward making payments on my new VW, which was brought home from the service.

Again, racing was put back for a few weeks; but the old Chevy was ready to go racing, and so was I. So Dad said, "How about you taking the Chevy out and race it in the hardtops class now since you got it running?" So thinking about it for a New York minute, and having some extra money now, I thought, Why not try it out? And we took it out the next weekend. Dad was racing his Ford, so Gary towed the Chevy for me to Ascot's track in Gardena, just off the 110 Freeway in his old Ford panel truck.

Jo Ann went along to watch, sitting up in the grandstands with my mother, and we were just starting to date then. So getting in the car with my heart beating, putting on all the seat belts, and putting on one of my dad's helmets without the face shield, I started it up and took a few "hot laps" with all the other cars roaring around the dirt track. Since the track was wet, there was mud flying everywhere. They always watered it down first to pack it before opening it up for the cars. Cars racing more on it would harden it like a pavement by the last race. Meanwhile, the track becomes drier and gets a groove as the racing continues throughout the day. So feeling the car and track out, I was gaining confidence while I went faster with each lap on this slippery, muddy freeway with cars passing me on both sides and others following along on my bumper. I was ready for the first race when the flag came out for us to clear the track, beginning the start of the timing for placement for each type of race qualification. Then they started the heat races after taking those three laps for your best time, which placed you in line according to your time. Now before all this and pulling into the pits, I was feeling pretty good until Dad started giving me a hard time; but he was also kidding me about not "putting my foot in" while I thought I had almost lost it once or twisted through a couple of turns but not completely because I was "out there on the edge" in my mind. Then waiting for my turn, checking out my car like a pilot does with his airplane before takeoff and before lining up for those timed laps, the butterflies started again.

The track was now getting drier, and the speeds were now getting faster with each car's attempts. In an open car with no windows and exhaust pipes straight to your head, there is nothing to gauge your speed other than the feel of the car since there's no speedometer—you don't have time to look at one anyway. They give you two laps, taking the fastest time; and if there's more time available after, you can come back and try again. I was slow but felt much faster. The slower cars are put in the front and the faster ones in the back in this type of racing, giving you a chance at holding off the pack. Plus that makes it more exciting for the crowd watching. So watching two races before mine, I carefully looked for the groove that the better drivers were

322

following while Dad was pointing to places in the track to follow and where to let go going into turns.

Climbing into the car and getting ready, we all pulled out on the track while the previous racecars came around into the pits. The flagman started placing the cars side by side and in their rows according to our time with our car numbers on his sheet. I was placed on the inside second row, and there were two other rows of cars behind me. This was where the faster cars were waiting. Then after the flagman checked our belts while pointing to us with the announcer giving our names and walking back to the front after the last car was announced, he got into his place too with those flags. We all started our engines and started rolling forward slowly around the track for that first lap before the flag. You could feel your heart, breathing, and mind gaining speed with the cars as we got closer together and faster. On the third lap coming around to the main straightaway, you knew that was the time to floor it, watching the flagman's arm coming down. I felt some bumping but was hanging in there on the first turn; and I had only one car directly in front of me as we came into the straightaway, but we had six more laps to go. These were called heat races, so you need only to put your foot into it because these were short ones before the semi and main events.

First and Last Race

By the fourth lap, I was still in second place; but there was one car coming up on my right side of the outside track, so I moved over in blocking him until we had gotten to the next turn. But that now gave just enough room for another car behind me to get his front wheel on the side of my door on the next turn, and he pushed through. We came into the turn all together with the other car holding me in on the outside, and the inside car now had his rear wheels throw a large chunk of mud from the lower apron inside track through my window, hitting my unshielded face while more followed, hitting me directly in the eyes. The shield would have protected me from the flying pieces, but the mud hit me directly in the eyes with force and impact; but I kept my foot to the floor, holding off the outside car while trying to clear my vision. It was just like the Golden Gloves bout many years before all over again. I could see some, but it was becoming blurrier with each second passing. Then I couldn't see anything at all with my left eye, but I finished the race in third place. I stopped before making it into the pits where everyone came running over laughing, but by then, it had completely become dark with pain and dizziness.

Upon their arrival there, the crew saw my face with me releasing the belts, trying to get out with the engine still running. "I can't see!" I exclaimed out loud, feeling my way out while someone was trying to help me get down to an ambulance that then rushed me off to Gardena Hospital. They took me in the ER while cleaning my face and reviving my vision; then they placed me in a room with bandages over my eyes. My parents with Jo Ann came in while they were admitting me, and they gave me a sedative while the doctor told us there was no way of knowing how much damage was done. "Your eyes are like empty eggshells." Mine had filled up with blood from the blow because of the hecatomb plus the lye mixture in the dirt track was causing blurriness with burning reaction in the eyes. I was kept sedated in order for the blood to dissipate in a few days, and on the third day, I was becoming more aware of those around me.

Now being very hungry, the nurse tried feeding me liver for dinner. I hate liver, and she told me, "If you can't see it or smell it, it's still just beef, and you can't tell the difference." Sorry, but I did; and my dad went out getting me a hamburger from the hospital cafeteria, making me a little happier. I was now thinking, "Maybe I'll be selling pencils from now on and can't sing either," But I was lucky after a week because my sight was returning.

The racing insurance paid for it all, but upon returning to work, I was told they turn down people from getting insurance coverage for that activity and that our insurance companies would add higher risk policies to ours as a whole company. "You must make up your mind—your job or racing, but not both." So needing the job, Dad sold the car. Both of us were disappointed from then on, but I did work on them and every once in a while got behind the wheel on occasions of "hot lapping Dad's cars." I never did tell them at work anything other than "I've stopped racing." For me, just guessing I was "driving faster than my angel could fly that day in traffic" was enough, and that is the closest to what I've seen on bumper stickers today.

Harbor Freeway

After going to work for the county of LA at Adams and Grand avenues, it was just another day of driving my daily route to work on the Harbor Freeway through downtown and coming up to the interchange with the Santa Monica Freeway where I normally would continue off to the South Figueroa off-ramp. But just before the Santa Monica, you must move into the two right lanes with the traffic traveling at 55-60 mph. There's also dividing island now coming up shortly with those right lanes, dividing the main south freeway from the west travel, or off-ramp, or continuing west on the Santa Monica. On this day, two cars directly in front of me banged together because one car had tried moving over into the right lane without seeing that the other car that was already there in his blind spot. Now myself being very close behind them while this was all happening within a split second, my dad's words and my experiences of driving on the racetrack told me "Drive straight through the hole" because when the two cars did hit side by side like that, the driver's automatic reaction is to "jerk the wheel" back away from the other car. This happened and with them back over in their reaction in the other directions, causing them to come back together again. If I'd tried stopping, that would have put me right in their moment too. Now flying between them in that split second and looking back in my rear mirror, I saw them coming back together, hitting again, with other cars piling up in a chain reaction. This taught me to expeditious while being awakened by my "angel in traffic," this time keeping me out of trouble again. I had learned defensive driving in Boston's circles and France, which had helped my angel.

VW Passing

Jo Ann had graduated from beauty school right after high school and before we had gotten married. Just recently passing the test for her license as a beautician, she found work in a beauty shop in Arcadia called Joey D's on Live Oak Avenue while we were still dating. I must say, this was still done with a great amount of resistance from her mother. Luckily, my job coverage was for all the surrounding towns east of Pasadena; therefore, we could arrange lunch together. I had just left her after eating and was now driving east on Live Oak entering the intersection at Second Avenue at the normal speed of maybe 30 or 35 mph in the left fast lane when an old flatbed truck filled with pipes and plumbing equipment decided to turn left in front of me. I may have had my head in the clouds, but they now went though the windshield of my car. Lucky for me, this was a VW from Europe where the windshields are made to fly out upon impact rather than those models in the United States that required them to be fastened and to stay in on impact. My face would have had to push it out, and I've seen this result happen many times, and they weren't good. My head did get cut upon coming back into the car after the first impact. I was unconscious for a few seconds then learned that the gas tank was crushed in front of me. Smelling gas now, I then got some help from some bystanders to get me out of the car, which was further crushed into a mass of metal below the passenger door of the truck. Because it was totaled, I could have been seriously hurt again without luck or angels. I got another ride to the ER at the Arcadia Methodist Hospital again with my parents and Jo Ann waiting while I was checked out, but this time, I went home with only minor cuts and bumps but with no car now.

It had been towed to my parents' house. Now I had no way of getting to work, and in my case, a car was part of my work. The next day, either my mom or one of my friends took me out looking for a car. Stopping at the nearby Longden's Pontiac used-car dealership lot on Huntington Drive, only a few blocks from the house, I found something fitting my style—a canary yellow 1964 Malibu Chevelle Super Sport hardtop with four-speed trans and black bucket seat interior but with only a 283 CI engine with a four-barrel crab. I wasn't looking for power but for something to be able to drive to work. It was in very good condition according to the salesman. It was a trade-in for a newer Pontiac. So I picked it up the next day and within a month, the truck's company insurance paid off my VW, leaving me with only three more payments left on the Chevelle. The settlement gave me enough money to buy the Chevelle and to keep the VW too. Now thinking with its stock 1,500 cc engine having two crabs, it would be perfect and was highly demanded for the use in dune buggies then. At the time, I thought I might build one of those someday too; but before getting around to it, my neighbor bought it for a buggy. I'd carried some of its parts around until just a few years ago, like taillights and other small parts, but I sold them at the swap meet in Pomona. It was just another passage for me cutting my ties with the past streams too, reflecting on that as one of my problems like my dad's.

THIRTY-EIGHT

The New Toy

Being a matter of nature for any young guy, this being one of the pioneering cars in the muscle car era, every time I could find the occasion to place that lead foot on the gas pedal, shift to four speed, and feel that speed was the start of bringing back that "American male car" relationship in my life again. After two years of driving around in small underpowered cars, it was time for sounds that shocked your soul. Also, Crazy Gene had a new 1965 Mustang Hi-Pro with a 289 CI with four-speed too; and we both would race anyone that throws down a challenge, depending on who was driving that night.

One night, using my portable tape recorder used for dictation in work, I picked up Crazy Gene for some fun. We drove over to the now-industrial part of town, next to where the airport was on lower Shamrock Avenue, around eleven at night. Now driving down slowly with Gene's nonstop talking and then turning around at the end, I turned on the tape recorder while making a U-turn. And now was the time. With just the streetlight watching, the engine revives response on the Tach. With my gas pedal hitting four grand with louder roars from the little small block then at the last time while releasing the clutch. We now were flying next to the old airport with each shift of gears as Gene was still talking every second until we hit over one hundred miles per hour in a little over a quarter mile, which I had measured during our driving down the street before making this charge, and then we replayed the tape again and again. Even deciding to double the speed on the tape machine to make it sound like Indy cars racing and shifting gears gave us greater laughter.

Gene was a racer too, putting in a bigger cam and some very low gears in that pony, winning almost all his races. I put my small block engine through many tests too, and it had enough on one occasion. Jo Ann and I were now married with two cars, with me driving the small 1966 Datsun 1600 Roadster for work. So it was time for something to improve that muscle. The same guy that worked for a Chevy dealership, whom we knew and where we later got my dad's 350 CI race crate engine, had told me about a 1965 Corvette that was brought in by some customer who wanted to exchange his 396 CI for a bigger 427 CI engine. I made a deal, and within a few weeks, it was now sitting in my Chevelle. I had dropped the starter on my foot while putting it in; and then some other problems developed, like too much weight up front with its greater engine weight. But the biggest one was that it was overheating within minutes upon starting up. It was easy with the weight problem to solve by putting in station wagon and air-conditioned Chevelle front springs and shocks in the front. But it took everything like changing radiators, fans, fan shrouds; and still, not much was changed in solving the other problem. The last straw happened one day when I opened the radiator cap only a few miles from our house before being forced to try something else. I was checking the cap, and it flew up like Old Faithful upon cracking open, with hot coolant gushing over my arm in an unexpected flash. My skin, like my mother's years before, was hanging and coming off with every screaming pain. So I was off to the ER again. After somewhat making a recovery, we put the car on a trailer and took it to Blair's in Pasadena, running it on his Dyno machine in attempts to find out what was going on with it. The first run showed it was running way too lean on fuel mixture. The problem was because I had ran new three-inch exhaust pipes and mufflers with a Holley 780 CFM double pump carburetor feeding it, causing the airflow to increase over the original Corvette's fuel mixture.

We drilled the jets, and it cooled down to running around 160 to 180 degrees. But now there was another problem; it was not getting enough gas from midrange up as well. So upon getting home, I replaced the fuel line to a three-eighths inch copper with more fuel being delivered. Later, Don Nicholson now returned back to Monrovia after living there and racing back east for Ford Motor Company, opening another shop on Foothill Boulevard in town. We now did some real turning on it before taking it to Irwindale for some racing. There was only one other 1964 Chevelle with a 396 CI engine, not rated at 425+ hp like mine. It was made under a special order through the factory for Dan Blocker of TV's Bonanza fame under his own special order. However, while also putting mine in, we had also put in a L88 clutch with a shielded bell housing, but with only a ten-bolt rear with poise traction and 373 gears. It was still badged with its "283" on the front fenders like my old '53 Studebaker with its "6." Many victims paid that price of believing its misnomer. It had around only two or three hundred miles on the new engine. During Christmastime, we drove it to my aunt Lemoyne's to Downey, knowing my cousins, especially Eddy, would be there. Now after "recovery" from Christmas dinner and being ready to go home, it was time to show off the car. This was the first time releasing those horses loose with my revving up this engine, like it's a precursor around the normal old engine's rpm like before at below four grand on the Tach. Releasing the clutch, the car jumped only few feet while the Tach. and engine went within another few seconds, flying seven to eight grand without the car moving much forward. Now seeing this, I let off the gas as fast as I could, not wanting to blow this engine.

Now I jumped out, thinking maybe the drive shaft had broken; so getting down on one knee next to the rear tire, I looked under the car, smelling the burned rubber, when the skin of my hand—by accident, not thinking it was placed close to the rear tire—became stuck to the melted rubber, which burned me again. These were eight-inch-wide redlines, and they couldn't hold the power from then on. I later let Dave help supply me with many tires that got burned by "testing in Sunny California smog." I learning after that it was only three and a half grand from now on while easing that clutch out and letting the car roll slowly five or six feet before wiping the ponies into action.

I found one day that Jo Ann was also just as guilty finding her lead foot too, and the first time it happened, she had to tell me about the event. She and her sister were driving somewhere; and upon letting out the clutch with a little too much gas, these tires sounded off again at a signal, bringing a little embarrassment. Then at the next light, the car that was next to them at the light before was revving up his engine; and she didn't know what kind of car it was, but again, the other car stepped on it as the light changed. Now Jo Ann and her sister were laughing, but then hitting the gas for a little fun, they went flying by his car to his amazement. She would drive it to her work in San Marino on Huntington Drive daily while I drove the Datsun to work. Anyway, one other day, after getting home again, she told me, "This Corvette kept bugging me." So at one of the signals, she again had to "punch it" a little, leaving it way behind her with the driver shaking his head in disbelief by the next light.

For myself, the most fun came with the new Boss Mustangs and the people's reaction with my ability to let them get through the intersection after the light had changed while just rolling slowly from the start of race then "punching" the yellow Chevelle, causing it to rise up on all fours, pouncing like a cheetah hunting its prey with a flash, passing them by for the kill. They just couldn't believe it with its stock "283" marking on the fender with the appearance of being stock. Other than that, rumbling sounds came from the exhaust while the Corvette Cam was making some uneasy lapping, awaiting their moment.

Under the Hood 396 C.I. On Grill

On another occasion, my dad was racing at Riverside Raceway with his stock car that weekend. With the big race on Sunday and Riverside being forty or more miles away from Monrovia where I was still living at the time, it was just when the sun was coming up that I had to leave to get there in time for readying the race car. As I was entering the 210 Freeway on-ramp from Myrtle Avenue, I punched it, shifting into third gear at around 100 mph and was ready to shift, now coming to the top onto the freeway. But next to the lane I was on, it just so happened there was a CHP traveling alone the freeway. I let off the gas after seeing him, but it was too late. He let me go for a little over a mile, and by then, I was now only five miles over the speed limit. But the lights came on anyway, and I pulled over to the side, at the same time watching my rear mirror. There were no other cars on the freeway. He got out, walked up, shaking his head, and asked me, "What's the big hurry?" He said, "You know, I don't have to clock you to know you were going over the 65 mph limit knowing you were coming up at over 80 mph and then slowing down by the time you were on the freeway."

I told him, "I'm on my way to ready my dad's race car at the Riverside Race," after asking me that first "What's the big hurry?"

He gave me a warning and told me, "The life you save maybe yours or mine," just like James Dean said on his TV safety spot just before his death. I raced the Chevelle at the drags a few times more, and my lead foot became much lighter on the street after that, thinking about Dean's ending.

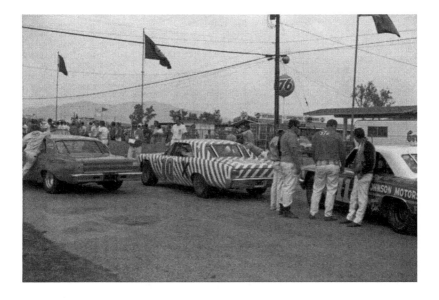

Another side story while at one of those yearly races at Riverside was that we had registered to race the '66 Chevelle, but its 396 CI engine had broken during qualifying laps. On the next day of the big race day, I found myself sitting in the stands beside and talking with James Garner during the Stock Car Time's Road Race at Riverside.

He had just made his Grand Prix movie by then and had become hooked on racing like Paul Newman after his movie. Now he was racing an Olds off-road car too, and I then asked him to autograph a card for my wife, who had stayed home. It said, "Sorry to have missed you, Jo Ann, signed James Garner." Because we had just seen his movie the night before and she was tired of racing, she didn't go and was very sorry to miss that day at the races. It was understandable after my working on the racecar for two weeks, and not making the race, she had enough racing for a while.

Goodbye, Chevy

Jo Ann became pregnant with our first child, Shannon. As the months rolled along, because of "that extra heavy duty clutch" and her sitting down in its bucket seats with her belly getting closer to the steering wheel, it was becoming clearer that she couldn't drive it any longer or push in that clutch. So one night, while we were out killing time before my taking her home for an arranged surprise baby shower for her by friends and family, we did some car shopping along the way and found our Olds Tornado. I'd also been looking at 1968 Dodge Chargers too, but she liked the Olds because of its luxury.

So I sold the Chevelle to a rich college kid in Pasadena; and once in a while, I would see it around, knowing it by that marked center rear-end housing that was painted red, letting those behind it know a "black widow" warning sign had pass, being a marker to warrant of its possibilities for all those left behind. It was now time for responsibility and concert some form of adult behavior with our child on the way.

Last Photos with Olds Tornado & our Datsun background

Jo's sister Kathy's Datsun & Dad's 59' Chevy across street

Also, not having the kind of money to compete any further with the rising of more and greater muscle cars from the factory cars was disconcerting. It was like being back into those O'l Santa Fe grammar school days of being the fastest or second fastest, but it now had become a big business—the playground had became faster and bigger.

The same was happening for my dad. Now he was racing at bigger places like Riverside, the Big O in Ontario, Las Vegas, and others speedways with just the cost of tires being a requirement alone, like two to four hundred dollars per set of tires per race without any big sponsorship. It was becoming harder, so Dad began doing more racing with his ministock Datsun 510 sedan with its sponsorship from the Arcadia Datsun dealership where I had gotten my Datsun too. They raced on the new Rivergrade Road Speedway in Irwindale, owned and operated by his old racing friend, Art Atkinson, alongside the new 605 FWY, mostly because of the lesser cost. It's now funny; the new racetrack across on the other side of the freeway is called Irwindale Raceway. Racing was just becoming too big for the little guys without factory or big money support from deep pockets. However, Dad did well within the points standing and was always within the top five racers of that class.

Our Datsun Family

The Chevelle was not a stop-and-go kind of car at any time. So Jo Ann drove it to work while I needed something better on gas and something dependable after my putting in that bigger engine. So in late 1966, through the local Datsun dealership, where Jo Ann's mother worked with for their finances through the bank she worked for, we got a good deal on a used 1966 Datsun 1600 cc Fairlady Roadster. It was fun to drive too, and there were just two of us then. Then Jo Ann's sister Kathy also later bought a 1967

Roadster from them as well, but after her getting married, she sold hers. But before getting married, she had also bought a St. Bernard puppy while she was living in a house with some of her girlfriends; and upon losing the house, Sam (Samson), her dog, came to live with us for some time too. He grew from a loveable puppy to a slobbering something that was larger than Cathy, which pulled her around the neighborhood on a leash during her days off from work while visiting her parents or us. We were now in our first house and living across from Jo Ann's parents at the time.

Anyway, like my friend with their Great Dane dogs, Sam would love riding in the passenger seat in both our (Cathy and ours) cars, with his uncontrollable slobber flying and his long hair in the wind; but before this dog, we also had Scamp too, the escape artist. Sam was given away to some friends of Jo Ann's mother so he could live on a ranch with more room; he had dug holes to China in our backyard, and I almost broke my leg in some of his holes on occasion in the dark. He was having trouble adjusting to being moved from one family to another and was becoming a problem.

For Scamp, he came about one day, only shortly after a few months into our marriage while just moving into our first apartment. So out on my job in a black neighborhood of Monrovia knocking on doors and interviewing people about a person living there, this little puff of fur, which was more gray than white at the time, followed me from door to door and then to the Datsun. Upon my opening the door of the car, he just jumped right in, as if saying, "I'm in need of getting out of here." So leaving him in the car, I went back out again knocking on doors, asking kids if anyone knew whose puppy this was; and nobody had any ideas. So we went home together, being my first surprise to Jo Ann.

We had rented the downstairs-end apartment in the Monterey Apartments with a small rear yard patio but did not think of having dog soon. So I had put him in the yard before she came home, and she found him there upon her coming home from work and before I'd returned from my workday. He was white with very curly hair. After giving him a bath, we still could not find any tags or a collar. He was some form of mixed poodle and cocker but a "little tramp" for sure; therefore, we gave him the name Scamp. He earned this name in many ways over the years too. Also, being in some form of Mr. Houdini, the escape artist walked fences and discovered ways in finding females like the great Casanova or other dogs' yards throughout his long life. He became our first baby and lived on until after all three of our other children were walkers and talkers. Without that Datsun, his love and companionship would not have ever been enjoyed. Later on, we received one of his sons whom we then named Tramp, who was the result of his romantic Casanova venture with the next-door poodle, costing the owner but was also a joy for us too. He was later also joined by our last dog, Princess, a mixed Springer spaniel and Australian shepherd who was always protecting the kids in the pool or just loving them.

Little Party Animal

However, still speaking of the original Scamp, we would have parties at that first apartment; and the first one with him was great. All the partiers just loved that ball of white fur. We didn't have much for furniture, like chairs and a table; but we did have an old TV, which I still have, a lot of pillows, and our king-sized bed. Anyway, we didn't notice at the time that Scamp was helping himself to any drinks found down on his level. While not paying much attention, as new parents should, it became quite noticeable when I invited an audience to watch him retrieve his ball. Now all were very surprised and laughed with him chasing it, but now he ran head-on into the wall on our shag rug having more then enough traction, and those four paws weren't going into same direction as his head. The next morning upon my getting up just before noon, Jo Ann and I had gotten something to eat, but Scamp still didn't move like he normally did and stayed in bed instead with his first learned hangover. Going outside to take care of his business and drinking a lot of water was all he could handle that day. We didn't have any further drinking problems with him after that. He died years later at ten or twelve after our moving to Glendora, but we soon had two other dogs to replace him as the kids' other pets. We also lost our German shepherd the first weekend after moving to Glendora. She was very protective of the kids too, and the vet believed she had a bad heart from birth because there were no other signs of cause of death. It's funny in a way that her father was a descendant of Rin Tin Tin, the strong movie hero; but he had almost killed Scamp on one of his outings into our friends' next-door backyard before we all rescued him. This dog was very protective of the pups, but Scamp had just gone over looking for company while the puppy had encouraged him. Scamp did recover and much later died of a heart problem. Jo Ann's parents got one of the other pups as well, "the biggest and blackest" German shepherd male I've ever seen. But he got to be too much to handle for them, and like Sam, he was given to my cousin Pee Wee and George. They couldn't handle him either. Pee Wee was too small, and he was too big, and they couldn't handle either. So he became a member of the U.S. Marine Corps, serving our country during the Vietnam War and becoming a real hero.

The Datsun Just Kept Going

For the Datsun, it's still outside in my yard now in Arizona, not running; but like Scamp, the kid's remember rides in it to the beach with the top down and with the wind in their faces. My oldest daughter had always wanted it, saying it was to become her car when she gotten old enough to drive; but it stopped running before that, getting her license too late. Next, my son took it apart with the intent of fixing it before getting his license, but he never did put it back together. My dad had gotten in on the act too and bought a 1967, which is still parked at his home in Washington with wild berries growing under and through it, with the annual rains wearing it down to rusty memories now. He was racing his 510 sedan with the same engine and frame from a Roadster under the body, and he still has some extra parts plus holds three older Datsun 210 models, which don't run in Washington. He's still that junkyard dog of not letting go.

Dad racing at 605 Speedway   Dad racing at Las Vegas

On one occasion while still racing Dad's stock car, we left it in Las Vegas because there was another race in a few weeks, and Dad needed the points for his year-end standings. So he and I drove up the next weekend in my Datsun for the race, and I was drafted on the tail of many big V8 cars and eighteen-wheelers at 70-80 mph in order to save gas. It was a little fun finding we would be pulled along with very lightly touching the gas pedal and them being unable to brake that chain of air behind them. This car with its small 1600 CI later on came the 2000 CI engine model, winning its class in many sports car competitions, being somewhat a copy of the English Austins cars in many ways. These cars put Datsun in many racing circles and in the public eye. Then they really did it by building the 240Z, which I could've bought for three thousand dollars new because of my dad's racing for Datsun in 1970, but mine now has over 250,000 miles on it before it stops. Its days are now numbered too. However, the 240Z is still one of the cars that brought Japan into the serious auto world.

Another Smaller Toy

After moving to Glendora, the Olds Tornado had problems with its front C cups and clips, and it cost too much for repair. I just happened on a 1974 LUV truck, which was the small truck made for Chevrolet in Japan with a four-cylinder engine, but this one had now a 327 CI Corvette V8 engine with a power guild auto transmission. We also had a nineteen-foot 1969 Tahiti jet boat with an inboard 455 CI Olds engine and were using the Tornado for pulling it to lakes and camping in a tent. So I kept the engine from the Tornado and a few extra parts just in case the boat engine had some problems. Because of them having same engine, as it turned out, it did; but that comes later with both engines becoming part of our extended family. I sold the boat only two years ago to Mark, the boyfriend of Kathy's granddaughter Heather, and gave the

Tornado engine to his brother for his 1968 Olds Cutlass, which is now an over 500 hp engine car.

The truck had a small camper shell with a bed box kit, a board bed with a three-inch foam to sleep on that I had custom-built, plus enough power to pull the boat at any speed over the Grapevine Mountains. One day, I tested it out after making a few changes to it. But because of it's stock low gears for its original four-banger engine, believing it had 460 rear gears, the front wheels went into the air after holding the brakes and pushing that lead foot almost to the floor. A little later, I replaced its transmission with a 350 tranny too, adding a shift kit and then an early-model eight-inch Ford Mustang rear end, giving a mixture of the different gears' ratio available to choose from. But choosing 325 gears plus adding an RV cam into the engine, it now gave me very good gas mileage, but I still had that pulling power. Of course, Jo Ann got this one to drive daily as well as to work again. It now also had a big ram air hood scoop with hairpin fasteners hiding its little scamper secret.

So on one occasion, she was pulled over by one of Glendora's finest—not for doing anything wrong, but just to find out what was under that hood. Later, a friend working at a shopping mall garage called us, telling us about an overhead camper coming off a small truck while hitting the overhead exit and just left it there in the mall where he worked. I went over to pick it up and then spent many nights rebuilding the damaged section for a few hundred dollars, and it came out surprisingly new looking. I'd gone to all the El Monte Camper builders getting replacement panels and siding.

We used it for a few more years until buying a four-door Chevy Crew Cab truck with a much larger overhead camper to sleep six because by now, all kids wanted to bring along their friends, adding also our friends, plus Jo Ann's mother who, of course, was always camping and boating with us. Again, we both had a lot of fun surprising people with that little truck "that could." Some teenage brothers down the street bought it, broke it, but then bought a 1969 Chevelle and added my engine in it for some more fun.

Our Family Autos

Later, Jo Ann bought a 1980 Buick Regal Sport Coupe with a V6 to drive to work after getting the bigger truck with its overhead camper because it was too much to drive to work, and gas prices were rising too. Later, the Regal became my middle daughter's first car. For Shannon, it was her grandmother's 1973 Nova, which Jo Ann's father bought for his wife in the Christmas of 1973, and Shannon drove it throughout high school. Now it was passed on to her and her younger brother, Mike, who was with me in the role of co-building an using Blair's speed shop machines, which now also came back to Glendora. We "hopped it up some" with "hot cams and a four-barrel carburetor for those guys' high school days." But it's now with me in Arizona, waiting to becoming another phoenix rising from the ashes. Mike went off to college, leaving me with a stripped-down paint job that hasn't been finished but is becoming closer into flashing the road.

After my son, Mike, finished his college days and my divorce and with my remarriage and having some money after my mother's death, it was my turn for fun again with the purchase of a red Dodge (Mitsubishi) Stealth sports car, driving it at around 150 mph while the sun was racing through my back on an early Sunday morning with no one else on the freeway in Arizona, testing its newly installed rear spoiler after our visiting and looking for future retirement property. After two trips and getting stopped twice for speeding, it was time to sell it too.

Also, I rebuilt my 1957 two-door Chevy Bell Air hardtop—the car of my dreams before moving here had became my latest toy. We brought it to our forty-fifth class reunion, and now its days are numbered, and I've sold it too. There is still a reproduction (kit car) 1967 Cobra 427 frame and body shell with some other parts outside my garage and another two-seated kit car, an English Lotus awaiting in the wings to be put together one of these days as well. Now we also added a little new fun with our 2005 PT Cruiser Turbo Convertible after having some other fun cars. Speed and cars have always been a part of my life's journey, and this era is becoming more a part of the past than the future, like me. As with the '57 Chevy, its more a memory of our past; and my lead foot, with its over 400 hp engine, has only became a thing for bragging to the world in times of our bygones.

Getting behind the wheel makes you think and gives that feeling of those times when you were at age sixteen or eighteen, but the mirror reminds you, it's just a silly old man sitting in the seat staring back at you now. While just watching those lower Honda rice cars flying past with their loud funny-sounding pipes brings us old men some anger, but we also know and remember those are their '57 Chevy's. Like their loud music, beating and pounding everything within range, our windows shake; and they are coming to surround you—it's their time, so move over before that window disappears for them too. Only the rich and pebbles with their memoirs in writing their and our days with our cars will be able to enjoy these joys for a little longer, and we all wish that would stay, but the world won't allow it.

THIRTY-NINE

The Real Treasury

Friends and family is the real treasury in our lives that have been our gold recovered and spent. So while we lived our times in our house on Fairgreen in Monrovia, there came a young couple buying and moving into the house next door to ours, giving us that German shepherd puppy before moving to Glendora; and they became one of our pure-gold friends. Steve and Burl were their first names. Steve was an ex-marine working toward his becoming a fireman, and Burl was an ER nurse working for Arcadia's Methodist Hospital. Steve was into jeeps and was a member of the Desert Rats, but they also had an Olds Vista Cruiser station wagon with that clear middle part top for family as well. They also had their young son, Scott, who was around the same age as our Shannon; and later when our middle daughter, Kellie, and son, Michael, were born at Arcadia Methodist Hospital, Burl was there with Jo Ann during both births. I got to be there only under a new policy for the birth of our son, but with Shannon, I was running back and forth from Jo Ann's bed to the waiting room. And her labor pains were going for hour after hour during the play-offs of the Lakers and Celtics championship game, but I was not allowed yet in the delivery room during those days. With each time, it become even more an event to share and savor with all of our family and friends.

Steve and Burl had their daughter, Holly, just a few months before our Kellie's birth too. So our kids grew up together until they moved to Ventura County where Steve became his dream by becoming a fireman, and Burl found work at a hospital there as well. They found a nice home in Santa Rosa with a swimming pool, but we still all went camping with them every Memorial Day. We also went with our other friends from the O'l retail credit company gang, like Bob and Mary Key Weston from my work, and with others too—like always with my mother-in-law at Carpinteria State Beach in Ventura or in the mountains. Shannon and Kellie are still close with Bob's daughters until their move with their parents to Georgia after Bob's retirement, and the grandparents can now be closer to their grandson too.

For Steve and Burl, only a few years ago while Kathy and I were at a performance here in Prescott, Arizona, at a college, there they were standing in front of me; and they only lived a few miles away in Chino Valley, Arizona, for over the last seven years. Just the other day at the Prescott hospital in the ER section, again there was that face I've known for the past thirty some years, working but with a little more gray hair; and Steve was now retired too. Then she told me that they're daughter, Holly, had married and that with her husband, they had four children and had built a house on the very next door to their property with Steve's help. But last November, her husband died of a heart attack at an early age without any known preconditions. Its part of this extraordinaire life to find them living so close again after all these years. This just joins the many other things that happened to me in the past ten years or more.

We were young in Monrovia, cooking barbeque and making hand-turned ice cream with fresh peaches while making drinks from our lemon trees, strawberry from our backyard, and then adding any kind of leftover liquor found in the house from parties. And as results, we chased one another down the street with buckets of water on hot summer days or nights for fun. None of us had much money, but we all had that youthful joy. Jo Ann's dad would hear us laughing. But being the "quiet man," he would quietly turn on his hose, surprising us when we ran by him as he came from the shadows with the hose hidden behind his back; and then he got into the fun too. Funny how you can lose your friends; and then out of the blue, they appear, like we all are just always behind a few mirrors down the way. Then they appear again but are now unable to reach through the glass, dead or alive, as just shadows in our minds.

My Rebel Family

They, our children, start so very small. Being a part of us, there is no other more special vision of beauty after counting the fingers and toes with the nurse. From then on, it becomes a special part of your life with responsibilities, challenges, and undertakings; and you will never be the same is so true.

Shannon

My first little girl, Shannon Kathleen, was born only a few days from each of her grandmothers' birth dates in August. They were all Leos in the stars. She was seen more like my mother with a lot of hair like the lion's mane. Being the first grandchild for both our parents, Shannon's every wish, whim, and sweet delight was granted by her grandparents, which was always against the wise controls put in place by her parents. My dad bought her a small electric racecar to drive and ride around at their house.

Jo Ann's dad kept a very watchful eye from across the street when she was allowed to pack up a bag and doll, saying she was running away from home then crossing the street and sitting on her grandfather's curb at her age of three or four. He called Jo Ann, telling her, "We are safe having a sandwich inside with Granddad." While weighing in, he told her why she might need to return home before it gets dark. She is very stubborn and can't be forced into any decision without some thought of her own first.

The grandmothers bought or sewed clothes for the little princess so that she will always be dressed properly. These were also later passed on to her younger sister or friends in the neighborhood. She became a model walking the catwalks at Henshaws Department Store in Arcadia at age five, like her mother who had modeled and then later worked at Mac Bratneys Department Store in Monrovia years before her daughter. However, she did not follow in her mother's collection of shoes during high school that used her earned money for the greatest reward with shoes. Jo Ann had forty-seven pairs of shoes when we had gotten married. Jo Ann's mother, Betty, also had to buy a drum set for Shannon, which she loved to bang away on while singing her made-up songs. This was maybe louder than being at any powwow in or out of our house. Shortly, the drums somehow were found to have a defective hole that appeared overnight after two or three weeks; but Betty got a big kick out it, knowing this would be an unwanted present to us, her parents.

Shannon appeared in the local newspaper articles doing her modeling poses and was mostly picked because of her long blonde hair with those green eyes, bringing smiles to all while flashing her own personality for the cameras. It's funny in a way how she was offered a scholarship to a design school in LA after graduation from high school, but she decided she would rather stay with her friends and attend junior college at Citrus. These friends became friends just like in the TV sitcom—male or female, supporting one another throughout their bad and good times in trying to find those steps in their own streams. She is now finished with college this year at Cal Poly Pomona and is going into teaching. She is married and brought us our first grandson into the world.

She was also my artist, having a measured IQ above 114 in elementary school—reading at a very early age, placed in advanced special classes, wanting to become an oceanographer at an early stage of her own vision, and receiving straight "A"s without much effort. But she turned into my "dippy, hippy flower child, who is caring with a passion of nourishing the soul for all humanity" throughout high school. She would read a complete romantic paperback novel in one day or night. I would see her bedroom light on in the middle of the night as a sign that she's reading, and she was never a morning person anyway. It was hard to figure out if it was because of the reading or it was just because of her.

I had always seen her becoming a teacher, but she is like her parents—more like her dad in that she mostly learns things by herself, can't be told what to do or not do, and does not duck under the tables in life. She is now married to the greatest man named Gene, who was first her friend with his heart full of love and was the biggest human teddy bear who has always been there for her since high school. It took her some time to see and understand that.

Funny again are these streams of time. His father was from the Basque Province in Spain and had kept their banquet feast and toasting alive with joining and caring of those traditions among families here in America and now. He is deceased, so his son is now in charge of continuing their cultural experience too. That is a forever-lasting memory in my life from my time spent there with those wonderful Basque men at their banquet many years before. Now adding and having my greatest gift, my first grandson, Tanner—who is amazing too—makes the world a brighter and better place for all of us at any time because of his great smile. Kathy and I wish there was some way of living closer being a part of his youth's daily life and deeper memory.

Shannon played sports, softball and soccer, starting very young; and once again, she had a very natural talent in abilities and leadership but did not apply all of those great gifts given to her within or to the highest level of her ability. She did play very intensively and with passion on the high school soccer varsity team and was an outstanding forward, sometimes a midfielder with strong presence. And she played second base in softball with the same intensive program within the city leagues.

During one of our (Shannon, her sister, and I) softball practices of throwing around and hitting balls at their grammar school behind our house, she was running after a ball. Then turning the wrong way during the throw back, she popped her kneecap out to one side; and she went down in pain, with me carrying her home and then making a trip to the ER. From then on, she repeated this popping out of her knee to one side on occasions, putting it back in place with great pain until after high school when she had arthroscopy surgery to fix it.

She also had a head injury, like her dad in football, during one of her soccer practices in high school in which one of her best friends, Vicky Matejzel, kicked the ball while Shannon dove for it too and got knocked out. Shannon could have done more with her sports or by going to college again if she wished. I never was her coach other than helping by being the assistant coach on some of her teams and on a few occasions, but Jo Ann and I were always standing watching and supporting her. Just living across the street from her grandparents with a pool, she grew up with her own pool in our own backyard. That made all of our kids very strong swimmers and types of pebbles with our dogs always checking and making sure they didn't stay underwater too deep or too long without coming up for air.

Kellie

Our second child, our middle child, Kellie Michelle, was born in April, a true Taurus, bull in heart and mind. Weighing close to ten pounds, she was with a lot of hair that surprised Burl, who was present there, encouraging and coaching Jo Ann to push out "our Little Buddha," with her rolls of skin and cheeks hanging down. There are almost two years and a few months between each birth of our children.

Jo Ann's sister, Cathy, enjoyed more time in caring and being a part of Kellie's world, probably because both were the second child, and also both had the capacity for holding their own against any odds. Kellie grew out of that extra skin, being very loving and caring, and also seeing that great fire seen in those beautiful big brown eyes rise without warning. She has her mother's dark brown hair and eyes and my darker skin coloring. She and her mother also have many of the same responses, which are mostly good and can be bad.

First growing up with girls and boys on her block at the Monrovia house, Kellie was more the "tomboy," climbing walls and trees and playing in the dirt, more so than Shannon, who just wanted to stay clean. On one of these occasions of climbing walls with the boys, a brick fell on one of her big toes and caused it to be deformed. On another time, I was home mowing our backyard the day before Shannon's birthday party and trying to watch them play while Jo Ann was away still at work. We had a large swing set, which I had lifted and rocked back with the "slider swing" holding it up in order to cut the grass around where the poles hit the ground. The phone rang in the house. I stopped the mower and told them both, "Stay way from the swing," while I ran to the house. I'd answered it, and then heard a loud crashing sound with Shannon yelling and Kellie crying. I dropped the phone, running back out and seeing Kellie penned under the swing set. She had climbed on the "slider swing" part, knocking down the hold set down around her. While I lifted it off her and picked her up, she was screaming in pain, and by the time we'd gotten into the house, her forehead had grown to three times its normal size and a crease between her eyes appeared. I called Jo Ann's parents to take Shannon while I was closing the house, rushing Shannon across the street, jumping in the car, speeding away to ER within minutes, and then waiting while she went to get an x-ray. Jo Ann had gotten home before I could get a hold of her and was very upset to find no one there. Then going across the street, finding Shannon at her parents', they told her what happened.

She joined us in the ER, and they told us that Kellie has a concussion with blood pushing her forehead out but no other signs of any other injuries. They kept her overnight for a few days, and being the only child in the children's ward, all the nurses stayed with her, giving her all their attention. She was like me at the police station of my childhood; she was now the prime star since there were no other children in the ward. We visited her, finding a smiling face with two black eyes; and upon her release, both eyes where now really "big black eyes" because the blood had now shifted down. Jo Ann's mother wouldn't go to the store with her until this changed because of all the looks from people as if we must be "child abusers." She and our other two kids got to be known by their first names at Glendora's ER, like their dad at Arcadia and Glendora as well.

When Kellie really gets mad now, that mark in her forehead appears like the bull getting ready for the charge. Kellie was not a student and would rather talk, socializing with anyone, than read or study things in books. She was able to convince her teachers that her helping in classes was enough, and this did get her passing grades. So later, she would use these same skills, moving her way up in the retail world and having great taste in color, design, and organization. Shannon would come home and find their shared bedroom rearranged every few months too. She is interested in all the things that are of value—clothes, food, cars, and vacations. She also values people, animals, and real friendships, plus family, and has compassion to help anyone too. She would go fishing but let the fish go afterward and hiking to see butterflies, and after getting over her fear of seeing fish swimming by her in the water, she became my longest enduring water skier, staying behind our boat at lakes longer than anyone else. She learned about fixing cars and helped in handing me wrenches and starting campfires. She still hikes and camps, loving the outdoor

Like her sister, Kellie was very good in sports too, playing soccer, softball, and volleyball. She and I started together, with me as her first soccer coach. It was my first attempt at coaching anyone, especially small girls, and it was her first time being a part of a team. We won the championship with her becoming one of that team's key features. We continued together in the following years, and then I stepping aside as she got older, but we continued our partnership in softball though. I was her first coach with that as well, and I went on with coaching her and the town's all-star team for a couple of years too. She continued playing on the high school varsity team, playing third base; she had a very strong throwing arm and was a very good slugger.

She has just gotten married to an LA sheriff, whom she tutored through his classes in the academy a few years back. Ivan is, in some ways, very much like me and is also dyslexic, making it very difficult for him, especially with those many writing requirements in his job. He works in the courthouse and has been awarded much recognition for his fine work there. He was born in Mexico, his father owns a ranch there, and they are Castilian in blood, with him having blue eyes, blond hair, and very light skin complexion. Maybe there's that "Black Irish" connection coming back around again with its threads in time. Now bring along new claims of family connection with Spanish blood and him having very strong ties with his mother, who is divorced from his father, and he wishes there can be peace among all his family.

Mike or Michael

Michael Keith, which in Hebrew means "who is like God"—who likes just being Mike and prefers to be called that way—while being the baby of the family, born in October and wham, it's true, he follows within his zodiac sign too, being Libra balances nature and labels, like his mother. He has those blue eyes, knowing very well how to use them, and they give him a greater edge while dealing with most women, with that hair that once was very blonde, but still "Our Golden Boy" with his hair turning browner, as know by close family and friends, which is now darkening with age, but he also had his mother's very light skin color, making him "sun burnable" more than the other two. Most of the summer, he does become somewhat bronzed, and while still in his youth, he had freckles across his nose and cheeks. With this one, I was present with his mother at that moment of coming into our midst, at birth, with some discomfiture waiting for that first moment of hearing his discord of crying, while again within Burl's watchful eyes. This became an ever-lasting moment, but then we heard a louder cry when they place him on a board and performed circumcision.

All three children carry on that very Irish-sounding first name, bringing a smile with his mother's approval, because she had always wanting a son named Michael from the very beginning, his mother's parents the same, and my feeling reflecting more deeply the memory of my friend Mike, always there would be a "Mike" in some part or form to remind me of that injustice, which was bearing down from blind prejudices that are still alive and around us today. Whether it being Irish, dark-skinned friends, or left-handed people it goes back to our O'l Clan groups seeing and wanting or trusting pebbles that are not the same as us. I also liked Michael for many other reasons, more than Carl or Orval or Gerald like his predecessors. I've always played with my name being changed to Cal from Carl for myself.

Boys are more of a handful than girls, and we both were very happy with the girls' training and performances before his arrival. Both of us, as parents afterward, said freely at different moments, "If he was first, we may not have had any more children after him," for many reason. From the start, he has been rushing himself around into harm's way with a disregard for dangers, willing to take chances, jumping right into things, and then afterward, for most of the time, coming out smelling like a rose, though with a few thorny cuts or injuries, but he was also known very well by his first name within the ER at Glendora's hospitals. He was just walking when we had moved to Glendora, beginning his first foray into the world by learning to swim in the pool underwater, coming up for a breath at the edges, keeping up with his sisters, or accepting any challenge.

Before my becoming evolved with the school activities, Mike was placed in his first class during kindergarten at the school, which had it's own playground facing the main street, where parents or anyone driving by could see the kids playing at recess times. But before his attending this first class or school, Mike and the girls were being babysat by nice family during part of the day before Jo Ann and I got home from work. The family had three boys older than him, with one girl in between our girls' ages and one boy close to Shannon's age. For the girls, they hated being babysat during that period, and through speaking with Kellie many years later, I learned later she had a problem with one of the older boys, which her mother or I never knew about. However, for Mike, the boys all played with him, and he learned about playing dead from them.

During our first week with Mike in kindergarten, we got a note to meet with the teacher after school. She began with there being a real problem, not so much something that can't be fixed, with her going on to a whole range of things, and with that came many wrongs possible within our minds. Next she was saying, "Mike during our recess and playtime, will play cops and robbers, shooting everyone dead, and now with everyone lying dead in the playground, while cars are driving by, he doesn't let anyone up until that last one is shot." Then she continued by saying, "That's not good because many people have stopped in the street and ran over to check on the kids." Also, he has a friend "doing his saves" place him in line for him while he runs around playing with others, and now his friend wants that place to be saved for him until that special friend gets to the swing or equipment he wants, and then it becomes his turn when the friend reaches that point." Now Mike was younger, and smaller because of his birthday, when starting school, and we didn't know if he was mature enough to handle it yet, but the teacher continued, "Usually the bigger boys will rule the rest, but Mike has learned to hold his own while taking control of what he wants from the rest. So please speak to him about shooting the whole class down." We went home laughing but did explain to him that same night what playing with others means—it's important to let others have their turns too, whether it's dying or swinging, and it's not good seeing all your friends die and difficult for their parents to understand. It's only a schoolyard game. Take turns dying too, like Jess James had to die as well.

His first two-wheel bike was ran into the curb to stop it during his early years, at any speed, without wanting to know how to push back on the peddles to engage them to stop at first. He fell out of trees, broke bones, got fishing hooks in fingers, did all things of the X-Games sports, like skateboarding, snowboarding, and water skiing later in life while we told him repeatedly, "You are not Superman or made of steel."

The day came, at around age five or six, I taught him to water-ski for the first time by preparing the skis by cutting down a pair of old wooden big skis and tying a small rope connecting them both together in the front. Now with him ready waiting, and in the water, the boat pulled the tow rope slowly into position to begin this journey, but just as I'd gotten to our starting point and looking back at him, another boat came running across our path at a very high speed in our front line to travel. In the meantime, I continued to hear him yell, "HIT IT! HIT IT!" but I let off the gas just to let the other boat pass before giving ours more power, but I also looked back at him. He was free standing up on top of the water now and had pulled himself up by just using the rope, without the boat moving more than a few feet in the water. I then hit the gas, but it was now too hard, and this just pulled him out of the skis, with him yelling at me as we all in the boat tried not to laugh. We tried again, and up he went again, refusing to let go with his little legs moving sideways but staying up as the boat was going so slowly, it wouldn't come up on plain because of the slow speed. However, from that day on, it wasn't long before he was up on one ski, cutting water looking for wakes to jump.

Also, at the same age of four or five, we signed him up to play soccer, and I became his team's assistant coach while still coaching Kellie's team. He and others would just stand in that assigned position watching the airplanes or birds fly over until the ball with its crowd, appearing like a herd of dogs, came their direction, after being told, don't go beyond your area from parents and coaches yelling what to do or where to run. Some boys or girls would either cry or fly into action, but Mike had been around watching and playing with Kellie and Shannon at their team practices for two years before getting a chance now to play on a team himself; he had seen and done much more learning than others of his age. The same is true with playing baseball—his watching, kicking, hitting, throwing, catching and learning brought him a few steps ahead of others of his age for a while. He was a "starter star," using his feet, running, and making goals. He joined a soccer traveling club, playing with the best of the city's all-stars; then in high school, he went to summer camps at Santa Barbara College, and then in junior college, he made friends with a goalkeeper on his Citrus College team, who got him playing on a mostly German men's team in the San Fernando Valley league with grown men from all different countries that had played ever since they started walking, and this is where he learned much more. He was seen, plus his coach helped him in getting a scholarship to San Diego State College, where he learned about girls, drinking beer, and joining his Sigma Phi Epsilon brothers while living on campus. He played soccer for only one and half years, but continued his education for five years in sports medicines and getting his degree, but going to work for Fox's sports TV station for a little over a year before being cut from his editing job because of the cutbacks a few years ago.

Baseball was his other love, and with this sport, I continue being lucky to be his first Little League coach, with two other neighbor guys—one having only girls playing softball, who was coaching against Kellie and me, so he jumped at coaching boys, and then other guy who had never coached and was the dad of his best friend, a neighbor and friend to me, with his son Tommy growing up and living across the street and being buddies with Mike through all those years of sports and school. He played on another soccer team too, so they wanted to be on the same baseball team. His dad was also the minister with the church around the corner, and being my friend too, who loved his team of the "Cincinnati Reds and James Dean," he later conducted my wedding to Kathy, with us having our marriage in his church without any charge. His son was a large kid and, of course, like his parents in their gene pool. He also had a younger sister, who played sports very well too. During their first few years, his son and mine did most of the hitting of home runs and pitching, but Mike liked being the catcher best. Like his sisters, he had played on the all-star teams as well, which I also coached or assisted on for three or more years as well. Mike moved up, but didn't like the high school coach, though he continued playing American Legion Ball. He wasn't alone with some others too, who wouldn't and didn't play for the high school team. He was never big enough for football. We had started him in school early because of his birth date being on October; therefore, he was younger than most in his grade and smaller because of that too, but of course, he would have liked to play. But like his dad, too many broken bones didn't help. One of Mike's buddies did go on in baseball at USC and becoming a winning pitcher in the College World Series and then playing in the Big Leagues, with three or more pro teams in the "Big Show." His other buddy, Tom from across the street, went on to Fullerton College, becoming a water boy on its winning baseball team and is now coaching baseball while teaching English at Glendora High School. Mike is still playing both soccer and baseball, but now has added golf with his love of fishing too, after some injuries from snowboarding.

FORTY

Fishing Past On

This was always his other great love before even getting our boat, and his first time was when we took the family to that same lake, Bass Lake, where I'd last fished with my dad, just before my last year in high school. Finding a camping spot and setting up our tent with the three kids, two dogs, and Jo Ann, who never camped before, it became a learning point for us all. While I was setting up the tent and Jo Ann was unpacking, the kids, with the dogs, wanted to go down to the lake. So Shannon, the oldest, being with them and all of them having the ability to swim—Mike around four years old—with the big dog always swimming next to them as their protectors also and the small dogs there to bark on leashes, we felt them to be safe. They could all swim, but we told them, "Don't go in the water and DON'T GO TOO FAR FROM CAMP!" Somewhere, Mike found a clothes hanger, string, and a long stick pole, and he hooked them all together before leaving with no bait, doing his very first fishing on his own while the girls and dogs played. He waited much longer than any normal kid his age would for those fish to jump on that wire hook. He kept hanging in there on a big rock overlooking the lake as it was now getting dark, which it does up in the mountains earlier, then in flat areas. Jo Ann started calling for the kids, and there was no response, so we drove down to the lake in the car, but we did not see any of them, so we started calling out in the dark, asking everyone if they had seen them anywhere. We had now covered about a mile in both directions, and the worry was increasing, setting in along with our louder calls when the car headlights caused one of the two dogs' red eyes to flash, reflecting back from behind a group of tree. They had gotten lost and kept hiding behind the trees when the car lights came in their direction. Stopping now and getting out to call again, the dogs appeared with the kids running after them, with Kellie crying and Mike with his fishing gear dragging behind.

Then we drove back to the campsite; it had a picnic table. We started up the gas lanterns to get some food and put on some jackets because it was becoming much cooler now. When one of the kids sitting bare-legged at the table for a while said, "Something is on my legs!" we put the light down closer to her, and I could see a large daddy long-legs spider, then a few more, with the kids and Jo Ann jumping back from the table, brushing their legs and arms. Now putting the light under the table, we saw there

were a few thousand in all sizes hanging down, swinging, and bouncing in their webs. Of course, there was that reaction from all, and we all sat in the car eating before retiring to the tent, with everybody laughing but still looking very closely at anything we touched. I got out the bug spray, covering the bottom of the table before going to bed. The next day, Mike still wanted to go fishing, and so we got him a real small pole with some worms, and that was our first fishing trip. He would try for hours, never getting one, just losing his bait to the smaller fish, but like all true fishermen, hoping just once that "big one" would take the hook. The girls and dogs didn't get lose again and went swimming in the warm summer afternoons until dusk.

From that time on, Mike with the Boy Scout troupe, or with the other kids, when we went camping or boating would try his luck. I've taken both Kathy's grandkids fishing too after my mother died and taken them to my mother's trailer up in Silent Valley, above Beaumont, California, to fish in their pond, where you paid by the pound and making it too easy, which their grandfather, John Hardin, said after hearing, "That ruined them from real outdoor fishing," because he learned what a real fisherman must do from his dad and from now being a real "fly fisherman" in Ketchum, Idaho, where "Hemingway" fished and had died. Kelly's boys have come over to Arizona, and we went fishing and camping at Dead Horse campgrounds one summer in Cottonwood in the Verdi River too.

The one grandson, David, is a real fisherman, like Mike, and has his grandfather, John, along with his great-grandfather, JC, before him, enjoying the sport. David, with his close childhood friend, would come over and we would go fishing while floating down the Verdi River, catching bass before the monsoons rains started bringing the winds and washed us, forcing us to finding shelter inside our tents.

David now goes up to Idaho and has learned fly-fishing with his grandfather, and passing on that strong bond, forever sharing time with each other. It is too bad Mike's grandfather, Saint George, hadn't lived long enough to go fishing with him, but I'm sure this is where it's carried on in his genes too. Because there is no real love of it on my part, but Mike with his other grandfather, my dad, did go fishing together on our visit with him in a campground in Washington while Mike was sixteen. I took pictures with them bonding with poles in hands waiting for that big bite. They did catch a few, cooking them together on the camp stove that night and having a candy bar for dessert.

The last time Mike and I went fishing on a Father and Son Day outing in San Diego on a fishing boat for the day with just his fellow brothers of Sigma Phi Epsilon and their fathers; this was in his next to the last year in college. We drank everything, fished, laughed, and brought the whole groups, combining catch for a cookout at their house, eating, drinking while watching the Mike Tyson fight for his first championship on cable TV, and that one didn't last very long. I learned of his being a part of their organizers' committee, showing his many other skills besides sports to his brothers. During his time living with them, he talked of his many hikes in the wilds, sharing with his many fellow "jock" brothers who played only sports like football and baseball or other sports in the inter-cities and had never been fishing, swimming, and hiking in winter to summer months and had never been out of the intercity. Sharing something, dads and sons or daughters have bonded together for the rest of those fish stories and myths, either long or short, caught or gotten away, which can never be forgotten. The small pebbles shine in the streams of early- or late-sunshine lights of our memory.

Mike got married last September to the love of his life, the wonderful Heidi, whom is from Fort Lauderdale, Florida, and brought Mike from his long life in Southern California sunshine to Wisconsin with its short summers after they met on joint vacations on a small island called Isle Mujeres in Mexico, which led them to a long-distance relationship. That's proof that love has no boundaries and can find you anywhere or bring you anywhere that you would never expect. The last child has begun a new stream there, but most importantly, they have found each other, which brings a renewal of "the Allen small chain or clan."

My "other kids" started during my teenage years. There was a boy who was friends with Don across the street and hanging around our house at the early age of ten or twelve. His home was that of a dysfunctional family, so he wouldn't go home until late and my mom or the Burkhart's would feed him. He was a good kid, and I wonder whatever happened to him at times. He looked up to me, and I was a "big brother" to him—taking him places, the drag races, park, or just playing ball with him, but mostly he just hung out with us guys.

During my marriage to Jo Ann, Shannon had many friends, who stayed over, eat, and went camping with us. However, two of them are worth noting. First, Elena became a family member too, her mother being single and raising two children while working and going out with boyfriends. Elena needed Shannon; Jo Ann supported her, while dealing with her lack of confidence. So she called me Dad, and she gained some feeling of someone caring for and about her, which helped during those hard teenage years for her. She was our fourth child. Then there was Pam, full of energy, full of life, strong, yet appearing somewhat like Marilyn Monroe, being very voluble in a childlike manner too. She was always stronger in her convictions than Shannon or Elena. She too hung out with our family and was always a daughter to Jo Ann and me as well, becoming our fifth child. She came from a larger Mormon family and was one of the younger children; her father controlled the mother and many of their beliefs. However, Pam was not about to let him control her, and one day, she had a very serious medical problem, but the mother did not come to her aid. Jo Ann, being a very compassionate person, took control of the situation, getting Pam medical care; and if it weren't done, Pam would have died.

Pam lived in our household for some time before returning for a short while with her parents before moving out on her own, but they are together again in some understanding. She was one of Shannon's friends, with Elena, who moved in together for their own first apartment. They are now all married and have children working on their lives, yet they are very dependent on friends, like the TV shows "Friends", which was also very popular with their generation.

With coaching, you get involved with many kids too, but being a Boy Scout leader gives you even closer views of boys and their families. You see rich boys, whose mothers died of cancer, trying to deal with the loss with their father, and boys so poor their clothes are in need of repairs with their hearts caught between their parents' morals and dealing with the unfair facts of their own lives. I spent time with these boys hiking up many mountains, leading and following them in their strides to make small or big steps crossing streams, caring heavy loads, tears held with sweat, as goals were reached or lost. Under starry nights with no TVs, they learn to cook and learn about themselves and nature's ways, sometimes helping find those new paths.

One or two became like my sons too. One was Brian, who was going through rough times because of his parents breaking up. He was a big kid in some way, and at first, I'd be following him up hiking paths while only seeing this big backpack with large feet swaying back and forth with each step, determination in his eyes and stance. Later in a few years, he was now up front a part of the leaders, as the troop climbed the peaks. He and I became close, and there were tears in our eyes upon my arriving at his wedding a few years back. He now, with his wife, counsels parents and children with troubles and trying to help them because of the things he learned during his teens.

The other was also a very big kid for his age too, but very thin-skinned to pain, but because of his size, you would think him much older and capable of handling anything, but he was still young and again, I would follow him, trying to make it up his mountains. He would cry in pain, so we would stop, so I would let him rest while the troop would continue. He would rest for only a few moments, with me coaching him on, until we caught up with the others. Also with time, his mind caught up with his body and would sometimes carry other smaller boys' loads. He and his parents still exchange Christmas cards with me, and he has, after going through schooling and training, been trying to become a rescue fireman. Matt, with a few others, had shown strength in becoming men to be proud of, and for me, being a part of their streams has given me richness. We played volleyball at our meetings and with other troops at outings. We were not the normal troop, rebels compared to most others or standard Boy Scouts troops. First, the boys and I eat "termites," tasting like Lemon Head candy, for their first step in becoming members in our true brotherhood, during any one of their first overnight hike in the Angeles National Forest. This gave trust and a feeling of something special, knowing they have taken a big step beyond their peers and becoming one of us. Getting past any fear is a beginning of knowing what can be accessible and accomplished, which is a part of any survival first steps in life's streams.

Brian compared me to MacGyver in the TV show, coming up with using the everyday items around us to solve problems. We would win most, but we were not driven by making Eagle Scouts out of them; we became a "high adventure" troop by rock climbing, shooting marksmanship, and fishing, going on a camping trip to Santa Catalina Island, canoeing fifty miles down the Colorado River, hiking fifty miles reaching highs of over twelve thousand feet in the mountain peaks of California, snow camping in Yosemite Park during the winter, and conquering 120 degrees in Needles, California, and paddling down the Colorado River; but most of all, we met challenges that pushed them a little higher to make them see another higher level, that many never have or would have seen or felt. I'm very proud of my time with them all, all my kids, and that's the gold in my stream.

My standing left & mike setting right with troop on top of Franklin Pass mountain across from Mt. Whitney at 11780 Ft.

I've been very lucky in sharing trips to the Boy Scout camp of Cherry Valley on Santa Catalina Island: the first three times with my troop years before my second marriage to

Kathy and the fourth time was with Kathy's granddaughter Heather when she was ten or twelve years old, spending a week there—I was the adult chaperon for her and her best friend while traveling with the rest of their school's class and parent chaperons. They had oceanography classes—like my Shannon, they studied fish most of the time—plus the fun of group camp fires, swimming, and snorkeling in the clear ocean while sleeping in tents on wooden platforms trying to keep the wild pigs from joining the campers. We bonded, but she had more freedom, taking chances and building more confidence, knowing I've been there before and is more experienced in camping than any other of her grandparents, but I did not tell her of my teenage experience with sharks or the boys' encounter with a large sting rays shadow gliding across the ocean floor during their snorkeling, which brought them flying to the surface, while I was chaperoning them in a rowboat over there.

Community Pride

My days in the community of Glendora brought an interest in my children's schooling and its effects for others of our neighborhood. My friend and minister living across the street got me involved on a committee covering the spending of government funds for children under title four act and programs it had at our grammar school, which was just behind my house, where my children attended, and all children surrounding our school would be affected. After Shannon's benefits within programs in Monrovia, this had become high on my horizon, a priority, and we where looking to continue these benefits for her and other children. This was again the below Old Foothill Boulevard section of town, yet just above the railroad tracks, as it was for me in my youth. Therefore, some of the housing was well below the hillside homes and incomes higher class were set surrounding unified schools in Glendora.

Becoming a committee person was just the start because in a very short time, there was a movement by the school board to close two or more schools in the city, facing a loss of revenue and believing it was necessary to cut them because of decreasing numbers of children as a whole here. It became a fight between our school and two other schools, but after considering the loss of federal funds because of our school having a mixture of lower-income families and some other arguments made during a long period of hearings and meetings, we stayed open. It was a fight between the North and South, with the school board finding more money and only closing one school, much further south of the tracks. This put me in a position of learning about our teachers, parents, and those of power with the energy to make a difference for our children. It also gave me influence with some teachers dealing with my children during their time at this school. Therefore, I became committed. I became the school's PTA president for one year and stayed on assisting the next co-presidents, which was a couple sharing duties, and later the husband became the mayor of the city and they became our family friends. It was fun attending meeting with all women PTA council members, being the only male other than those in the school boards, the superintendent, or school principals. At one of our school assemblies with parents and the kids, I had gotten a free football film to show after our PTA meeting one night without screening it first. It came with beer commercials at the ending, and I was thinking, Oh, oh, I'd hear about this! Funny, the kids never noticed, and most of fathers asked, "When are you going to have another film on sports because they'll be back." Some mothers weren't happy, but we all got notes at our next meeting, mostly favorable, but I did screen any of our films before showing them after that. I continued as a member of the PTA board into the kids' high school days there as well.

There was other involvement community pride of courses, like the "Scout hut" being torn down and replaced in the main town park, which our troop used monthly, more than any other groups, because our troop was the very first Boy Scout troop found in the city, going back to its beginning. We raised money for our trips by using it and making a haunted house for the city every year, keeping kids in the park and off the streets on Halloween.

FORTY-ONE

The Strings of Time and Meeting Streams

The war went from 1964 and through the 1980s, with many losing their lives, with President Johnson trying to keep his great society war and the Asian war going along on two paths affecting deeply America's heart, but the end was coming for both. The pain was too great a task, and the country was pulling itself a part under the greater burden of so much death, seen in everyone's nightly TV news within their living rooms, without any end in sight. Therefore, Johnson made his announcement to the nation of not running again, facing his own misjudgments. This war killed his sprit and heart, but now came hope for the country again with another Kennedy, Robert Kennedy, building a new direction, new visions, new hope, and picking up the baton with its flame growing larger in each state, larger than his brother's, until that night in Los Angeles after his winning California's election primary. Like his fellow brothers—Abraham, John, and Martin—he became only flames after being killed with a bullet like them all. Bobby was of our generation, with those visions gathering for the old and young, the black, tan, and white, looking toward peace, a future with vision, and willing to lead this country out of that muddy quagmire of war. The country and its people were robbed by an angry young man from the Middle East, this time with our country's policy being wounded again. Instead, we got Nixon's treachery and dragging on with the war while telling the country, "I'll bring an end to this war" and then becoming out of control by his own blindness and weakness that surround him. "I'M NOT A CROOK," he said until the attempts to cover up his mistrusts and mistakes; it was the mask of paranoia that brought down his presidency and brought down our county too. He only received a pardon from his former vice president, who had taken over the rest of his second term, before leaving office, and then our country moved on to Carter, who was also too honorable and honest, not understanding the world's evil, and got caught up in the Middle East tangoed mess, which we are still dealing with now.

Those strings of time for Nixon started after becoming a part of Senator Joseph McCarthy's committee, searching and using America's paranoia toward Communism while looking among us and within its borders until the press cleared the smoke, but then and later, a larger tear of broken glass was staring him back in his own mirror because of the people surrounding him and his youth of misgivings.

It's now happening again with another president with some of these same men, who studied next to Nixon, Reagan, and Bush Sr. and who are still dividing the country even more now, based of fear. Why do men, with these strong conviction, believe that their "God" gives them guidance to cleanse us low pebbles and streams without knowing that its their own reflections of evil they see, hiding their own lies of evil having long legs and dirty feet beholden of their "truths," stomping around in the waters, making it muddy within man's mind and affairs. Time shows them for what they are, men with arrogance, with false pride, believing they are privileged because they are part of the aristocracy without real logic or humble appreciation of their status given or received. Events prove that a pebble can change the world and being wrong before discovering the truths were used to fool only their selves.

Wars are brought on by the great misunderstandings, greed, maybe a form of freedoms and aspirations, but more often in the name of a beliefs of gods and man's god, weather it be money, oil, power, or what my brother owns or believes should follow my beliefs. It will continue until our hearts see all men want the same basic jewels of real treasures set forth in the family, the Ten Commandments, and our bill of rights, but men must be ready within their own minds and hearts to accept this as truths. We must stop being blinded by our selfish gains without helping our brother humans climbing out of mud to a higher ground. Building a better world is more important than building safety net around us because there will always be holes and the streams continue to change around us all, losing that gold.

Next Generation

Hoping, as all parents do, we can leave the next generation with a better world while holding on to our own memoirs is what drives most of us. We are all a part of the "greatest generation" in our thinking—and we begin growing larger in the numbers of children—but our children or grandchildren don't know those streams we have lived. For them, it's not possible to really feel ours because they are now on their own, traveling faster and only seeing what's around them now, which is far larger than our world was when we were at their age. This book can be seen as bridge of our experiences during our generation, but now because their worlds are larger, faster, and filled with so much information, we can only hope that they get a small view of ours. Those of the older generations are at some point supposed to have the wealth of wisdom, but that's not true from the blind, those with deaf ears, or those with nearly closed minds surrounding all.

So what we pass on to our next generation can or will shape their streams still, but there's so much more now shaping their world too, and some of it is what we have left them. Good or bad, let us have hope in the next generation; it's their turn to shape their world for they're the next generation with much more improvement for all generations. Most of us gave them too much without them knowing the cost, hoping they won't have to pay a price later, but we now know they will carry the burden of the baby boomers' cost and change our dirty diapers while we decline in our generation. So be wise on how we spend their love.

Returning Streams

Kathy and I took the '57 Chevy to a car show in Cottonwood, Arizona, after my retirement, where we were living before moving here to Prescott. A man around Kath's and my age came over sitting down at our little table while I was sitting behind the car reading, and we started talking about cars. Then I later learned he lives in Camp Verde now, just a few miles away, living there for a few years, but before that, he came from Southern California too. Kathy came back, and we started talking more about California, then we found out he had lived and went to high school in Alhambra and then he told us about the loss of his first wife before moving over here. His wife, it came out, was the sister of Kathy's best friend when they both lived in Arcadia and before Kathy's came to Monrovia-Duarte High School. This type of thing happens very often to us at these car events with us old folks.

The next year, when we brought the '57 Chevy over to Prescott for another car show, Kathy spotted two guys near our age again, walking by wearing T-shirts with MONROVIA on their backs. I walked over and asked them, "Monrovia, California?" They both looked puzzled and said, "Why yes," with a big smile. We exchanged names, and at first they didn't ring any bells because they had graduated in 1955 from Monrovia High, older than us, but then the light came on for both names for me. The one has changed his last name for some reason, to "Jack" now, so I looked at our school annuals, and there he was—Turner, Bob, or Reggie Turner, being one the best friends of the Van Gundy's and that of Pee Wee's brother Lawrence. They both live here too with their hot rods. Also, it comes to light that Bob Walsh, the other guy, had also worked at Kathy's first husband's Chevron gas station in Arcadia and with her ex-father-in-law too.

Again, later at another reunion for all of the classes of Monrovia High School, held at the San Dimas Park a few years back, there were more cars, and we fount at this show a few other school mates from a lower batch, a year behind us; there is Ronnie or Ron Barrett with his hot rods and few guys from my car club with their cars too. Coming from nowhere again, we found out that Ron had started after his high school days working for Kathy's ex-father-in-law, "JC" at the Chevron gas station too, but later on opened his own station in Barstow and worked up the ladder. He then went to Dune Buggies and off road racing making that into a business, with his love of cars. We brought Bob Walsh with his car to the next reunion, and both talked about their years of going to Citrus Junior College together and common beginnings of working with Kathy's well-loved father-in-law and was John Hardin's dad, who had died at an early age with cancer. We used to visit with her ex-mother-in-law, Mrs. Hardin, who was still living in her Monrovia house all this time, with us stopping by and bringing her a hamburger for lunch because of her inability to leave her house, and we would visit with her until her death came this last year too.

The Jukebox

Years ago, my Uncle Frank was visiting me, while I was still living in San Bernardino, and we went to a old antique store in Riverside looking for some old gas pump items of interest to him. They also had some old jukeboxes, which Frank also owned, and I've always wanted one of them from the fifties. We then went to other stores when I started thinking that's something I should look into too. We had a store in Glendora and Azusa selling them too at the time.

Then after moving to Arizona, now being retired, Kathy and I made a trip back to California for a family visit, and we stayed in Riverside, only a few miles from that same first store. We had some time, so I returned to the shop where now the owner had died and his son with his mother was now running the store. There it was, a 1952 Seeburg 100C setting with three other jukeboxes, one from the forties and the other two from the sixties. This is the same model and year seen on "Happy Days," with the Fonzy giving a loving kick or knock; and later on, while we were in Laughlin at the Riverside Casino, we saw they had the real one from the show for sale at five thousands dollars, and I didn't pay that much for mine, but I did have to do a little work restoring mine. We got it home, and I then started collecting 45 records, still having some of Jo Ann and her sister's small box of records, plus some of my own that I already had. From this start, I now have a collection of over seven hundred or more and growing with continuing finds of more records at garage sales, goodwill stores, swap meets, and retrieving some very-known or very-little-know record memories.

Standing on a Corner

A few years ago, we where at another car show with the '57 in the nearby city of Prescott Valley, and while walking around looking at swap meet items, I came across a couple from Kingman, Arizona, selling car parts and other collectable items. I was going through a stack of their 45 records and was asked by them, "Why do you want 45 records?" Then after telling them it's for my jukebox, he asked, "What kind?" That led to him telling me he had one of the same year and model but sold it a few years ago. He then began telling me, as a "junk looker," he was driving down an alley in Winslow, Arizona, about ten years ago and spotted a jukebox sitting here in an alley. He then drove around to the front, knocking on the door; a woman open the door, and he asked about the jukebox. She said, "Just a minute, you needed to speak with my husband." He walked up and just asked, "Do you have a truck?" With that they loaded the jukebox into the back of his truck, lying in on its back, so as not to damage the beautiful design at the front with it's changing color lights, but it's very heavy and took all three of them to get it in the pickup truck. The problem that occurred while traveling in this manner had resulted in the big curved front glass on top, cracking by the time it was delivered to Kingman. The old man told him, it was in an O'l bar there in Winslow for many years. Like the Eagles' record, "Just standing on a corner in Winslow, Arizona . . . looking for a ride in a pickup . . ."

He replaced the cracked glass with Plexiglas and his wife painted it pink and sat for a few more years in their den until it wouldn't play any longer. He then took it to Riverside, California, and sold it to the same son, whom had it painted black, replacing the Plexiglas top, and fixed it so it's now playing again. As soon as I heard that story, I knew mine had at one time a Plexiglas top replaced by the son, and now I know where it had spent most of its spinning time for cowboys, maybe a few Indians, railroad workers, and other travelers along Route 66, which had made it even much more valuable to me. Finding things too can make trips in streams in time and return again. It's not the destination, it's the road traveled getting there that is most important, and finding 45 records to continue its stream of memories has been my quest.

The Watch

Just one more story, which some may not believe; however, it had started with Kathy's daughter buying me a James Dean's face wristwatch for Christmas in the Ontario Mills in California, and we both were very excited with my present. All my kids, Kathy's kids, and her grandkids don't know what to buy us old guys, and so knowing my pleasures with him, I've now have a good size collection that is far reaching and over well-meaning with his pictures, his books, cookie jar, coffee cups, and other items, but now telling everyone there's no more space left to hang or display all my items. Also there are my car trophies and cars and airplanes models in this one small room with the jukebox and its records, including all in small surrounding capsule holding me or anyone else who wants to travel in my own time machine back to the fifties.

I wore the watch for a few years, and one day it just stopped. So I just put it in my dresser drawer, with it sitting there for over six to eight months, while returning to just putting on my old Timex. However, one morning, getting ready for work at 5:00 AM and in a rush for work, I opened my drawer, seeing it running again at the exact correct time, so putting it on, assuming Kathy had taken it in somewhere, having it fixed, and had just forgotten to mention it to me. That night, after getting home and getting ready for bed, taking it off, I said, "Thanks for having my watch fixed." She gave me a look and then said, "I didn't have it fixed!" Now I thought maybe it just started running because of battery or some other reason, like being bound in there, but how was it set at the exact right time? I laughed and then said, "OK, you know what today's date is?"

She then replied, "September 30th." Then, I reminded her, "The day he died." The watch ran until almost somewhere into February of 1999, the month of his birth, and I haven't taken it anywhere to have it fixed; it just stopped again. It's just better to let things stay in their own zone.

On the next day after it started running again, I did tell everybody and anybody about its story while showing them the running wristwatch, and they would either get chills or just laugh, thinking I must be pulling their leg. However, I thought, "How, why, or where does these extraordinary events like this come from? Do they just happen?"

FORTY-TWO

Mom's Death

After my parents divorced, which was something I had seen coming, mainly because my father was becoming more out of control with everything in his life, my mother received the 548 Alta St. Monrovia house as part of their settlement, but within a few years, Monrovia forced her to be one of the last sellers of her home through "interim domain." She bought a home in Covina with that money and also found another man named Martin, who was living in a trailer park at the time in El Monte and had become her new husband before selling her house. They kept their own things separate and apart, but my mother did become closer with his youngest daughter and her family. However, cancer took the daughter's life at a very young age, just only a few years after the birth of her youngest daughter, leaving her husband with a young son and his younger child to rise. Mom stepped up with now there being two new step-grandchildren and my children to share love.

Then Martin's oldest daughter showed up on the scene, which had been closest to his previous wife and had been and was still an alcoholic. Later, I also found there were many other dark securities unknowns within this man, but he had a drinking problem too. She still didn't like her father, but she did become very close to my mother, especially after her father's death from a massive heart attack. She was strong because of her parents' problems, but like Jo Ann's sister, she had many issues, a daughter, and, after my mother's death, her true reason or wants became even clearer. My mother had taken my word with others' advise regarding the protection of her estate before her death. I received my half and the house; she only received one-fourth with the other daughters' two children, which receiving together, their one-fourth each. Martin had very little, but my mother had invested, while working part-time, in order to make her once-a-year trips in some part of the world and visiting China, telling me after her being there, "That's why Timpani Square occurred after my leaving and laughing." She and my father had always loved traveling.

She always loved people, and it wasn't enough with the Women's Club in Monrovia, which she stayed active in until her death, or her church, where she became a deacon, very active with Martin there as well. The two of them went camping year round and had a travel trailer, camping with a travel club, and they are both very active members, doing the organization of one or two trips a year. They had another trailer kept all year round in Silent Valley, California, for any weekend and getaways beside the one for traveling.

After her death, Kathy and I took her grandkids fishing and camping there before selling the trailer. John Hardin, being a "real" fisherman, took them fishing afterward, but it was in the real wild, and they just couldn't wait around to pull them in and then release, you just paid by the pound at Silent Valley, they would almost jump on the hook. However, one grandson, David or "Chunky," as he is called, did become a real fisherman, with his friend coming over here; and they both fished with me in the local Verde River. Then he continued going on to Idaho during summers learning to fly-fish with John, the real fisherman. My son, middle daughter, and I would fish on our camping trips while their they were growing up too, but my son loves it more than me, and he may do some ice fishing in Wisconsin now. I've shared some of those stories of my kid's fishing with you, but I've found that fishing is something about conquest, pacification, and patience to make a true fisherman.

Both Martin and my mom came to all my family events and holidays, always sharing in my family's times of treasures. My father had also remarried but moved on up to the state of Washington. Martin liked my son Mike very much, giving him things, which I don't think he gave to his own grandkids. After his death, my mother still came, also with Jo Ann's mother, and they always got too much more than they're share of things and more than most other kid's families could give. My mother gave love and interest in their well-being while combining a lot of pride in the people they where becoming. They where the gifts to her soul, and she was always standing near, bring light with a smile of approval to them and my family.

On the night before her death, she had called me, and we talked for a while before telling me she wasn't feeling well but had a doctor's appointment the next day with her heart specialist. She had some problems and was receiving medication and close treatment for it and also receiving some sculling from him about her weight gain, being borderline diabetic too, which was held under control with diet. I was divorced, telling her about meeting Kathy at our reunion. She was very happy about that, asking me about the kids, and was thinking about her next trip for this year back to Europe.

The next night, receiving a telephone call from one of her neighbors, there was something wrong at her house and then receiving contact from the police while getting myself together to go down there. She was dead. "I'll be there in twenty minutes," I said, hanging up and driving there in some heavy traffic. It may have been longer or much sooner, but my mind was trying hard to keep focus on driving and trying to keep any feelings under control. I drove up with the ambulances and fire trucks' lights flashing in the driveway with two police cars in front in the darkness of early light. Walking up the front steps and being met at the door by one policeman, I told him whom I was, showing my wallet ID open with my picture and my LA County badge facing his flashlight. The TV was still on, and she was in her la-z-boy blue chair as if asleep. The attendant started telling me, "It was her heart," as I walked closer and bent down on my knee, reaching out and touching her wrist and then her hand as if this would wake her up, but she was cold with a small smile on her face. Now going over to her telephone, I found her doctor's card and gave the policeman all the information they may need. They then called the doctors while I went outside, where a few neighbors were standing and talking in disbelief, as was I. They told me how much they all liked my mom and asking if there was anything they could do. I thanked them all and shook hands with them, making my way back into the house, but after that no tears came while thinking what must be done next.

Later getting home, I made some short telephone calls to tell family, friends, and Kathy what had happen, but always saying to all, "She just fell away asleep watching TV, and I was told by the paramedic there must not have been any pain involved because of the smile." Who knows who may have come to help her in crossing over—mother, father, sister, or baby daughter—but this is the easiest of all ways for it to happen, I thought. The next day, I called work and then contacted the funeral home for appointments and setting those wheels in motion. She and Martin had prepared buying their plots together at Oakdale Memorial Park in Glendora before either had passed away. She was always a planner and ready for the future.

Kathy was with me but had never met her. Shannon was living with her close friends in an apartment in San Dimas, leaving our home before my divorce, and Kellie was living with Jo Ann in her condo in Glendora. So it was just Mike, the two dogs, and one cat in the house in Glendora with its three bedrooms, two baths, over 2000 sq. ft., and pool. It's funny, after Kathy saw photos of Sylvia saying there was defiantly a similarity in appearance between the two. I'm sure my mother would have approved and been close to her just like she was with Sylvia. Kathy had lost her parents—first, her mother from cancer and, only a few years later, her father due to a complication with his heart condition. Like Jo Ann and Patricia, Kathy and Jo Ann got along well without any problems too after our marriage.

It was Jo Ann's mother who had some form of problem with Kathy and me, but no one had any clue why. Jo Ann's mother passed on a few years later from Alzheimer's after some time too, but at first Jo Ann had to move in with her in a larger house in Glendora until Jo Ann couldn't take care of her any longer. Then she moved her into a care home for a couple more years before her passing, and she was buried in the same cemetery with my mother and Martin.

The last of the Allen clan, Dad with his friend Albert, Eddie, and Pat, with some of my other cousins, came to Mom's funeral. Jo Ann with her mother, sister, and my children shared the front rows with Kathy and me. The Mitchell family, Myron and his wife, Paul and his wife, and Mom's other two sisters with Frank sat with pain and disbelief regarding her passing as well because she was the eldest of the children but also the rock in the family before her own marriage.

All of Jo Ann's and my friends and Mom's church members with her pastor gave a nice but short eulogy with anyone who felt their heart must speak words to share about her life and theirs. There were people standing with no place to sit and some waiting outside. Next came the drive to the grave site and then on to my mother's house in Covina with family and neighbors stopping by with food. This was the last time all the Mitchell family came together before the next loss in their clan a few years later. The pebbles moved on while my mother's was placed into our joined memory; we all had of her and believed she became a part of the universe of angel sprites, surrounding us. No tears, just a thank-you, and an Irish toast of honor, but still no tears came; however, I know there is now some emptiness.

Last Race Reunion

Racer's Reunion Gary, Dad and my 57' Chevy together for the last time

In 2003, just the "O'l Man" and I had gone for his last racer's reunion. After driving my '57 to California to give us some class and then flying up to Washington, picking him up in a rental car then returning flying back to San Bernardino, we then drove the '57 to "Big Gary's" house in West Covina and stayed the night with them. That is when I first saw the effects of the beginning stages of his debilitating disease; I woke up with him yelling for my help in the middle of the night and I tried to get him into the bathroom from the next-door room.

We visited with some of our other old friends in Monrovia and tried locating others in one day, but we had to drive and stay the night in Victorville at the hotel the day before the California Racer's Reunion, which was held at the racetrack next to the fairgrounds. I showed off my car while seeing and talking with many other fellow old racers, and many would look at Dad's old racing photo albums that my mother had compiled for over nineteen years. Hida Sweet, one of the organizers, brought some candy canes, passing them out, while he waved to all; when they announced his name, he stood to one side of the room during the presentations. This made him feel very important, and this was his last chance to link with this part of racing history. We started out for Arizona the next day, after also seeing another old friend, with his wife, Emil, who worked on his car at our house in Monrovia and lost his keys because of our earlier poor work, during those high school years, and was now retired living here in the high desert.

We had a problem with my car's steering bolt because it kept falling out just as we started out, but we got back on the road after a short stop. Dad thought that was just great too; it was like old times. We were driving to my house in Prescott, Arizona and had stopped in Palm Springs for a hamburger at In-N-Out, and there was a guy standing in line hearing us talking while I was saying something about In-N-Out in Glendora, where I ran into another guy who was in the same car club, "The Intakes," as me, though he joined much later on after me, and he had became the auto shop teacher at Monrovia High School. However, now this guy in Palm Springs had also been a member of our club as well, and it was again funny at one of the Goodguys car shows in Scottsdale a year before when a 1940 Ford Coupe had came in after Kathy and I, parking behind us, and it had the same car club plaque as ours—he too was a member of the club during the later 1970s. I asked how and why do these occurrences happen at these moments?

Dad stayed a few days with Kathy and I before we flew back to Portland's airport, where I turned him over to Carmyn and her son, Diane. Then as it happened, Diana passed away from a heart attack just two years ago while still being a very young, which hit his mother and my dad very hard. My dad treated him as one of his own blood, his son, but Diana had health problems and had been discharged from the air force because of his physical problems and was receiving disability payments all that time after his service. He needed watching but had too big a heart in many ways and didn't tell his mother of his heart problem, having died in a bathtub under unclear circumstances.

Dan's

Later my dad was driving one of his cars from Diana's house after his death when Dad got lost. A sheriff found him in a dazed state, and Carmyn came after getting a call, and then with the sheriff drove Dad in her car to their house; this resulted in Dad losing his driver's license, never to drive again. His dignity and condition just kept digressing into a worse state from those years. I'm very happy I could give him some very happy moments in that last trip, and we still had fun as the fog was beginning to find its way within him, losing his visions of the present. I told Kathy and Carmyn of my diagnosis while they both explained it as stress or old age, but I knew his streams had made a big change in direction, taking him deeper into its inescapable darkness.

Dad's last Racer's Reunion days
Dad standing with me on Dan's Mustang like when I was twelve years old

Losing a Son

Last summer, spending time for a week with my father at his house in Washington, while relaxing and talking about my deceased sister, his daughter, he looked at me and told me he never had another child or a baby girl. I could see Carmyn's surprise while I tried telling him about her death, but the more we both tried telling him more information, the more his mind would not accept our truths, and he became very upset with both of us. We dropped the subject, and within a few moments, he then told us his son had died a few years ago too. Carmyn was further in shock and kept telling him I was his son and hadn't die, standing right in front of him, but he didn't believe us now either. After a night's rest, he had accepted me as his son, but still didn't believe us. From others close to me, I knew that this happens with people with Alzheimer's. Also afterward, my thinking about this, maybe in his mind, he had confused the death of one of his best friends with the same name, Carl, with me, who had died just a few years ago. However, on his birthday, this March 13, my daughter Shannon called, wishing him a happy birthday, and as they where talking, he told my daughter, "Did you know my son, Carl, had died a few years ago?" She had spent time with Jo Ann's mother, who also had Alzheimer's and knew about this type of loss of memory too, but also she tried telling him, "That's my dad, and he's not dead!" I had talked to him too that same day, and he wanted me to drive over for some ice cream and cake, but I had to tell him that was too long a drive from Arizona for the day. Since that day last summer, I've become lost deeper in his foggy mind and have died, joining my sister. He has lost his son, and it's harder to see the pebbles deeper in his stream. It's painful for Carmyn and me, but it's a new day for him every day.

I was invited to attend another California Racer's Reunion after this, which we had gone to three years ago, but I told them Dad could no longer attend, but I would be there with my cousin Eddy. It was held on May 7, 2006, being my fourteenth attendance, but I arrived late and made it just in time for dinner and the ceremonies. I sat with Eddy, listening to the speakers talk about their past parts in our old racing days, which was of some interest. However, it was at Joe's Garage in Tustin, California, and having mirror paintings reflecting those early wooden board racetracks where dad began the racing days until more recent days with different kinds of cars, some racers, and others types that were a few real historical cars sitting in front and along the walls. On one wall were race posters, and below them was a table with photos and books of all kinds of people and cars from the fifties and sixties. One button had my dad's face on it, wearing his racing helmet, and there next to it was a photo of my dad being announce with the flagman pointing to him for the crowd's interdiction while in his car that we had built together, plus there was also one of me standing in the background behind the side of the car, but with my head cut off at the side of the track. Some guy standing next to me at the table tried making a joke after. I said out loud, "That's my dad and me." He said, "No, that's Jim Shearington," meaning the starter, then laughed, but most of these people never took my dad seriously anyway.

After getting home, a week later, I called Carmyn to talk with Dad, for our monthly talk. She told me after a few minutes that he was not there and she had placed him in a care home on that same day, May 7, 2006. She was unable to care for him any longer, and he was having trouble by falling among other troubles. I knew it was hard to make that decision, with me expecting it to come soon, we carried on talking for another ten minutes and agreed that sometime during the summer, I'd make a trip up to visit with them both. She'll have time to go through his things because I'll want the family photos and his racing book albums. She had already talked to Jim Penney about some of his things before my call.

I think she blames me for his changes and declining condition, after that last summer before, but I knew it was coming. He lost a son then, and now I've lost a dad, while she lost her husband of twenty-eight years this last month. Well, maybe next month, around Father's Day, I'll fly up for one last time to visit with him and bring home the photo records of his time and mine.

However, we lost him before that on July 8, 2006. Carmyn called, saying she had gone home for some rest after being with him until past midnight. They called around three, telling her he had passed away. She wished that she was there, that someone was there, but as I've seen on the TV shows with John Edward, they won't go or will wait until their loved ones are gone before passing away. She had told him earlier, "It's OK to leave." Some pebbles become stuck in their surrounding clouds before they become finest sand because of the wearing down of time, and his body has been worn down—it was time to go.

This was on a Saturday. I got a flight on Monday to Portland and rented a car, driving under clouds with some light rain at times, but there were sunnier skies, as I got closer to Rochester. A frog announced my presence at the door; she opened the door, and there was some joy in both our faces with some sadness. Her sister came over, and we had something to eat at a nearby new restaurant, which was serving just frozen food warmed up, but we laughed with stories of what he was doing in those past few months, like a young little child with his odd behavior and sad with the pain before the end came. I brought my work boots and did some leftover "honey dos" request by her from last summer, which kept us busy, but still remiss his presents. His wish was to be cremated, and they had sent him from the mortuary to another city to do it, but my return flight plans was set, with my going home on Friday, and he wouldn't be back until Monday or Tuesday. We wrote his obituary, giving it to the mortuary on Tuesday before my leaving, and I placed the family photos, his racing albums, three trophies of meaning to me—one he received during 1957 for being a "crowd pleaser," the other one won with the Corvette for our day at Riverside with Dyno Don (who died in January of this year as well), and the other one won from Eddy driving his roadster at Orange County drags, which was given to Dad in the fifties. Now all of these are placed in my suitcase within a heavy box. When I got home, both had been inspected with little sheets from the government before flying on our plane for home.

She will keep his ashes close to her for a while, maybe a cookie jar because of his love of them, before placing them in his final resting place. Again, no tears, I'd said my goodbyes long ago, and now she will have to find the time that's right for her, but I did have a "shot of good whiskey" again saying, "Have a fast drive home O'l Man. There's a big crowd awaiting you at the finish line," while I was flying home in the clouds.

There was no tears for my mother's death either, only my happiness for the way she passed, and as for my father, I'm sure there will be very little or none as well, except for those who feel the loss of memories in memorable times. For him, there would have been more of those days of torment inflicted within, his mental and physical agony, before his passing. That has ended now after all those many years in his lost places of every day. There should be an O'l Irish wake, but most of his friends have gone on before him; there's now only the younger members of my family—two cousins and three racing buddies. Then came his closer family—his wife Carmyn and her daughter, who had looked upon him in some form, a father for her because she never had one—plus his grandchildren, my children. So if I have a drink to when the body's end comes, it doesn't matter—I will face it only with joy that it has ended. His mind is gone, and neither one of us will see his special sunshine ever again, other than as faint memories of our past. Maybe I'll sing "You Are My Sunshine" to myself at his grave or in the wind or over a cool stream in Wyoming. Here's to the long life of Orval F. Allen, the last of his mother's children and his father's family of pebbles clan, riding into their last streams.

With this, it's time to continue my stream and my family's travels in their own pages while hoping this has given all following or reading this some received snapshot memories of my family and friends. But more so, I hope it will bring back the history of our shared times. I am hoping as well to place photos in my book to complete these story visions, which are closer to myths and truths to bring greater understand more then just words. For everyone else, please write your memories for your family—a page with a photo or scrapbook—because pebbles are very important and are extraordinary in our togetherness or for just one loved human before they become lost forever.

FORTY-THREE

Epilogue

I've been very lucky, enjoying my trips in life's streams, having adventures while learning something that was never known before or found just that day, and yet remembering events of those days of my past brings some balance. They may have become clouded, but there's still a new day and hope that my mind doesn't lose completely the memory of those past moments. It's very hard seeing others lose their selves, like my father, while the mind is being shattered though injuries, illness, decay, or dementia without them knowing that something is affecting them, or how or why, while yet still finding some happiness into that moment before it will disappear. Those moments, now lost and forgotten because of that slow process known as Alzheimer's, with its coming without peace in your own present state of mind, yet all along not seeing, while our memories are sliding into darkness or not being able to see within our own minds until that forthcoming brightness becomes lost completely. As it also has brought on to others, family, friends, or our own identity to be taken and gone from them, they are washed away into the sands of time or nights without any trace of present thoughts. What confusion and despair come in this process? We don't understand the mind or this disease as yet.

I'm saddened by the passing of those who are no longer among us to continuing in our streams, but they are still as much a part of us because sometimes a thought or a reflection brings them back. Like the leaves of a great oak tree, the winds of time has taken many of us far away and continue to push us on our own journeys farther by carrying us in time and place from them, yet seeds are still planted. Many have disappeared into many unknown places, places in time, places beyond what we can ever be able to know, and places many of us can't think of ever entering or ending or believing we can understand or wanting to know in the end. We hang on until our season comes, not knowing what the winter will bring.

With age comes unexpected pains of joints or muscles and the slowing of moving from moment to moment without any known reasons with the brain's unexceptional disbelief. This subject becomes more a part of our daily conversation with age too. But again comes our fifty class reunion again this year, and we still get together, still sharing the best of times, the worst of times, with some things of our old memories, some things being myths, with some unforgotten fantasies, but always our own experiences to record and recall. Yet if we're still lucky, we now have our children or grandchildren and friends filling those days and years with joy. There still is a feeling of somewhere, there's renewed friendships to be found, and there is a gathering of our friends and family here or in the stars or at the streams for us pebbles in time.

We all feel pain in that loss of ourselves, lovers, family, and friends, but that's what life reflects more and more at our age, with each coming year, and coming before our own years of winter come upon us. This pebble has been polished smother with the experiences of life's traveling streams and others surrounding me, rubbing shoulders and bringing a clearer vision that just keeps getting richer with the human experience too. We must learn to carry what we feel, know, enjoy, and dislike, earning that right with age, and also brings sadness to us or our heart knowing there is no escape. With as much happiness in understanding that's life too. So try to sing, dance, and drink the wines of life before the winds of winter become too strong for us to stand, without the sands of time completely covering us. Staying in the streams as long as we can, whether in pain or dreams, but holding love with its joy closest to our breast helps us become extraordinary into our selves. My own toast to all pebbles, "May love find you on your path and bring warmth into your soul that opens the clouds to sunshine and finds an easy path to travel up or down life's dreams—while finding pure love with others, while holding a loving hand." I'm just another traveler with a vision of myths and truths, looking for dreams in my extraordinary life's gold within the coming of another day.

UNTIL THE END

INDEX